Asian Cult Cinema

Asian Cult Cinema

Thomas Weisser

Boulevard Books, New York

Asian Cult Cinema

A Boulevard Book / published by arrangement with
Thomas Weisser

PRINTING HISTORY
Boulevard trade paperback edition / April 1997

The Putnam Berkley World Wide Web site address is
http://www.berkley.com/berkley

ISBN: 1-57297-228-9

BOULEVARD
Boulevard Books are published by The Berkley Publishing Group,
200 Madison Avenue, New York, New York 10016.
BOULEVARD and its logo are trademarks
belonging to Berkley Publishing Corporation.

B&W illustrations and photographs by various
institutes, organizations and companies.

Grateful acknowledgment is made to the following companies,
whose properties illustrate this book in the spirit of publicity:
Film Workshop Co Ltd, Golden Princess Films, Golden Gate Film,
Magnum, Shaw Brothers Co., CineMart Publishing, Atlas World Sales,
Long Shong Distributing, Ko Chi Sum Films, Worldwide Films Corp,
Team Work Productions, Mandarin Films, DeChance Ltd, Golden Way,
Media Distributing, Golden Harvest Limited, Ocean Shores Film Ltd,
Silver Bird Films, Chun Sing Company, Star Entertainment Co Ltd,
Sil-Metropole Organisation, Win's Films, Lau Kun Wai Productions,
Bo Ho Films, David Lam Company, Hong Hwa Films & Seasonal Corp

Book design by Richard Oriolo

PRINTED IN THE UNITED STATES OF AMERICA

10 9   8   7   6   5

This book is dedicated to
Yuko Mihara Weisser
my wife and best friend

Contents

Foreword   ix

Acknowledgments   xi

Introduction by Max Allan Collins   1

A Note on the Text: Deciphering the Chinese Language   5

The Films   9

The Roots: Martial Arts   217

Director Filmography   261

The Major Players   283

Foreword

Initially, a series of my Asian mini-reviews was published in the fanzine *Naked! Screaming! Terror!* (1989). Those reviews, along with a couple hundred more, were reprinted for the premiere issue of *Asian Trash Cinema* in 1991 (now called *Asian Cult Cinema*). This marked the birth of America's first magazine on contemporary Asian cinema.

My early writings were labors of love, filled with exuberance and awe. But they also contained some unfortunate inaccuracies. I was traveling in uncharted waters, armed with limited information about the Chinese culture and even less knowledge of the language. So unavoidable mistakes were made.

Thanks to valuable correspondence with the rabid readers of *Asian Cult Cinema* magazine, intensified by my eye-popping Hong Kong *vacation* (with special thanks to my persevering daughter, who helped me explore every nook and cranny), strengthened by the dedicated assistance from my Asian translators Derek Cheung and Jonathan Wong—many of the initial errors were cleared up.

I expanded some of the original critiques. And, in many cases, revamped my thoughts completely. I wrote another 300 reviews and then spent time creating a director filmography. All this was published as *Asian Trash Cinema: The Book* in 1992.

Three years later, I wrote a sequel that included a listing of *Roots Films* (mostly martial-arts movies lensed between 1969 and 1982). It's impossible to appreciate where Hong Kong cinema is today without seeing where it was yesterday. I also wrote a couple hundred new reviews for movies released after the publication of Book #1, plus some that had slipped through the cracks the first time around.

Now, with much pride, we present this current volume, published by Boulevard Books. Essentially, it's a combination of everything from the original two books (upgraded yet again) plus about 200 new listings. As with the former books, these entries range from Horror to Action, Sexploitation to Fantasy. Each review also includes a *star* rating system, from ★★★★ [the best] to ★ [the worst], which is based on the film's entertainment value *within the intended genre* and not necessarily on the *artistic* merit compared with other titles. For example, I've tried to judge a horror film on its peculiar characteristics as a "horror" film, consisting of certain qualities considerably different from that of a "drama." It is conceivable that a (★★★) horror film would be worthy of only (★★) in a more conservative rating system.

This book also contains an upgraded and expanded Director Filmography consisting of titles from this volume *plus* many obscure entries not found in the publication. There's also an equally valuable Major Players Filmography, complete with multiple listings and ID photos.

The emphasis in *Asian Cult Cinema* is almost exclusively on Hong Kong cinema. But, allow me to take a moment and mention that my wife, Yuko Mihara, and I have recently completed an extensive book on Japanese cult movies called *Japanese Cinema: The Essential Handbook*. Look for it at your favorite bookstore.

Lastly, I want to thank you for your continued support. And, as usual, your comments are always encouraged and appreciated. You can reach the ACC staff c/o Vital Books, PO Box 16-1917, Miami Fl 33116.

Acknowledgments

I wish to thank my daughter Jessica Weisser, Scott Williams, Jonathan Wong, and Derek Cheung. Without their help this book could not have been written.

Special thanks to the following writers who contributed reviews to many issues of *Asian Trash/Cult Cinema* magazine. Edited and condensed versions of the following original critiques have been reprinted in this volume:

John Bowie (*He's a Woman, She's a Man*)
Brian Camp (*Fire Dragon* and *Most Wanted*)
Forrest Chan (*Arrest the Restless*)
David Chute (*Five Element Ninja*)
John Crawford (*The Adventurers*)
Travis Crawford (*Bride With White Hair 2; Dragon Inn; C'est La Vie, Mon Cheri* and *Green Snake*)
Steve Fentone (*Hong Kong Godfather, That's Money,* and *Cops & Robbers*)
Mark Giguere (*Red to Kill*)
Jason Gray (*Fatal Rose* and *Romance of the Vampires*)
Lim Cheng Tju (*Swords of Many Loves, Full Contact, Warrior's Tragedy* and *Rock & Roll Cop*)
Steve Sanders (*Fist of Legend*)
Jeff Segal (*Remains of a Woman*)

I wish to also thank the following people for their help:

Jonathan Wong and Derek Cheung, who spent hours unifying and translating the text from the Chinese *hanzi* symbols.

Maria Chen at Tai Seng, who assisted and contributed to the cause; and Elizabeth Beier, the Boulevard/Berkley editor, who helped every step of the way.

Richard Akiyama and his staff at *Cineraider*, Bob Sargent, Ric Meyers, George Patino, Scott Williams, Tim Lucas, Max Allan Collins, Michael Weldon, Jerry Chandler, and Craig Ledbetter (for being there in the beginning).

And my daughter, Jessica Weisser, my wife, Yuko, Amber Golden, and Carlos Vargas, who did the cross referencing and the painstaking detail work.

Introduction

by Max Allan Collins

A few weeks ago (as I write this), the local theater here in Muscatine, Iowa, had playing on two of its four screens the following: *Broken Arrow*, directed by John Woo, and *Rumble in the Bronx*, starring Jackie Chan. And both of these action-filled films were packing 'em in.

For longtime aficionados of Hong Kong fare, this seemed at once a triumph and something of a farce. For those of us who love the work of Woo and Chan, it was glorious to see their work on mainstream, middle-American movie screens, overcoming ethnocentric (i.e., racist) attitudes about Asian films, and particularly (in the case of *Rumble*) films starring "yellow people." But it was also a bit of a bitter pill, because *Broken Arrow* is one of Woo's worst films, a hodgepodge self-parody with lousy bigtime American movie acting (John Travolta is no Chow Yun-Fat) and rotten screenwriting (Woo, a wonderful writer, has not yet been allowed to write for himself in the U.S.); and, fun as it is, *Rumble in the Bronx* is decidedly second-rate Jackie Chan fare, chosen for distribution because of its American setting (though it was filmed in Canada) and multitude of white faces in the cast.

Still, it's hard to believe it was just a few years ago—1989, to be precise—that Thomas Weisser began writing about Hong Kong cinema in the pages of the now defunct fanzine *Naked! Screaming! Terror!* A good writer writing about movies makes the reader want to see those movies—and Tom, with his witty, unpretentious, cogent comments about the likes of John Woo's *A Better Tomorrow* and Tsui Hark's *I Love Maria* (two of my favorites, by the way), sent the small but fanatical following of that fanzine out into the Chinatown sections of major cities searching for (and spurred underground mail-order sources to start providing bootleg copies of) these wild movies with their blood–spurting action scenes, their hopping vampires, their martial-arts magic, and their unabashedly *un*-Western sexual mores.

Eventually, Tom's own magazine affectionately labeled this material, by way of the magazine's own title, *Asian Trash Cinema*; but the hard-core cult-movie audience raised on British horror movies, Godzilla sequels, George Romero zombie epics, and artily incoherent European thrillers (called *giallos*) was well aware that Weisser's tongue was in cheek. By using "trash," he invoked snobby movie critics dismissing any genre fare as beneath contempt.

In fact, the Hong Kong cinema discovered by Weisser and a handful of others (Ric Meyers introduced me to John Woo's gangster movies about the same time Tom began writing about them) has more than its share of treasures among the trash. What Hollywood fantasy can live up to the visual poetry and sheer exhilaration of Tsui Hark's *Chinese Ghost Story*? *I Love Maria*, with its flashy effects, zany humor, and keen characterization, rivals *RoboCop*, and easily outshines its sequels. The various Bruce Willis and Arnold Schwarzenegger blockbusters, for all their action, pale next to Jackie Chan's *Project A* or *Armour of God 2*.

And, of course, these movies were made for peanuts—the catering budget on *Die Hard 3* could fund three or four Hong Kong action flicks. On top of this is the unlikelihood of seeing Bruce or Arnold actually take on a dangerous stunt. In Hong Kong, it's required—Jackie Chan is not the only star who does his own "gags." The late Brandon Lee once told me of a Hong Kong director's insistence that Brandon do his own quite dangerous stunts, or risk being laughed off Hong Kong screens; Brandon complied, and it's a bitter irony that he braved those dangers only to have Hollywood sloppiness kill him.

Broken Arrow aside, John Woo is a brilliant filmmaker; such films as *The Killer*, *A Better Tomorrow 1 & 2*, *A Bullet in The Head*, and *Hard-Boiled* signal a talent worthy of ranking alongside such American action *auteurs* as Don Siegel, Robert Aldrich, and Howard Hawks. Woo is an odd amalgam of Sam Peckinpah poetic violence and Douglas Sirk over-the-top soap opera melodrama, and it's a combination uniquely Asian despite its very American sources (though in truth the great French director Jean-Pierre Melville ought also to be cited).

Jackie Chan is the most popular movie star in the world (already a cliché but, like many clichés, true), with a unique ability to combine outrageous comedy (marked by mugging that sometimes makes our man Weisser uneasy) with mind-bogglingly staged and death–defyingly executed stunts. He's a bizarre combination of Buster Keaton and Evel Knievel, with some Douglas Fairbanks thrown in; or, as Donald E. Westlake so aptly described the actor/athlete's ability to walk up walls and careen off the surface of anything, "Jackie Chan is Fred Astaire and the world is Ginger Rogers."

But John Woo and Jackie Chan are not the whole story. There's Tsui Hark, the Steven Spielberg of Hong Kong, a director, producer, even occasional actor, and enormously successful and skilled at all three. There's charismatic Cynthia Khan, a female action star whose stunt work rivals Jackie Chan's, and whose *In the Line of Duty* series (and its offshoots) presents her as a credibly tough police inspector without losing any sense of humanity, much less femininity. There's Samo Hung, the chubby everyman whose martial-arts skills are dazzling and dizzying, equally proficient at comedy and action melodrama. There's Ringo Lam, a director whose gritty approach took John Woo's trademark "heroic bloodshed" into darker, more troubled waters (waters into which Quentin Tarantino dipped for the "inspiration" for his *Reservoir*

Dogs). And of course there's Chow Yun-Fat, the Asian superstar who, in work for John Woo and Ringo Lam, among many others, radiates presence like heat off asphalt.

Those great talents are only the beginning of what you can discover. If you're already a buff of these films, *Asian Cult Cinema* will be a handy reference guide to familiar, beloved territory. For the uninitiated, this will be a travel guide to an exotic but surprisingly accessible foreign land, an alternate universe of filmmaking that has the energy, talent, and enthusiasm that Hollywood long ago squandered.

Best of all, your guide on this fabulous journey is the man who introduced Hong Kong "trash cinema" to the underground cultish audience from which it spread to the mainstream. He has received little praise or notice for this not inconsiderable feat, which was a stunt worthy of Jackie Chan himself. I am proud to have played a small role in the publication of this book, which with its fun, informative mini reviews of hundreds and hundreds of movies, is an overdue introduction to a wider audience of another worthy facet of Hong Kong cinema: the entertaining and unpretentious film criticism of Tom Weisser.

A Note on the Text: Deciphering the Chinese Language

Since Hong Kong was part of the British Commonwealth during the period these movies were made, the law states "any film shown theatrically must have accurate English subtitles." However, often these films are transferred to videotape with little regard for the readability of the translations. Sometimes they are duplicated sloppily, with subtitles disappearing below the TV screen or chopped at the sides (especially in full-screen dubs). Simply, the videos aren't intended for Anglo consumption; the average Asian viewer couldn't care less if English subs are legible.

The two major spoken languages of the Chinese people are Cantonese (a dialect of southern China, the official language of Hong Kong) and Mandarin (the language spoken in the People's Republic of China). Although they sound similar to the untrained Western ear, they are as different as Spanish and Italian. A Hong Kong Chinese cannot communicate orally with a mainland Chinese. However, the written Chinese symbols (called *hanzi*) have the same meaning to both groups. For example, both a Cantonese speaker and a Mandarin speaker can read the same newspaper, but they can't discuss what they read with each other.

This results in almost insurmountable problems when trying to Romanize the written Chinese symbols (application of Western letters to *hanzi* characters). The English translation is achieved by applying alphabet sounds to the spoken interpretation of the *hanzi* symbol. Depending on whether the translator speaks Mandarin or Cantonese, the result can be as different as night and day. For instance, here is the *hanzi* for a popular Taiwanese actress: (王祖賢). This name can be interpreted as either Wong Ki Chang (Cantonese) or Wang Zu Xian (Mandarin). To further complicate the situation, often a performer (or a production company) will anglicize a name to avoid international confusion. Thus, Wong Ki Chang/Wang Zu Xian is better known as **Joey Wang.**

Another peculiar problem lies in haphazard alias choices, resulting in two different actors with the same name. Both Leung Chiu Wai and Leung Kar Fai are **Tony Leung** (and they both star in ***Ashes of Time*** and ***Eagle Shooting Heroes***). And sometimes a performer may decide a name change would be nice. For seven years, Lin Ching Hsia was known as Lin Ching Hsia. Now, she is **Brigitte Lin** (but, in the past, she also made films under Lin Quig Xia and Venus Lin). Obviously, this can play havoc when compiling a book like this one, especially when there doesn't appear to be any accepted correct standard.

For this text, we've attempted to identify and use anglicized names, if that seems to be the choice of the performer. **Samo Hung** is Samo Hung, not Hung Kam Bo or Hong Jin Bao. And if the person chooses to use the Cantonese interpretation rather than the Mandarin, we have also followed the lead. Thus **Tsui Hark** remains Tsui Hark (Cantonese), not Xu Ke (Mandarin). However, if there is no clear-cut choice, we have opted for the Cantonese interpretation because it is more universally accepted in the entertainment arts media. But if the actor/actress is making films for mainland Chinese production companies, we have used the Mandarin form.

Last, there has always been confusion in the Western world regarding the placement of "family" name and "given" name. As a rule, if the name of the person has not been anglicized and consists of three words (e.g., **Chow Yun-Fat**), the first word (Chow) is the family (i.e., last) name. If the complete Chinese name is only two words (e.g., **Wu Ma**), then the first (Wu) is the family name (we would write it Wu, Ma). Anglicized names like **John Woo** are exceptions; Woo is obviously the family name. And, a bit more confusing, in combination anglicized/traditional names (e.g., Clifton Ko Sum), the middle word (Ko) is the family name.

Asian Cult Cinema

The Films

ABOVE THE LAW.
> See *Righting Wrongs*

THE ACCIDENT.
> See *Blood of the Black Dog*

ACES GO PLACES (1982)
director: Eric Tsang. Sam Hui·Karl Maka·Dean Shek·Carroll Gordon·Chen Sing·Tsui Hark ★★★

ACES GO PLACES 2 (1983)
director: Eric Tsang. Sam Hui·Karl Maka·Sylvia Chang·Suzanna Valentino·Yasuaki Kurata·Joe Dimmick ★★★½

ACES GO PLACES 3:
MAN FROM BOND STREET (1984)
director: Tsui Hark. Sam Hui·Karl Maka·Sylvia Chang·Peter Graves·Richard Kiel·Jean Mersant·Tsunehara Sogiyama ★★★½

ACES GO PLACES 4 (1986)
aka **YOU NEVER DIE TWICE**
director: Ringo Lam. Sam Hui·Karl Maka·Sylvia Chang·Sally Yeh·Roy Chiao·Ronald Lacey ★★★½

ACES GO PLACES 5:
THE TERRACOTTA HIT (1990)
director: Lau Karl Leung. Sam Hui·Leslie Cheung·Nina Li Ch·Conan Lee·Karl Maka·Danny Lee ★★
A stalwart series with major emphasis on caper-type adventures and espionage action. At times there are unique SciFi elements (especially in #2), but mostly these films are madcap, daredevil escapades usually involving an intricate master plan to steal some mega-valuable artifact. Or zillions of dollars in diamonds. Most of the installments have been released internationally under the title *Mad Mission*. The Chinese name is *Choi Gai Pat Dong* (roughly translated as Best

Partners). The series follows the exploits of a superthief named King Kong (played by Sam Hui throughout) as he teams up with bumbling police detective Albert Au (Karl Maka) and his wife Ah Tung (Silvia Chang) to retrieve an array of valuable treasures and foil the criminal masterminds in the process.

In #1, the three sleuths are on the trail of diamond smugglers. The only clue is a sprawling map tattooed on the butts of two pretty girls (an idea seemingly inspired by the similar Spaghetti western *Stranger and the Gunfighter* [1973] with Lee Van Cleef and Lo Lieh).

#2 is probably the best of the series, with some exceptionally funny sequences and an exhausting action-oriented script. Filthy Harry (Joe Dimmick, doing a precise Clint Eastwood imitation) is a mercenary hired to retrieve the diamonds stolen in #1 and, at the same time, kill King Kong, Albert, and Ah Tung. The plot bounces all over the place, from motorcycle chases to car chases, bike chases to foot chases. Plus there are giant robots, martial arts, and an ending that diligently spoofs *Shaft* (with Isaac Hayes music to match).

#3 is a significant departure from the others. Directed by **Tsui Hark,** this one is a frenzied parody of spy films in general and James Bond and *Mission Impossible* spy films in particular. The Asian regulars **Samuel Hui** and **Sylvia Chang [Chan Chia-Ling]** are joined by Peter Graves and a variety of familiar faces, including Richard "Jaws" Kiel. The plot has our Hong Kong heroes being tricked by James Bond and Queen Elizabeth look-alikes who steal the precious "Star of Fortune." The film tends to be unnecessarily confusing and far-fetched. After an incredible opening 30 minutes, it drifts into nonsense involving Santa Claus, skateboard shenanigans, and a parody of *Mad Max 2: Road Warrior.* In the middle of all the action, Albert and Ah Tung have a bouncing baby boy, Baldy Jr., who also returns as a regular in the next entry.

#4 emerges as one of **Ringo Lam**'s best early efforts, with larger-than-life sets and Indiana Jones-style action (in fact, Ronald Lacey re-creates his Nazi role from *Raiders of the Lost Ark*). In this one, King Kong volunteers from some superman experimentation conducted by scientist Roy Chiao (from *Indiana Jones and the Temple of Doom*), but terrorists interrupt the proceedings. After an extensive helicopter-speedboat chase, King Kong manages to escape with the scientist's daughter (**Sally Yeh [Yip]**). Eventually, the action switches to New Zealand, when the bad guys kidnap Ah Tung. Everything escalates into an explosive finale as the Best Partners battle the terrorists in an underground lab/fortress. Incidentally, Albert is transformed into a supermonster during the fracas.

Aces Go Places: The Terracotta Hit (#5) is a return to a smaller-scale martial arts film. Chop socky director **Lau Kar Leung** spends a lot of time with kung fu scenes and, unfortunately, with lackluster parodies of *The Last Emperor* and **Prison on Fire**), but not much thought is given to character development or plot structure. King Kong and Albert, tired of the rat-race, open an investment firm but soon are framed for a robbery by a brother-and-sister criminal team (**Leslie Cheung** and Nina Li Chi). Eventually Conan Lee, playing a supercop from China, forces everybody to become friends and join him in a fight against traffickers. This results in an extensive kung fu battle in a warehouse filled with terra cotta statues. Silvia Chang is nowhere to be seen. Apparently she and little Baldy have migrated to

Sam Hui (L) with Karl Maka in *Aces Go Places*

Canada, where they are waiting for Albert to join them.

Before the Aces films, Sam Hui enjoyed a profitable career as a singer. The films brought him new notoriety. Karl Maka (sometimes Mak Kar or Karl Mak), although he certainly is not a newcomer to HK cinema, made a quick name for himself via these films. This is probably due to his unique bald appearance and his ability to overact with charm. He was (and still is) a successful film producer.

ADVENTURERS (1995)
director: Ringo Lam. Andy Lau·David Chiang·Rosamund Kwan·Wu Chien Lien ★★★
This film opens in 1975 Cambodia during the Communist takeover. A young boy sees his parents killed by a traitorous CIA double agent. Twenty years later, the kid grows up to become **Andy Lau**. He's rescued from the war-torn country by his Uncle Shang (David Chiang), who trains him and guides him on the path to vengeance against the evil Chun Pui, now a crime boss in San Francisco's Chinatown.

Some critics have chastised this **Ringo Lam** film for being too derivative of John Woo's ***A Bullet in the Head*** (1990), and others have complained about Andy Lau's wooden performance (but when hasn't he been wooden?). But neither of these criticisms take away from the scope and intensity of the film. While it's not the objet d'art that **Full Contact** or **Burning Paradise** was, this movie is both massive in scope and visually breathtaking. It also benefits from the inclusion of two strong, well-defined female characters, the multidimensional **Rosamund Kwan** as a crime lord's girlfriend who is dangerously attracted to vengeance-seeking Andy Lau, and the hauntingly beautiful Wu Chien Lien (certainly the brightest thing about **Chow Yun-Fat**'s ***Treasure Hunt***) as the daughter of the Chinatown bad guy.

It's also great to see David Chiang in a film again. He was a major kung fu star throughout the '70s, starring in many top-notch **Chang Cheh** productions. He has aged well, and the part fits him perfectly.

ALL ABOUT AH-LONG (1989)
director: Johnny To (Tu). Chow Yun-Fat· Silvia Chang ★★½
Chow Yun-Fat won the Asian Best Actor award for this film, but the movie tends to be a Hong Kong version of *Kramer vs. Kramer*, as a successful career women (**Silvia Chang**) attempts to reclaim custody of her son from her former lover, Ah-Long (**Chow Yun-Fat**).

The ending is particularly noteworthy for its unexpected downbeat twist. After being reunited with his boy, Ah-Long is killed in a bike race.

ALL IN DIM COLD NIGHT (1974)
director: Yao Fengpan [Feng-Pang]. Qin Meng·Yue Yang·Jin Lingai ★
A rich landowner has an affair with a girl. She's pregnant, but he refuses to marry her. On a cold night, the girl

and her child go to him for help, but he won't let them inside his house. They freeze to death at his doorstep and return as ghosts. They torment him until he finally drowns. Sadly dated by today's standards. The entire thing is a tedious bore.

ALL IN THE FAMILY (1980)
director: Chu Mu. Jackie Chan·Shek Tin·Linda Chu ★★
If there's a skeleton in **Jackie Chan**'s closet, this is it. Studio boss Raymond Chow thought it would be a good idea for the popular chop socky star to get some mainstream attention, so Chan was added to the cast of this turn-of-the-century sex farce. The film is a series of vignettes dealing with a family who has gathered to be with the dying patriarch during his last days. There's lots of coy talk and heated bickering, but it doesn't get sexy until Jackie Chan arrives (which is about an hour into the film). At that point, playing a bumbling rogue, he seduces the pretty daughter first and then her mother.

Jackie and his lovers are the only ones who take their clothes off and do the nasty in this otherwise silly sex pic. If you've been dying to see Jackie in bed with a woman (especially a totally nude Jackie), this is your only chance in his 40+ motion pictures.

Also, this movie remains the only Jackie Chan film without one fight scene. And there are no stunts, unless you count Chan's gyrations in the sack.

ALL THE WRONG SPIES (1984)
director: Teddy Robin Kwan. George Lam ·Lin Ching Hsia·Tsui Hark ★½
Here's a difficult movie to like, especially if you hate the Hong Kong brand of slapstick. It's the story of a goofy private eye named Yoyo (George Lam) and his haphazard escapades dealing with the disappearance of Hitler's secret war document (the formula for an atomic bomb), allegedly stolen by the Jewish underground and stashed in Hong Kong.

Kinder critics have referred to this film as a *Casablanca* spoof, but the humor is painfully obvious and forced. Too much of it relies on pratfalls and broad sight gags.

It's nice to see **Lin Ching Hsia** in an early role; she looks great in her slinky cat-burglar outfit, and she certainly knows how to crack a mean whip. Future filmmaker **Tsui Hark** stars as a sadistic Japanese spy; he's probably the best thing about the film. Incidently, the set design is credited to **Tsui Hark** and his wife, Nansun Shi. Director **Teddy Robin Kwan** (with Dennis Yu) made the humorlessly grim ***Flesh and the Bloody Terror*** four years later.

Director Kwan is a powerful HK producer who broke into the entertainment business through music. He fronted a mega-popular bubblegum group called Teddy Robin and the Playboys, whose popularity in Hong Kong rivaled that of the Beatles.

ALOHA, THE LITTLE VAMPIRE (1987)
director: Ng See Yuen. Law Yoi·Lee Ting Hing·Chen Yu Chiao ★
A children's movie? With jokes about AIDS, gays, and illegitimate babies? What's wrong with this picture?

It's the story of a vampire kid who runs away after his uncles embarrass themselves in a duel for the opportunity to bed the child's mother. Not much going on here, except for pretty Chen Yu Chiao.

AMAZON COMMANDO.
See *Golden Queen Commando*

AMAZONS OF HONG KONG (1980)
director: James Cheung. ★
How can a documentary about Chinese women wrestlers be so-o-o-o bor-

ing? You'll be begging for G.L.O.W. reruns.

AMERICAN SHAOLIN.
See *Treasure Hunt*

ANGEL (1986)
aka **IRON ANGELS**
aka **FIGHTING MADAM**
director: **Raymond Leung/Teresa Woo.** Moon Lee·Elaine Lui·Hideki Saijo·Yukari Oshima ★★★

ANGEL 2 (1988)
aka **IRON ANGELS 2**
aka **FIGHTING MADAM 2**
director: **Raymond Leung/Teresa Woo.** Moon Lee·Alex Fong·Elaine Lui ★★★

ANGEL 3 (1990)
aka **RETURN OF IRON ANGELS**
director: **Teresa Woo/Stanley Tong.** Moon Lee·Alex Fong·Ralph Chen· Kharina Isa ★★
Obviously inspired by *Charlie's Angels* and the HK hit *Deadly Angels,* this series features three incredible special-agent policewomen, including endearing **Moon Lee [Lee Choi Fung].** It's mostly wall-to-wall, frame-to-frame action with loads of shootings, mayhem, explosions, and (of course) girls with guns.

In #1, **Yukari Oshima** plays the sadistic villainess, Madame Su, involved in drug trafficking. And she steals the show.

#2 is the best of the three; the final half hour is an exhausting, roller-coaster ride through an amazing display of cinematic violence as the girls go to war.

The third film is a disappointing venture that relies more on Bondish-type gimmicks than the powerful exuberance of the female leads. Watch **Killer Angels** instead.

ANGEL ENFORCERS (1991)
director: **Ho Chi Mao.** Anh Lee·Yeung Pan Pan·Mon Choi·Chui Wai Ling· Dick Wei ★★½
Here's another variation on the popular **Angel** motif. This time four Kung Fu babes (one with a very trendy garter holster) try to stop a gang of diamond thieves directly associated with the mob. Lots of excessive gunplay, violence, and thrilling stunts. Plus the girls look great.

ANGEL FORCE (1991)
director: **Simon Yun Ching.** Moon Lee· Yukari Oshima·Sibelle Hu ★★½
Moon Lee continues the **Angel** charisma in this action-packed tale of special police squad versus Mafia gun traffickers.

Lots of well photographed fight sequences (with and without guns), mostly shot in the Thailand jungles, probably back to back with *Dreaming the Reality*. Light on plot, but very heavy on visual thrills and stunts; an extraordinary array of finely choreographed action scenes. Just relax your brain and enjoy the mayhem.

ANGEL HUNTER (1991)
director: **Sun Chung.** Anthony Wong· Vivian Chow·Lau Ching Wan·Ng Mau Tat ★★★
Devil worship is the central theme here. When a pretty student commits suicide it's because of her association with a secret cult of Satanists. The underground religion is thriving among teenagers due to their nihilistic attitude toward the forthcoming Chinese takeover of Hong Kong in 1997 (they compare it to the "end of the world"). Detective Chow (**Lau Ching Wan**) investigates when another student (**Vivian Chow [Zhou Hui Min]**) gets swallowed up by the teachings of the cult.

A blasting assault against all types of organized religion cleverly disguised as an action pic. Featuring high production standards, a superb soundtrack, and a stunning *girls-with-guns* conclusion!

ANGEL MISSION (1990)
director: Chris Li (Lee). Yukari Oshima· Yeung Pan Pan·Dick Wei·Kao Fei ★½
A dismal drug-trafficking/female slavery story highlighted only by an undaunted performance from **Yukari Oshima**. She plays an undercover cop from Japan trying to find some girls who have mysteriously disappeared in Hong Kong. In this preposterous script, her mother is a whorehouse madam behind the whole thing. What a coincidence! What crap!

ANGEL OR WHORE? (1990)
director: Raymond Leung. Emily Chu· Bao Yi Tu· Bai Ying ★★
A very evil magician, Hsi Chian (Bao Yi Tu), is doing nasty things. Finally, he's confronted by a beautiful female fighter (Emily Chu). She is actually a legendary superwoman known as Eighteen Virgins because of her ability to divide into 18 clones, each with specialized fighting skills. However, magician Chian manages to defeat her (them?) in a frenzied battle, but he is also killed in the process.

Switch to the afterlife. . . .

The Eighteen Virgins are in heaven; Hsi Chian goes to hell, where he tricks the devil (he doesn't consume an amnesia drug) and returns to Earth ("With Eighteen Virgins in heaven, I can do anything I want on Earth," Chian muses). But a local vigilante, named Stone Head (Bai Ying), and a young prostitute (the reincarnated superwoman in a reversed role, thus the title) eventually stop his reign of terror.

One of the perverse highlights of the film is when the old whorehouse madam, training her new prostitutes,

puts watermelons between their legs. "If you can break melons with your thighs, then surely you can take money from a man," she cackles. Mmmmm.

ANGEL TERMINATORS (1990)
director: Wai Lit. Clare Wai·Carrie Ng ★½

ANGEL TERMINATORS 2 (1991)
director: Simon Yun Ching. Moon Lee· Sibelle Hu·Yukari Oshima ★★
Maybe if the production company had hired mix-n-match expert **Godfrey Ho** to edit these two films into one slick feature, they'd have something worth talking about. But as they are, these movies only demonstrate how barren the girl-with-guns genre has become. Neither film covers new ground, but that's not surprising. The real crime here is watching these accomplished fighting divas in productions clearly beneath their talents.

Even though #2 has the same cast and the same director as *Dreaming the Reality* (also 1991), it definitely is lacking the same production standards. If you're given the choice, watch that one instead.

ANGEL THE KICKBOXER (1992)
director: Godfrey Ho. Moon Lee· Cynthia Rothrock·Yuhari Oshima· Waise Lee ★
Mix-and-match specialist **Godfrey Ho** is at it again! This time he takes pieces of a lackluster Cynthia Rothrock actioner (available in the United States as *Honor and Glory*) and combines it with **Yukari Oshima** fight sequences, plus large helpings of unreleased footage from an early **Waise Lee** heist caper. The result is, as expected, awful.

ANGEL'S BLOOD MISSION (1987)
director: Benny Ho [Godfrey Ho]. ★
Producer Joseph Lai strikes again! Here's another dreadful composite,

the unlikely combination of at least three different films attempting to tell the story of Hong Kong gangster families at war with each other.

The title is an obvious attempt to capitalize on the popular *Angel* series. And the opening cast credits is an illogical anglicized nightmare with names like Mark Watson, Mike Abbott, Gary Carter, Eric Hopper, etc.

ANGELS WITH GOLDEN GUNS.
See *Anger*

ANGER (1988)
aka **TERROR IN A WOMAN'S PRISON**
aka **ANGELS WITH GOLDEN GUNS**
director: **Leung Poeh [Pasan]**. Bill Lau·Eva Bisset·Gigi Bouce·Emma Yeung ★★½

The rating is based strictly on the sleaze factor and definitely not on the technical attributes of this film. It emerges as an accidental homage to Jess Franco, with hatchet edits and lots of pan-and-zoom nonsense. But the lurid camerawork adds to the overall trashy effect.

Boss Ho King (Bill Lau, looking a lot like an Asian Elvis without the gold chains) is deeply involved in the white slavery racket, supplying prostitutes and "thrill kittens" to the seedy underworld. Eventually three of the captive women lead a bloody rebellion (resulting in bullet-riddled bodies everywhere) and then join forces with an adventurous detective for the ultimate vengeance, which involves a rather unconventional use for firecrackers.

It's one of the sleaziest, with an amazing amount of nudity (especially during a bizarre love dance to the song "Je T'Aime"), bamboo-box torture, cheap sex, and sordid S&M sequences (highlighted by a disturbing male-scrotum whip scene).

ANGRY RANGER (1988)   **15**
director: **Lo Wei**. Iwanbeo Leung·Ben Lam ★★½

Ping-Wen (Iwanbeo Leung) returns to the old neighborhood after doing time in prison for a youth gang rumble. While he was in the slammer, things got worse and his former friends are now the "terror of the streets." They are members of a HK triad causing severe problems for the community. Ping-Wen tries his best to keep out of their way until they attack his family. Then he unleashes his own justice.

Reenactment of the '60s USA juvenile delinquency flicks, with an unsettling ultraviolent Hong Kong slant.

ANIMATION SEXITATION (1990)
director: **Lu Tung-Lo**. ★½

While a group of friends are playing Sexitation (an Asian adult boardgame similar to Truth or Dare with dominoes), they relate their private sexual fantasies. None of the stories are very exciting but the standouts include one about a man who gets his penis caught in a mousetrap, and another about three nude girls with guns, *Angel* fashion. Some of the vignettes feature X-rated animation, thus the title.

APARTMENT FOR WOMEN (1995)
aka **HOW DEEP IS YOUR LOVE**
director: **Chin Wing Keung**. Charlie Yeoh [Young]·Max Mok·Joyce Jiang Selena M.·Peta Marie·Jimmy Wang ★★

A bittersweet tale of single working girls (especially focusing on pretty **Charlie Yeoh [Young]**, introduced in **Tsui Hark**'s *The Lovers*) and the men in their lives. Sometimes funny, sometimes gritty, but not very original. It's mostly a collection of the standard soap-opera clichés, including both an unwanted pregnancy and an abusive boyfriend.

There's also a halfhearted jab taken at the inequities in the workplace, but

16 director **Chin** isn't as interested in issues as he is in characters. Or perhaps "caricatures" would be more correct.

ARMAGEDDON (1990)
director: Shao Jun-Huang. Alex Man ·Tsui Siu Keung ★★
A gang of Chinese criminals (led by **Tsui Siu Keung**) migrates to Hong Kong in search of easy pickings. After pulling a few jobs and killing a couple of cops, they turn their sights on the Tse Sui Luen Jewelry Company. But the robbery is miserably botched. Some of the crooks are tricked and killed by police supersleuth, Detective Yuen Shiu (**Alex Man**). The criminal boss vows vengeance on Yuen and his family.

Sloppy direction and stilted acting destroy any semblance of creativity in this routine actioner.

ARMOUR OF GOD (1987)
director: Jackie Chan. Jackie Chan· Alan Tam·Rosamund Kwan ★★★★

ARMOUR OF GOD 2:
OPERATION CONDOR (1991)
director: Jackie Chan (with **Frankie Chan**). Jackie Chan·Do Do Chen·Eva Cobode Gracia·Ikeda Shoko ★★★
Jackie Chan initially made a name for himself as a talented kung fu fighting stuntman, starring in many old school chop socky flicks including **Drunken Master, Dragon Fist, Fearless Hyena, Half a Loaf of Kung Fu**, and **Shaolin Wooden Men** (to mention only a few). He cemented his career throughout Asia (and much of the Western world) by making stylized, contemporary stunt-laiden, martial-arts action films (initially movies like **Dragons Forever, My Lucky Stars,** and **Wheels on Meals** followed by the exceptional **Police Story** saga).

These two "Armour" films, however, deviate from his usual fare into supernatural-thriller--adventure-spy yarns, similar to the *Indiana Jones* series.

Jackie plays Asian Hawk, who used to be in a rock band called The Losers, but now he works for an auction house. A former member of the band (now a big pop star) goes to Asian for help when his girlfriend is abducted. It seems that the kidnappers don't want money; rather, they want the valuable "Armour of God" which Asian has just secured for a museum auction. Lots of outlandish action follows, including a cannibal confrontation, monks with machine guns, and a particularly thrilling fight sequence between Jackie and a coven of female kickboxers.

Armour of God 2: Operation Condor is a loosely related sequel to #1 with even greater over-the-top FX and breath-taking stunts, especially during the deadly wind tunnel sequence inside an underground Nazi fortress. The plot deals with an international adventurer played by Chan (plus his two beautiful sidekicks, pretty Do Do Chen [Chen Yu Ling] and blonde Eva Cobode Gracia) and their search for 200+ tons of gold bars hidden by the Germans during World War II.

The film emerges as, reportedly, one of the most expensive Hong Kong productions of all time (Chan went way over budget on this one). And, in typical big-bucks fashion, it is extravagant in style and scope. But it also borrows far too much from *Indiana Jones* for it to be called original.

Lots of stunts, car chases, chop socky action, and bike chases. But the biggest problem lies in Chan's bedroom comedy sequences. These scenes are surprisingly lackluster. He seems incapable of generating any kind of romantic spark with his female leads.

ARREST THE RESTLESS (1994)
director: Lau Ka Chang [Larry Lau].
Heung Wah Keung·Leslie Cheung·Vivian Chow ★★½

This film, like many Hong Kong movies, is a combination of different genres. Its title alone implies a somber crime movie. And indeed, the movie begins that way. Sergeant Lam (**Heung Wah Keung**) crosses a powerful triad boss and finds himself demoted to the Police Juvenile Division.

At this point the tone of the movie changes, from a serious tough-cop-vs-organized-crime flick to an Asian *Rebel Without a Cause*. Teddy (**Leslie Cheung**) and Sic Man (**Vivian Chow**) are two kids who get mixed up in gang trouble, which results in the murder of a rival leader. A rotten cop pins the youth's death on Teddy, but Sergeant Lam knows the truth. After wrestling with his conscience, he decides that he can't stand by and watch an innocent boy become the victim of police corruption.

There's a lot going on in this movie, but most of it is yesterday's news. Ultimately, Leslie Cheung is handsome and Vivian Chow is great to look at. Perhaps the rest is unimportant.

AS TEARS GO BY (1988)
director: Wong Kar Wei. Maggie Cheung ·Andy Lau·Jacky Cheung ★★★

A darkly serious look at a gangster's life in Kowloon, with none of the excessive machismo so often cluttering HK crime movies. Director **Wong Kar Wei**'s style is slow and plodding (although not boring like his later *Days of Being Wild*). Through its deliberate pacing, the film manages to deliver a mean punch.

The somber story is helped by terrific performances, especially from **Andy Lau**, who walks an emotional tightrope between vulnerability and

Maggie Cheung in *As Tears Go By*

savage brutality. **Jacky Cheung** is also surprisingly good as the hotheaded gangster brother; and, of course, **Maggie Cheung** is a welcome sight in any film.

ASHES OF TIME (1994)
director: Wong Kar Wei. Leslie Cheung· Brigitte Lin·Tony Leung [Kar Fai]· Maggie Cheung· Tony Leung [Chiu Wai] · Jacky Cheung ★★★★

It's been described as "chop socky for the art theater crowd." But hiding behind this snooty moniker is a martial-arts film of epic proportions directed by **Wong Kar Wei**, arguably HK's most celebrated filmmaker.

This story of mercenary folk hero Ouyang Feng (**Leslie Cheung**) is told in a free-form, nonlinear narrative, featuring some of the world's most extraordinary cinematography (by Christopher Boyle) with breathtaking action to match.

Brigitte Lin [Lin Ching Hsia] plays a woman spurned. She initially hires Ouyang to kill her unfaithful suitor Huang (**Tony Leung [Kar Fai]**). But then, mysteriously, she changes her mind and hires him to protect the rogue.

Another subplot involves the *other* **Tony Leung [Chiu Wai]** as a heroic swordsman slowly going blind. He's been hired to protect a town from brutal horse thieves, but he really wants to make enough money to return home and see his wife before completely losing his sight.

Director Wong has come a long way since his early minimalistic movies like **Days of Being Wild** (1991). Without selling out to the lowest common denominator, he has created the definitive action film filled with meaty characterizations and brilliant performances. Some exploitation fans will still complain about Wong's methodical pacing, but these are the same people who bitch about Sergio Leone Westerns as being slow.

Ashes of Time also features **Jacky Cheung** and **Maggie Cheung** in supporting roles.

ASSASSIN (1993)
director: Cheng Siu Keung. Mok Siu Chung·Rosamund Kwan ★★★½

Here's a unique twist on the *Femme Nikita* story, this time with a male in the pivotal position. This epic action adventure film, set in the 18th century, tells the bloody story of Tong Po Ka **(Max Mok [Mok Siu Chung])** whose forbidden love is the catalyst turning him from a simple farmer into the region's number one killer/swordsman.

Po Ka's forbidden love is Yiu **(Rosamund Kwan)**. And before they can run away together, the hero is arrested on trumped-up charges. In prison, Tong demonstrates his brutal fighting ability and his unflinching disregard for human life, so the ruler appoints him as an undercover government assassin specializing in delicate exterminations. Tong becomes a heartless killing machine. But a chance reunion with his old flame Yiu makes him reassess his violent behavior. The warlord can't allow this transformation in Tong's personality, so. . . . Well, you get the idea.

The final sequence is, perhaps, the best in any martial-arts pic. But the movie is full of classic kung fu battles and intense swordplay with many beheadings, torso splittings, severed limbs, poison drinks, beautiful young girls, giant dildos, perverted eunuchs, betrayals, and gruesome revenges. Director **Cheng** keeps the action moving with fluid camerawork and crisp editing. A great-looking production, rated Category III for excessively graphic violence.

ASYLUM OF LOVE (1987)
director: Lu Tung-Lo. ★

Somewhere in the middle of this mess there's a story about ghosts haunting a man who has just returned from a campaign in the Manchurian marshlands. It all takes place in the 19th century, and he lives in a bizarre castle filled with hunchback men and beautiful women. (Well, kinda beautiful, anyway.) There are some unexpected XXX scenes, but none of it is very interesting or entertaining.

ATTACK OF THE JOYFUL GODDESS (1982)
director: Chiang Sheng with Lu Fong. Chien Tien Su·Hsu Chung Fei·Lee Chung I·Lee Chien Sheng ★

This is a very confused (and confusing) story, set in ancient China, about a troupe of traveling performers and a town general who wants to have sex with the leading actress.

It also has something to do with evil spirits being rejuvenated by placing a doll face-up inside a suitcase. Go figure.

AU REVOIR, MON AMOUR (1991)
director: Kenneth Tsang. Tony Leung [Kar Fai]·Anita Mui ★★

A big-budget soap opera starring **Tony Leung (Kar Fai)** and **Anita Mui [Mei Yan Feng]**, set against the backdrop of Japanese-occupied Shanghai during

Michiko Nishiwaki, Yukari Oshima, Cynthia Khan, and Moon Lee (L to R) in
Avenging Quartet

World War II. Former lovers, Mui Ye (**Mui**) and Shun (**Leung**), reunite in the midst of revolutionary violence.

AVENGING QUARTET (1992)
director: (Stanley) Wing Siu. Cynthia Khan·Moon Lee·Yukari Oshima· Nishiwaki Michiko·Waise Lee ★★½
If you're content to bypass plot in favor of watching fighting divas pound the shit out of each other, then this is for you.

Chinese female cop **Cynthia Khan** teams up with powerhouse **Moon Lee** to stop two bad girls from Tokyo, **Yukari Oshima** and Nishiwaki Michiko, who are plotting to steal a valuable painting from Waise Lee. But, as you might expect, the plot isn't as important as the frenzied kung fu action. These girls kick major butt!

AWAKENING (1994)
director: Cha Chuen Yee [Cha Fu Yi]. Anthony Wong·Simon Yan·Lee Yuen Wah ★★
What a dream project! And how sad

to see it turned into a nightmare. Here are Hong Kong's two leading psycho actors, **Simon Yam** and **Anthony Wong** together again for the first time since *Full Contact* (1992). Their chemistry alone should have turned this into the cult hit of the year. But no such luck.

Early on, the relationship between the two characters is intriguing, punctuated by crisp dialogue and clever rivalry. However, long before the incoherent close, this project is seriously derailed. **Cha Chuen Yee**, a director with a flare for crime and ghastly horror, should stay away from comedy. His timing and camera angles are miscalculated, often detracting from the punchline.

Awakening begins as a very dark thriller. Fung Shui (**Simon Yam**) stands by helplessly, watching his wife and baby as they are ripped apart by an unseen force. Apparently they were given bogus exorcism advice by a celebrity necromancer, Liu Sheng Ming (**Anthony Wong**). Fung vows vengeance against the phony priest.

Years pass, and an elaborate trap has been concocted. Fung hopes to publicly humiliate Liu and steal his wife and child in the process.

Somewhere in the middle of this quirky story, director Cha felt the need to add comedy. Not dark humor (which would've complimented the hoodoo witchery), but out-of-character nonsense involving cross-dressing, lamebrained assistants, car chases, and even some slapstick. But what happened to the plot? The whole thing ends with Fung and Liu becoming friends, ready to embark on a cleansing mission against the phony wonderworkers of the world.

We're left with dreams of how good it could've been.

BAMBOO HOUSE OF DOLLS (1977)
director: Kuei Chih-Hung. Birte Tove·
Lo Lieh ★★★

Never flinching, the Shaw brothers jumped into the exploitation market full-tilt for this ultraviolent misogynist tale of women brutalized in a Japanese prison camp during World War II.

Obviously designed as an international project [the uncut print was banned in Hong Kong for over 10 years and it's never been shown uncut theatrically in the United States], this production has a bevy of attractive women, including Anglo beauty Birte Tove. She plays a captured Red Cross nurse who tries to mastermind an escape from the horrors. Veteran actor Lo Lieh is a camp officer (secretly a double agent) who assists the girls.

The movie is a parade of vicious torture sequences and gratuitous, unabashed nudity. Shockingly savage, this film remains the granddaddy of the women-in-prison atrocity flicks. Definitely not for the casual viewer.

BANQUET (1991)
director: Tsui Hark. ★

It was a good idea. It just isn't a good movie. Almost every major actor and actress in Hong Kong (with the conspicuous absence of **Jackie Chan** and **Chow Yun-Fat**) offered their names and talent to this film, with all proceeds donated to the victims of the disastrous flooding in mainland China earlier that year.

The plot, dealing with a ruthless businessman and his attempt to secure a contract to rebuild Kuwait, is virtually nonexistent. It's little more than an excuse for a parade of endless cameos and unsatisfying vignettes.

Stargazing is the only reason anyone would watch this lame comedy. Just for the record, here's a list of some participating stars: **Tony Leung,** Eric Tsang, **Rosamund Kwan, Jacky Cheung, Samo Hung, Joey Wang [Wong], Maggie Cheung, Sally Yip [Yeh], Anita Mui, Simon Yam, Karl Maka, Leslie Cheung, Stephen Chow,** Waise Lee, **Ti Lung,** Richard Ng, and Willie Chan.

BAREFOOTED KID.
See *Young Hero*

BATTLE CREEK BRAWL (1980)
director: Robert Clouse. Jackie Chan ·Mako·Jose Ferrer·Kristine De Bell· Ron Max·Rosalind Chao ★½

Here's a weak 1980 attempt to break **Jackie Chan** into the American marketplace.

In 1930 Chicago, a Chinese immigrant (Jackie Chan) pisses off a gangster boss (Jose Ferrer), and he proceeds to make the mob henchmen look like dunces during countless encounters, including a ludicrous fistfight on rollerskates. Eventually, the whole thing ends up in a predictable bare-knuckles boxing competition.

This film was met with lukewarm response from both the critics and the martial arts fans. Jackie Chan went on to star with Burt Reynolds in both *Cannonball Run* and the disastrous *Can-*

nonball *Run 2* before returning to Hong Kong. In 1985, he returned to America to make **Protector** with equally disappointing results.

BATTLE IN HELL (1989)
director: Wen Hua/Girao Fan. Yang Bao Ling·Fan Ji Rao·Fang Zhong-Xiu ★★½

Three beautiful Mongolian sisters kill themselves when their father's army suffers a defeat at the hands of the invading Chinese hordes. Their spirits are resurrected in contemporary times, but they have become vicious vampires bent on revenge.

The film is handled in traditional horror fashion, with loads of atmosphere and good visual FX—unnecessarily complicated by a routine thread-bare "love through reincarnation" theme.

BEASTS.
See *Flesh and the Bloodrum Terror*

BEAUTIFUL DEAD BODY
aka **SPOOKY KAMA SUTRA** (1987)
director: Xin Ren. Cheryle Chung· Tiajia Han ★★

A girl (Cheryle Chung) kills herself after being drugged and raped by a sinister warlock named Tong (Tiajia Han). But, in this instance, death is not the final stop. The evil sorcerer breathes life into the young victim and continues to seduce her (in rather boring but decidedly X-rated fashion).

When a good magician threatens him, Tong activates an army of zombies to fight the battle. In the end, white magic triumphs and wicked Tong is defeated. Big surprise, right?

BEAUTY EVIL ROSE (1994)
director: Lam Wuah Chuen. Usang Yeong Fang·Suen Chi Wai ★★★

In Thailand, an evil witch named Da-Shaie (Usang Yeong Fang) and her leather-clad female followers are kidnapping and brainwashing nubile young girls into joining their cult. A man, Ah-Kang, and his fashion model girlfriend, Manna, arrive from HK, looking for his missing sister. The two join forces with a disheveled priest and a cop to do battle with the cult. Manna is used as bait to help locate the group. After repeated attacks involving witchcraft and Uzis, they succeed in destroying the witch and her followers.

Simply, *Beauty Evil Rose* is a demented Hong Kong delight. It's a sexy S&M thriller, featuring every possible gratuitous element HK fans could want. There's wagonloads of nudity. Witchcraft. Torture. Monsters. Guns. Plus knockdown gorgeous women in various stages of aggression, domination, and nakedness, highlighted by the extraordinary charms of newcomer Usang Yeong Fang. She's the kind of cold-blooded beauty who could give the Pope a wet dream.

The monsters are cheesy. But what else can we expect from protruding penis creatures? And the unexpected girls-with-guns finale serves as icing on an already delicious cake. Turn off your brain, and have fun.

BEAUTY INVESTIGATOR (1992)
director: Hsu Hsia. Moon Lee· Yukari Oshima·Sophia Crawford· Melvin Wong ★★½

Once again, **Moon Lee** is a cop who goes undercover as a nightclub singer (i.e., **Killer Angels**). And once again, she ends up fighting **Yukari Oshima**, who plays a (you guessed it!) Japanese hitwoman (as in **Angel**). Plus, once again **Yukari Oshima** turns out to be a police double agent (**Book of Heroes**).

Despite this incredibly tired plot, the girls look great and the action is swift. So, damn it anyway, it's still a lot of fun.

BEFORE DAWN (1988)
director: Clarence Fok Yiu Leung. Loletta Lee·Yi Wan (Dean Ip)·Yip Tak Hu
★★
"Why did my son become such a monster?" cries Kian's mother (Yip Tak Hu). And in this low-rent thriller/soap opera we get the answer. It's a disjointed tale of a boy (Yi Wan) who flirts with homosexuality, drugs, and the underworld as he rebels against his well-meaning but slutty mom.

Filmmaker **Fok** has vastly improved his style since directing this film (simply compare this one with his marvelous **Naked Killer** in '93), but his fascination with disturbingly violent images and alternative sex practices has remained consistent through the years.

BEHEADED 1000
director: Ting Shan Si. Joey Wang· Anita Mui·Wang Yu·Gian Xiao-Lao
★★
Amateurish special effects mar the credibility of this ambitious fantasy epic (clocking in at almost 2 hours). It's the story of a grand executioner (Gian Xiao-Lao) who beheads his 1000th criminal, and in so doing is responsible for unleashing a demon army controlled by the Blood Lotus (beautiful **Joey Wang [Wong]**, who seems to be having the time of her life).

Anita Mui is totally wasted in her cameo as a ghostly messenger. **Wang Yu** tries hard, but he isn't very convincing as the executioner's apprentice. Yet, nothing is more irritating than the cheesy FX, wildly incongruous in this otherwise striking production.

BEST IS THE HIGHEST (1990)
    aka **HE WHO'S THE BEST IS THE**
    HIGHEST
director: Samo Hung. Chin Ka Lok· Lam Ching Ying·Samo Hung·Wu Ma
★★
Basically, it's a battle for the Palace of Heaven between Against-Nature Boy of the Evil Religion and DeaLei Lama, the Sharp-Witted Buddha. Evil A/N-Boy has given Master Mud-Yuet (**Lam Ching Ying**) an ultimatum: Deliver the challenging Buddha for a death match within seven weeks or relinquish the throne. Mud-Yuet joins forces with arrogant Chak-Fei (**Samo Hung**) to train a young fighter (**Chin Ka Lok**) for the grand battle. Silly fantasy nonsense with wacky charm.

BET ON FIRE (1988)
director: Tony Cheung [Cheung Ren-Jie]. Joey Wang·Cherie Chung·Cheung Man ★★★
Cherie Chung (from **Once a Thief**) and **Cheung Man** (the only pleasant thing about most **Stephen Chow** films) are two young women forced into a life of prostitution. Mostly this is a sensitive melodrama about loyalty and female bonding. Until the end, when it becomes a graphic ultraviolent revenge flick.

A BETTER TOMORROW (1986)
director: John Woo. Chow Yun-Fat·Ti Lung·Leslie Cheung·Emily Chu ★★★★

A BETTER TOMORROW 2 (1987)
director: John Woo. Chow Yun-Fat·Ti Lung·Leslie Cheung·Dean Shek ★★★★

A BETTER TOMORROW 3 (1989)
director: Tsui Hark. Chow Yun-Fat· Anita Mui·Tony Leung [Chiu Wai]· Saburo Tokito ★★★½
Because of this incredible series, especially #1 and #2, **Chow Yun-Fat** is a major star in Asia (see **The Killer, Full Contact, Hard-boiled**, etc). And **John Woo** is now making big budget films in the United States for Twentieth Century Fox.

These are gangster films that focus on criminals as heroes, but not in a pandering fashion like the "USA-Scarface-type" films. Rather, these movies are Hong Kong's answer to the macho Italian Western, with refreshing emphasis on loyalty and camaraderie. Here, the characters live in a bittersweet yet gallant world where violence is the only way of life. In fact, violence IS life.

Chow Yun-Fat is Mark, a gangster who dauntlessly lives by a strict code of honor and loyalty even though his world is filled with corruption and crime. However, his partner Ho (**Ti Lung**) is wrestling with his conscience, generally suffering from guilt feelings, mostly due to his father's disapproval of the syndicate. He is also afraid of potential problems with his younger brother Kit (**Leslie Cheung**), a naive rookie cop currently ignorant of Ho's true profession. When a trafficking deal goes sour, the double-crossing bad guys retaliate against Ho's family, killing his father. Ho winds up arrested and imprisoned. Mark retaliates against the evil gang (one of the best examples of John Woo's incredible heroic bloodshed gun mania), but he ends up critically wounded. When Ho gets out of prison, he finds Mark is now a cripple, reduced to a subhuman position with the mob. He tries to help his friend, but soon realizes the crime lords will never leave them alone. Mark, Ho, and brother Kit arm themselves to the hilt and attack the gang in a blazing finale.

Even though Mark is killed in #1, Chow Yun-Fat returns as cousin Ken in #2. This is a mere contrivance in the plot as charismatic Chow plays the role in the same fashion, with the same attitude. Mark or Ken?—it's truly insignificant. This time Ken is operating a Chinese restaurant in New York and gets mixed up with the HK triads. The whole thing escalates into another gang war in Hong Kong. The conclusion of #2 is staggering (and emotionally fascinating) with its bewildering, blood-drenched body count that goes on forever. These movies are anthems to heroic bloodshed. They contain the most over-the-top bullet-spitting, machine gun-cracking, blood-splattering scenes of all time. In any movie. From any country. Ever.

#3 is a deviation from the first two films, as producer **Tsui Hark** becomes director; the pace is much slower and the movie takes on a saga feel. This is not necessarily a negative, but is a departure from the initial exploitive nature of the series. #3 is more correctly described as a "prequel" [circa 1974] with heavier concentration on character development (a field day for Chow Yun-Fat and **Anita Mui** [sometimes **Mei**]) and less emphasis on action.

BEWITCHED (1981)
director: Gui Zhihong [Zhi Hong].
Lily Chan·Melvin Wong·Ai Fei·Fen Ni
★
While under an evil spell, a man kills his daughter; an investigating police detective also becomes possessed. A good monk fights and defeats the spell. Humdrum amusement.

BIG BRAWL.
See *Battle Creek Brawl*

BIG HEAT (1988)
director: Andrew Kam/Johnny To.
Waise Lee·Kwok Choy·Joey Wang· Chu Kong ★★★½
Produced by **Tsui Hark,** this graphic blood-and-gore spectacle features an amazing barrage of nonstop mayhem, as Detective Wong (Waise Lee) and his cohorts try to stop a gangster kingpin from importing drugs into Hong Kong.

The crime lord is determined to go full throttle, bent on making his fortune before crime-and-punishment changes in the 1997 Chinese takeover. Detective Wong tries desperately to find witnesses who will testify against the big boss, but they are eliminated as

Chow Yun-Fat in A Better Tomorrow 2

quickly as they are discovered. The killings are especially graphic; truckloads of gore and HK blood. It's an incredible display of action and brutal violence.

BIG SCORE (1990)
director: **Wong Ching (Jing).** Joey Wang· Danny Lee·Lam Chung·Kwok Shing Hong ★★★
Another ultraviolent cop/action flick, notable for an unusual computer espionage plotline. But, undoubtedly, the main attraction is the ruthless gangster hit squad featuring an incarnately evil villainess (**Joey Wang**).

Amazingly, at one point, she says, "Short life, huh?" as she blasts a child cowering in the corner of the room. No doubt about it, this is a very nasty woman!

However, the film is seriously marred by an awkward buddy motif between the two policemen. It's a contrived relationship that doesn't ring true, cluttered with annoying comic relief and unnecessary slapstick.

BITE OF LOVE (1990)
director: **Stephen Shin.** George Lam· Rosamund Kwan ★★★
Director **Stephen Shin** (of **Black Cat** fame) creates an effective, lethargic vampire tale—more akin to the Euro horror films than to the HK variety.

George Lam is a lonely bloodsucker who is repulsed by the concept

of killing to live. Instead, he stays alive by becoming the blood bank's best customer. But eventually the bank runs dry, and he is forced to take a harder look at his predicament.

BITTER TASTE OF BLOOD (1986)
director: **Albert Lai.** Tong Chun Yip· Cher Yeung ★★
After a successful robbery, one of the young thugs slips away and retreats to his uncle's home in the country. There he falls in love with pretty Ling and attempts to start a new life. But his former gang won't leave him alone. He decides to take the law into his own hands, eliminating his ex-partners but dying in the process.

You've seen it a thousand times before. Or at least it seems that way.

BLACK BUTTERFLY (1990)
director: **Raymond R. Lu.** ★
The low rating is a backlash response. This film begins with stirring promise (almost like a female version of **The Killer**), but too quickly it degenerates into a very predictable, claustrophobic gangster flick. You'll feel cheated.

BLACK CAT (1991)
director: **Stephen Shin.** Jade Leong· Simon Yam·Thomas Lam ★★★★

BLACK CAT 2 (1993)
director: **Stephen Shin.** Jade Leung· Robin Shou ★★
#1 is an incredibly violent and immensely satisfying film from the director of **Bite of Love**. This is an Asian version of the controversial French motion picture La Femme Nikita (Point of No Return for the Bridget Fonda fans) with some unforgettable scenes. And in many ways, this story of a misunderstood nonconformist in a brutal world emerges superior to the original.

Scientists install a microchip (called Black Cat) inside the brain of a violence-prone girl named Catherine (convincingly played by newcomer **Jade Leung**) in an attempt to refine and control her fits of rage. Their plan is to turn her into the perfect government secret agent "killing machine." It's a detailed look at how the system creates its own brand of madness. Yes, this movie is very strong stuff. It goes straight for the jugular. Perhaps the best example is when her CIA trainer, Brian (**Simon Yam**), decides to test Catherine during a romantic holiday. They stop at a church, where she is instructed to kill a just-married bride. And she does so without flinching. Plus, the ending will give you a jolt.

#2 is a disappointing mixed bag with Jade Leung returning in the title role, but it's sadly marred by the inclusion of an unbelievable supervillain—plus the espionage plot is already dated by the fall of Russia.

BLACK DRAGON.
See *Mr. Canton and Lady Rose*

BLACK MAGIC (1980)
director: **Ho Meng Hua [Ho Menga]**.
Ti Lung·Lo Lieh·Lily Li·Ku Feng·Linda Chu ★★½

BLACK MAGIC 2 (1982)
aka **REVENGE OF THE ZOMBIES**
director: **Ho Meng Hua [Ho Menga]**.
Ti Lung·Lo Lieh·Linda Chu·Liu Hui Tu ★★★

BLACK MAGIC 3 (1985)
aka **BLACK MAGIC TERROR**
aka **QUEEN OF BLACK MAGIC**
director: **Lawrence Chen (L. Sudjio)**.
Suzzanna·W.D. Muchtar·Teddy Purba ·Wil Sofia ★½
Basically *Black Magic 1* and *2* (aka *Revenge of the Zombies*) are "black magic vs white magic" movies with some totally outrageous elements. There's a warlock with an army of female zombies (brought to life by

Jade Leung in Black Cat

pounding spikes through their skulls), nests of worms and centipedes multiplying under the skin of a hapless victim, an evil magician who drinks human milk to keep from aging, plus exploding bodies, love potions, crocodiles slit open, fireballs, and much more. Both 1 and 2 are groundbreaking horror entries from the Shaw brothers' production company.

#3 (also known as *Queen of Black Magic*) is a Philippines/Indonesia co-production. It's a sequel in name only, the by-product of an Asian distribution deal. For the true sequel to Black Magic 1 and 2, see a film called *Seeding of a Ghost* (1986), also produced by the Shaw brothers.

BLACK MAGIC WITH BUTCHERY
aka **BLACK MAGIC WITH BUDDHA** (1989)
director: **Lo Lieh**. Lo Lieh·Candy Yu· Chaun Koon Tai·Chau Sing ★★½
Here is a cheap exploitation film that succeeds totally on that level. Director **Lo Lieh** must be trying for Hong Kong's Herschell Gordon Lewis award, delivering the goods with a very gory version of *Fiend Without a Face*.

The story is about two explorers who invade a temple in the dark of a jungle. They find a mummy, remove its brain, and return to the mainland. The blood and fluid from the brain are used in black magic rituals that result in a series of bloody murders throughout the city . . . committed by the brain! Seeing is believing.

Incidentally, director Lo began his career as a martial arts actor. He also starred as the villain in the legendary *Black Magic* movies and *Human Skin Lanterns*. He also directed *Summons to Death*.

BLACK SHEEP (1988)
director: Wen Lap Kuen. Cheung Hing Wong·Lin Wai Ken·Yuen Ken Chui·Foo Wai Yu ★★
This is a stark (yet emasculated) story of a high school gang and their assault against society. Although it tries to be realistic, the movie never really rises above the *To Sir with Love* sugary sort of message film. This is no *Boyz N the Hood*.

BLADE OF FURY (1993)
director: Samo Hung. Ti Lung·Cynthia Khan·Ngai Sing·Samo Hung ★★★½
Big budget, well-written, expertly directed chop socky fare. **Samo Hung** has created a stunning motion picture here, aided by the brilliant fighting/acting ability of veteran **Ti Lung**.

The plot pits brother against brother in the land of the Black Flag, a nationalistic sector of China where isolationism is the political law.

If you're looking for incredible martial arts action, brutal swordplay, and fistfighting combat—this is the movie to see.

It's also good to catch **Cynthia Khan** dressed in something besides a cop uniform. She shines as Ti Lung's servant, Nine Catties. But it's still Samo Hung's movie. He wrote, chore-ographed, and directed it with frenzied precision, plus he stars as the maniacal villain.

BLESS THIS HOUSE (1986)
director: Donny [Rentai] Yu. Bill Tung ·Loletta Lee ★★★
A good haunted house story, similar to Tobe Hooper's *Poltergeist*. The FX are enjoyable and the action is swift, especially in the last half hour. Worth the watch.

BLIND SWORDSWOMAN (1982)
aka BLIND SWORDSWOMEN
director: L. Titus. ★½
This is a variation on the Japanese blind Samurai films, with two blind women in the lead roles. It's the story of their effort to retrieve the *Book of Sanho*, stolen by evil dictator, Vita Lee.

Sounds like **Tsui Hark's The Swordsman** (1991), doesn't it? Well, interestingly, it includes some of the same stunts later used in Hark's expensive production, especially the candle-flame gag.

BLIND WARRIOR (1987)
director: Ratno Timoer. Enny Beatrice ·Rudy Pusha·Nenua Roiser ★★
So much potential, most of it wasted. The biggest problem with the film *is* the Blind Warrior hero. He's incredibly lackluster.

But on the plus side, in typical Hindu/Indochina fashion, there's an (over)abundance of gore. Primarily, severed limbs, squirting blood, and decapitations (at least five, some very unusual). And the villain, Radna Parna, is quite good. He's a religious dictator who uses his power to oppress the poor and satisfy his lust for women. The virgin-sacrificing scenes are top-notch.

Incidentally, Barta the Blind Warrior (Enny Beatrice) also lumbers his way through a sequel called *Warrior* and *Blind Warrior* (teamed with Barry Prima).

BLONDE FURY (1987)
aka LADY REPORTER
director: Mang Hoi. Cynthia Rothrock·Chin Siu Ho·Roy Chiao·Mang Hoi·Wu Ma·Jeff Falcon ★★½
Perhaps one of Cynthia Rothrock's best films, tailormade for the blonde kickboxer. She's a newspaper reporter who decides to investigate charges against a top banker (Chin Siu Ho) when she senses his conviction was trumped up. Cynthia and the banker's daughter (Elizabeth Lee) eventually clear his good name, but the road to righteousness is lined with countless bad guys, including popular kung fu villain Jeff Falcon.

If the story appears more convoluted than necessary, it's because the film was (for whatever reason) shot over a two-year period, with different writers and cinematographers. And Cynthia's hairstyle changes at least twice during the production.

BLOODBATH 23 (1990)
aka LIFE'S GAMBLE 23
director: Oli Nicole. Anna Veyama·Max Mok ★★★
Writer, producer, and director **Oli Nicole** creates a highly unusual Asian thriller here, starring pretty **Anna Veyama**. She plays a dance teacher stalked by a vengeful escaped killer.

There is also a collection of sex-oriented subplots (reminiscent of Russ Meyer's *Beyond the Valley of the Dolls*); however the story is definitely inspired by bait-and-stalk films. It's a weird combination, but it works with a style of its own.

BLOOD DEMON (1988)
aka TALE FROM THE EAST
director: Len Tsu Chow. ★★
It's a curious attempt to mix *Friday the 13th* with *E.T.* (!?!) A bunch of high

school kids have a barbecue/campout (sound familiar?). They are visited by extraterrestrials, including a vicious superstrength monster yearning for blood. There are also some good E.T.s being chased by the brute. However, it's a pair of wacky electricians who really make the movie work.

BLOOD MANIAC (1986)
director: Tong Wai Sing. Ching Wong Mui·Min Fung Fun·Wai Lan·Ko Ling ★½
Cheap. Cheap. Cheap.
Gory. Gory. Gory.

A man (Wai Lan) brings home his new wife (Ching Wong Mui) and is faced with an icy reception from his parents. His devil-worshipping brother has recently died, but the warlock's spirit is haunting the house. Soon the man becomes possessed and (somehow) creates a mental link with a zombie buried in the backyard (!).

The result is a bloody free-for-all, including an outrageous hand-through-a-belly segment. The whole thing ends with his wife giving birth to a monstrous fanged creature that rips its way through her stomach. This is no easy childbirth.

The film wins the "Worst Use of a Musical Soundtrack" award. A pause button is distractingly pushed every time there's a line of dialogue. But, honestly, the film is such an abomination, even that distraction adds to the fun.

BLOOD OF AN INDIAN FETISH CULT (1984)
aka INNOCENT NYMPHS
director Man Kun Boa. Oi Wai Nai·Hong Yu Hong·Moan Fung·Chung Tai Bil ★★
Words like "bizarre" and "odd" can't do justice to this outlandish Chinese/Samoan coproduction. A cult of Chinese, who idolize American Indians,

retreat into the wilderness, where they build a Jonestown-type reservation.

Their religious rituals soon get out of hand, and at one point, the priestess (Oi Wai Nai) loves her mate to death (in graphic XXX-rated fashion). Surrounding the ceremonies are a series of goofy vignettes including a martial arts fighter who strengthens his penis by slamming it into a tree trunk! Not for the easily offended.

BLOOD OF THE BLACK DOG
aka **THE ACCIDENT** (1987)
director: Stanley Tong. Kent Cheng·Ai Di ★★★

This movie's attraction relies on its ability to surprise. It begins as Disney-type fluff showing a tender relationship between a young girl (Ai Di) and her uncle (fatty **Kent Cheng [Cheng Chuen Yan]**); but after a scene with a ritualistic slaying of the family dog, it explodes into an amazing frenzy of ghost and demon terrorism punctuated by a frightening crucifixion sequence. It's a roller coaster ride.

BLOOD RITUAL (1988)
director: Li Yuen Ching [Li Siu Wah]. Chiu Siu Keung·Gina Lam·Dion Lam·Lam Ki Yam ★★

The first 15 minutes pack a wallop as a gang of delinquents stalk and rape a girl in the dark ruins of an old building. Then, unfortunately, the film regresses into a routine, preachy police drama about how "our youth is turning to devil worship and worse." When a cop (Chiu Siu Keung) is exposed as a member of a demon cult, it's all downhill. Too bad.

Also starring Dion Lam as the police detective investigating the case.

BLOOD SORCERY (1986)
director: Pan Ling Tong. Gu Feng·Bai Biao ★★

Two explorers (Gu Feng and Bai Biao) are cursed when they steal a magic jade statuette from jungle natives in Borneo. Lots of gross and gory FX, including blood dripping from unusual bodily orifices, leeches swimming around under the skin, and, while a man is eating, his dinner turns into a plate of worms. Oriental hoodoo.

BLOODSTAINED TRADEWIND (1990)
director: Chu Yuan. Waise Lee·Carrie Ng·Lo Lieh ★★★

If you are still searching for the ultimate gun movie, take a close look at this one. It's a virtual whirlwind of bullets, as a Japanese gang attempts to gain control of Hong Kong's underworld. There's an impressive cast (Waise Lee, **Carrie Ng**, Lo Lieh, Alex Fong, and **Ng Man Tat**) and not much chance of a sequel. They all end up dead at the film's conclusion.

BLOODY BEAST (1994)
director: Yueng Kuen. Lawrence Ng [Ng Kai Wah]·Eugina Lau·Tong Chung Yip ★★★

Lawrence Ng, usually relegated to supporting roles (e.g., **Sex and Zen, Underground Banker**) catches the ball this time and runs with it.

The structure is similar to all the other HK true crime films (from **Dr. Lamb** [1992] to **Untold Story** [1992]. There is no doubt as to who the killer is, merely how heinous were his crimes. And with regard to Chen Siu Hsiong (Lawrence Ng), his crimes were monstrous.

The film opens with Chen already in prison. He is constantly beaten and tortured by the warden, who is trying to get a full confession out of him. Finally, Chen agrees to tell all if three conditions are met. First, the name and address of his family must be kept secret; second, there can be no media coverage; and third, he must be executed immediately after his confession. The warden agrees, and Chen tells his story.

He was a nerdy kid, mistreated by both his father and sister. When his mother dies, Chen assumes the household chores, which confine him to the home. Secretly, he longs for the touch of a woman and satisfies himself by spying on his sister as she undresses. Chen finds the opportunity to be alone with a pretty widow and her little girl. He brutally kills them both and rapes the dead woman. His next victim is a woman bathing on the riverbank. Once again he kills and violates her.

After sneaking a peek at his sister making love to her boyfriend, Chen decides he'd like to try sex with a living girl. He attacks a woman and forces her to perform oral sex. But when she bites him, Chen figures it's best to kill first and then screw.

Eventually he picks the wrong victim, a girl who's proficient at martial arts. She fights him off and then fingers him for the police. With his story completed, the film concludes as Chen is executed in prison.

Filmmaker **Yueng Kuen**, long associated with chop socky films (he directed *Shadow of the Tigers* [1979]), is a diligent craftsman. It's obvious that he understands this genre, as he has imitated it so precisely. There's plenty of gross-out violence, lots of nudity, and a bit of humor from the incidental characters. The real difference between this one and the many other similar ventures is **Lawrence Ng.** His performance is both varied and poignant, a difficult task while maintaining an aura of lunacy.

BLOODY FIGHT (1990)
director: Wilson Tong. Tsui Siu Keung •Liu Chu Yuen ★★
Yet another reworking of **The Killer**. A hitman teams up with a cop, to fight the triad after his family is killed. The action is intense and the gunplay state-of-the-art, but there's nothing new going on here. This is especially dis-

appointing after director Tong's wildly original horror film **Ghost Nursing** (1988).

BLOODY GHOST
aka **FUNNY GHOST** (1988)
director: Yuen Chun Man. Sandra Ng• Chang Pak Cheung ★★★
A gangster buys two canisters from a witch. Inside bottle #1 lives a female ghost; the spirit of her unborn son is in #2. Meanwhile, a beautiful but penniless waitress (Sandra Ng) attempts suicide by leaping from a building top. Her fall is broken by the gangster's car, and (miraculously) she ends up with canister #1. The chase is on.

Eventually the bottle is broken and the ghost escapes to wreak havoc. The evil spirit is destroyed when the heroine drips blood on the small bottle, somehow making the mother ghost's stomach expand (as if pregnant) until she explodes. By the way, this is a comedy.

BLOODY HAND GODDESS (1985; released in 1994)
director: Leung Kay. Ching Wan Lau •Leung See Ho ★
The evil Bloody Hand Goddess had a baby girl who was kidnapped by a brave swordsman. But the goddess took revenge by killing the man. Luckily, his friend had hidden the child so the villainess couldn't find her. Eventually, the girl seeks the help of Pure Man of Mount Wang to assist in a challenge against her evil mother.

This dreadful martial arts fantasy had been collecting dust on a shelf somewhere for almost ten years before it was finally released in 1994. And there's only one reason it's available at all. It stars current Hong Kong heartthrob **Lau Ching Wan** (the brooding lead from **C'Est la Vie, Mon Cheri** [1993], **Doctor Mack** [1995], and **Tears and Triumph** [1994]). But you can be sure Lau would've preferred for this one to stay buried.

BLOODY SMiLE (1980)
director: Park Yoon Kyo. Chung Se Hyuk·Chi Mi Ok ★★
During childbirth, a family sacrifices the life of the mother to save her baby. She returns from the grave and takes possession of another woman to get revenge.

After a collection of humdrum horror films, director **Park** returned to his original profession, cinematography. He lensed **Tsui Hark's** *Once Upon a Time in China* series.

BLUE JEAN MONSTER (1990)
director: Jimmy Li (Ivan Lai). Shing Fui On·Amy Yip ★★★½
This film vacillates so wildly between tasteless sexual humor and brilliantly choreographed action sequences, you'll wonder if you're watching one movie! But it's all part of the mix for one of Hong Kong's best black comedies.

Okay. Let's cut through the crap— this movie is one of the prime reasons for watching Hong Kong films. It's filled with all the outrageous elements we've come to love from Asian cinema. In fact, everything about this film is outrageous.

It's the story of a cop who is killed during a daring bank robbery (a segment shot in gory, ultraviolent fashion). But wait! The gods are smiling on Tsu Hsaing (Shing Fui On, top bad guy from **The Killer**), and he's revived by an electrical storm. Now, he's become an indestructible superpowered creature who must recharge himself daily with heavy doses of electricity.

Among other things, he has to worry about the gaping wound in his belly that refuses to heal. He hopes to stay alive long enough to see the birth of his baby (his wife is ready to pop any day), and of course he wants to capture the remaining bad guys who robbed the bank.

Immersed in this demented *Dead Heat* (1988) story line are some of the sickest, most offensive gags you'll see in contemporary cinema—lampooning everything from homosexuals to paraplegics, childbirth to virginity, Jackie Chan to Madonna.

Plus, there's **Amy Yip**, who makes an appearance as Death Ray, a sexy prostitute. The monster accidentally squeezes her huge tits so hard they squirt milk like a water pistol, reducing her famous megabust to a flat-chested wasteland. Sure, it's in bad taste! But what'd ya expect?

BLUE LAMP IN A WINTER NIGHT (1985)
director: Yao Fengpan [Feng Pan]. ★★½
A good, atmospheric, turn-of-the-century horror story with ghosts, vampires, and an impossible love triangle.

BLUE VALENTINE.
See *Rose*

BOMB DISPOSAL OFFICER: BABY BOMB (1995)
director: Jamie Luk. Anthony Wong· Lau Ching Wan·Esther Kwan Wing Ho·Chan Mong Wah·Lung Tin Sung ★★½
An Asian hybrid of *Speed* crossed with *Three Men and a Baby.* An unlikely amalgamation? Not for a Hong Kong movie.

Two members of the HK bomb squad, John Wong and Peter Wan (**Anthony Wong** and **Lau Ching Wan**), are infatuated with the same girl (Esther Kwan Wing Ho). Mary is a homeless waif who agrees to become their roommate, and soon she's the target for their wolfish affections. During a night of to-o-o much drinking, they both score with Mary; she ends up pregnant.

Meanwhile, there's a mad bomber (Chan Mong Wah) running around the city blowing people-n-places to smithereens (including a little boy who is too inquisitive for his own good during the opening sequence of the film). But the evil bomber is upset with the two cop heroes because they are constantly foiling his best work. So he kidnaps the pregnant Mary and attaches a bomb. The device is kept from activation by the combined pulses of mom and unborn child. Without constant stimulation from each heartbeat, it will detonate.

Director **Luk** has created an uneven mixture of broad comedy and thrill-oriented action that works because of the performances. It's nice to see Anthony Wong step out of typecast and play the hero for a change. Lau Ching Wan uses his sleepy-eyed good looks to best advantage as an alcoholic bomb-squad officer. And Esther Kwan manages to look both perky and sexy at the same time.

BOOK OF HEROES (1987)
director: Chu Yen Ping. Yukari Oshima·Hu Kwa·Yang Hui San·Kurata Yasuaki ★★
Very talky, with an intolerably slow first half. Things liven up when beautiful **Yukari Oshima** is hired as a bodyguard for a wicked Japanese Mafia boss. Unfortunately, she has little to do until the end, when she is exposed as an undercover cop. Forget the movie and watch sexy Oshima in action during the final ten minutes.

BOXER'S OMEN (1983)
director: Gui Zhihong. Phillip Kao· Wang Lung Wei ★★½
A sequel to **Bewitched** (1981), made by the same director toward the end of the powerful Shaw brothers' production empire. In this one, the boxer returns to Thailand to avenge his brother

but very quickly he finds himself caught up in black magic and evil spells.

Chopscary fare. Interesting special effects and more gory than most.

BOYS ARE EASY (1993)
director: Wong Ching (Jing). Lin Ching Hsia· Maggie Cheung·Chingmy Yau·Tony Leung·Jacky Cheung·Lo Hei-Kong ★★
Director Wong Ching (Jing) (**Fight Back to School, Royal Tramp, Last Hero in China, City Hunter,** etc.) strikes again! But at least **Stephen Chow** is nowhere in sight.

This is an inoffensive piece of fluff with an all-star cast, reminiscent of countless American comedies from the '50s.

Daddy Chin (Richard Ng) is afraid his daughters are taking their various careers too seriously, leaving no time to smell the roses. [At this rate, he worries, they'll never get married.] So he pretends to have a fatal illness, and his last request is that they come to a special dinner—with boyfriends. The plot deals with how these single, liberated women find escorts for the party.

The daughters are played by a stunning cast of HK starlets: **Maggie Cheung, Brigitte Lin [Lin Ching Hsia],** and **Naked Killer's Chingmy Yau.** Their lucky dates are **Tony Leung [Kar Fei], Jacky Cheung** and Lo Hei-Kong.

BRAVE YOUNG GIRLS (1990)
director: Luk Kam Bo. Yukari Oshima ·Hsia Chi Ling·Leung Kar Yan·Hui Ying Hung ★★
The brave girls are an unsuccessful robber, a prostitute, and a Japanese detective (played by **Yukari Oshima**). They join forces to eliminate a gang of international flesh peddlers. But after the smoke clears and the bad guys are

crippled, the police arrest the female robber and cart her away. Crime doesn't pay, Hong Kong style.

BRIDE WITH THE WHITE HAIR (1993) aka **JIANG-HU [RIVER-LAKE]: BE- TWEEN LOVE AND GLORY** director: **Ronny Yu.** Leslie Cheung·Lin Ching Hsia·Elaine Lui·Ng Chuu-Yu ★★★★

Filmmaker **Ronnie Yu** is back! And he's back with an extraordinary motion picture, easily his best film to date. After the pitiful **Shogun and Little Kitchen** (1991), it's refreshing to see this contemporary master sparkle with style and vigor again.

The strong cast (**Leslie Cheung, Brigitte Lin [Lin Ching Hsia]**, Ng Chun-Yu, Elaine Lui and Nam Kit-Ying) is just the beginning. Director Yu has also tapped the talents of the industry's best production specialists for this project. From Academy Award-winning costume designer Emi Wada, to filmmaker Dennis Yu (**Evil Cat**) as scriptwriter, to meticulous composer Richard Yuen, the team is exceptional.

Yu's collaboration with cinematographer Peter Pau [director of photography for **To Be #1, Saviour of Souls, Legend of Wisely,** and **Terra Cotta Warrior**] is one of the screen's most compelling marriages. Together they've created a fantasy epic that crackles with originality. For example, in order to give a surrealistic fresh quality to the film, all the daytime exteriors were shot at night under artificial lighting.

The story is based on a two-volume Chinese novel written by Leung Yu-Sang in 1954, the official source material for **Chang Ling**'s **Wolf Devil Woman** (1982). It tells the story of a beautiful girl/witch, Lian (Lin Ching-Hsia), raised by wolves in the Wu Dang Mountains. At one point she rescues a young warrior, Zhuo Yi-

Hang (**Leslie Cheung**), from a wild animal attack, but disappears before he can thank her. Swordsman Zhuo joins forces with revolutionary armies who are trying to defeat the evil Mo Dynasty, governed by a mutant Siamese twin named Ji Wu-Shuang [a bisexual amalgamation played by Ng Chun-Yu and Elaine Lui].

Meanwhile, Lian is recruited by King/Queen Ji to defeat the rebels. But when she refuses to attack the swordsman, the emperor orders his army to torture her. Left for dead, she is nursed back to health by Zhou. The two fall in love. This angers the emperor (his male side is secretly infatuated with the witch). And through black magic, he/she prepares a deadly revenge.

In addition to the twisted romantic plot, this film is filled with robust action and frenzied fight sequences. The kung fu and swordplay are so realistic that the audience winces from the impact.

BRIDE WITH WHITE HAIR 2 (1993) director: **David Wu** with **Ronny Yu.** Brigitte Lin·Leslie Cheung ★★

David Wu (editor for **Bride with the White Hair**) is credited as director for this film, although insiders insist that most of the film was orchestrated by **Ronny Yu**, who decided it wouldn't be a good career move to be associated with the sequel.

There are serious problems with the basic structure of this film, not to mention its uncompelling story line. This time **Brigitte Lin**'s character is relegated to the position of irredeemable villain (bad move, folks). She's a one-dimensional, vengeful witch leading her clan of women warriors against their male tormentors.

This sequel has two obvious strikes against it from the start. (1) The visual bravura made the original Bride with the White Hair so distinguishable is

Brigitte Lin in *Bride with the White Hair*

abandoned. And (2) the chemistry between Brigitte Lin and **Leslie Cheung**, which fueled the emotional fire of *Bride 1* is difficult to conjure this time, given that they only share one scene.

BROKEN HOUSE (1976)
director: Ho Meng Hua [Ho Menga].
Ya Gui·Ma Sha·Meng Ding Ge ★★½
An early terror film from veteran filmmaker Ho Meng-Hua, who later directed many of the Run Run Shaw classics, including **Goliathon** and the **Black Magic** movies.

In this one, a bad kid becomes an even worse adult. As a child, Yun throws acid in the face of his father. And as an adult he kills his girlfriend (with a Coke bottle to her genitalia).

Meanwhile, dad has gone insane. And to prove it, he's stalking and decapitating pretty female victims. Yun's brother puts an end to the entire ugly mess by killing them both.

THE BROTHERHOOD.
See *Code of Honor*

BRUTAL SORCERY (1986)
director: Pan Ling Tong. Lai Hon Chi ·Lily Chan ★★
A taxi driver gets involved in black magic after he has a streak of bad luck. Good title; so-so movie.

BUDDHIST SPELL (1982)
director: Chu Yuan [Chew Lu Kong].
Liu Chia Yong·Hong Min·Wu Ma ★★
According to the Holy Book of the Buki Cult, when the Blood Kid sucks the blood of 99 children, it will be resurrected and become the true God. Of course, the end result is, at that point, the Buki Cult can rule the world. So a high priest recruits the aid of an evil warrior to help him find children (especially those born under the sign of the dragon) for the sacrifice.

Meanwhile a good master (Liu Chia Yong), in possession of the sacred wood, has reincarnated the soul of a beautiful songstress, Yuyi (Hon Min), who assists him against the Buki Cult and their zombies.

It all sounds so much better than it really is. Way too much talking makes this slow going, although if you make it to the conclusion (the birth of the Blood Kid), you'll be glad you came along for the ride.

BULLET FOR HIRE (1991)
director: John Cheong. Simon Yam· Jacky Cheung·Elaine Liu ★★½
Triad hitmen (**Simon Yam** and **Jacky Cheung**), disguised as cops, kill an American ambassador and his delegation in a very violent gun battle. A beautiful Chinese bodyguard (**Elaine Lui**) is the only survivor, but soon she is stalked through the streets of HK by the professional killers who fear that she can finger them.

BULLET IN THE HEAD (1990)
director: John Woo. Tony Leung [Chiu Wai]·Waise Lee·Jacky Cheung· Simon Yam·Fennie Yen·Yolinda Yam ★★★★
Sprawling. Intense. Melodramatic. Brutal. Each describes this epic tale of loyalty and betrayal from one of Asia's premier filmmakers, **John Woo**

(best known for **The Killer, A Better Tomorrow**, and **Hard-boiled**).

This 2-hour-plus saga tells the story of three friends (**Tony Leung** [Chiu Wai], **Jacky Cheung,** Waise Lee) who flee Hong Kong after a gang-war confrontation circa 1967. They escape to Saigon and quickly find themselves in the middle of the bloody Vietnam war, resulting in a series of absolutely harrowing torture sequences at the hands of the Viet Cong.

Despite the good performances from the three leading actors, this film will always be remembered as the one that catapulted **Simon Yam** into stardom. Although Yam had been making films for years, this was his first meaty role. He emerged as the star to watch. His portrayal of a Eurasian mercenary trying to smuggle gold out of Vietnam crackles with an intense charisma.

BUNMAN.
See *Untold Story*

BURNING AMBITION (1989)
director: Frankie Chan. Frankie Chan· Yukari Oshima·Simon Yam·Hui Ying Hung ★★

Actor-turned-director **Frankie Chan** presents yet another gangster versus gangster (or if you prefer, triad versus triad) action melodrama, aided by the always welcome **Yukari Oshima**.

This time, Chan and Oshima are brother and sister, fighting for control of the gangland empire, when the youngest member of the family (**Simon Yam**) is given the position of boss. Only the action sequences save this film, especially the match between Shaw Brothers' vet Hui Ying Hung [Wai Ying-Hung] (fighting with broken glass protruding from her foot) and bat-swinging Yukari.

BURNING PARADISE (1994)
aka **DESTRUCTION OF THE RED LOTUS TEMPLE**
director: Ringo Lam. Lee Tien San·

Willie Kwai [Chi]·Carmen Lee·Yang Sheng ★★★★

Once again, **Ringo Lam** expands his directorial vision and infuses an exhausted genre with new verve. Just as he rewrote the guidelines for heroic bloodshed flicks with his astonishingly fresh **Full Contact** (1992), Lam adds a new dimension to historic action films with *Burning Paradise.*

By combining darkly sinister villains with immortalized legendary heroes Fong Sai Yuk and Hung Shi Kwan, Lam has created a top-notch action film that breaks with the traditional chop socky formula. With no apologies, Lam quickly sets up the story (hundreds of Shaolin monks have been taken prisoner by the evil Red Lotus sect, and the two heroes invade the enemy fortress to free them).

The real star of the movie is the Red Lotus stronghold itself, a virtual maze of traps, poison gases, booby-trapped blades, bottomless pits, and boxing zealots. It's like a living, breathing, menacing villain. Inside this beast, Fong Sai Yuk and Hung Shi Kwan are pitted against every possible type of obstacle in scenes reminiscent of the best moments from Steven Spielberg's *Indiana Jones* adventures.

This is a cult favorite waiting to explode.

BURNING SENSATION (1989)
director: Wu Ma. Kenny Bee·Do Do Cheng·Wu Ma·Richard Ng·Carol Cheng ★★★

The ghost of a dead TV actress, A-Ying (Do Do Cheng), continues to live in the netherworld of television signals. This wonder woman (jumping through the television set into a living room!) comes to the aid of a family when they are threatened by a waspish Vampirella-type ogre who kills her victims by strangling them with her 6-foot tongue. Amazing, right? And because of the

TV motif, there are some mind-bog-gling musical numbers that add to the excitement. It's directed with visual glee by famous character actor **Wu Ma**, who also costars.

BURY ME HIGH (1991)
director: Tang Chi Li. Moon Lee·Jacky Cheung·Tan Chi-Li·Sibelle Hu ★★★
Regardless of the title, this one has nothing to do with death under the influence of drugs. Instead, it deals with a magical burial ground in the Carrigan Mountains. If a man is planted there, his descendants will benefit heartily—through an abundance of wealth or intelligence.

In this instance, the beneficiaries are Anna Wong (**Moon Lee**) and her brother, Wisely (**Jacky Cheung**). She becomes a rich director of a large conglomerate; he's a computer wizard. But after 24 years of continued success and happiness, their luck is starting to change. Her company is beginning to falter, and he has developed a brain tumor. It seems nobody told them about a special provision of the pact, which demands they must perform a sacred ritual at the burial site before the 25th year. After a college professor (played by director **Tang Chi Li**) sheds light on their predicament, the three travel to Carrigan.

In the mountains they are confronted by an evil dictator named Nguen (**Yuen Wah**, popular HK villain from **Dragons Forever** and countless chop socky films). He has his own ideas about harnessing the supernatural power. But Nguen's militant sister (**Sibelle Hu**) and her band of revolutionaries aid the desperate trio, igniting a spectacular state-of-the-art battle sequence, filled with lots of ultraviolent action and frenzied gunplay. Resulting, of course, in a happy ending for all the good guys.

BUTTERFLY AND SWORD (1993)
director: Tang Chi Li. Michelle Yeoh·Donnie Yen·Tony Leung [Chiu Wai]·Joey Wang ★★★½
One of **Michelle Yeoh**'s best performances, allowing her the freedom to show her talents as both a top-notch dramatic actress and an action starlet. She's a loyalist trying to keep the king's empire safe from a revolutionary gang attempting to overthrow the government.

An exceptionally strong cast (including Donnie Yen, **Tony Leung**, and **Joey Wang [Wong]** as Butterfly), coupled with over-the-top adventure sequences, make this essential HK viewing. From the director of **Legend of Wisely** and **Bury Me High.**

BUTTERFLY MURDERS (1979)
director: Tsui Hark. Lau Siu Ming·Michelle Mei·Wong Shih Tong·Zhong Guozhu·Chen Qiqi ★★★½
Brilliantly filmed, this **Tsui Hark** classic is regarded as a landmark in contemporary HK cinema. It's a complex murder mystery about strange occurrences within the walls of Shum Castle. It appears bloodthirsty butterflies are responsible for a rash of killings. But can that be true? Folk hero Fong Sai Yuk (Lau Siu Ming) and the delightfully sassy Green Shadow (Michelle Chan) investigate.

The real stars of this period thriller are director Tsui Hark for his keen vision and cinematographer Fun Chin Yu for his ability to capture it.

CAGED BEAUTIES (1988)
aka **FIGHT FOR LOVE**
director: Yuan Ching Lee. Derek Wan·Chan Sing·Heung Gwo Chi·Jeff Falcon ★★½
Oddly, the women-in-prison exploitation film is a rarity in Hong Kong cinema. In fact, this movie is one of a mere handful (also see *Women's Prison 1991*, plus the World War II

entries ***Excessive Torture in a Female Prison Camp, Girls in the Tiger Cage***, and the Shaw Brother's classic roughie ***Bamboo House of Dolls***).

This one tells the story of an oppressive revolutionary government (the country and locale remain undisclosed) randomly arresting unsuspecting citizens. The men are used for target practice, and the women become prostitutes. There's an ample amount of torture sequences. Lots of whips, chains, bondage, and other typical prison-oriented mayhem.

CALAMITY OF SNAKES (1990)
director: William Chang Kee. Yunpeng Xiang·Luo Bi-Ling ★★½
If snakes make you queasy, avoid this film. Thousands of them are featured throughout the movie, including a 50-foot monster-serpent at the film's conclusion.

The plot is simple. After many years of man's cruelty to snakes (we're subjected to countless examples as we see them squashed and chopped, beheaded and skinned), it's time for the slithery creatures to get even. And they do.

CALL GIRLS '94 (1994)
director: Lai Yat Ching. Lau Ho Man· Ng Yee San ★½
Here's another entry in a long-running HK series. *Call Girls '88* introduced **Maggie Cheung**, and *Call Girls '92* featured **Veronica Yip, Carrie Ng**, and **Cheung Man**. Somehow, the same kind of future stardom doesn't seem likely for Lau Ho Man, based on her performance in this tired opus.

The daughter (Lau) of a gambling addict is sold to a madam of a whorehouse, where she becomes a prostitute to make money for her dad's habit.

The plot is merely an excuse for a lot of category III nudity and sexual bopping, plus some S&M stuff when she refuses to service the clients.

There's also a silly subplot about a blind man who needs an operation, but you don't really care, do you?

CANNIBAL MERCENARY (1983)
director: Hong Lu Wong. Lee Song-phon·Sugia Namchan·Soraud Charazcheu· Rom Rachon ★★★
Former Special Forces Sergeant Tony Kong, desperately needing money for an operation to save his daughter's life, accepts a mission that takes him into the jungles of Vietnam again. His orders are to hunt down and destroy an army of vicious, bloodthirsty cannibals headed by a demented war criminal.

Incredibly violent. Extremely graphic. And the final half hour packs a wallop.

CAPRICIOUSNESS (1980)
director: Kim Young Hyo. ★
A gambler faking his death comes back as a ghost to scare his wife to death. He then marries her best friend, but his dead wife returns to haunt them. Familiar story, wearisome execution.

CASH ON DELIVERY (1992)
director: Terry Tong. Simon Yam· Veronica Yip·Sandra Ng ★½
This one plays like a melodramatic soap opera, with **Simon Yam** and **Veronica Yip** having an affair (she secretly wants to have a baby in order to claim a trust fund, but her husband is impotent). Soon she becomes obsessed with her new lover. And through a series of contrived situations he is implicated in her husband's accidental death. Simon's lawyer girlfriend (Sandra Ng) ends up representing him in court. The whole thing is ludicrous [but Goddamn it!], Veronica Yip sure looks great.

CAT (1992)

director: Lan Nai Kai. Waise Lee·Gloria Yip ★★
UFO researcher Waise Lee is hot on the trail of two female aliens and their monster cat. The extraterrestrials are in Hong Kong to steal an octagon on display in the Museum of Natural History. They need it to destroy a blob creature that has followed them through space to Earth.

THE CAT LIVING TEN TIMES (1992)
aka DEVIL CAT

director: Leung Lee. Wong Mai Shi·Chu Ping Fun·Chui Shin Ha·Yeung Chi Fu ★★
The director of the atmospheric *Scare the Living* proves that horror is a delicate balance between the frightful and the absurd. Unfortunately, he also turns up lacking in the demonstration. This is essentially a reworking of the same ideas successfully enacted in *Evil Cat*, but poor production standards and unintentionally funny dialogue create snickers instead of chills.

A murderous feline creature (sometimes in the persona of a beautiful, white-haired cat woman) seeks revenge against the decedents of Chow Sung, who savagely raped an innocent virgin in ancient China. A missed opportunity.

CENTER STAGE (1992)
aka THE ACTRESS

director: Stanley Kwan. Anita Mui·Maggie Cheung·Tony Leung ★★★
An effective docudrama directed by **Stanley Kwan** (best known for his superb *Rouge*, starring **Anita Mui**). This one tells the story of a legendary Chinese actress Ruan Ling-Yu (played by **Maggie Cheung**), who committed suicide at age 25 in 1935, following vicious attacks by the media over an adulterous relationship.

But the real story seems to be that of dependence. **Maggie Cheung**

gives a remarkably low-keyed performance as a woman who needs men in her life in order to feel important. As expected, it's a bitter tale, darkly depressing.

CENTIPEDE HORROR (1988)

director: Keith Li. Margaret A. Li·Mui Ki Wai·Hussein Hassan·Wang Lei ★★½
There're some freakish moments in this film. An evil priest torments his enemies with nasty crawling creatures, especially centipedes. They crawl everywhere, thousands of them. The final 20 minutes are an absolute endurance test. Certainly, nobody will ever want to kiss the heroine (**Margaret A. Li**) if they've seen this movie!

C'EST LA VIE, MON CHERI (1993)

director: Derek Yee Tung Sing. Lau Ching Wan·Anita Yuen ★★★
Many of you reading this probably couldn't give a damn about this movie. Writer/director **Derek Yee Tung Sing**'s smash hit tearjerker (one of the biggest HK hits of 1993) represents a style of American melodrama that you probably turned to HK cinema in an effort to avoid, but if you can get past your initial prejudices, you'll find a surprisingly mature and expertly crafted love story.

It's a down-to-earth portrait of the relationship between a jaded jazz musician (excellent **Lau Ching Wan**, nailing the self-pitying tortured artist routine down pat) and an eternally optimistic street performer (**Anita Yuen**).

The film's strength lies in director Derek Yee Tung Sing's willingness to allow time for these emotionally wounded characters to *like* each other before they fall in love (they don't actually kiss until almost an hour into the film). Even when the narrative threatens to take a climatic plunge into well-worn cliché territory (a disease is involved; 'nuff said?), the warmth of the film manages to keep it on track.

Anita Yuen in *C'est La Vie, Mon Cheri*

CHALLENGE OF LADY NINJA (1979)
director: **Lee Tso Nam.** Chen Kuan Tai·Yang Hui San·Chen Kuan Tai·Pok Ying Lam ★
The real challenge here is to watch this film all the way to its conclusion. **Chen Kuan Tai** looks okay, but her kung fu shenanigans wear thin in this unremarkable might-vs-right tale. Lady ninja Lee Tun retaliates against Japanese warriors after they invade China and kill her father and his resistance group.

CHEETAH ON FIRE (1992)
director: **Choy Fat.** Donnie Yen·Carrie Ng·Chueng Man·Lan Hui Kwong ★½
Good cast wasted in a lackluster film about a stolen computer chip and a breakneck chase to retrieve it.
Donnie Yen tries to revive his slumping career while **Carrie Ng** and **Cheung Man** stand around and look cute. For martial arts fans, there's excellent action from Lan Hui Kwong, the

kickboxing bodyguard who became famous after his bout with **Jackie Chan** in the conclusion of *Drunken Master 2*.

CHINA DOLLS (1992)
director: **Jimmy Li.** Lam Ching Ying· Amy Yip·Wu Ma ★★½
This is a mixed bag of sex and violence, featuring **Amy Yip** in a full-fledged (tailor-made) role. She's May Lin, an unfortunate victim of gunplay between her husband and the HK cops, who gives her baby to a policeman (**Lam Ching Ying**) before escaping to mainland China. Throughout the rest of the film, she tries to get back to Hong Kong to retrieve her son, but she finds herself victimized by gangsters (especially big boss **Wu Ma**). They want her for a prostitution ring [big surprise, right?].
The downbeat ending finds May Lin surviving yet another gun battle, only to be deported back to China after getting a glimpse of her child.

CHINA DRAGON (1995)
  aka **SHAOLIN POPPY**
director: **Chu Yin Ping.** Kam Shing Wu·Sik Siu Loong·Fok Siu Man·Yip Chuen Chung ★★
I wonder—does **Chu Yin Ping** know he's a very strange filmmaker? Does he recognize the cockeyed quality of his movies? Or do they seem normal to him?
All of his films have a foundation planted in reality, but his character development and plot execution are always slightly off-kilter, making even tired stories seem freshly different. The interesting aspect of Chu's productions is that this quality appears to be effortless and, more important, unintentional. For instance, in *Golden Queen Commando* (1984), it seems natural that Elsa Yeung would be wearing chic sunglasses as she escapes on horseback through a desert with her five

cohorts while the soundtrack blares music stolen from a spaghetti Western. Director Chu has a way of getting his audience to bite on any morsel of absurdity and devour it without question. Without a doubt, this is a talent.

Here we have a traditional story line. Two students of Shaolin Temple, a ten-year-old brother and his older teen sister, qualify to attend the World Martial Arts Competition in Hawaii.

Only in the demented world of Chu Yin Ping could this tournament be The World Martial Arts and Supernatural Power Competition; only here could we have villains attempting to use the students in their hunt for a missing key that opens an abandoned nuclear power plant on the China/Russia border. Plus, there are a variety of other eccentric ingredients, including an uncle who used to be a Buddhist monk but now is Catholic, a scientist who enjoys sticking things up his ass, and a little boy who wears an elephant mask over his genitalia, allowing his little trunk to stick out.

Unfortunately, these idiosyncrasies don't necessarily equate to good moviemaking. And with the exception of an amazing Shaolin Temple sequence early on, this film fails to generate much of a soul. Even the tournament conclusion doesn't reach the same level of excitement as the Shaolin footage, which means the film runs out of steam somewhere along the line.

Lately, child actors have made a comeback in Hong Kong films. I'm thinking particularly of Tse Miu, who led this trend with **New Legend of Shaolin** (1994). But now here's China Dragon with two kid actors. It seems to me—this time—we're dealing with at least one too many.

CHINA WHITE (1989)
director: Ronnie Yu. Russell Wong·Ku Feng·Ronnie Yu·Alex Ma·Billy Drago· Andy Lau ★★★

Amy Yip in China Dolls

This film was virtually ignored when it played theatrically in the United States. What a shame. It's a competently made actioner from one of HK's best directors, **Ronnie Yu (Bride with the White Hair** [1993]), chronicling the rise to power of two Chinese gangsters in Amsterdam's Chinatown and their conflict with the Italian Mafia. The gun action is swift and chaotic, accentuated by a bittersweet love story. In fact, their downfall is orchestrated by an angry girlfriend who gets a violent revenge on the courthouse steps.

CHINESE FEAST (1995)
director Tsui Hark. Anita Yuen·Leslie Cheung ★★★
Perhaps this one was inspired by the success of the Juzo Itami's Tampopo (1986/Japanese). The similar story deals with a grand contest between two chefs, with the winner receiving either a million bucks (50 million HK$) or ownership of the restaurant, depending on which master impresses the judges more. Lots of slapstick and implausible situations, but the result is entertaining and stylistic.

Anita Yuen turns in a terrific performance, all the more effective due to the satirical freedom allowed by the script (especially the punk variation on her now-classic **C'Est la Vie, Mon Cheri** character).

The idea for this film probably originated from **Tsui**'s '91 star-studded bomb **Banquet**. With one major difference, of course. This one is actually entertaining.

CHINESE GHOSTBUSTER (1993)
director: Wu Ma. Wu Ma·Cheng Ho Nam ★★
Director **Wu** is caught up in this world of hopping ghosts and spiritual mumbojumbo (see reviews of his earlier films **Burning Sensation** and *Exorcist Master*). This time he plays a ghost priest who is trying to keep two mortal lovers away from each other. But unfortunately he brings nothing new to this overexposed genre.

CHINESE GHOST STORY (1987)
director: Ching Siu Tung. Leslie Cheung·Joey Wang·Wu Ma ★★★★

CHINESE GHOST STORY 2 (1990)
director: Ching Siu Tung. Leslie Cheung· Joey Wang·Jacky Cheung ★★★½

CHINESE GHOST STORY 3 (1991)
director: Ching Siu Tung. Tony Leung [Chiu Wai]·Joey Wang·Jacky Cheung ★★★
It's probably true that **Tsui Hark** is a better producer than director. His best productions (**Roboforce, Dragon Inn, The Killer, A Better Tomorrow 1** and **2**, and this series), were each directed by someone other than himself.

While it's been speculated that he totally controls his projects (apparently going as far as reshooting "unacceptable" scenes), **Hark**'s participation in Asian film more closely resembles the role perfected by Roger Corman in American filmmaking, particularly demonstrated by his willingness to give a variety of competent directors

their chance to prove themselves and then sharing in the notoriety.

This series is an impassioned creation from director **Ching Siu Tung** (also see **Witch from Nepal**). It's an adventure-oriented romance that incorporates the classic Chinese man-in-love-with-a-ghost motif, but the whole thing seems fresh and original. Actually, this is a brilliantly conceived fantasy featuring two very likable Asian performers, **Leslie Cheung** and Joey Wang. But the real star is director Ching Siu Tung and his extraordinary camerawork.

Part 2 is a true sequel. **Joey Wang** returns as the beautiful ghost **Sian** and **Leslie Cheung**, once again, is **Ning,** the hapless hero. The film begins with the words *The Story Continues. . . .* and it's packed full of great FX, including a giant centipede monster at the exciting conclusion and the soul-eating Tree Devil.

Part 3 jumps ahead 100 years. Director Ching Siu Tung centers the story on a new character: a timorous monk (played by **Tony Leung [Chiu Wai]**, best known for his performance in **Bullet in the Head**). Ghostly vixen Joey Wang and swordsman **Jacky Cheung** return in similar but decidedly different roles. This installment relies more on detailed characterization and exciting beginning-and-ending adventure sequences, but the middle section drags. The story is starting to show signs of wear.

CHINESE LEGEND (1992)
aka **MOON LEGEND**
director: Mak Yai Kit [Peter Mak]. Jacky Cheung·Joey Wang·Cheung Man·Wu Ma ★★★
A young swordsman (**Jacky Cheung**) is plagued with a reoccurring dream featuring a beautiful vampire, Moon Cher (**Joey Wang**). These dreams are so vivid that at one point he awakens holding part of her bracelet.

Joey Wang in *Chinese Ghost Story*

He's positive that she is alive somewhere, and he knows she is in danger. Determined to find and rescue her, he embarks on a remarkable journey.

Distinguished photography, tremendous state-of-the-art special effects, and completely innovative scenes (e.g., the female vampire stabs her victim with a hollow reed and then, using it as a straw, sucks his blood) elevate this film to an elite status.

CHINESE TORTURE CHAMBER STORY (1994)
director: Wong Ching [Jing] with **Lam Hing Lung [Bosco Lam].** Yung Hung·Ng Kai Wah ★½

Little Cabbage (Yung Hung) is found drenched in blood next to the body of her dead husband. She was at one time the concubine of a pharmacist named Yang (Ng Kai Wah). His wife, in a fit of jealousy, married Little Cabbage off to one of the locals (the one found dead at the film's beginning). Yang's wife, being unfaithful, schemes to implicate Little Cabbage and Yang

for murder. They are arrested and put through a series of tortures in an effort to extract confessions. Since the judge in the case has a son who is involved with Yang's wife, there is no way he can get a fair trial. After numerous torture sessions, Yang's sister is able to convince a new judge to rehear the case, and Yang and Little Cabbage are found innocent.

Even when director **Wong Ching [Jing]** delves into sordid serious trash like this film, he does it so broadly, so irresponsibly, that the entire production suffers. His fascination with goofy slapstick and heavy-handed humor defuses any atmosphere generated by the subject matter at hand.

Wong Ching [Jing] has spent his career scurrying through genres like a rabid squirrel, making a mess of everything he touches. A quick look at junk like *Fight Back to School* (1991), *Royal Tramp* (1992) and *Last Hero in China* (1993) proves the point. He even managed to make **Jackie Chan** look like a clodknocker in *City Hunter* (1993). And now he has homogenized S&M! Don't be taken in by the exploitive title—you won't even find a torture chamber in the film.

CHUNGKING EXPRESS (1994)
director: Wong Kar Wai. Takeshi Kaneshiro·Tony Leung [Chiu Wai]· Brigitte Lin [Lin Ching-Hsia]·Faye Wong ★★

Two steps forward, one step back. After praising filmmaker Wong Kar Wai for *Ashes of Time*, I feel somewhat reluctant to criticize the director for this film made earlier the same year. But, damn it, this movie is so slow and ponderous—and so-o-o-o goddamn self-important—it can't possibly be recommended.

Here are two stories, both dealing with quirky explorations of human relationships. In the first, **Brigitte Lin** is a trafficker who picks

Singer Faye Wong in *Chungking Express*

up a self-pitying cop (Takeshi Kaneshiro) and spends the afternoon in a hotel room. Apparently they aren't interested in doing the nasty; she promptly falls asleep, and he whines about how unhappy he is. In the second part, **Tony Leung [Chiu Wai]** plays a detective who mopes around his apartment every night, talking to stuffed animals about how lonely he is, while every afternoon a girl (Faye Wong) sneaks into his place because she has a crush on him.

In the middle of all this there's a message about love in the modern world. But we're too bored to care.

CIRCUS KIDS (1994)
director: Ma Sui Wai. Yuen Biao·Donnie Yen ★
Drug traffickers cause trouble for a fledgling circus. Silliness personified.

Times must be getting rough for **Yuen Biao** and Donnie Yen if they're making crap like this. And, as surpris-

ing as it may seem, they're not even given a chance to brighten things up with their martial arts magic.

CITY COPS (1990)
director: Liu Chia Liang. Cynthia Rothrock·Mui Ka Wei·Michiko Nishiwaki·Mark Houghton ★★
Generally considered a lesser film for Cynthia Rothrock, yet it's one of the few that allows her to be sexy. But let's face it . . . her fans don't really want sex from Cyndy. They want her to kick some butt. Right? And she does. The problem is, director **Liu** seems to have forgotten to include a plot.

CITY HUNTER (1993)
director: Wong Ching [Jing]. Jackie Chan·Joey Wang·Chingmy Yau·Leon Lai·Goto Kumiko·Lo Wai Kwong ★★½
This **Jackie Chan** comedy/adventure is little more than a lightweight version of *Die Hard* on a luxury liner.

Jackie is private detective Rye Saeba, who, with his assistant, Kaori (**Joey Wang [Wong]**), follows the trail of a runaway girl to a cruise ship that becomes the target for a group of armed robbers. Watch for **Chingmy Yau** (of *Naked Killer* fame), who plays an undercover government agent named Saeko.

The most talked-about sequence is the *Streetfighter* video gag near the film's conclusion. Through a contrived plot tangent, Jackie transforms into the various characters of the popular *Streetfighter* video game (E. Honda, Gulle, Dhalsim, and [embarrassingly] female kickboxer, Chun Lee).

Filmmaker **Wong Ching [Jing]** directs this movie with the same heavy-handed goofball intensity that predominates in his silly (but highly popular) **Stephen Chow** vehicles, *Royal Tramp* and *Fight Back to School*. But the bottom line: Jackie Chan deserves better.

By the way, all the gay-bashing jokes in the original theatrical version have been removed for the video release.

CITY ON FIRE (1987)
director: Ringo Lam. Chow Yun-Fat· Danny Lee·Sun Yeuh·Roy Cheung ★★★
An effective cop/action story, but more important, it's a somber (perhaps gloomy) look at the reckless, tragic life of an undercover detective named Ko Chow.

Costars **Chow Yun-Fat** and **Danny Lee** play the opposite roles that they would (2 years later) portray in **The Killer**. This time Chow Yun-Fat is the cop who gets too emotionally involved with his thief/killer quarry, Fu (Lee). Interesting, the plot of this film surfaced in America as the uncredited source for *Reservoir Dogs*.

CITY WAR (1988)
director: Sun Chung. Chow Yun-Fat· Ti Lung·Tien Niu·Tsui Siu Keung ★★★
Hong Kong hero **Chow Yun-Fat** stars in this story dealing with two cop partners secretly stalked by a now-out-of-prison gangster looking for revenge.

The excellent rapport between **Ti Lung** and Chow Yun-Fat elevates the film above the tired script. Beware of a sugary-sweet ending.

CLOSE ENCOUNTER OF THE VAMPIRE.
See *Dragon vs Vampire*.

CLOSE ESCAPE (1989)
director: Chow Chung Wing. Kwok Fu Shing·Max Mok·Yukari Oshima· Dick Wei ★½
A routine action drama about diamond thieves and gangsters distinguished only by **Yukari Oshima**'s brief appearance as a Mafia hitwoman.

Jackie Chan with Joey Wang (L) in City Hunter

CODE OF FORTUNE (1990)
director: Kent Cheng. Andy Lau· Anita Mui ★★½
A light-comedy adventure tale with top-rate fight sequences divinely choreographed by **Samo Hung** (who also produced the film and costars). **Andy Lau** and **Anita Mui** are secret agents, sidetracked in a prison camp, while on the trail of a missing fortune.

Director **Kent Cheng** is better known as an actor, usually playing a character named Fatty (**Run and Kill, Crime Story, Dr. Lamb**, etc.). Two years later, he would direct another film with his friend Andy Lau, **Dragon in Jail** (1992).

CODE OF HONOR (1987)
aka **THE BROTHERHOOD**
aka **TRIAD SAVAGES**
director: Benny Chan. Chow Yun-Fat· Danny Lee·Shing Fui On·Mei Fei-Lung · Dick Wei ★★½
A needlessly confusing tale of dissention in the ranks of Hong Kong's powerful underworld. Big Boss Ho

Chen-Tung (Mei Fei-Lung) is tired. He wants to retire ["We used to gain power through ethics, not violence"] and join his son, Hui (**Chow Yun-Fat**) in Australia. Before he's given a chance for that, one of his officers (Shing Fui On) squeals to the cops, and the old man finds himself arrested.

After successfully fighting the charges in court, he's mysteriously assassinated. The Japanese Mafia, recognizing the weakness of the HK triad, attempts to move against the gang. Hui arrives from Australia and unites with his brother to save his father's empire.

Danny Lee is featured in a cameo as an undercover cop.

COLOSSUS OF THE CONGO.
See *Goliathon*

COMFORT WOMEN (1992)
director: **Wong Kong.** Wong Kong· Wan Man Ying ★★½
This film goes to great lengths to confirm it's worthiness by supplementing the narrative with stock World War II footage and noble discussions of the whys and hows, but the final result remains something slightly shy of a geek show.

Not as shocking nor disturbing as **Man Behind the Sun** (although it's directed by the star of that film, **Wong Kong**), this movie attempts to expose the sordid subject of organized brothels on the Japanese front lines. The story centers on the horror of it all, as the women are duped into believing they are truly serving their country, while the military treats them like vermin. When venereal disease begins to run rampant, the whores are transferred to Camp 731, where they are used as human guinea pigs.

Surrounding the nastier segments are bland condemnations of the inhuman behavior, but the knee-jerk liberal attitude is sorely out of place, calling attention to the exploitative nature of the film. It's reminiscent of the preacher who gives sermons about the evils of sex in order to ensure a large attendance at his church.

COMMANDO FURY (1991)
aka WOMEN'S PRISON 1991
director: **Chester Yang.** ★★
Women prisoners are tortured, whipped, and beaten inside a World War II detention camp. Apparently, the commander (Bernard Tsui) is trying to get someone to talk about the location of an important microfilm.

Vicious brutality, typical women-in-prison fare.

COPS AND ROBBERS (1979)
director: **Alex Cheung.** Teng Mei Feng·Fung Hoi ★★½
Former TV director **Alex Cheung**'s first theatrical feature, *Cops and Robbers* was executively produced by Hong Kong's "little big man," the tiny but mighty **Teddy Robin Kwan**. This was Kwan's first production assignment following his return to Hong Kong after a lengthy tenure in Canada. But what starts with much promise soon becomes a routine policier; yet for followers of modern HK criminal action who are interested in witnessing the rough-around-the-edges roots of the genre, it could be essential viewing.

In a lyrical opening sequence, street kids chant "eenie-meenie-minie-mo" to select who plays the good guys and who plays the bad in an innocent game of cops and robbers. The heavy-handed message isn't lost on the audience.

The film is mostly notable for its unglamorized perspective and gutter's-eye worldview. Violence is swift and relentless: cops are chopped with butcher knives, a hand is severed. A preteen kid is threatened with a handgun to the head. Police brutality is casual and unquestionably accepted as a justifiable law enforcement procedure.

As a trivia sidebar, producer/actor/musician (etc.) Teddy Robin Kwan performs live in a discotheque, playing lead guitar in a band and singing a brazenly pro-police anthem while the hearty heroes sing along. Robin had once fronted a real-life bubblegum pop group (Teddy Robin and the Playboys) whose teenybop popularity reportedly rivaled that of the Beatles in Hong Kong.

CRAZY BLOOD (1988)
director: Li Siu Wah. Olivia Cheng·Eddie Chan·Kwan Lai Ye ★★★
This one really pays off. It's a riveting no-nonsense thriller, not afraid to wallow in the muck. And wallow it does.

Chen (**Olivia Cheng**) is a dedicated social worker who has allowed her job to dominate her personal life. Inadvertently, she neglects her devoted husband, Lo-Wei (Eddie Chan), and their young son, Chia-Pu. Although he dislikes his wife's patients ("they're just street trash"), Lo-Wei is tolerant of his wife's workaholic situation and takes the opportunity to develop a strong bond with his son.

Then, Lo-Wei's sister (**Kwan Lai Ye**) offers to baby-sit the child while the parents respond to an emergency case. While they're gone, one of Chen's delinquents breaks into the house and rapes the sister. During the assault, baby Chia-Pu climbs out the window and falls to his death.

Lo-Wei is over the edge with grief. His brain snaps. He withdraws into himself except at night, when he stalks the "street trash," gruesomely killing them, sending them to the afterlife to keep his son company.

CRAZY SAFARI (1990)
director: Lo Weng Tung. Lam Ching Yip·Ni Xau·Sam Christopher Chan ★★★★

Holy shit! What a demented hybrid this film is! A *The Gods Must Be Crazy* variation of the standard Chinese horror story complete with hopping vampires and magic spells, set in Africa!

Magical priest HiSing (played by **Lam Chang Ying**, the sapient hero of the **Mr. Vampire** series) accompanies his young ward, Leo (Sam Christopher Chan), to an auction in England, where they purchase a mummified vampire. Much to the crowd's amazement, the creature is rejuvenated before their very eyes. However, the priest is wise to the ways of the undead and quickly brings the creature under control.

After a short racial-slur subplot involving jive black delinquents and their attempt to rob the vampire, Hi-Sing and Leo are aboard a plane heading back to their Hong Kong home, along with the vampire passenger. And a very incompetent pilot.

Midflight, they run out of gas and the airplane goes down in the African jungle. They are separated while parachuting. The vampire comes tumbling from heaven during a vicious attack against a native tribe by some Anglo diamond thieves. His arrival creates such a commotion that the bad guys (including an uncredited British bitch in mirror sunglasses) retreat. The vampire is immediately elevated to village god status.

Meanwhile, HiSing and Leo are miles away in a thorn bush, fighting off lions and a rhinoceros. Eventually, everyone is reunited in the village.

Then, the evil diamond thieves return to rob the natives. They have brought their own superhuman zombie for the battle. In an especially marvelous sequence, HiSing transfers the spirit of **Bruce Lee** into the native chief (actually played by **Ni Xau**, star of *The Gods Must Be Crazy*), and through some imaginative trick photography Bruce Lee takes on the bad guys! One of a kind.

CRAZY SPIRIT (1986)
director: Chien Yueh Sheng. Ray Lui
★
Lame *Poltergeist* rip-off, with a Buddhist priest trying to exorcise suburban home. Yawn.

CRIME STORY (1993)
aka **SERIOUS CRIMES SQUAD**
director: Kirk Wong. Jackie Chan·Kent Cheng·Chong Fat ★★★
This **Jackie Chan** police/action tale is far superior to his previous **City Hunter**. The goofball humor and impish mugging are gone (does Jackie even smile in this one?), replaced by truckloads of action, stunts, and chases. The ending, although remarkable, is perhaps too close to **Hardboiled** for its own good.
The story, apparently based on a true kidnapping case in HK, is relatively basic. A policeman (**Kent**

Jackie Chan in *Crime Story*

Cheng) is tired of being poor, so he and his gang snatch a wealthy, unscrupulous businessman for a large ransom. Eddie Chan (**Jackie Chan** in a decidedly adult role) is a no-nonsense detective assigned to the case.

CRIMINAL HUNTER (1988)
director: Frankie Chan. Danny Lee·Eric Tsang·Dick Wei·Nina Li Chi·Lo Wei·Sing Fui On ★★★
Here's one of Hong Kong's blackest comedies, certainly a major departure for director **Frankie (Armour of God 2) Chan.**
A homicide detective (Eric Tsang) accidentally stabs his girlfriend during a scuffle with a killer. While she's recuperating, the killer returns and squeezes the bandaged wound until it bursts, thus murdering her. But then, the detective tricks the killer into thinking the girl's still alive by taking a picture of her in a wedding dress. When the killer returns to finish her off, he walks into a trap. The detective, like a demented puppeteer, has rigged a gun in her hand. By pulling the strings, he shoots the killer dead. Does this sound remotely like a comedy?

CRIPPLED HEROES (1983)
aka **OUTCASTS OF KUNG FU**
director: Ling Akuri-Lu. Wang Hop·Ka Hai·Yu Hen ★★

CRIPPLED HEROES: MORTAL COMBAT (1983)
director: Chan Cheh. Lo Wang·Kou Chu·Sun Chen·Chan Cheh ★½
Kou Chu is the blind warrior. Lo Wang is the deaf-mute fighter. Lu Fang plays the no-armed kickboxer. Sun Chen is the legless female boxer. And Chan Cheng (yes, the director) is unbearable as the village idiot. They all band together, using deadly tiger-style kung fu, to fight evil Tin Tan Wong in this chop socky hybrid.

CRIPPLED MASTERS (1984)
director: Ho Wang Muri. Wang Hop
·Ka Hai·Jackie Conn ★★
These two movies are essentially made for people who visit carnival freak shows. Both films are identical in scope, set in medieval China. They tell the story of two men. One had his arms chopped off by the evil king; the other, his legs. They join together (actually one upon the other's shoulders) to take revenge. Fascinating for about 20 minutes, until the novelty wears off.

CROCODILE HUNTERS (1989)
director: Andy Lau. Andy Lau·Alex Man·Sandra Ng·Lung Fong ★★
Don't be misled by the title. It's not an Everglades travelogue. Nor a horror film. Rather, it's a vapid police action flick, saved only by a very good opening sequence dealing with gun-wielding crazies who take over a theater complex. What a shame that the rest of the movie doesn't measure up to the slambam beginning.

THE CRUEL KIND (1990)
director: Chin Sing Wai. Chang Kuo Chu ·Shi Kai·Ho Pi·Claire LeVert·Ho Man Ying ★★★½
Filmmaker **Chin Sing Wai**'s homage to European thrillers, this Hong Kong production was in fact completely lensed in Paris for the full effect. The result is a psychological horror tale of the highest caliber.

Shen Chiang (Chang Kuo Chu) is an erotic photographer haunted by the ghostly apparition of a girl (Shi Kai) murdered in an adjoining apartment. He lives in a swirling nightmare of perverse sex and Daliesque images. He no longer knows the difference between reality and fantasy. In fact, Shen doesn't even know if he's dreaming or if he's awake.

Paintings bleed before his eyes. Women are viciously beaten. Lesbians frolic with strapped-on dildos. Prosti-tutes are brutally slaughtered. But is it really happening or not? Perhaps the answer lies with his girlfriend/model (Claire Le-Vert).

This is one of those rare gems that demands to be watched more than once. And it gets better with every viewing.

CRYSTAL FORTUNE RUN (1994)
director: Li Kin Sang. Cheung Man· Simon Yam·Anita Yuen·Kirk Wong·Li Kin Sang·Kent Chow ★★★
I admit it. The three-star rating isn't based on story. It's strictly a show of appreciation for **Cheung Man** (in her best role ever) and for **Anita Yuen** (just having fun and not taking herself too seriously for a change).

Unfortunately, the story really sucks. Well, perhaps the story doesn't suck as much as the execution does. The haphazard direction and (seemingly) unfinished script are an insult to a terrific cast.

Master criminal Ko Kit (Anita Yuen) and superhero Wind Yip (Cheung Man) steal the diamond of Emperor Chan from a triad stronghold. They eventually join forces with an alcoholic cop named Kwong (**Simon Yam**) in a battle against the vengeful mobsters, led by Lung Yu (cult director **Kirk Wong**).

The reason everybody wants the diamond is that it will open the grave of Emperor Chan. And inside that grave is reportedly a treasure equivalent to half the money in the world. There's an additional problem, however. Emperor Chan had built so many graveyards that nobody is exactly sure which one houses the fortune.

The audience never finds out either. The movie ends with Ko and Wind flying off to look for the treasure. Maybe the producers are hoping for a sequel, but—damn it—the movie should not be over yet. It would be like

The Killer ending before the final shootout. What kind of crap is this?

CUPID ONE (1984)
director: Ringo Lam. Sally Yip [Yeh]·Mark Cheng·Erik Chan ★½

Even beautiful **Sally Yip** can't save this one, as filmmaker **Ringo Lam** vacillates wildly between sophomoric humor and embarrassing melodrama. Yip plays a girl who, after an argument with her boyfriend, accidentally stows away on a yacht [*Cupid One*] bound for Thailand. Of course, she and the captain (**Mark Cheng**) initially hate each other, but then fall in love.

In the final 20 minutes, Lam tries to breathe life into his dying project when the leading characters are suspected of slave trafficking by the authorities. At least this results in some welcome action sequences. They're tediously predictable, but welcomed nonetheless.

CURRY AND PEPPER (1990)
director: Blackie Ko. Jacky Cheung·Stephen Chow·Ann Bridgewater·Eric Tsang ★★½

Cop buddy flicks have a built-in problem. They are formula entertainment. And, as such, they have become a cliché unto themselves. This kind of film offers nothing new to the action genre; instead it merely serves as a vehicle for aspiring actors. The best buddy pictures have managed to create "overnight" sensations out of their leading, often mismatched, partners. And this film is a prime example.

In the same style as Richard Donner's *Lethal Weapon* (1987), this one is an explosive mixture of black comedy and red-hot action, punctuated by the charming relationship between two quirky hard-boiled partners. *Curry and Pepper* launched the careers of **Stephen Chow** and **Jacky Cheung**. Some critics of HK cinema don't nec-

essarily consider that a favorable occurrence.

A Part 2 was expected, but rising salaries (and egos) of the two leading men kept it from happening. However, **Jacky Cheung** starred in a sequel of sorts called *Hot Hot and Pom Pom*, which incidentally is a much funnier, more satisfying film.

CURSE (1987)
director: Kong Yeung. Li Sua·Kwon Hoi San·Lai Hon·Chang Hoi ★

A young woman named Tu (**Maria Jo**) is married to a repulsively disgusting, wheelchair-confined, old man (why the hell did she marry him in the first place? he doesn't even appear to have money!). There is also a repugnant cousin who takes advantage of the situation and rapes her.

But she is really in love with the gardener. When lust-driven cousin murders the gardner, Tu kills herself to join her boyfriend in the afterlife. The story is preposterous and the acting abysmal. Horrors.

CURSE OF THE WICKED WIFE
aka **WICKED WIFE** (1984)
director: Wong King-Fang. ★★

A confused tale about twins separated at birth: one lives with a rich family and the other with a poor family.

There's also a subplot involving a vampire, and another about an evil landowner who kills people with death bugs.

The movie is reminiscent of *Centipede Horror* when the heroine spews up the death bugs at the conclusion, but getting to that point is a long and winding road.

CURSE OF THE ZOMBI (1989)
director: Hao Lee. Shaojun Lau·Xiao Yan Ze ★★½

A surprising film. Certainly not great, but definitely a lot of fun.

A young archaeologist (Shaojun Lau) agrees to a working vacation. His wife, Zuan (Xiao Yan Ze), wants to visit her family in the wilds of Thailand. So together with his brother and his brother's girlfriend, they go.

But there's trouble ahead, *Straw Dogs* fashion. A jealous punk named Lo remembers how Zuan had rejected him when they were children. He decides to make trouble for her and her foreigner husband by convincing an evil magician to rejuvenate a zombie. This creature then kills some of the villagers and Lo tries to blame the outsiders for the deaths. But the village leader sees through the plot and executes the magician.

Lo retaliates by devouring a bunch of worms; thus he becomes supercharged. In the end, however, he is defeated when a local witch puts an invincible spell on the archaeologist.

CYPRUS TIGER (1990)
director: Gao Fei and **Lui Jun-Gu.** Simon Yam·Conan Lee·Philip Ko·Joey Wang ★½
Was *Tango and Cash* a big hit in Hong Kong? Well, this one features the same tired story about a clandestine politically-protected bad guy (Philip Ko) exposed by two hotshot cops, Cyprus Tiger (Conan Lee) and Climax (**Simon Yam**).

Plus, even though she has very little to do, you'll find **Joey Wang [Wong]** slumming in this mess.

DANCES WITH THE DRAGON (1991)
director: Wong Ching (Jing). Andy Lau· Cheung Man·Chu Kong ★
Filmmaker **Wong Ching** travels the same ground trampled in his *God of Gamblers* series. This time **Andy Lau** plays an unfortunate amnesia victim who is mistaken for an immigrant, but after countless mistaken identification gags (none of them as convincing as the amnesia ruse in *God of Gam-*

blers), he confronts the evil business-   49
man Chow Tai Dang (Chu Kong). Beautiful **Cheung Man** is the only reason to tolerate this junk.

DANCES WITH THE SNAKES (1992)
director: Lee Han-Chang (Richard Lee). Wong Shun Jun·Fan Li-Chiu·Shu Man Hua·Lee Chong Ning ★★
This one could easily qualify as an *Erotic Ghost Story* sequel. Although it's not as well made, conceptually they're the same. Three beautiful sisters (Shu Man-Hua, Fan Li-Chiu and Lee Chong-Ning) are tormented by a sexually charged ghost named Old Yinsan (Wong Shun Jun). When they get tired of "sucking" him, they decide to escape to a nearby kingdom where new adventures await.

Lots of nudity and soft-core sex. There's a particularly dynamic nude female oil fighting sequence that culminates in a four-way orgy. Incidentally, regardless of the title, there are no snakes in the film. Rather, it's an obvious reference to a certain part of the male anatomy.

DARAWASA (1983)
director: Tulsi Ramsay. ★★
The goddess Kali gives birth to a werewolf who becomes hopelessly addicted to a serum created by a mad scientist. Sounds better than it is.

DARK LADY OF THE BUTTERFLY
aka **DARK LADY OF KUNG FU** (1983)
director: Chang Ling. Chang Ling·Tien Peng·Wang Moon Lun ★★½
Chang Ling (star and director), known as **Pearl Cheong** in the USA (see the *Wolf Devil Woman* series), is Hong Kong's most captivating, enchanting export. This is a combination Batwoman and Robin Hood tale with some delightful fantasy overtones. But the contrived plot of mixed identities makes it difficult to endure even for Chang's fans.

50

DAUGHTER OF DARKNESS (1993) director: **Lan Nai Kai [Ivan Lai].** Anthony Wong·Lily Chung ★★★½

DAUGHTER OF DARKNESS 2 (1994) director: **Lan Nai Kai [Ivan Lai].** Trin Dien Li·Dick Lau ★★★
Anthony Wong is lecherous, borderline inept Police Captain Lui. He asks questions like "Do all your family members have big tits?" to a girl who just lost all her relatives to a psycho killer. And he poses for media photos with his arms wrapped around bloodied dead bodies. But somehow he gets the job done.

As irreverent (and sometimes plain silly) as these two films tend to be, they are also chilling. *Daughter of Darkness 1* is the more repugnant of the two, wallowing in its own excess of degradation, incest, torture, and kinky sex. But both movies deliver enough cheap thrills to keep the most jaded Asian cult fan satisfied.

And both films are similar in style and composition. Ever since the success of **Dr. Lamb** (1992), numerous Hong Kong filmmakers have developed their screenplays in a similar fashion—essentially backward. A suspect is arrested, followed by investigation, information slowly unravels, and the movie ends with a graphic visualization of the crime.

Perhaps the biggest difference between these two films and other horror/crime flicks is the amazing amount of brutality and sadistic violence inherent in both, contrasted with the nonchalant attitude most of the characters have for it.

These are both rated Category III (for excessive sex and gore); not everyone will be amused or entertained by them. But if you enjoy the demented work of **Lan Nai Kai** [the **Erotic Ghost Story** series and **Rikki O**], don't give it a second thought.

DAUGHTER OF THE DEVILFISH (1984) director: **Aag Mang.** Yu On On·Lam Chia ★
There's a family in turn-of-the-century China. It consists of a man and his two wives, good and evil.

One day, the husband is in a foul mood because he's having trouble catching fish. He decides the best thing to do is beat the hell out of his first wife and throw her in the river. Even though she dies, her soul is quickly reincarnated. First as a fish, then a tree, and finally a gold bush. Her high mortality rate is due to the evil second wife catching on to her reincarnation act. However, once she reaches the bush stage, she is fairly safe. Golden bushes are pretty good at defending themselves.

Perhaps it should be called *Daughter of the Golden Bush*, but who cares one way or another?

DAYS OF BEING WILD (1991) director: **Wong Kar Wai.** Leslie Cheung·Maggie Cheung·Carina Lau· Tony Leung ★★½
It's a rambling story of a heel (**Leslie Cheung**, the unappreciated other male star of **A Better Tomorrow**) and his absolutely shameful behavior toward most of the female cast members, who include **Maggie Cheung** and **Carina Lau**. Director **Wong Kar Wai** is recognized as one of the new breed of Hong Kong art directors, but in this film (and his earlier **As Tears Go By**) he clearly opts for atmosphere with little regard to the story.

Although **Tony Leung** is prominently featured in the credits, he doesn't show up until the end of the film.

DEAD AND THE DEADLY (1982) director: **Wu Ma.** Samo Hung·Wu Ma·Lam Ching Ying·Cherrie Ch ★★
A dead man (played by Asian kung fu action/comic actor **Samo Hung**

[Hung Kam Bo] allows a ghost to take over his body so that he can get revenge against his murderers. Especially interesting is a segment wherein he escapes detection by transforming into a bug and hiding in his wife's sanitary napkin. Too bad the rest of the movie isn't equally as outrageous.

See **Eastern Condors** or, on the lighter side, **Dragons Forever**, for the best Samo Hung films.

DEAD CURSE (1985)
director: Zhuang Bao Wen. Pan Zhen Wei·Tianer Shang ★★½
Although similar in style to the less effective **Blood Ritual** and **Brutal Sorcery**, fast-paced direction and interesting characters make this film one of the better demonic/possession pix.

A beautiful (but incessantly cackling) witch (Tianer Shang) becomes even stronger after she is killed by a police detective (Pan Zhen-Wei). "I cast a bloody spell on you and your family!" she had cried while dying. Now she is keeping her promise.

DEAD END OF BESIEGERS (1991)
    aka **STEEL HORSE**
director: Ronnie Yu. Cynthia Khan·Yu Rong Guang·Cheung Feng Ni·Li Fai ★★½
Cynthia Khan is engaging in an active (yet supporting) role as a woman who rescues the hero (played by Yu Rong Guang) and other kung fu fighting youths from a gang of Japanese pirates who are preparing to attack turn-of-the-century China.

This is the debut film for martial arts boxer Yu Rong Guang. Many genre enthusiasts are predicting he will be the next Asian superstar. Since this film, he's been carefully placed in a variety of hit vehicles. And, interestingly, Yu's been the villain in each— purposely given the opportunity to growl, snarl, and go ballistic against Hong Kong's biggest box office

draws. In **Project S** (1994), he confronted **Michelle Yeoh** (and indirectly **Jackie Chan**), in **Rock 'n' Roll Cop** (1994) he fought **Anthony Wong,** and in **My Father Is a Hero** (1995) he took on **Jet Li.** Perhaps there's a method to the madness.

DEADLY ANGELS (1984)
director: Pao Hsueh Li. Yen Nan-Hsi· Evelyne Kraft·Shaw Yin Yin·Dana Lan ★★★½
By all accounts this was the first of the contemporary HK girls-with-guns flicks, obviously inspired by America's "Charlie's Angels" (ABC, 1976–1982). Produced by the prolific Shaw brothers, it stars Yen Nan-Hsi, Shaw Yin-Yin, Dana Lan and **Goliathon**'s beautiful female Tarzan, Evelyne Kraft (who wears the most incredible pair of skin-tight short shorts imaginable!).

Horror writers I Kuang (**Black Magic, Seventh Curse**, etc.) pulls out all the stops and concentrates on fast-paced action, fierce gun battles, deadly kung fu fights, and spectacular explosions to tell the story of an undercover female police squad trying to thwart a gang of jewel traffickers.

DEADLY DREAM WOMAN (1992)
director: Wong Ching (Jing) with **Wong Tai Lai.** Cheung Man·Jacky Cheung·Yo Chok Ching·Yip Duk Han ★★½
Cheung Man (the only good thing about most **Stephen Chow** films) gets to wear a superhero costume, complete with a black cape and catwoman mask, in this contemporary tale of triads and gangsters in Hong Kong.

Her name is Nightingale Wong, and she hails from San Francisco. In HK, she attempts to help her father, who is being bullied by Jaguar Lui and his gang. But after taking a mean tumble, Nightingale develops amnesia. (Director **Wong Ching** really likes this ploy; he also used it in **God of Gam-blers** and **Dances with the Dragon**.) A band of prostitutes befriends Nightingale and introduces her to the business. Her memory returns when Jaguar visits the nightclub (brothel) and she launches a frenzied assault at his spacious estate. Two years later, **Cheung Man** would star in a similar (although much better) superhero role as Wing Yip [see **Crystal Fortune Run**].

DEATH CAGE (1988)
director: Robert Dai/Chen Wen Sun. Mark Long·Robin Cho·Angela Tsai ★★
Obviously inspired by the early **Bruce Lee** movies ("He insulted our school, master!"), this film is a violent remake of *Karate Kid*. It's the Wai Chai Gym versus the Hunter Gym. And the ring is a huge steel cage. Yikes! no one gets out alive! Where's Hulk Hogan?

DEATH TRIANGLE (1992)
director: Albert Lai. Moon Lee·Cynthia Khan·Melvin Wong·Yukari Oshima ★★★
Golden Sun Films, a company that has always held the sleaze-n-action banner high, unites their three most popular female stars for a major kick-n-smack fest. Yes, it's **Moon Lee, Cynthia Khan**, and **Yukari Oshima** (called **Cynthia Luster** in the credits), all battling against each other for 90+ pulverizing minutes.

For the most part, the ridiculous plot has to do with two cops, Yang (Cynthia Khan) and Lee (Moon Lee), who are in love with the same man (Melvin Wong). Lee kills the boyfriend and puts the blame on Yang. Then Yang recruits help from her gangster friend Koko (Yukari Oshima).

It's all just an excuse for the girls to kick some butt for a while. You could find worse ways to waste an evening.

Cynthia Khan (L) with Moon Lee in Death Triangle

DECEPTION (1988)
director: Tsui Hark. Lin Ching Hsia· Joey Wang·Pauline Wong·Elizabeth Lee ★½
A lesser film for filmmaker **Tsui Hark**, who tries desperately to capture the atmosphere of a Hitchcock thriller. He succeeds only in presenting an unattractive portrayal of very catty, self-centered women, none of whom are very interesting.

In *Deception* he delivers the dark side of the **Peking Opera Blues** concept. These women are vicious, conniving, and desperate. But, sadly, they are never clever or appealing. A good cast (**Lin Ching Hsia, Joey Wang [Wong]**, Pauline Wong [Wang Xiao-Feng] and Elizabeth Lee) is wasted.

DEMI-GODS AND DEMI-DEVILS (1985)
director: Chang Shing. Choi Si Kun· Lam Chun Kay ·Wai Tin Chi ★
A rather standard costume action/drama set in medieval China with a few fantasy overtones. Ho hum.

DEMON FIGHTER (1984)
director: Chang Peng-Ye (Chu Yen Ping). Lin Ching Hsia·Zheng Shaoqiu· Wong Tao·Lung Fei ★
This is more a collection of unrelated (but outlandish) special FX segments than a cohesive film. But (for a while, anyway) it has something to do with a search for a jade horse statuette in me-

dieval China. Starring **Zheng Shao-qiu** (from *Invincible*) and a young **Lin Ching Hsia** (using the Mandarin of her name in the credits, **Lin Quig Xia**).

DEMON INTRUDER.
See *Nocturnal Demon*

DEMONESS FROM THE 1000 YEARS (1989)
director: Patrick Yeung. Joey Wang· Jacky Cheung ★
It begins as a delightful fantasy tale about a beautiful good witch named Yun Yu Yi (**Joey Wang [Wong]** in a thankless role) who escapes into the future after stealing the Bead of Hell from an evil demoness.

But it very quickly degenerates into an absolutely demeaning, sophomoric comedy with an astonishing collection of *very* unlikable characters, especially pseudo cool Captain Mambo (**Jacky Cheung**) of the Severe Crime Division.

DEMONS (1993)
director: Leung Tung Ni. Ko Mei Han ·Yan Ho Lin ★
A girl is kidnapped and taken to a ghostly underworld. She tries to escape, but soon discovers that she's dead and living in the afterlife. Unfortunately, this pretty soul is damned to an existence of perpetual wandering unless she can avenge her death and thus become reincarnated.

When two mortals attempt to help her, she mistakes them for her killers. This results in bothersome jokes dealing with methods of haunting, until the truth comes out and the girl enlists the men in her vengeful quest. It's mostly a series of uninteresting sight gags and lots of music stolen from *Goblin* soundtracks.

DEMONS FROM FLAME MOUNTAIN 53 (1983)
director: Tyrone Hsu [Hsu Hsia]. Yu Lin· Wu Ma ★★½
An impish female spirit (Yu Lin looking a bit like an Oriental Debbie Gibson, God forbid) is banished from Hell by her mother, the Queen of Flame Mountain.

The girl-devil causes a litany of problems for Earth folk (e.g., disguised as a giant fireball, she rolls through a village, destroying everything in her path) until she is finally reinstated in Hades.

Incidentally, she has the ability to breathe fire and, at one point, demonstrates by blowing into the tail of a dog until the animal explodes.

DESCENDANT OF THE SUN (1986)
director: Chu Yuan. Cherie Cheung· Yuan Biao·Lon Tin Chi·Kwan Fung ★★
Hsuan Shu-Shang (**Yuen Biao**), a good and holy magician, fights the evil Black Queen (Cherie Cheung) for control of the netherworld.

Obviously, he wins. But first we are forced to watch a long and predictable flashback summarizing his mystical life. A lesser film from the Shaw brothers.

DESTRUCTION OF THE RED LOTUS TEMPLE.
See *Burning Paradise*

DETECTIVE IN THE SHADOW (1991)
director: Lai Guo Jian. Waise Lee· Carina Lau ★★
Lightweight romantic action/comedy about the unlikely relationship between an undercover cop (Waise Lee) and a club hostess named Miss Witty, the Queen of Silver (**Carina Lau**).

Violent gangster hijinks unsuccessfully mixed with a silly love story.

DEVIL AND THE GHOSTBUSTER (1989)
director: **He Lian-Chow**. Wan Wen Zheng •David Wei ★★
Beautiful Wan Wen Zheng plays a ghost bent on revenge. Killed while being raped, she gives supernatural fighting powers to a kung fu boxer (David Wei) in this rather slow, atmospheric, serious film.

There's more than the usual amount of nudity, which mercifully makes it a tolerable cinematic journey.

DEVIL CAT.
See *The Cat Living Ten Times*

DEVIL DESIGN (1987)
director: **Yuen Cheung Yan**. Ko Sun Chu• Sui Kim•Chung Long ★★
After retreating from a battle, a band of Mongolian soldiers take refuge in a cemetery, where they are slaughtered by reanimated zombies from the underworld. But the leader (**Ko Sun Chu**) is possessed by the Devil, and he levels an assault against a nearby Chinese village. Local monks cover themselves with writings from the sacred scriptures in an attempt to stop the marauding warlord and his demon army. They succeed in an anticlimactic finale.

DEVIL FETUS (1985)
director: **Liu Hung Chuen**. Eddie Chan•Loy Sau Fan•Lau Tan•Au Yang ★★
Yes, the scene that everybody talks about features a possessed boy, split down the middle, as a demon jumps from inside. But the film is actually a demented, medieval variation of Larry Cohen's *It's Alive* (1974).

On the Feast of the Hungry Ghost a monster rapes the family's mom. She dies, but the possessed fetus lives. For a while, anyway.

DEVIL HUNTERS (1989)
director: **Tony C. K. Lo**. Moon Lee• Alan Tam•Sibelle Hu ★★★
Regardless of the title, this is not a horror (or fantasy) flick; it's a good police action opus from deft director Tony (**Haunted Madam**) Lo, similar to the many **Angel** clones.

A policewoman beauty (girl-n-gun diva **Moon [Mona] Lee**) goes undercover to capture a mob boss. Of course, she succeeds.

DEVIL TWIN (1988)
director: **Shao-Ji Long**. Cui Xian Mai •Hiang Hua Long ★
An incredibly slow, shot-on-video horror film about two sisters (Cui Xian Mai and Hiang Hua Long), sort of an Oriental *Juliette and Justine*. But if de-Sade were alive today, he would spit on it. Or worse.

DEVIL YIELDED TO GOD (1984)
director: **Shen Liu Li**. Ya Lei Gui•Yu Yang ★★
After his girlfriend (Ya Lei Gui) dies, a young swordsman (Yue Yang) visits the home of her parents, but they are harboring a big secret. Namely, her spirit.

DEVIL'S BOX (1988)
director: **Tommy Chin**. Simon Yam• Flora Chung•Allen Fong•Alfred Cheung ★★½
Trouble begins during a movie shoot. An assistant director falls to his death shortly after moving a mysterious ornate box. A curse is unleashed when the box is opened, resulting in strange occurrences and numerous deaths (including a movie editor strangled by film).

The movie fluctuates uneasily between traditional horror and black humor, saved by **Simon Yam**'s performance as the harassed director, Tang. He plays the role with uncharacteristic deadpan restraint, adding an air of intelligence to the film.

DEVIL'S OWL (1988)
director: Liu Kuo Shin. Chia Ling· Leung So Sin·Kong Chin Ha·Lone Fade ★½
Before the opening credits, the audience is informed: "This moving picture is specially for World Wide Animal Protection Associations." Yet, in the opening scenes bats are beaten to death, chickens get their heads chopped off, and ducks are gutted before the unflinching camera eye, (perhaps the producers don't consider these as animals?).

At any rate, a girl (Chia Ling) gives birth to an owl creature, and this monster rallies all its furry friends into a bloody revolt against the humans for their savage behavior. Cheesy special effects add to the unintentional laughs, but you'll also find lots of gore and carnage in this no-budget *Day of the Animals* (1977).

DEVIL'S SWORD (1987)
director: Ratusan Fagurant Lainnta. Barry Prima·Gudhy Sintara·Advent Bangou ★★½
A fantasy film about crocodile people and a beautiful but evil witch queen who rules them. A winner with cult favorite Barry Prima (also see his *Warrior* series).

DEVIL'S VENDETTA (1986)
or **DEVIL'S VINDATA**
(according to credits)
director: Liu Kuo Shin. Cheung Man· Chow Ken Bo·Fung Sui Fang ★★
The devil interrupts a Buddhist prayer session. While under a hypnotic trance, one of the priests slices open his chest and pulls out his pulsing heart. The devil devours it, whereupon he transforms into a gorgeous demoness. Heavenly rays suck him/her into the afterlife, where she

opts to become a vampire and return to earth.

The film is filled with glitzy Asian FX and outrageous transformations. Plus a young **Cheung Man** (did she take Pat Benatar look-alike lessons?) as the demoness.

The plot, although obviously intended as incidental exploitation, is uncomfortably similar to **Tsui Hark**'s later epic productions *Swordsman 2* (1992) and *Swordsman 3: East Is Red* (1993).

DIAMOND FIGHT (1987)
director: Lee Tso Nan. Meng Fei·Norman Chu ★
A needlessly confusing story of intrigue and double-crossing. Valuable jewels belonging to a Japanese exporting company have vanished in Hong Kong. Three different criminal organizations are scurrying about trying to find them, but only the mysterious Suzie Mazuda (Meng Fei) knows their true whereabouts. A suave HK police detective (*Lewd Lizard* star Norman Chu) befriends her to crack the case.

DIARY OF A BIG MAN (1988)
director: C Yun How (Chow Yuen). Chow Yun-Fat·Sally Yeh (Yip) ★★½
Without **Chow Yun-Fat**'s ever-growing popularity, this film *wouldn't* have been made. Without his diverse acting ability, this film *couldn't* have been made. But his critics suggest that, maybe, it *shouldn't* have been made at all.

Fundamentally, it's an Asian remake of Blake Edwards' *Micki and Maude* (1984) as a man tries to juggle marriages to two different women. And it's pretty funny, mostly because of Chow Yun-Fat's comic timing and his willingness to poke fun at his own skyrocketing career (a radio announcer reports that "Chow Yun-Fat has once again been named the most popular actor in Hong Kong," to which Chow mutters, "It must have been fixed").

DIARY OF A SERIAL RAPIST (1995) **director: San Hui Wing.** Chan Man Wen· Shi Yue Niang ★★★
Of course the subject matter is exploitive. And some people would argue that such a movie shouldn't be made in the first place. But this film is a surprisingly effective docudrama based on the vicious crimes committed by the Tuen Mun District rapist in 1992/93.

As with most true crime films, one always wonders how many liberties are taken with the script. But this time that question doesn't seem important. Authenticity takes a back seat to the characterization. Director San manages to create believable circumstances plus flesh-and-blood people.

That is especially true of the rapist. Regardless of his vicious, brutal acts, he's not a monster. He's a dimwitted sap who never seems to understand the severity of his crimes. And that makes him an even more menacing character.

During his interrogation at the film's conclusion he calmly insists, "Pretty girls deserve to be raped." To which the detective replies, "If that's true, Cherie Chung and Lin Chin Hsia must be very busy." But the rapist misses the point and continues, "Yeah, why are women so bitchy?"

It doesn't make any difference if this is based on a true story or not; the message comes through loud and clear. But be forewarned that despite the unexpected maturity of the script, this is a Category III exploitation film. It does not shy away from graphic scenes of brutality and nudity. Unflinchingly, the movie illustrates how this rapist's appetite becomes more ravenous with every assault.

DR. LAMB (1992) **director: Danny Lee** with **Billy Tang.** Simon Yam·Danny Lee·Kent Cheng ★★★★
This is easily one of the best Hong Kong films around: both barbarous and stylish—at the same time.

Based on a true story, **Simon Yam** plays Lam Gor Yu, a demented serial killer on a mission from God to eliminate bad women from the world. He's a taxi driver who has the opportunity to see street walkers putting their worst foot forward. After he begins his murderous behavior, he can't stop. And he's not content to simply strangle and forget. Lam Gor Yu takes the bodies back to his apartment, where he systematically dismembers, photographs, and (in some instances) has sex with them. His photos eventually get him into trouble with the law. When he takes the negatives to be developed, the concerned store owner contacts the police. The result is a harrowing police-procedural study.

Actor **Danny Lee** surprised critics and audiences alike with his assured direction, never flinching from the savage portrayal. His characterizations and camerawork add an air of credibility and class to the brutal subject matter. Yet it should be mentioned that this filmmaking debut was obviously aided by the talents of his codirector, **Billy Tang** **[Tang Hin Sing]** of *Vengeance Is Mine* and *Run and Kill* fame. The film was produced by **Parkman Wong** [director of *Passionate Killing in a Dream* and **Red Shield**].

Also starring **Kent Cheng**, identified as **Cheng Jui** in the credit sequence.

DOCTOR MACK (1995) **director: Lee Chin Gai.** Tony Leung [Chiu Wai]·Richard Ng·Lau Ching Wan·Christy Chung ★★
Tony Leung [Chiu Wai] is Doctor Lau Mack, an unconventional surgeon

who got his medical degree from the University of Africa after getting kicked out of a Hong Kong college. He was actually expelled because of an accident caused by his friend Roger Jaw (**Lau Ching Wan**). And in the ten-year interim, Roger has become an important hospital CEO, while Mack is content running a small storefront clinic.

Secretly, Roger has grown to hate Mack. When a turn of events makes Dr. Mack the toast of HK high society (specifically, his unique mixture of tribal and conventional medical techniques), Roger takes credit for the achievements, causing friction with his girlfriend, who eventually falls for the loveable Dr. Mack.

This is a melancholy drama, saved from turgid sentimentality by excellent performances from all the principal actors (especially Tony Leung in a believable three-dimensional characterization). But the problem still remains, nestled deeply within the soap-opera script. It's inoffensive and, worst of all, predictable. This is the kind of meaningful cinema embraced lovingly by the *M*A*S*H* generation. Was there really anyone in the audience who didn't think Dr. Mack would save the poor Boy Scout hit by the stray bullet? It's so corny that it almost works better as a parody.

DOCTOR VAMPIRE (1991)
director: Lu Jian-Ming. Guo Jin En·Chan Ya Lun·Peter Kjaer ★★★
Here's a very enjoyable tale about vampires (the Western variety, not the hopping kind) with a decidedly decadent overtone, nudity, and a captivatingly romantic plot.

A young doctor (Guo Jin En) from Hong Kong is stranded in the wilderness when his car breaks down. He stumbles upon a house that turns out to be a brothel run by vampires. After being seduced and drained by a gor-

geous one named Cora (**Chan Ya Lun**), he's sent on his way (memory erased and car repaired).

Later, the evil boss vampire (Peter Kjaer) is sampling blood from his whores when he discovers the delightful virgin juices mingling inside of Cora. "This is better than ginseng!" he cries, "bring me this human!"

So Cora is sent on a mission to Hong Kong. But after arriving in HK, she falls in love with the doctor (who is now beginning to show signs of vampirism) and the two outcasts try desperately to escape the clutches of the bloodsucking pimp.

DR. WEI IN THE SCRIPTURE WITH NO WORDS
director: Ching Siu Tung. Jet Li·Rosamund Kwan·Charlie Young·Takeshi Kaneshiro ★★★★
Inevitably, this film will be compared to Steven Spielberg's *Indiana Jones*, but that's less than half correct. There's also a clever homage to story-within-story movies like *La Magnifique* (1974) and *Stunt Man* (1980). Yet, the bottom line is this film stands on its own and emerges as one of the best HK productions of 1996. Director **Ching Siu Tung** (best known for his *Chinese Ghost Story* films) delivers an intelligent, great-looking, effect-laden actioner filled with an impressive array of endearing characters.

Everybody is worried about Chow Si Kit (**Jet Li**). He's a writer with *writer's block*, and even though he's under contract to produce a 9-volume series within a year, based on the adventures of his fictional character Dr. Wei, three months have passed and, after one installment, he's out of steam. His editor is pissed off, his agent/wife is concerned, and his assistant writers are beyond frazzled.

Most of Chow's problems stem from his crumbling marriage; wife Monica (**Rosamund Kwan**) is demanding a divorce. At one point, assistant Takeshi Kaneshiro tries to get the writer back on track by explaining, "A tortured life is the food of a creator." But Chow's heart is broken, and he can't concentrate on writing. Chow and his two assistants (the forementioned Takeshi Kaneshiro and popular HK starlet **Charlie [Yeoh] Young**) fly to the Chinese wilderness in search of inspiration. En route, while their boss is sleeping, the two helpers begin writing for him. This starts the ball rolling; Chow, inspired by the out-of-kilter direction his story has taken, adds his own twists and turns. Soon, the literary work becomes an amalgamation, with three different authors propelling the story in unexpected but delightful directions. As they individually try to be more and more outrageous, the plot shifts constantly and the characters (each based on real-life people) change personalities (e.g., Rosamund Kwan drifts effortlessly from a "nice woman" to a whip-wielding bitch and back to nice again).

Most of the screen action takes place within the visualization of the ongoing novel, wherein the king of adventurers, Dr. Wei (also **Jet Li**), is searching for a sacred scripture that must be kept from the invading Japanese patriots. But the story, obviously due to the fertile multiwriter input, is a roller-coaster ride with incredible stunts, explosions, train wrecks, magic swords, flying sumo wrestlers, monsters, plane crashes, ninjas, fireballs, and much more—simply, this is the most impressive collection of special effects ever amassed for one movie, including some very good monster makeup (a far cry from the rubber centipede lurking at the end of **Chinese Ghost Story 2**).

In the past, Jet Li has been criticized for his stoic no-nonsense presence, in direct contrast to the more accessible light-n-breezy performances of top competitor, **Jackie Chan**. This time, Jet Li is very likable. He actually smiles a number of times in the film.

Plus, as if accepting a direct challenge from Jackie himself, Jet Li even finds himself in a drag segment (remember, Jackie Chan's gender-bender scenes in **Project S** and **City Hunter**?). But, as a girl, Jet is definitely the prettiest.

DON'T GIVE A DAMN (1995)
director: Samo Hung. Samo Hung·Takeshi Kaneshiro·Cathy Chow·Yuen Biao ★

Frankly, my dear Samo . . . we don't give a damn either.

There's goofy slapstick comedy and mindless kung fu action, but not a plot anywhere in sight. It's mostly a series of vignettes dealing with a haggard cop (**Samo Hung**) and the problems he has with his youthful boss (Takeshi Kaneshiro), a customs agent (**Yuen Biao**), and a girl who won't give him the time of day (**Cathy Chow**). The whole mess escalates into a slipshod gang war involving the Triads, the Yakuza, and the Mafia.

Another film in the minus column of Samo Hung's uneven directorial career, joining other misses like **Ghost Renting** (1992), **Owl Vs Bumbo** (1985), and **Paper Marriage** (1988). But these failures are easily forgivable when he dilutes them with such great films as **Pedicab Driver** (1990), **Dragons Forever** (1986), and **Eastern Condors** (1986).

DON'T PLAY WITH FIRE (1981)
director: Tsui Hark. Lo Lieh·Lim Ching Chi·Chung Chi Man·Bruce Barron ★★★

A no-nonsense look at a very bleak world. If we're to believe **Tsui Hark**'s narrative, Hong Kong is on a collision course with Hell. Crime and degradation, lunacy and vengeance pollute the crowded streets. Terminal depression lurks in every hallway, amid decaying animals and human entrails. This is an ugly film, shot with jarring close-ups and hatchet edits—far removed from his sprawling epics like *Once upon a Time in China*.

Three kids on a joyride accidentally hit and kill an innocent man. The collision is witnessed by a rebellious teenage girl named Pearl (Lim Ching Chi), who blackmails them into helping her pull a few robberies. Inadvertently, their activities compromise a vicious triad gang who attack the youths with ferocious intensity.

Shaw Brothers veteran **Lo Lieh** plays Pearl's brother, a frustrated cop who's too preoccupied with his own problems to notice his sister's descent into corruption and madness.

DON'T STOP MY CRAZY LOVE FOR YOU.
See *My Crazy Love for You*

DRAGON CHRONICLES (1994)
aka **SEMI-GODS AND SEMI-DEVILS**
director: **Cheng Siu Keung.** Brigitte Lin· Gong Li·Cheung Man ★ ½
Here's an example of a big-budget flick trying to seduce an audience with special effects and to hell with continuity. What a shame to see three of Hong Kong's biggest actresses wasted so badly.

Brigitte Lin [Lin Ching Hsia] and **Gong Li** are two rival sisters looking for the ultimate martial arts technique; **Cheung Man** is the assistant to the king, and she's also looking for the precious kung fu chronicles. They all meet in a netherworld where they battle each other and fly around a lot. In fact, they fly around so much, you'll forget about the plot (unfortunately, a remarkably easy thing to do). Instead, you'll be trying to figure out where all the wires are hidden.

DRAGON FAMILY (1988)
director: **Lau Kar Wing.** Andy Lau·O Chung Hung·Max Mok [Mok Siu Cheung] ★★
You've seen it all before. In fact, the ending is a direct rip-off of *A Better Tomorrow 2*. **Andy Lau** and his small band of betrayed gangsters invade the mob boss's house and, although wildly outnumbered, they manage to wreak complete havoc on everyone inside.

Director **Lau Kar Wing**, brother of action filmmaker **Lau Karl Leung**, doesn't have the cinematic style of **John Woo** (nor that of his sibling). His actors slip hopelessly into melodramatic performances that border on preposterous. Lau seems to be hopelessly lost in the slower tender moments, and he overcompensates in the action scenes. More gunfire doesn't necessarily make a better film. In the **A Better Tomorrow** films, the action works because—first—the audience cares about the characters. *Dragon Family*, while it attempts to retrace the same bloody steps, is incapable of delivering any of the personality.

DRAGON FROM RUSSIA (1990)
director: **Clarence Fok Yiu Leung.** Sam Hui·Maggie Cheung·Carrie Ng· Nina Li Chi·Lai Chun Lee ★★½
The rating is perhaps kind. But the action is swift and the FX are good. Unfortunately, the irrationally confusing story leaves much to be desired.

Loosely based (very loosely based) on the Japanese comic book *Crying Freeman*, this one tells of a secret clan, Eight Hundred Dragons, whose members hunt down and assassinate "untouchable" criminals all over the world. Starring Samuel (*Aces Go Places* series) Hui as Yao, the clandestine hitman. Lots of thrills and spills, but short on substance.

Brigitte Lin (L) with Gong Li (R) in *Dragon Chronicles*

DRAGON IN JAIL (1992)
director: Kent Cheng. Andy Lau·Ho Kar King ★★½
Predominantly, it's a character study of a loser named Henry (**Andy Lau**), an ex-con who tries desperately to fit into society after being released from prison. But his personal battle with drugs, and then with local gangsters, compromises the relationship with his girlfriend, Winnie. Eventually, he's framed for killing Winnie. But after beating the rap, he seeks revenge and loses his freedom again. Downbeat and ugly, with the best moments coming early on—during the prison sequences.

DRAGON INN (1992)
director: Raymond Lee (Li Hui Min).
Tony Leung [Kar Fai]·Lin Ching Hsia· Maggie Cheung· Donnie Yen ★★★½
During the King Tai era of the Ming government, the numerous eunuch courts hold much of the country's power. The strongest of these, the East Chamber, is led by Tsao Siu Yan, who orders the wrongful executions of

those who protest his power, using his court to frame them. As the film opens, two innocent children imprisoned by the East Chamber are rescued by imperial swordsman Chow Wai-On (**Tony Leung [Kar Fai]**) and his companion, Yau Mo-Yan (**Lin Ching Hsia**). Wai-On and Mo-Yan whisk the youths away, with the eunuch's soldiers in close pursuit. The paths of the two opposing factions cross at the Dragon Inn, the lone shelter for travelers in an unending stretch of barren desert.

The inn is run by Jade King (**Maggie Cheung**), a self-absorbed, apolitical swindler who is bumping off some of her male customers so that chef Duo has fresh ingredients for his meat dishes.

A vicious thunderstorm forces the East Chamber men to stay several days at the inn without knowing Wai-On and Mo-Yan are in their midst. Wai-On pleads with Jade to reveal the inn's hidden passageway so he may ensure a safe escape for the children. She agrees, but only if he satisfies her lusty cravings—a prospect that sits none too well with Mo-Yan. The escape doesn't go as planned, and the tensions erupt in an exciting, fast-paced, gory battle amid a desert storm.

Essentially, this is a remake of **King Hu**'s 1972 epic (also called *Dragon Inn*), which starred Pai Ying and Shang Kwan Ling Fung. Some critics complained that the new version lacked the subtleties of the original, abandoning intricate character development for mindless action and blatantly exploitive elements (especially citing the cannibalism subplot). But, the film is decidedly a new adaption of the original and not intended to be an exact copy.

DRAGON LORD (1980)
aka **YOUNG MASTER IN LOVE**
director: **Jackie Chan.** Jackie Chan· Hseuh Li·Huang Ing Sik·Barry Wong ★★
This one is generally considered to be **Jackie Chan's** transition film, from the kung fu fighting pics to movies that relied more on stunts and straightforward fist/kicking combat. In fact, he purposely downplays martial arts for a new cinematic direction, the frenzied mayhem he stylized over the next decade.

Jackie plays Dragon, an innocent nationalist who attempts to capture a gang of political thieves. Don't expect the kind of flashy special effects and expert filmmaking that mark Chan's later career. Basically, this is an ambitious, low-budget adventure film. It is significant only because Jackie Chan became the world's biggest action star, and this film was the springboard.

DRAGON PEARL (1989)
director: **Chung Leung.** Kim To·Che Kim Chu·Wong Chung Yu·Chan Chi Keung·Marilyn Chow *pick your own rating*

There are seven dragon pearls (opaque jewels the size of golf balls). "I own two of them," proclaims the evil Tarus King from outer space. "When I own all seven, the god of the Dragon will appear and the universe will be mine!"

He recites these words shortly after his army (led by a muscular black man and a beautiful blonde girl in Superwoman garb) attacks a Buddhist temple and massacres everyone. Thus begins one of the strangest low-budget Asian films of them all.

Mere words can't describe the cockeyed spectacle that follows as a band of good witches and wizards attempts to find the pearls first. Your jaw will drop in total disbelief.

DRAGON VS VAMPIRE (1985)
aka **CLOSE ENCOUNTER OF THE VAMPIRE**
director: **Lionel Leung.** Yuen Cheung Yan · Yuen Sun Yi · Jan Chi Jing · Carrie Lee ★
A routine comedy horror film set in medieval China. Nothing new here. An incoherent mess from start to finish. Don't be fooled. Stay away.

DRAGONS FOREVER (1986)
director: **Samo Hung.** Jackie Chan· Samo Hung·Yuen Biao·Yuen Wah· Deannie Yip·Crystal Kwok·Dick Wei ★★★★
Perhaps the best of the **Jackie Chan** transition films [the ones made between his early chop socky days and his later crime-story period], *Dragons Forever* mixes great fight sequences and back-breaking stunts with endearing, charismatic performances. The camaraderie among the three lead characters (Jackie Chan, **Samo Hung**, and **Yuen Biao**) is so obviously genuine the screen seems to crackle with their relentless enthusiasm.

A gangster, Wah Hua (legendary bad guy Yuen Wah), is using his

62

chemical factory to refine narcotics. But the waste is killing the fish in Catherine Yeh's lake, destroying her business. So she sues. Lawyer Johnny Lang (Jackie Chan) decides to abandon Mafia client Wah in favor of Catherine (Deannie Yip) when he falls in love with her cousin, Nancy (Pauline Yeung).

The key to this film's success lies in personalities and the way they interact with each other, aided by **Samo Hung**'s deft direction. Despite some nasty roughness, the movie never loses sight of its goal—to entertain.

Plus there's a plethora of cameos including, Fung Shui-Fan as Yuen Biao's psychiatrist, Roy Chiao as the no-nonsense judge, and Shing Fui-On as one of Jackie Chan's hood clients. Also watch for Dick Wie and a young Billy Chow as two of Yuen Wah's thugs.

DRAGONS OF THE ORIENT (1993)
director: Rocky Law. Jet Li·Wu Ben ★★
This one is essential viewing for kung fu enthusiasts. In fact, if you are mesmerized by martial arts tournaments and know the names of all the different fighting techniques, add another (★) to the above rating. This movie was made for you.

It's a documentary following the journey of news reporters Wang Chun and Yang Ching as they travel all over mainland China in search of accurate information on the secret world of martial arts. The film devotes a good amount of time to **Jet Li**, the boxer who become popular via **Tsui Hark**'s *Once upon a Time in China*, and also his trainer **Wu Ben**.

But for viewers who don't care much about kung fu, the most interesting thing about the film will be the amazing scenery, including the famous Shaolin Temple, the Great Wall, the Lukao Bridge, and much more.

DREAM LOVERS (1986)
director: Chen Ching Lo. Chow Yun-Fat ·Lin Ching Hsia ★★★½
A musical composer played by **Chow Yun-Fat** is haunted by the ghost of a girlfriend from a previous life. It seems that she expects him to keep his promise of eternal love, even through reincarnation. Surprisingly, he does. He breaks up with his long-time (and loyal) girlfriend, but in a very somber scene. ("Whether 2000 years or 9 years, it's still love") she kills herself.

Truly unique story, plus there are some very steamy love scenes in this poignant film.

DREAMING THE REALITY (1991)
director: Simon Yun Ching. Moon Lee·Sibelle Hu·Yukari Oshima·Eddie Ko ★★★½
If you can sit through the endless array of boxing sequences in the middle of this film, you'll be otherwise impressed with this crackerjack action flick. A diva cast (**Moon Lee, Yukari Oshima,** and **Sibelle Hu [Hu Hui Chung]** helps to make it one of the better girls-n-guns HK films.

Moon Lee and Yukari Oshima play hitwomen working for their gangster father. While traveling to Thailand on assignment, Lee has an accident and suffers from amnesia. She is befriended by Lan (Sibelle Hu) who introduces her to a "normal" life. Thinking that his daughter has betrayed him, the ruthless father sends Oshima to find and eliminate her. When she can't pull the trigger on her sister, dad retaliates by ordering her stepbrother to snuff Oshima. This is the final straw. Lee and Hu join forces to eliminate the patriarch and his Triad empire.

DRESS OFF FOR LIFE (1986)
director: Lee Han Chang (Richard Lee). Jimmy Wang Yu·Shelia Tu ★★
Chen Yuen (**Jimmy Wang Yu**), a pro-

fessional boxer, goes into hiding when his career takes a nose dive. His loneliness has bred impotence and, ultimately, insanity. Now he stalks the city streets, attacking and slaughtering unsuspecting females.

The chilling horror of the crazed misogynist is offset, unsuccessfully, by the silly meanderings of two Hong Kong detectives.

DRUGS AREA (1991)
director: Cheng Siu Keung. Gao Xiong· Sibelle Hu ★★½
Action flick about illegal drug dealing in Hong Kong and the undercover cops who risk their lives and their relationships to capture the bad guys. Specifically, it's the story of narcotic agent Wong (Gao Xiong) and his cop girlfriend, Nancy (**Sibelle Hu**). Her Triad father is murdered in a botched drug deal and they try to find his killers.

Good, well-choreographed gun

sequences highlight this rather routine thriller.

DRUNKEN MASTER 2 (1994)
director: Jackie Chan (partially directed by **Lau Karl Leung**). Jackie Chan·Ti Lung ·Anita Mui ★★★★
Jackie fired director **Lau Karl Leung** halfway through the production, resulting in some glaring continuity problems. But, that aside, this is the quintessential **Jackie Chan** film. Perhaps it is the best chop socky movie of them all.

The plot is truly insignificant (although for the sake of critique, it deals with a gang of criminals trafficking in Chinese antiques and Jackie's attempt to expose the bad guys). This is an action film, and as such, it contains some of the most extensive jaw-dropping stunt work and martial art magic ever amassed together in one feature.

If you aren't yet part of the initiated, and you'd like to see why Jackie

Jackie Chan's **Drunken Master 2**

Chan is the number one box office draw in the world, watch this film's amazing conclusion. The fight sequence between Jackie and his real-life body guard, Lan Hui Kwong, is the most intricately choreographed spectacle you're likely to ever see.

DRUNKEN MASTER 3 (1994) **director: Lau Kar Leung.** Willie Kwai [Chi] • Andy Lau • Michelle Lee • Liu Chia Hui • Adam Cheng • Simon Yam ★★½
After **Jackie Chan** fired him from **Drunken Master 2**, director **Lau Kar Leung** promised he'd make the real Drunken Master sequel. Although this one is identified as #3, it more accurately would be the second in the series, telling the story of a teenage Wong Fei Hong (played by Willie Kwai, known as Willie Chi in **Burning Paradise**).

Rabid Jackie Chan fans, who wanted to see director Lau fall on his face for pissing off their hero, will be disappointed. While he hasn't made an epic here, Lau Kar Leung has done what he promised. He's re-created an old time chop socky flick—devoid of slick stunt work, loaded with martial arts fighting.

Of course, his cast helps. Lots of seasoned kung fu stars mix it up with such perennial favorites as **Andy Lau, Simon Yam**, and **Michelle Lee**. But, in reality, the filmmaker didn't need to prove anything to anybody. His reputation was already secure in the annals of HK moviemaking after starring in Legendary Weapons of China (1982) and directing such actioners as **Tiger on the Beat** (1988).

The major weakness in this film is its disregard for historical accuracy. The movie is filled with the kind of embarrassing mistakes that plagued the Italian sword-n-sandal productions (e.g., somebody in a tunic wearing a watch). This time, in one sequence, Wong Fei Hong gives an explanation to the princess by saying: "It's just like seeing a movie," when clearly movie theaters didn't exist circa 1900. Or there's a costume party where someone is dressed like Boris Karloff's Frankenstein monster. Plus automobiles from the Roaring 20s and clothes from the '60s are commonplace in turn-of-the-century China.

EAGLE SHOOTING HEROES (1993) **director: Jeff Lau.** Lin Ching Hsia • Leslie Cheung • Joey Wang • Maggie Cheung • Veronica Yip • Jacky Cheung • Carina Lau ★½
It should be a crime to put so many great actors and actresses in a movie this bad! Director **Jeff Lau** was riding the train to success in his early career [with genuinely funny entries like **Operation Pink Squad**], but he seriously derailed in 1990 (**Mortuary Blues**) and, judging from this attempt, he hasn't gotten back on track yet.

The cast is an amazing who's who, including **Lin Ching Hsia, Leslie Cheung, Joe Wang [Wong], Maggie Cheung, Veronica Yip, Jacky Cheung,** and **Carina Lau** [as a man!]. But the story [an evil villain named Wicked trying to kidnap the daughter of a king] is one mindless sight gag after another, with absolutely no regard for continuity. In the wrong hands, this film could single-handedly destroy the current rage for Asian cinema. Avoid it at all costs.

EAST IS RED.
See Swordsman 3

EASTERN CONDORS (1986) **director: Samo Hung (Hung Kam-Bo).** Samo Hung • Yuen Biao • Lam Ching Ying • Joyce Godenzi • Billy Lau • Wu Ma • James Tien • Dick Wei ★★★½
The Dirty Dozen theme, Hong Kong style. Probably the best of the **Samo Hung** films, this action/adventure flick tells the story of death-row convicts

sent into Vietnam to recapture an army base.

The final 20 minutes are among the most over-the-top, balls-to-the-wall finales in Asian cinema. A good introduction to the genre. Costar diva Joyce Godenzi became Mrs. Samo Hung in 1995.

EASY MONEY (1987)
director: Kent Cheng. Michelle Yeoh (Khan)·George Lam ★★
Not a bad movie, it just isn't very original. This is a clone of Norman Jewison's *Thomas Crown Affair* (1968), the story of a bored millionaire who masterminds an intricate bank robbery only to be dogged by a hotshot insurance investigator, which results in an unlikely romance.

The biggest difference between this version and the original lies in the gender switching of the lead characters. In Jewison's film, Steve McQueen is the bank robber; this time it's **Michelle Yeoh**; and George Lam plays the insurance agent, originally Faye Dunaway's role.

Directed by popular character actor **Fatty Kent Cheng.**

EDGE OF DARKNESS (1988)
director: Lo Lieh. Chin Siu Hao·Alex Man· John Sham·Lo Lieh ★★★½
Veteran Shaw Brothers actor **Lo Lieh** has created a tight, suspenseful thriller about an undercover cop (**Chin Siu Hao**) who becomes the right hand of a vicious triad boss. The gun action is state-of-the-art and often breathtaking, but this film also benefits from an intelligent script that explores the Asian concept of loyalty.

This subject is often the focal point of **John Woo**'s heroic bloodshed films, but here it is put under a microscope and dissected. Rather than endorsing the patented machismo melodramatics found in many contemporary HK cop/buddy movies, Lo Lieh attempts to cast a critical eye at the follies of such errant endorsements.

A different type of film from director Lo who has, in the past, made such diverse motion pictures as **Black Magic with Buddha** and **Summons to Death**.

EDGE OF FURY (1985)
director: Lee Cuo-Nan. Ti Na·He Cong Dao ★★
Lily (Ti Na), a cop's ex-wife, gets mixed up with the mob in this kung fu intensive action flick. He Cong Dao plays policeman Johnny Tu Lung, who infiltrates the triad organization in order to destroy their empire and rescue his former wife.

ELUSIVE SONG OF THE VAMPIRE (1987)
director: Lu Bin. He Hong Tong·Zi Quiang Qu·Chu Hong ★★
This movie ranks high on the wacky scale; unfortunately it is also severely disjointed and dreadfully inept. But, frankly, there's a lot to be said for wacky.

It's the story of Xiao Fan (He Hong Tong), who discovers that his home is haunted by four hopping zombies. He enlists the aid of a kung fu sorcerer to get rid of them.

Meanwhile, the transvestite king (Zi Quiang Qu) has stolen the soul of the castle priestess, Xiao Cui (Chu Hong), while making love to her. He refuses to return it until she can replace it with the soul of a male virgin.

She eventually finds the man (who is still having zombie problems) and removes his soul. But he isn't a virgin for long, because they fall in love and nature takes its course. So the priestess, the man, and the kung fu sorcerer join together to fight the transvestite king.

What about the vampire mentioned in the title? Now that's a good question. There's none to be found.

ENCOUNTERS OF THE SPOOKY KIND (1981)
director: **Samo Hung.** Samo Hung·Wu Ma·Wong Har·Yuen Biao·Chung Fat· Chan Lung ★★★½
A classic. Perhaps the first important martial arts horror film, expertly realized by one of the genre's greatest director/stars, **Samo Hung.** Here is the forerunner of *Mr. Vampire* (1984) and the countless clones to follow.

In this one, Chang (**Samo Hung**) and his silly friends conduct a seance. But it actually works as the group conjures up some real monsters. Inspired by the accidental spooky encounter, Chang's unfaithful wife and her lover go to a black magic priest and request his supernatural power to kill the goofball husband. Soon, every ghost, mummy, zombie, and vampire in the immediate vicinity is chasing poor Chang, in a wild frenzy for his head. Chang retaliates by asking a white magic priest to help him. The resulting battle between the two wizards is a textbook example of the genre.

ENCOUNTERS OF THE SPOOKY KIND 2 (1991)
director: **Samo Hung** with **Ricky Lau.** Samo Hung·Lam Ching Ying·Meng Hoi ★★
Ten full years after the first one, **Samo Hung** directs Part 2. As one might expect, it's really not a sequel at all.

Instead, this is the story of a transient named Po (played by **Hung**) who tries to help a little girl ghost become a real person before her senile mother discovers that her daughter is dead. When all else fails, Samo shows off his kung fu. At least that makes up for the lame story.

ENTER THE FAT DRAGON (1978)
director: **Samo Hung.** Samo Hung· Yuen Biao ★★★
After **Bruce Lee**'s death, there were countless films that both honored and

ripped off the superstar's mystique (see the Roots section of this book). This one, with bumpkin **Samo Hung** as a Bruce Lee fanatic who has several encounters with Mafia hoods when he moves to Hong Kong from the country, is easily the best of the batch.

The treat of the film is Samo Hung himself. Regardless of his rotund size, he is one of the most agile fighters in HK cinema.

EROTIC DREAM OF THE RED CHAMBER (1978)
director: **Li Han-Hsiang.** Lo Bao·Lin Ching Hsia·Sylvia Chang ★★★
An original piece of Asian erotica comparable to the Euro soft-core classics, *Story of O, Emanuelle,* and *The Fruit Is Ripe.* But it's definitely Oriental in mien. Based on a Cantonese opera, this lavish production from the Shaw Brothers tells the story of 15-year-old Pao Yu and his preoccupation with bedding beautiful women.

Much of the Chinese opera music is toned down to contemporary Mandarin (and inadvertently Western) taste, making this a very palatable *and* spicy audio/visual experience. Some of the beautiful woman who visit Pao Yu and his dream quest are Li Ching Hsia and a young **Silvia Chang [Chang Chia].**

EROTIC GHOST STORY (1990)
director: **Lan Nai Kai.** Amy Yip·Ha Chia Ling·Man Su ★★★

EROTIC GHOST STORY 2 (1991)
director: **Lan Nai Kai.** Anthony Wong ·Lui Siu Yip·Clarine Chan ★★★

EROTIC GHOST STORY 3 (1993)
director: **Lan Nai Kai.** Noel Chin· Huang De Bin·Pauline Chan ·Shing Fui On·Chi Jing Wen ★★★
In #1, Wutung is a demon. When visiting the Earth's netherworld, he is attracted to three beautiful ghost/fairies

(one of them is voluptuous **Amy Yip**). Disguised as a scholar, he seduces the three fairies; Hua Hua, Fei Fei and So So.

According to Oriental folklore, fairies exist on the first level of immortality and because of their "close relationship to humanity," they have a more difficult time controlling themselves from carnal pleasures. Regardless, these fairies are seduced through deceit and eventually band together and destroy Wutung.

In Part 2, Wutung transports himself into another body and is now called Chiu-Sheng. He seduces a mortal named Hsiao-Yen. Heaven sends two militant fairies to stop the relationship.

#3 adds monsters and cannibalism to the mix, keeping the series alive for yet another go around. But Wutung is gone. A young couple, Chu Chung and Hsia Hui (Huang De Bin and Pauline Chan [Chan Bao Lian]), takes refuge in a haunted temple during a thunderstorm. There they meet the keeper of the flame, a Buddhist monk named Reverend Wick (Shing Fui On, sporting an uncharacteristic bald head). Wick has the ability to transport the curious travelers into magical realms of extraordinary sexual pleasures. But they must heed his warning ["Return to me before the incense burns cold"] or they will be forced to live forever in the dark void of space.

Chi Jing Wen plays I-Meng, a beautiful siren who convinces Chu Chung to rescue her from the clutches of an evil queen in the fantasy underworld. Also with Cheung Jing Hua.

This adult fairy tale (also released in some markets as **Tale of Eros**) is heavily saturated with loads of gratuitous nudity and soft-core sex scenes, a virtual bevy of Chinese beauties. Plus there's some unsettling blood and gore. Make sure you see the Mandarin version; it's uncut.

Pauline Chan (R) with Huang De Bin in *Erotic Ghost Story 3*

EROTIC JOURNEY (1993)
director: Lau Kwok Hung. Wong Yuet Ling·Dick Wei·Melvin Wong·Yuen An Yam ★★½
If you like sleazy exploitation, give this one a higher rating.

It's the story of three female tourists who find themselves incarcerated in a Thailand jungle prison after they witness a drug trafficking caper. You'll find all the requirements for women-in-prison fare, including sadistic warders, tortured captives, and of course a generous amount of whipping, bondage, and degradation.

EROTIC NIGHTS (1990)
director: He Fan. Bei Gi Keer·Wang Yung Fen·Chan Pui Ki ★★★
An insufferably slow beginning fools you. This one actually develops into a compelling study of three girls and the paths they choose to stardom in the HK film world. Wildly sexy with an abundant amount of nudity. Lily (Bei Gi Keer) is especially charismatic as the sexpot who will sleep with anyone to achieve her showbiz goal.

ESCAPE FROM CORAL COVE (1988)
director: T. Chang. Iwan Beng·Bee Lee Tan ★★★
A nondescript, generic title hides this diamond-in-the-rough horror tale. When

a drunkard urinates on sacred ashes in an abandoned churchyard, an evil sex killer is resurrected from a watery grave in the Coral Cove Lagoon. The ghostly creature begins stalking unsuspecting teen vacationers, particularly Irene and Alex (Iwan Beng and Bee Lee Tan) plus their nubile friends. Incredible underwater photography and a healthy dose of graphic gore.

ESCAPE FROM HELL HOLE.
See *Hell Hole*

ESCAPE FROM THE BROTHEL (1991)
director: Wang Lung Wei. Alex Fong ·Pauline Chan·Billy Chow·Sophie Crawford ★★
If you're looking for trash, look no further—especially if you want to see a naked kick-boxing prostitute try to beat the shit out of her client. And, as if that's not enough, there's wall-to-wall nudity plus some truly bizarre sex positions and vicious S&M activity.
But the real plot is quite tired. It's the story of three young men from mainland China who escape to Hong Kong after getting framed in a robbery. In HK, one of the accused, Sam Ma (Alex Fong from *Angel* days) looks up his old girlfriend Bi Bi Chow (*Erotic Ghost Story 3*'s Pauline Chan). He finds that she and her sister are trapped in a life of prostitution. Of course, he's willing to help them get out.

ESPIRIT D'AMOUR (1986)
director: Ringo Lam. Alan Tam·Cecilia Yip ★★
A horror fantasy about a young man who falls in love with the ghost of a girl via a ouija board. Despite an unexpected, surprising finale (he loses the girl in an exorcism), there's really not much going on here. Filmmaker **Ringo Lam** is a much better action director. See his **Full Contact** or **Burning Paradise** for good examples.

ETERNAL COMBAT (1991)
director: Cheng Chang Yip. Joey Wang· Zheng Ying Lin·Yuen Wak ★★★½
Wow! A magician (Zheng Ying Lin) recruits the spirit of a macho soldier (who, incidentally, died from a heart attack while making love to five women) to help him fight a powerful, sinister ghost named Cici. Cici is a beautiful dominatrix (**Joey Wang [Wong]**) who, during an exuberant battle, whisks everybody into the future, where she has gained control of an insane asylum. The inmates call her the Evil Woman, and she proceeds to live up to her name.

EVIL BLACK MAGIC (1991)
director: Yao Fenpan [Fen Pan]. ★½
The director of **Spirit Vs. Zombie** rips off the HK classic **Black Magic** series, substituting nudity and softcore sex for gore. It's the story of a sorcerer's apprentice who knocks off his master and uses the secret spells to snatch the heart of a pretty, but snobbish, girl.

EVIL CAT (1986)
director: Dennis Yu [Yun Kong Yu]. Lau Kar Leung·Tang Lai Ying·Mark Cheng ★★★
A fascinating film that is also very scary. There are a lot of plot twists, but the final 20 minutes is especially memorable. The villainess (Tang Lai Ying) transforms into an incredibly powerful cat that, in her fury, destroys the police station.

EXCESSIVE TORTURE IN A FEMALE PRISON CAMP (1988)
aka **GREAT ESCAPE FROM WOMAN'S PRISON**
director: Wong Kong. Linda Chong· Lung Wong ★★
A brutal tale of strife in a female prison on the Amur River at the Korean/ Chinese border during World War II.

Yuen Fung Go, a Korean who defected to the Japanese three years before, has taken over the command of the enemy prison camp. He's torn between tradition and his patriotic alliance, but becomes merciless in sadistic torture techniques to prove his dedication to the Japanese cause. Overly melodramatic, but grim.

EXCUSE ME, PLEASE (1989)
director: Xung Fe Lei. Ching Lee· Richard Ng ★★
A group of flimflam friends (morticians by trade, more correctly cremators) are chased by the mob and then by ghosts in this horror comedy (with enough subplots to confuse even the most rabid Oriental enthusiast).

Especially bewildering is a graphic rape committed by the heroes (!), after which the violated girl (Ching Lee) kills herself and returns from the grave to seek revenge. It's tasteless by Western standards, and culturally fascinating for the same reason.

EXORCIST MASTER (1993)
director: Wu Ma. ★★½
A British priest, practicing in China, is killed in the churchyard by a falling cross (shades of *The Omen*?) and is buried in the church basement. Many years later, the church is reopened by a Vatican-trained Chinese priest, Father Wu (director **Wu Ma**).

Master A-Chiou (**Lam Ching Ying**, Mr. Vampire himself) is skeptical of Western religions and fights to keep the Catholic doors closed. But he's overruled. Sure enough, the village should have listened to him—the dead priest is resurrected as a vampire. The creature infects the new priest and members of his flock, until finally Master A-Chiou saves the day.

It's not nearly as good as **Wu Ma**'s *Burning Sensation*. And some sequences (e.g., Master A-Chiou dressed in drag, creating a distur-

bance during Mass) are supposed to be funny but instead are painful. Both Wu Ma and Lam Ching Ying have played these roles so many times, they could do it in their sleep, but they continue to make it seem fresh. Their interaction with each other is top-notch. The production is also top-notch, and the special effects are a cut above the standard HK horror fare.

EXPOSED TO DANGER (1988)
director: Wong Kuo Chu (Parkman Wong). Lu Hsia Fen·Yon Lin Tam ★★★
After being falsely accused of killing her best friend's father, a girl (Lu Hsia Fen) serves time in prison. She tries to start her life over again, but becomes the target for a psycho (in fact, the same one who did the original murder). Lots of gore and maggot-infested bodies. Plus a girl fight that culminates with a beheading!

Parkman Wong directed only a few films (his most notorious is *Passionate Killing in a Dream*); he's best known as a producer and collaborator with **Danny Lee** on the classic trendsetting mid-90's Category III films *Dr. Lamb, Run and Kill*, and *Untold Story* (in which he also appeared as an actor).

EYE FOR AN EYE (1990)
director: Ke Sing Pui. Joey Wang· Max Mok Siu Cheung·Lam Chun Yin· Melvin Wong ★★½
If you're the kind of person who wonders how somebody can take six bullets to the chest and still keep fighting, this movie isn't for you.

But, on the other hand, if you'd like to see **Joey Wang** smack someone with a baseball bat so hard that he lifts off the floor and smashes through a picture window, crashing into a swimming pool 10 stories below, don't hesitate. This one will make you happy.

69

It's an ambitious gangster story, in the tradition of the many *Godfather* clones. This one deals with the quest for power (*i.e.*, greed) as young mob members, unhappy with the conservative Mafia system, attempt to carve their own niche by dealing drugs. **Max Mok** is an anti-triad cop; **Joey Wang** is the daughter of the big boss.

In the film credits, Joey Wang returns to her given name, **Wang Zu Xian** (at least temporarily). Perhaps this is in response to the Taiwanese tabloids and their insistence that she had turned her back on her country by abandoning her family roots. Joey Wang constantly seems to find herself in the midst of controversy. In 1995, she was blasted in the Hong Kong gossip columns for her romantic involvement with a considerably younger pop singer. That incident hurt her considerably at the box office, and many studios began to view her as unbankable, resulting in a motion picture dry spell for more than a year.

FAI & CHI: KINGS OF KUNG FU
aka **KUNG FU VS ACROBATICS**
(1990)
director: Wong Tai Loy. Charles Fai·Charles Chi·Andy Lau·Joey Wang·Yuen Wah ★★★
Despite the cumbersome make-it-up-as-you-go story line, the Hong Kong comedy team of Charles Fai and Charles Chi is loads of fun to watch. Besides the expected slapstick, there are moments of satire ["Who's she?" referring to a picture of Britain's Queen Elizabeth. "So ugly . . ."] and "in" jokes ["We need a killer for protection!" cries Chi. "How about **Chow Yun-Fat**?" his girlfriend asks]. Plus there's even a clever live-action/cartoon-animation sequence (à la Roger Rabbit) in a ghostly cemetery. But, unfortunately, the rambling plot keeps the film from reaching its potential.

Two men (Fai and Chi) go deep into the uncharted regions of China in search of a mythical hair tonic of the gods. They discover an ancient tomb and (through a series of accidental heroics) they revive beautiful 1000-year-old Princess Wendy and her aide, Mandy. The four return to Hong Kong, but so does an all-powerful and very jealous suitor from Wendy's past.

FAMILY HONOR (1990)
director: Norman Law. Joey Wang·Shing Fui On·Richard Ng·Lo Lieh ★★
Another gangster film. Another familiar theme. Two brothers, loyal to each other, are on different sides of the law but end up with a common enemy—the mob.

This one begins as whimsical comedy fluff, but takes a sadistic turn when loan shark Tao (Shing Fui On) blows his short fuse and seeks retribution on a rat-fink pusher. This puts his police captain brother (Lo Lieh) in a difficult position. But when Tao is killed by the mob, the captain and his girlfriend (**Joey Wang**) take the law in their own hands and retaliate.

The story is flimsy and the acting pedestrian; the only saving grace is the expansive gun fest at the conclusion.

FANTASY MISSION FORCE (1984)
director: Chu Yin Ping. Jackie Chan·Chang Ling·Wang Yu·Lin Ching Hsia ★★★
Director **Chu Yin Ping** also made *Golden Queen Commando* and *Pink Force Commando* the same year. Maybe he was into some weird hallucinogen drugs—who knows? But his cockeyed vision of the world remains unparalleled in Hong Kong cinema.

This one teams **Jackie Chan** and **Chang Ling** (see *Wolf Devil Woman*) as soldiers of fortune trying to rescue a band of generals held captive by the

Japanese during World War II. Of course, our heroes are in it for the money. But so is another, less scrupulous gang headed by **Wang Yu** and **Lin Ching Hsia** (aka **Venus Lin**). The plot is further complicated by a tribe of Amazons, plus a variety of *Mad Max* apocalyptic goons, and an unrelated adventure inside a haunted house.

The finale, identical to Chu's two other '84 epics, ends in a massive balls-to-the-wall battle sequence that leaves almost everybody dead or dying.

FATAL CHASE (1992)
director: Chik Ki Yee. Robin Shou· Phillip Kao·Waise Lee·Yukari Oshima ★★½
Lots of gunplay and machismo as the cops battle a counterfeit ring in the Philippines. The chase initiates in HK, where the Filipino and Chinese triads are fighting for control of drug and gun trafficking. But soon the action switches to the islands, where the police agents find themselves in a deadly fight with the conflicting gangs.

Notable for a gun-toting midget and cameos by Waise Lee and **Yukari Oshima**. It's not art, but. . . .

FATAL LOVE (1988)
director: Leung Poeh [Pasan]. Leslie Cheung·Cherie Chung·Melvin Wong ★★
It all begins as a ghost story (a man meets a beautiful girl who supposedly died a month ago), but soon it degenerates into a silly love triangle involving Chi Wing (**Leslie Cheung**), Cecilia (**Cherie Chung**), and her gangster boyfriend, Sam Tsao (Melvin Wong). Don't ask how. And after watching the downbeat ending, don't ask why.

director: Chan Chi Suen. Ellen Chan· Michael Wong ★★★½
As of last count, there are at least three more Hong Kong films called *Fatal Love* (including one with **Cherie Chung** and **Leslie Cheung**, another with Clare Wai, and a third with Chan Wing Gee). This one stars **Ellen Chan** and, on the gratuitous level, she gets naked a lot. That's a real big plus, because she's incredibly beautiful. But the big surprise is she can act, too.

Novice policewoman Debbie Fung (Ellen Chan) goes undercover to expose Law Fuk Tin (Michael Wong), a young business tycoon suspected of drug trafficking. Debbie manages to gain his attention and confidence; soon she's living in his house. But when it looks like her cover is blown, she's ordered off the case. However, Debbie is convinced that Law is innocent, and she secretly continues dating him.

Unfortunately for this undercover female cop, the man is guilty as sin. Not only is he guilty of drug trafficking, but also of murder. Specifically, he likes to murder girls after intense bouts of sado sex games. At one point Law says to Debbie: "I forgot to tell you, I enjoy watching girls die." And apparently he really enjoys watching girls die in gruesome, messy fashion. One of his victims is bound, gagged, and stabbed 164 times.

I'm not going to tell you how this one ends. But I must say—it shocked even a jaded enthusiast like myself. I think you'll be surprised, too.

FATAL PASSION (1990)
director: David Ho. Alex Man·Cheung Man·Nancy Cheung ★★★
Tim Wong (Alex Man) has a shitty marriage. His career-driven wife, Diana (**Cheung Man**), is more interested in her TV scriptwriting job than in her husband. Tim suddenly finds

72

himself involved in a torrid affair with an old girlfriend, sexy Siu Man (Nancy Cheung). Unfortunately for Tim, she has a very jealous boyfriend who is secretly a hitman for the triad.

Violent Hong Kong twist on the *Fatal Attraction* concept.

FATAL ROSE (1995)
director: Tong Ky Ming [Wilson Tong]. Clare Wai·Charlie Cho ★★½
There's a cycle in every commercial film industry around the world: if a film is successful, copy and imitate it until audiences grow tired and stop buying tickets. It also seems that the worst (and sometimes weirdest) cash-ins crop up in the dying days of a trend. *Fatal Rose* is a soft-core revenge romp that barely attains mediocrity, riding on the coattails of higher-profile films like **Remains of a Woman** (1993) and **Legal Innocence** (1993).

The first scene has Scarlet (Clare Wai) coming home and being ambushed by an intruder. It turns out to be her husband, pretending to be a rapist on their wedding anniversary! After a bout of sex, her husband leaves and has his throat slit in the underground garage.

Through a series of coincidences that would even make Perry Mason's head spin, Scarlet eventually finds her husband's killer, a man named Spicy (Charlie Cho, the star of HK sleaze fests *Devil of Rape* and *Haunting Evil Spirit*), and she gets revenge.

But not before being attacked by Spicy's psychotic wife (the woman kicks Scarlet in the stomach so hard that she aborts her child) and, as these films tend to go, she's betrayed by the undercover cop in charge of the case.

There's plenty of blood, knives, fisticuffs, and sex. But it just feels so tired. Sometimes cash-ins at least try out a few new twists or hybridize genres to make things more interesting.

Fatal Rose is all math; predictable and formulaic.

FATAL TERMINATION (1989)
director: Andrew Kam. Moon Lee· Ray Lui·Philip Ko·Cheung Chi Tak ★★½
Superb action sequences, an intelligent plot, and beautiful **Moon Lee** are the components that boost this entry above many other shoot-em-up competitors.

Regarding the FX stunts, one scene is particularly mind-blowing. The villains are dangling a little girl (by clutching only her hair!) from the window of a speeding car while Moon Lee is simultaneously grasping the hood and pounding away at the windshield, desperately trying to break the glass to reach the crazed driver inside.

Unfortunately, the film suffers from a very slow beginning, perhaps a necessary evil, to establish the complex plot dealing with a corrupt customs official, the mob, the cops, and a missing shipment of illegal weapons.

FATAL VACATION (1988)
director: Eric Tsang. Eric Tsang·Irene Wan·Lee Tse Hai·Lee Kim Chung ★★★
Just when you thought it was safe to go on vacation. . . .

Tour guides Bob and Candy (Lee Tse Hai and Lee Kim Chung) are escorting a diverse group of HK tourists to the Philippines. Trouble erupts when a few mischievous youths wander off and, inadvertently, get trapped in the crossfire between Filipino cops and a gang of ruthless, gun-trafficking revolutionaries. The bad guys, after blowing the hell out of a nightclub, take the busload of vacationers hostage and retreat into the jungle.

Loads of action, exploding gunplay, vicious brutality, and savage rape highlight this creative twist on

Hong Kong's contemporary ultraviolent cinema. It's a traveler's worst nightmare.

FIGHT BACK TO SCHOOL (1991) director: **Wong Ching (Jing)**. Stephen Chow·Cheung Man ★

FIGHT BACK TO SCHOOL 2 (1992) director: **Wong Ching (Jing)**. Stephen Chow·Cheung Man ★

FIGHT BACK TO SCHOOL 3 (1993) director: **Wong Ching (Jing)**. Stephen Chow·Cheung Man·Anita Mui ★★ This series is an example of the Hong Kong film industry cloning really bad USA productions.

Remember the Hollywood junk movie *Hiding Out* (1987)? At least when **David Neidorf** played a cop going undercover as a high school student, it was to break up a juvenile drug ring. In this Asian version, it's to find out who stole the police commissioner's favorite pistol.

#3 has the same goofy intentions as the first two, with huge hunks stolen from *Basic Instincts* (1992). It's a parody, I guess. More insufferable nonsense from Hong Kong's favorite clown, **Stephen Chow (Chiauo Sing Chi)** and proletarian director **Wong Ching (Jing)**.

FIGHT FOR LOVE. See *Caged Beauties*

FIGHTING MADAM. See *Angel*

FIGURES FROM EARTH (1988) director: **Gin Luang**. He Mei Wei· Feng Cui Fan·Wan Xiu Liang ★★½ In feudal China, two undercover agents (Feng Cui Fan and Wan Xin Liang) are trying to capture grave robbers, but instead they fall into the clutches of an evil vampire seductress (He Mei Wei). Bloodsucker Chung

(who attacks her victims during oral sex) is challenged by a professional demon hunter who saves the captured officers by mummifying them, and then propels her into the future.

As these tales go, the agents are reanimated in contemporary Hong Kong, where the ageless vampire is continuing to cause bloody havoc. The horror sequences are surprisingly effective (and in some instances, downright scary), but silly Feng and Wan spoil the film.

FINAL JUDGEMENT (1993) director: **Otto Chan**. Simon Yam·Cecilia Yip·Tung Ping·Chun Pui·Anthony Wong (cameo) ★★★ **Simon Yam** is Au Peng, a decent family man who won't even look at a girlie magazine. It comes as a shock to everybody when he's arrested for the sexual assault and death of a high school girl. The charges are based on flimsy scientific evidence (cloth fibers and the like) that is publicly rebuked by the chief of police.

The federal cops torture Au Peng mercilessly. At one point, they stick a live rat in his mouth, but Au Peng continues to insist on his innocence. No matter how hard the feds try, circumstantial evidence is all they've got. But the case goes to court.

Is he innocent? Or guilty?

Director **Chan** once again creates an interesting, thought-provoking film (also see **Pink Lady**), but he has no qualms about mixing moments of pure exploitation with his poignant story. He could be the up-and-coming Asian trash director.

FINAL RUN (1988) director: **Philip Ko**. Simon Yam· Yukari Oshima·Cheung Kwok Keung· Kao Fei·Dick Wei ★★★ This is **Midnight Angel** without the female caped crusaders. Once again, **Yukari Oshima** steals the show as she seeks revenge against the drug overlord who killed her fiancé.

FINAL TEST (1987)
director: Lo Ke. Wai Tin Chi·Cynthia Pulley·Chin Siu Ho·Chung Chi Wai
★★½
Here's a nifty scifi thriller that's a cross between *Logan's Run* (1976) and *The Terminator* (1984). Good FX include a semi-mechanical cyborg villain.

FINALE IN BLOOD (1991)
director: Chan Kwok. Nonie Tao · Lawrence Cheng · David Wu · Chikako Aoyama ★½
Yet another HK ghost story in a genre already overcrowded with high-caliber product. There's no room for mediocre efforts. This one, telling the story of ghost Fang Yin (Nonie Tao), who saves the life of a goofy radio announcer (Lawrence Cheng), is tediously hackneyed.

She's a lost soul killed in a three-way love triangle, and if you make it all the way to the end, you will be able to see how she wound up dead. But the finale in blood isn't worth the wait.

FIRE DRAGON (1994)
aka **FIERY ROMANCE**
director: Yuen Woo Ping. Brigitte Lin · Mok Siu Chung ★★★
After turning out such superior historical kung fu epics as *Drunken Master* (1978) and **Tai Chi Master** (1993), director **Yuen Woo Ping** has created yet another high-flying costume adventure, with more than a passing nod to *Swordsman 2* (1992). It offers the now-familiar mixture of flying sword-wielding females, kung fu heroes, and an all-powerful villain who single-handedly takes on all the good guys in a climactic, destructive death battle.

It's not as spirited as **Swordsman 2**, nor as well-scripted as **Tai Chi Master**, but the battle scenes easily rank with those previous films. The plot is

set against a background of court intrigue and politics, as young fortune teller Yuen Ming (**Max Mok [Mok Siu Chung]**) carries an important letter to a regional prime minister warning him of visiting Prince Wan's plans to betray the Emperor. Ming's attempts to deliver the letter serve as the catalyst for a heady mixture of romance, comedy, and numerous sword and kung fu battles, replete with the usual flying and leaping stuntwork so much a part of these films.

Brigitte Lin [Lin Ching Hsia] stars as the mysterious and evasive Fire Dragon, a veiled and colorfully costumed superassassin, whose attempt to kill the benevolent Prime Minister on behalf of the duplicitous Prince leads to a battle with Ming. But, as with most Yuen Woo Ping films, the female characters are not well defined or very interesting.

FIRE FIGHT (1988)
director: Gian [Chien] Rue Sheng. ★
A swordsman makes a bet that he can stay overnight in a graveyard, where he falls in love with a ghost. There's lots of new age romanticism, ridiculous philosophical clichés that sound like verses from sugary Hallmark greeting cards like "If there are ghosts, they're in your heart." Yuck.

FIREFIST OF THE INCREDIBLE DRAGON (1983)
director: Wang Yung Ling. Maple Lin· Jerry Young·Keith Lee·Chin Lung·Paul Chan ★★½
The debut film by director **Wang Yung Ling** (two years later he would make the outrageous **Lewd Lizard** [1985]). This one features his own brand of misogynist mayhem as a psycho is raping and killing a series of women. After he's finished with them, the brute dumps their bodies in a wooded swamp. But then he discovers one of the victims is missing.

As it turns out, she wasn't dead after all. She organizes a vigilante group of kung fu fighting friends and they go after the freak. He conjures up spirits of the dead girls to help him in the ensuing battle. As it turns out, one of his victims had been pregnant when she was killed, so a ghost flying, punching fetus joins his spooky gang. Yes, the whole thing is tasteless. But it ranks high in the bizarre category.

FIRST MISSION (1985)
director: Samo Hung. Jackie Chan·Samo Hung·Emily Cho·Lam Ching Ying·Dick Wei·Man Hei ★★★
A film with more heart than sense, but that's really not so bad. **Jackie Chan** leaves the S.W.A.T. team to join the C.I.D. Police Force in order to keep a closer eye on his retarded brother, Danny (**Samo Hung**). The mandatory stunts and kung fu seems out of place in this quaintly tender story, but Samo Hung plays his role to perfection.

Also starring Emily Chu, Man Hei, and Lam Chang Ying as the S.W.A.T. team commander.

FIRST SHOT (1993) 75
director: David Lam [Lam Di Yu]. Ti Lung· Maggie Cheung·Lau Shek Ming ·Simon Yam·Waise Lee ★★★★
A great-looking, bombastically scored action film of the highest caliber from filmmaker **David Lam** (**Powerful Four**). It tells the story of corruption within the HK police system, circa 1970s. **Ti Lung** gives the performance of his career, glistening with tragic heroism. He's a hard-nosed cop, Wong Yat Chung, who fights both the mob and the political establishment for his staunch beliefs. **Maggie Cheung** **[Cheung Man Yuk]**, looking her all-time best, plays a government agent who befriends him. **Simon Yam**, Waise Lee, and Lau Shek Ming round out the exceptional cast.

Essentially, the film is a remake of Brian DePalma's award-winning *The Untouchables* (1987). Police corruption is the centralized crime, replacing the prohibition and bootlegging theme of its American counterpart. And '70s Hong Kong is an effective substitute for the Chicago of the late '20s. Waise Lee plays Faucet, the top mob

Ti Lung (R) in *First Shot*

boss, who is both sinister and brazenly powerful. His confrontation with Wong (Ti Lung) crackles with electricity that the imitated Robert De Niro/Kevin Costner confrontation failed to generate.

The intelligent (albeit plagiarized) script adds purpose and determination to the dynamic action sequences. The film is a genuinely effective study of morality and loyalty in an increasingly unscrupulous world.

FIRST TIME IS THE LAST TIME (1988) **director: Raymond Leung.** Carrie Ng ·Ma Sze Chen ★★★½

A very dark, realistic women-in-prison film from **Angel** director, **Raymond Leung. Carrie Ng** plays Winnie, a young woman who is jailed after avenging her boyfriend's death at the hands of some ruthless gangsters. Once in prison, Winnie befriends another inmate, Yuk, who, secretly because of the underworld massacre, wants her dead.

FIRST VAMPIRE IN CHINA (1990) **director: Yam Chun-Lu.** Lam Ching Ying·Yi Yuen ★★

The initial 10 minutes and the final 30 minutes are exceptional horror fare, but the middle section is tedious to the point of intolerable. At the conclusion, when the vampire comes back to life, all hell breaks loose. The scene with the bats attacking the front door is frightfully wonderful.

Also worth mentioning: when the vampire finally does return, he looks a lot like the zombie in Ray Dennis Steckler's *Incredibly Strange Creatures Who Stopped Living and Became Mixed-up Zombies.* Just a coincidence?

FIST OF LEGEND (1995) **director: Corey Yuen.** Jet Li·Yasuaki Kurata·Chin Siu Ho·Ada Choi Siu Fun ★★★½

With more than a genuflection to **Bruce Lee**'s *Fists of Fury* [known as Chinese Connection in the United States] (1972) **Jet Li** is Chen Zhen, a student studying abroad during World War II who returns home to avenge his master's death at the hands of those sinister Japanese.

Once Chen discovers his teacher was poisoned, all hell breaks loose. While kicking some ass, he even uncovers a secret Japanese plan to invade China.

The cast is exceptional. But the real reason you're watching this flick is to see **Jet Li** fight. And he fights like a son-of-a-bitch.

The final sequence is nothing short of amazing, pitting Chen against the evil Japanese kickboxing general (Yasuaki Kurata). This is incredible old-time, butt-stomping kung fu, with minimal wire effects and optimum fists of fury.

FISTFUL OF TALONS.
See *Wind, Forest, Fire, Mountain*

FISTS OF FURY 1991 (1991) **director: Ching Siu Tung.** Stephen Chow· Cheung Man·Kenny Bee· Corey Yueu· Nina Li Chi ★½

Terrible! Here's proof that **Stephen Chow** can make a mess of anything. Even director extraordinaire **Ching Siu Tung** (*Chinese Ghost Story* series and *Swordsman* series) can't keep this loose-cannon actor under control.

Things heat up at the Sifu Fok School when a group of Japanese kung fu fighters, accompanied by their unscrupulous teacher, show up for the big martial arts tournament. **Stephen Chow [Chiauo Sing Chi]** goofs off, mugs for the camera, initiates a food fight, and is generally an embarrassment, all in the name of entertainment. This godawful film even inspired a sequel, *Fists of Fury 1991 Part 2* (1992).

FIVE DEADLY ANGELS (1989)
director: Danu Umbara. Yati Octavic
·Lydia Kandou·Debby Cynthia Dew·
Dana Christina·Eva Arnez ★★½
A conscientious scientist (Cok Sim-
bara) develops the deadliest explosive
the world has ever known, but soon it
falls into the hands of a wicked criminal, Bruto (Rakhmat Hidayat). The five
angels (brunette sharpshooter Yati Octavic, Lydia Kandou the crossbow specialist, kickboxer Debby Cynthia Dew,
cycle daredevil Dana Christina, and
Eva Arnez the knife expert) band together to stop Bruto's reign of terror.

A good jazz score by Gatot Su-
darto keeps the action swift and fast-
paced, regardless of Umbara's banal
script. According to the credits, the
girls' costumes were supplied by Rimo
Jeans Corner. I don't know why that
strikes me as humorous.

FIVE ELEMENT NINJA (1982)
aka **SUPER NINJAS**
director: Chang Cheh. Cheng Tin Chee
· Lo Meng·Yu Tai Ping·Chan Wai Man
★★★★
Wild, stylish, bloody stuff. This is the
kung fu equivalent of the *Baby Cart*
films. It's a colorful Shawscope picture
with lush early-Chinese-restaurant
decor and exteriors filmed on garishly
phony studio sets (perhaps the secret
aesthetic link between Shaw and
Hammer). But the action is lavish,
bloody, and inventive. And it's thrill-
ingly staged, the filmmaking integrates
all the potential shortcomings into a
style, which results in director **Chang
Cheh**'s most impressive movie. Of his
100+ films, this one is Chang's masterpiece.

The steady flow of ritualized sequences—and spurting blood—gets a
compelling momentum going. The fun
elaborates on a typical plot: A martial
arts school is challenged by a band of
nasty ninja, devilish Japanese bad
guys divided into five elemental

units—Gold, Wood, Water, Fire and
Earth—each with a totem color and
appropriate killing method.

Hero Hsiao (Chien Tien Chi)
learns some secret ninja tricks in order
to defeat them, but not before his best
pal (Lo Meng) is all but disemboweled
by a Japanese Mata Hari (Chen Pei
Hsi). One great early shot has a
fighter, speared from below by the evil
Earth Ninjas, fighting on manfully as a
length of intestine dangles down to his
ankles.

FLAMING BROTHERS (1988)
director: Joseph Cheung. Chow Yun-
Fat· Alan Tang·Lin Ching Hsia ★★★
This is a lesser-known **Chow Yun-Fat**
gangster flick, sandwiched between *A
Better Tomorrow 2* (1987) and *The
Killer* (1989). While director **Joseph
Cheung** doesn't have the cinematic
style of filmmaker **John Woo**, he's
made a movie that works nicely *because* it never strays far from the basics.

The plot is simplicity personified.
Alan Tang and Chow Yun-Fat play
brothers who choose different walks of
life. Chow gets married and settles
down, while Tang develops a Triad
business. Tang's life is threatened
when a rival mob tries to move against
him, and Chow comes to his aid. The
ending is an impressive display of
heroic bloodshed as the two brothers,
bound by a personal code of honor,
embark on a suicide mission against
the enemy.

Based on Chow Yun-Fat's enormous popularity, especially as a result
of other machismo mayhem flicks, it remains a mystery why this film never
received the attention from the bloodshed fans. It's better than most of the
Tomorrow clones.

FLASH FUTURE KUNG FU (1984)
director: Kirk Wong. Wang Lung
Wei·Ko Hung·Lui Leung Wai ★★

Somewhat of a rarity in Hong Kong films, a futuristic scifi pic (also see *Final Test* and, to some extent, **Wicked City**).

In this future world, everyone seems to be wildly bonkers, living lives of extreme decadence. Mind-altering drugs are as common as candy bars. In the midst of all the mania, a traditional kung fu school is determined to stick with the old ways. They reject drugs and concentrate on their studies and vigorous martial arts training. A rival cyberpunk girl gang takes on the old school in a wild and bloody kung fu battle. The bad girls eliminate almost everyone. Good-guy leader Lau (Wang Lung Wei) and his assistant survive the scrimmage and plan a counterattack. They are aided by one of the rival females when she leaves the cybergang because the other members want to use experimental drugs on her baby.

An early effort from director **Kirk Wong**, relying on strong visuals within a corrupt chrome-and-glass world. With lots of smoke, glistening surfaces, and mind-numbing music.

FLESH AND THE BLOODY TERROR
  aka **BEASTS** (1988)
director: Teddy Robin Kwan with **Dennis W. K. Yu.** Fong Ling Ching· Teresa Woo ★★½
This is an interesting (and very graphic) rip-off of *The Hills Have Eyes* plus *Last House on the Left*, and a big steal from *I Spit on Your Grave*, by two HK filmmaking vets, **Teddy Robin Kwan (All the Wrong Spies)** and **Dennis Yu (Evil Cat)**.

A group of teens go camping in the woods, where they are stalked by some backwoods mutant psychos (called, amazingly enough, Disco Boys). These frenzied weirdos rape (in shocking and explicit "X" detail) one of the girls, and then gruesomely kill her brother.

When the local peace officer re-fuses to cooperate ("We don't have no Disco Boys in these parts . . . only outsiders messing up our countryside"), the girl's father (scriptwriter Fong Ling Ching) takes justice into his own hands. He hunts down the sickos and eliminates them with brutal (and gory) ingenuity.

If your taste leans toward this type of sadistic fare, then add an extra star (★).

FLYING DAGGERS (1993)
director: Chu Yin Ping. Ching Siu Tung· Tony Leung [Chiu Wai]·Maggie Chung·Jacky Cheung ★★
Regardless of the strong cast, this is a lesser film for director **Chu Yin Ping**. He has always taken a maverick approach to filmmaking, and because of his cockeyed vision, he's produced some of the classic HK cult films (e.g., **Golden Queen Commando, Island Warriors, Fantasy Mission Force**).

But this time his script is so meandering, and at times incoherent, that struggling through it simply isn't worth the effort.

Perhaps it's more the fault of the scriptwriter, Hong Kong hack director/ producer **Wong Ching [Jing]** than of Chu. But this story of bounty hunters on the trail of Fox O'Nine Tails (**Jacky Cheung**) is so preoccupied with goofy slapstick the overall plot becomes secondary to a collection of forgettable sight gags.

The film was promoted in some markets as **Holy Weapon 2** because of the similarities in cast.

FONG SAI YUK (1993)
director: Corey Yuen. Jet Li · Sibelle Hu · Siu Fong Fong · Josephine Siao ★★★

FONG SAI YUK 2 (1993)
director: Corey Yuen. Jet Li·Sibelle Hu· Josephine Siao·Adam Cheng· Yuen Kwai ★★

These films are traditional chop socky fare dressed up with state-of-the-art fight choreography, proving once again that the genre is still very much alive. And, based on the box office receipts, immensely popular.

The plot deals, primarily, with Fong Sai Yuk's conflict against Tiger Lee's family and the promise of Lee's daughter to anyone who can defeat his wife (**Sibelle Hu**) in combat. **Jet Li**'s portrayal of the legendary hero is whimsical and somewhat introverted, as opposed to the more traditional zealot portrayal in countless earlier films. The emphasis is on martial arts and light comedy. As with most films directed by **Corey Yuen (Yuen Kwei)**, the action sequences are superb but the other dramatic scenes tend to be treated as filler.

#2 is broader in scope, but **Jet Li** continues to play the role with wide-eyed innocence. It tells the story of Fong Sai Yuk's attempt to woo the Emperor's daughter in order to snatch

heavily guarded political papers that would guarantee his teacher's claim to ruling power. The whole thing gets derailed when both Fong's wife and mother show up to help him and make sure he doesn't fall in love with the daughter. Much of the movie tends to be silly, but the fight scenes make it watchable.

FORBIDDEN ARSENAL (1991) **director: Yuen Chun Man** with **Cheng Siu Keung.** Cynthia Kahn·Waise Lee· Loletta Lee·Too Shu Chun ★★★ Despite the generic title, this cop actioner delivers the goods. In this case, the goods are huge quantities of guns being smuggled into Hong Kong from China.

There's a task force of two cops, one from mainland China (Too Shu Chun) and one from Taiwan (handsome Waise Lee), plus a policewoman from Hong Kong (action star **Cynthia Khan**, playing the same character from **In the Line of Duty** series) in

Jet Li and Sibelle Hu in *Fong Sai Yuk*

charge of stopping the Mafia-controlled shipments.

There's lots of ultraviolence and excessive gunplay. Plus great cinematography and good characterization, but unfortunately, it's a very familiar story. Yet, overall, it's more quality stuff from producer Dickson Poon. Released in some Euro markets as *In the Line of Duty 6*.

FORCED NIGHTMARE (1992)
director: Lau Sze Yu. Sandra Ng·Lam Ching Ying ★★
Sandra Ng is the local soothsayer and telekinetic wonder child. Through ESP, she can gain control of everything, including people's bladders. The local constable asks her to go to Hong Kong, where her services have been requested. But en route the bus is involved in an accident and she, along with everyone else, is killed. Her powers go astray, reanimating all of the bodies. They descend on HK as indestructible criminals.

Once she realizes what has happened, Sandra seeks the aid of **Lam Ching Ying** (in his patented **Mr. Vampire** role). The results are supposed to be funny. But instead—as the title suggests—they are merely *forced*.

FREEDOM FROM THE GREEDY GRAVE (1989)
director: Cheng Ren Sheng. Yang Ching Huen·Chu Bao Yi ★★½
A fairly good horror comedy from director Cheng Ren Sheng that borrows liberally from *Beetlejuice*, as a family (played by Yang Ching Huen and Chu Bao Yi, as his wife) moves into a haunted house possessed by the ghosts of the former occupants.

A particularly shocking (read: disgusting) sequence features a geekghost biting off the heads of live frogs and snakes.

On the lighter side, in the begin-

ning of the film, a young ghost/vampire asks his father, "Why do we always jump?"

"Because that's what the living dead do," answers Dad.

"Can't we change that now?" replies the child. And they begin walking. So much for tradition.

FRIED FOX (1991)
director: Willie Chung. ★½
Gangsters and gamblers (God! I'm getting tired of this!) in a typical Hong Kong action flick. The minuscule plot finds a man trying to quit working in a crooked casino. The card tricks during the opening credits are the best part of the movie.

FRIEND FROM INNER SPACE (1986)
director: Ricky Chan. Wen Hsai Chi· Chien Jen·Ti Lung ★½
Perhaps the Shaw brothers' biggest goof.

While at summer camp, a kid (Wen Hsai Chi) is separated from the other children when he chases a white rabbit (inspired by *Alice in Wonderland*?). He finds himself in a strange netherworld of bizarre creatures, a haunted house, and the ghost of his dead uncle (Chien Jen), who eventually helps the kid patch up the problems between his quarreling parents.

Also with **Ti Lung** in a thankless costarring role.

FROM BEIJING WITH LOVE (1994)
director: Li Kin Sang. Stephen Chow [Chiau Sing Chi]·Anita Yuen·Pauline Chow ★★★
When a dinosaur skull is stolen from the Chinese authorities, Agent Chow (Stephen Chow) is deployed to find it. Aided by his assistant (she's secretly a double agent), he battles a virtual army of thieves, traitors, and beautiful vixens.

A surprisingly violent screwball comedy with HK's favorite clown,

Stephen Chow [Chiauo Sing Chi]. It's better written than most of his goofy flicks (perhaps he should have dumped **Wong Chin [Jing]** a long time ago), and many of the sight gags actually work (I'm admitting this grudgingly).

Seemingly, Chow made a conscious decision to break from his parade of mindless slapstick comedies with his previous *King of Beggars* (1993). And now comes *From Beijing with Love*, a spy spoof with a genuine sense of humor. It's well written, featuring as many tongue-in-cheek witticisms as silly hijinks. What a pleasant surprise.

FULL CONTACT (1992)
director: Ringo Lam. Chow Yun-Fat· Simon Yam·Anthony Wong·Ann Bridge-

water·Bonnie Fu·Chris Lee·Frankie Chin ★★★★

Filmmaker **Ringo Lam** delivers his masterpiece. While it may be too violent and bleak to woo the mainstream audiences, it emerges as a film that simply can't be ignored. Unquestionably, it's the final word on the ultraviolence craze in HK cinema. Plus the pic benefits from, perhaps, **Chow Yun-Fat**'s finest performance.

This tale of double-crossing and retribution blasts away at the archaic "honor among thieves" cliché while it establishes a new order of Darwinism, depicting the secrets of survival in life's sewer.

Jeff (**Chow Yun-Fat**) and Sam (**Anthony Wong**) are small-time Chinese gangsters working in Bangkok. Sam offended a local crime lord and, to make amends, he and Jeff are forced

81

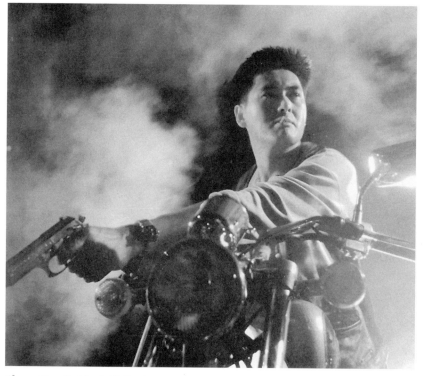

Chow Yun-Fat in *Full Contact*

THE FILMS

to join an operation assault against an arms convoy. They team up with nihilistically insane Judge (**Simon Yam**) and his gang of misfits, including a muscle-head, Dean (**Frankie Chan**), and a yummy slut inappropriately named Virgin (Bonnie Fu). After the heist, Judge convinces Sam to double-cross his friend Jeff by killing him in a burning building. But Jeff manages to escape, recuperating in a monastery. He returns to find that his girlfriend, Mona (Ann Bridgewater), has now taken up with two-timing weasel Sam. Jeff closes the book on his former relationships and takes his revenge against Judge and his gang. This confrontation in a triad nightclub features the most incredible gun battle ever captured on film, as the camera actually *rides* the bullets across the room to the targets (after this film, the trick was used in other HK films [e.g., **Heroic Trio**).

Full Contact is a sleazy, street-level excursion that plunges deep into the darkest realm of criminal anarchy. It's constructed like a spaghetti Western, a cynical world where a gangster like Jeff can actually be seen as a good guy. As such, it's no accident that director Lam has set this film in Thailand, perhaps the last untamed frontier in Southeast Asia.

FULL THROTTLE (1996)
director: Derek Yee Tung Sing. Andy Lau·David Ng·Gigi Leung·Chin Ka Lok ★★★
For the most part, in the '90s, HK cinema split into three different genres: (1) kung fu action films (a resurgence spearheaded by **Tsui Hark**'s *Once upon a Time in China* [1991]), (2) ultraviolent psychological thrillers known as Category III movies, designed for an adults-only audience (for example, Billy Tang's *Dr. Lamb* [1992]), or (3) sensitive relationship movies (popularized by **Derek**

Yee Tung Sing's *C'est la Vie, Mon Cheri* [1993]).

Here, director Yee takes his predilection for the "gentle touch" melodrama (which he elevated to an art form in *Mon Cheri*) and applies it to a rather predictable story of two motorcycle racers and the women in their lives. **Andy Lau**, who has spent the better part of his career playing shy and diffident parts, once again follows suit. This time he's a misunderstood garage mechanic named Joe whose only joy in life is racing his bike. Obviously, he has trouble communicating with his girlfriend (Gigi Leung), and she's tired of playing second fiddle to a motorcycle. Coincidentally, Joe's estranged father owns a successful bike business and also sponsors a high-ranking racing team, but daddy and son don't get along. Ironically, another biker named David (David Ng) befriends Joe in hopes of hooking up with his father and thus getting a chance at the big competition.

It's a long and winding road, but David does get to ride in the Macau Race (which he wins). Joe wasn't in the competition because of an injury. In fact, the injury has convinced him to never ride a bike again. Instead, he has decided to put his energy into maintaining both the garage and his rocky relationship with girlfriend Yee. But when his business partner is killed in a racing accident, Joe straps on his helmet and goes into competition against David. The girlfriend, who is angry over the life-risking decision, leaves Joe. But, after the smoke clears, they make up and presumably live happily ever after.

This would be the makings of a maudlin soap opera if it weren't for the director's love for the characters he has created. These are multidimensional people who come alive, demanding attention and concern from the audience. It's not a terrific movie, but it's populated with some terrific people.

FUN AND FURY (1992)
director: **Frankie Chan.** Leon Lai· Frankie Chan·Vivian Chow·Kent Cheng ★★½
In the same spirit as **Frankie Chan**'s earlier **Outlaw Brothers**, this is a martial arts comedy, vacillating between action set pieces and goofy sight gags. Similar to countless other HK flicks, it tells the story of a cop (pop singer **Leon Lai**) and his girlfriend (**Vivian Chow**) who find trouble from her triad-boss father (played by **Kent Cheng**).

FUNNY GHOST.
See *Bloody Ghost*

FURY IN RED (1990)
director: **Wang Lu Wei [John Ni].** Conan Lee [Lee Yuen Bah]·Ng Ngai Cheng·Robin Shou ★
Robin Shou is a colorful villain, a sadistic hitman with a weakness for masochism. But he can't carry the show by himself. Besides the rambling, incoherent story line (half of it was shot in Hong Kong and half in Los Angeles, with no regard for continuity), the biggest problem is Conan Lee's lackluster presence. Once touted as the successor to **Bruce Lee**, Conan in godawful this time. It's particularly disheartening after his impressive performance in *Tiger on the Beat 1* (1988) and *2* (1990).

FURY OF THE HEAVEN (1986)
director: **Luo Lin.** Li Shai·Luo Man ★★½
One of the better possession movies, filled with hexes, spells, and exorcisms. It also contains a crucifixion (well, sorta), lesbian sex (Li Shai and Luo Man), and flying skulls.

FUTURE COPS (1993)
director: **Wong Ching [Jing].** Andy Lau·Sim Yam·Aaron Kwok ★★
Director **Wong Ching [Jong]** seemed to be preoccupied with the arcade game Street Fighter 2 in 1993. Besides this film, he also directed **Jackie Chan**'s *City Hunter*, which featured versatile Chan playing parts of each video character (E. Honda, Gulle, Dhalsim, and [amazingly] female kickboxer Chun Lee).

But with this film, he hires HK's hottest male stars and inserts them into the various parts. Dhalsim is **Simon Yam**, **Andy Lau** plays Vega, plus there's **Jacky Cheung** as Gulle, **Aaron Kwok** as Ryu, and Richard Ng as E. Honda. Oddly, sexy kickboxer Chun Lee is missing in action (was director Wong fighting with his girlfriend protégée **Chingmy Yau** this week, or what?).

The plot is basic. These superhero cops from the future go back in time to rescue their chief, who's being held in a maximum security prison.

Is it any good? By now, you've probably seen enough Wong Ching films to answer that.

GAMBLING GHOST (1991)
director: **Samo Hung.** Samo Hung· Mang Hoi·Nina Li Chi·James Tien ★★
Samo Hung, the Peter Sellers of Hong Kong, directs and plays three roles in this feeble horror/comedy. He's a dreamer, a young man with high hopes but without the drive to achieve the goals. Plus he also plays the lad's useless father, *and* the ghost of the roguish grandfather who eventually teaches the grandson to become a gambling expert known as the Saint of Gambling obviously inspired by 1989's *God of Gamblers*. Craps.

GANGLAND ODYSSEY (1991)
director: **Charles W. M. Chan** suspected pseudonym for **Andy Lau.**

Andy Lau·Alex Man·Cheung Man· Alan Tang ★★
A man (**Andy Lau**) returns to Hong Kong after a 16-year exile. In 1974, he had eliminated a gangster boss, and now he's back to join his family as they fight to maintain control in the middle of a messy kidnapping. Also staring Xin Liang Wan and sexy **Cheung Man [Chan Wai Man]**.
Most of it looks good. But the script is tired. Very tired.

GANGS (1987)
director: Larry Lau (Lau Ku Chang).
Ho Pui Tung·Wong Chung Cheun·Tse Wai Kit·Ma Hin Ting·Eleven Leung ★★★
A grim look at teenage violence in Hong Kong, similar in many ways to the rash of gang pics popular in the USA. However, it's very different from the gangster films of **John Woo/Tsui Hark** (*The Killer, A Better Tomorrow*, etc.).
This one doesn't glamorize the violence. The idea of heroic bloodshed is lost on these hapless characters. Instead, this film is actually the study of a gang-in-demise as the members of Sung/Sing are destroyed. Certainly one of the best. Especially when compared with other genre films like **Black Sheep**.

GANGS '92 (1992)
director: Larry Lau [Lau Ku Chang].
Aaron Kwok·Jimmy Lee ★½
A loosely related sequel to **Larry Lau**'s own '87 HK film [*Gangs*], but it lacks the conviction and grittiness of the original.
The biggest problem with *Gangs '92* is its inability to create sympathetic characters. Pop singer **Aaron Kwok** plays an arrogant rich kid who joins a Hong Kong street gang. This group of bad-ass kids become the heroes when they are framed for murder,

finding themselves at odds with both the cops and the triads.
Of course, it's a tired plot; obviously derivative of Walter Hill's *Warriors*. Plus it's not helped by a very bad performance from another Asian pop singer, Jimmy Lee.

GENERAL INVINCIBLE.
See *Invincible*

GHOST BALLROOM (1990)
director: Tong Ky Ming. Sandra Ng· Lau Kar Fei ★½
A prostitute is killed. She returns from the grave to take revenge. But it takes her a while. Quite a while.

GHOST BUSTING (1991)
director: Wong Ching [Jing]. Sandra Ng· Lolanto Chan ★
Wong Ching [Jing], Hong Kong's leading hack, directs a ghost story this time. Students at a magic school are threatened by evil spirits, but they fight fire with fire. The kids transform into powerful icon gods for the confrontation. They become Elvis Presley, Charlie Chaplin, **Bruce Lee**, and Jesus Christ. The bad ghosts don't have a chance. Right?

GHOST FESTIVAL (1985)
director: Stephen Wu. ★
A psychopath solicits ghostly help to find out who killed his wife, and then concocts a bizarre plan (involving murder and reanimation) to get vengeance. Contains some nudity, unusual in films of this type, but who cares?

GHOST FEVER (1990)
director: Nilson Cheung. Rosamund Kwan·Wong Jing·Lau Szu Yu ★★½
It begins as a routine happy-couple-buys-a-haunted-house tale and develops into a supernatural version of *Fatal Attraction*.
Soon after they move into the house, the pregnant wife is hospital-

ized. The husband, a squirrely slug (**Wong Jing**), takes the opportunity to seduce a woman that he meets in an elevator at his office building. Unfortunately for him, the woman is actually an insecure ghost with a jealous streak (played to the hilt by shapely **Rosamund Kwan**).

She also has a very vengeful family. Her mom retaliates by biting off the adulterous husband's penis.

GHOST FOR SALE (1987)
director: Guy Lai. Ricky Hui·Shing Fui On ★
Complete nonsense! A camera crew finds real ghosts when they arrive at a cemetery for a movie shoot. They capture the spirits and return to the city, where they try to sell them to the highest bidders. Ricky Hui and Shing Fui On are totally wasted in this junk.

GHOST HOSPITAL (1988)
director: Yu Kong Yun (Dennis Yu). Choy King Fei·Leung Sui Long·Kwan Hoi San·Cook Fung ★
Because of a hospital hex, whenever a certain patient (why this one only?) sleeps, he visits a supernatural world of hopping zombies and warring priests. A pathetic film. It's so disjointed that it looks like two different movies spliced together. And it probably is. A major disappointment from Dennis Yu.

GHOST IN THE MIRROR (1974)
director: Sung Tsun Chow [Song Cunshou]. Shin Chie·Ku Wen Tsung ★★½
A scholar (Shin Chie) falls in love with a beautiful girl (Ku Wen Tsung), who may or may not be a ghost. This familiar theme in Chinese literature works well in this arty horror film. Visually stylish.

GHOST KILLER (1987)
director: Hwa I-Hung. Shing Fu On· Chi Ho ★
When gangsters (led by Shing Fu On) kill Chi Ho, his ghost possesses the body of a young taxi driver. The mission, obviously, is revenge. Dull and tedious.

GHOST MANSION (1987)
director: Yuen Cheung Yan. Charlie Cho ·Wu Kwan Yu · Lam Chin Ming · Lau Lam Kwong ★★
Obviously it was inspired by the success of the *Haunted Cop Shop* series, but this tiresome comedy has much more in common with the American *Police Academy* films. The S.W.A.T. trainees (a coed group of goofy guys and buxom babes) are living in a haunted house. Shivers.

GHOST NURSING (1988)
director: Wilson Tong. Suit Li·Norman Chu·Mei Wong ★★★
When loan sharks kill her boyfriend, Jacki (Suit Li) goes into hiding with a group of prostitutes. But her luck continues to go bad. Inadvertently, she's responsible for the death of a client at the hands of a crime boss. Jacki seeks advice from a holy mystic known as the God of Gold. He informs her that she was a gangster in a former life, and she can change her destiny only by nursing a ghost [i.e., by pricking her finger once a month and allowing a few drops of blood to fall on the head of a deformed embryo].

After performing the ritual, the baby's ghost begins to protect Jacki. Her enemies meet tragic and unpleasant deaths, including zombie attacks and the perennial HK favorite: vomiting up maggots.

Eventually Jacki meets the man of her dreams, Raymond Cheung (Norman Chu, who seems to enjoy starring in bizarre films; see *Lewd Lizard* for another example). But the baby becomes wildly jealous and possesses Raymond's body, with murderous (and graphically gory) results.

GHOST OF THE FOX (1990)
director: Wong Kong. Wong Kong·Sibelle Hu ★★½

A thinly disguised martial arts extravaganza as Taoist monks prepare young Tapo (Wong Kong) for the ultimate battle with the evil Manyuan and his demon army. Lots of bloody kung fu action, swordplay, and Chinese fantasy dealing with Tapo and his fighting foxes from Lunsan Temple. Also starring **Sibelle Hu** in a throwaway role.

GHOST RENTING (1992)
director: Samo Hung with **Corey Yuen.** Samo Hung·Yuen Biao ★½

A jealous gangster husband kills his wife's boyfriend but then suffers a screwball vengeance (body sharing) in this underdeveloped HK comedy.

GHOST SCHOOL (1987)
director: Kam Ling Ho. ★

Could a movie be any worse? At least it wasn't shot on video, but the story is a very unsatisfying blend of preppie humor and preppie horror about the ghost of an ancient warrior who tries to communicate with some vacationing fraternity boys. Obviously this was intended as a takeoff on the *Happy Ghost* series. Abysmal.

GHOST SNATCHER (1989)
director: Xung Fe-Lei/Lan Nai-Kai. Richard Ng·Joey Wang·Joyce Godenzi ★★½

An absolute, unabashed *Ghost Busters* rip-off. But it's so much fun that the similarities are soon forgotten. Good FX, too. And rubber-face **Richard Ng**'s mugging is always welcome.

GHOST STORY OF KAM PIN MUI (1991)
director: Richard Yang. Chan Pui Ki·Wu Ma·McLaren Lu ★★½

A quartet of naked, sexy vampires (including beauty McLaren Lu) and their ghostly family, helmed by Wu Ma, haunt the village of Kam Pin Mui in this traditional tale of good and evil.

The big difference is its brazen concentration on nudity and sexual relations, routinely avoided in period HK features.

GHOSTLY LOVE (1990)
director: Wu Kuo Ren. Hui Tien Chee·Emily Chu·Lam Wei·Mark Long ★★½

Director **Wu Kuo Ren** has made another fine horror movie here (also see *Who's Killer* [*Who's The Killer*]), this time mixing large helpings of sex/nudity with ghostly goings-on.

It's a period film with lots of sword fighting and some chop socky tomfoolery, but the real treat is the special effects and the extended sex sequences, notably between the hero (Hui Tien Chee) and the ghostly ladies of his concubine (especially beautiful Emily Chu).

GHOSTLY VIXEN (1989)
director: William Chang. Danny Chan·Wu Ma·Amy Yip·Sandra Ng ★★★

They call her the Evil Girl. And she comes from an alternative dimension. Her goal is to suck the sperm and devour the life from 100 human virgins. Once her mission is completed, she will receive an eternal body. Currently, she is at #98.

A leather-clad gladiator has been sent by the Netherworld to stop her. The opening clash between these two superpowers in a glitzy disco/nightclub restroom is wonderfully chic. And, incidentally, Evil Girl is incredible knockout **Amy Yip**, a stunning big-breasted

Hong Kong beauty. You'll dream about this performance.

Plus, there's more. This movie features some of the strongest (or perhaps, most objectionable) sex gags in Asian comedy, including a man cursed with a magic penis spell. His staff grows so long that it literally drags on the ground. He has to tape it to his leg, but that leads to severe walking problems (just imagine!) when he gets sexually aroused. With **Danny Chan.**

The same cast (and director) also made *Our Neighbors Are Phantoms.*

GHOSTS GALORE (1987)
director: Hsu Hsia. Lo Lieh·Linda Chu · Huang Cheng Li ★★
Veteran **Lo Lieh**, once again playing an evil black-magic priest, unleashes some particularly nasty Japanese ghosts on a peaceful Chinese village. There's lots of action in the grand Shaw Brothers style, but too much slapstick tends to spoil the film.

GHOST'S LOVE (1990)
director: Kenneth Lu. Sin Yun·Tian Wu ★½
A shorthanded mix of gangsters and ghosts in a film riddled with reprehensible special effects.

Sin Yun is a girl who unwisely chooses triad boss Tian Wu as a boyfriend. When he drugs her and tries to involve her in his nasty trafficking caper, she is accidentally murdered. Her ghost battles the guardian of heaven's gate for a chance to return and seek revenge.

GHOST'S LOVER (1984)
director: Yeung Kuen. Tong Gen Chung· Lee Jung Jung·Hui Lan·Lo Yun ★
An uneven marriage between contemporary values and ancient sorcery as a man becomes involved with a girl

who could be a ghost. Or then, maybe not. A familiar story in Oriental films.

GINSENG KING (1989)
director: Rotar Ru-Tar.
A rating is impossible for this film. I loved it—for all the wrong reasons; you may hate it for the same reasons.

A synopsis can't do justice to this fractured Thai tale. I won't even try. If you want to amaze your friends and test your sanity at the same time— don't miss it.

The plot has to do with the resurrection of a 1000-year old Ginseng King (looking a lot like a walking tree with bug eyes) who helps a young couple fight off flesh-eating zombies. He's aided by his son, a Pillsbury Dough Boy lookalike.

GIRL GANG (1994)
director: Tao Ten Hong. Lo Wu Tung· Sally Yuen ★★
This one isn't about a girl gang at all, but a boy gang. And the leader of this boy gang is Danny. He's a big shot because he has connections with the mob. Danny's gang makes a few bucks by doing some lightweight triad business, but mostly they sit around, smoking and talking trash.

Eventually, they decide to make some extra cash by getting a couple babes and whoring them out. This works fine until Michelle, the sister of a prostitute, goes to the cops. When the police retaliate, the mob disowns the gang. So Danny decides to make some getaway money by kidnapping Michelle, and . . .

Well, that's enough. Right?

This is either good or bad, depending on your criteria. As a crime/gang actioner, it's rather awful. But if you're looking for Category III type of sex, nudity, and rape, it delivers.

GIRLS FROM CHINA (1993)
director: Wong Tai Loy. Kwan Sau Mei·Lee Li ★★
More appropriately this one should be called *Girl from China*, since all the action revolves around one young woman named Chow Ying (Kwan Sau Mei).

After numerous bouts with lecherous males and bitchy coworkers, Ying eventually discovers the joys (and profits) of making a living on her back. Even though she becomes a prostitute, Ying still has hopes of landing a wealthy mate. Eventually, she does.

The cast is uniformly good, but obviously the standout is Kwan Sau Mei. She better be—the movie revolves around her as she switches from cool to sexy, hot to devious. There are enough twists and turns in the plot to keep it interesting. But unfortunately, when all is said and done, the film just doesn't offer anything new.

GIRLS IN THE TIGER CAGE (1985)
director: Tai Ng Ok. Shen Yi·Chen Hung-Lieh·Chang Shan·Karen Yeh ★★½

GIRLS IN THE TIGER CAGE 2 (1986)
director: Tai Ng Ok. Shen Yi·Chen Hung-Lieh·Karen Yeh ★★½
This familiar story of a Japanese female detention camp in China during World War II serves merely as an excuse for an array of savage S&M tortures inflicted upon a bevy of attractive prisoners (particularly Chen Hung-Lieh, Chang Shan, and Karen Yeh) as they long for freedom.

#1 concludes with their escape, while #2 begins with their recapture, followed by more brutal tortures—culminating with Chen's guerrilla assassination of the camp's hero commandant (Shen Yi) after the war ends.

GIRLS UNBUTTONED (1995)
director: Wong Tai Loy. Loletta Lee·Hong Yu Lan·Wu Mia Oyi·Yan Yu Mei ★★

Girls Unbuttoned

The (mis)adventures of three boy-crazy girls as they get involved with an unlikely collection of losers. The plot is little more than an excuse for a lot of soft-core frolicking and a ton of nudity.

This is a popular cult film due to the uninhibited coyness of frequently naked **Loletta Lee** (costar of *Remains of a Woman*). Not to mention her sexy costars Hung Yu Lan (Miss Asia 1993) and Wu Mia Oyi (Miss Hong Kong 1993).

Director **Wong Tai Loy** seems to have drifted a long way since his early chop socky days of *Born Invincible* (1978) and *Deadly Blade* (1980).

GOD OF GAMBLERS (1989)
director: Wong Ching (Jing). Chow Yun-Fat·Andy Lau·Joey Wang·Ng Man Tat ★★★

GOD OF GAMBLERS 2 (1990)
director: Wong Ching (Jing). Andy Lau· Stephen Chow·Ng Man Tat·Cheung Man ★½

GOD OF GAMBLERS 3 (1991)
director: Wong Ching (Jing). Stephen Chow·Gong Li·Ng Man Tat·Sandra Ng ★★
Once again, **Chow Yun-Fat** elevates a so-so script into an exceptional film. #1 is a routine gambler-takes-on-the-

casino tale with an unexpected amnesia twist, plus there's a riveting conclusion.

#2 is chowless. And misguided. It's a slapstick action comedy that revolves around the antics of two inept gamblers, played by **Andy Lau** and **Stephen Chow**. Apparently, they have special magical powers (e.g., being able to change the face value of any card at will), but they can use these talents only for benevolent purposes. The whole thing is a silly, humiliating sequel. But it made money at the Hong Kong box office, so along came another sequel.

Certainly #3 is a better bet. Ever so slightly. Andy Lau is gone; Stephen Chow is totally in charge (just for the record, I'm not a fan of Chow's goofy shenanigans, and I wish he'd get caught jerking off in a dark movie theater), but this time the script is a bit more creative with a clever time-travel twist. Most of the action takes place in 1937 Shanghai, and costar **Gong Li** (the Chinese beauty from *Raise the Red Lantern*) helps take your mind off Chow.

GOD OF GAMBLERS' RETURN (1994) **director: Wong Ching [Jing].** Chow Yun-Fat·Tony Leung [Kar Fai]·Chingmy

Chow Yun-Fat in *God of Gamblers*

Yau·Cheung Man·Wu Chien Lien·Wu Hsin Kuo ★★

Chow Yun-Fat returns as God of Gamblers, bent on revenge after Devil of Gamblers (Wu Hsin Kuo) kills his wife (**Cheung Man**). His quest takes him and his rogue ward Tsu-Miu across mainland China to the fabulous casinos of Taiwan for the ultimate showdown.

It must've seemed like a great idea—bring Chow Yun-Fat back to one of his best screen characterizations, and then surround him with an all-star cast. How can it miss?

The answer is simple: the problem is **Wong Ching [Jing]**. Typical of all Wong's recent productions, this film can't decide whether it's a comedy, a drama, an actioner—or whatever. The result is a schizophrenic nightmare, yanking the audience from one unrelated sequence to the next, thus breaking any sense of drama through countless scenes of slapstick, interspersed with violent psychotic outbursts.

If director Wong would have enough faith in any one genre to build a cohesive film around it, the result might surprise even his toughest critics. But this irrational all-things-to-all-people style only frustrates everybody, including the actors, who tiptoe through their parts like a soldier in a minefield, fearful of the next explosion.

And further, the cameo appearance by Tse Miu (the precocious brat from *New Legend of Shaolin*, currently being groomed by Wong Ching for future stardom) is a blatant example of a production company's despotic manipulation. These are simply scenes of crass publicity with little regard for the plot.

GODFATHER'S DAUGHTER MAFIA BLUES (1989) **director: Fan Tsui Fen.** Yukari Oshima ·Mark Cheng·Wan Xin-Liang ★½

If the Godfather's daughter (**Yukari Oshima**) is blue about anything, it's probably the lame script for this miserably written crime/action/comedy. Essentially, it's a contemporary chop socky flick masquerading as a story of two gangs (one Chinese, one Japanese) trying to gain control in Hong Kong through the lucrative nightclub scene.

GOLDEN DESTROYERS (1985)
director: Gordon Chan. Anita Mui·Casanova Wong·Roger Seller ★

An early effort from singer **Anita Mui**, obviously made at a point in her career when selection of songs was more important than selection of scripts (it wasn't until 1989, with **A Better Tomorrow 3**, that she would be recognized as a serious actress).

Gordon Chan is another suspected pseudonym for director **Godfrey Ho**. This film has the look of his other patchwork productions, a bit of this movie and a bit of that one . . . and poof—a new film. It's the disjointed story of a greedy priest who goes into cahoots with a Thai entrepreneur as they steal the precious artifacts from a sacred temple. A caretaker tries to stop them by raising golden zombies from the dead.

Although he receives top billing, popular kung fu boxer Casanova Wong appears only in a fight scene during the opening credits. Anita Mui fares a bit better, coming and going when the story turns to Hong Kong, but most of the time she's nonessential to the plot.

GOLDEN LOTUS: LOVE AND DESIRE.
See *World's Foremost Banned Novel*

GOLDEN NUN (1987)
director: Hsu Tien Yung. Land Lo·Ti Tau Hung ★

The Golden Nun (Land Lo) rescues a village carpenter (Li Tau Hung) from a band of vampires. But, is she really the good witch she pretends to be? Do you care?

GOLDEN QUEEN COMMANDO
aka **AMAZON COMMANDO** (1984)
director: Chu Ping. Lin Ching Hsia·Sally Yeh (Yip)·Elsa Yeung·Teresa Tsui·Hilda Lau ★★★★

The movie begins by introducing the seven female fighters, now behind bars in a maximum security prison for a variety of offenses. Each woman has a specialty, ranging from explosives to burglary. And each can also kick some serious butt. In jail, the women fall under the leadership of Black Fox (Lin Ching Hsia, wearing a very chic eye patch), who plans their escape and convinces them to join her in a top-level undercover mission against an oppressive military general and his dangerous chemical plant.

Despite the derivative-sounding plot, filmmaker **Chu Yin Ping** infuses it with his own brand of cockeyed freshness as he turns this story into a spaghetti Western, complete with Ennio Morricone music borrowed from *The Good, the Bad and the Ugly* and *Duck You Sucker*. These Asian beauties on horseback singlehandedly save a village from bandits (in an obvious nod to *Seven Samurai/Magnificent Seven*), encounter ghosts in an ancient burial ground, and then take on the entire cavalry of black-caped soldiers. Plus these girls still have time to bicker among themselves, flexing muscles as they jockey for control of the group.

Director Chu made a sequel, *Pink Force Commando* (see separate review), later the same year. Lin Ching Hsia (called *Venus Lin* in the credits) and Elsa Yeung also star in the police thriller *Phoenix the Raider* (1985).

GOLIATHON (1977)
 aka **MIGHTY PEKING MAN**
 aka **COLOSSUS OF CONGO**
director: **Ho Menga-Hua [Ho Menga]**
called **Homer Gaugh** on Euro prints.
Evelyn Kraft·Danny Lee ★★★★
Even if there hadn't been a giant ape
in this movie, it would've been a four
star extravaganza. Even if the film
weren't an unabashed Asian clone of
King Kong, it would've been don't-
miss-it entertainment.

The ads for *Goliathon* screamed:
"Action! Excitement! Spectacle beyond your wildest dreams!" Certainly,
these accolades were meant to describe beautiful Evelyn Kraft. She's the
blond jungle girl who steals the show!
She is mesmerizing.

Fresh from her performance in
Franz-Joseph Gottlieb's German horror film *Lady Dracula*, Evelyn brings
an incredible amount of screen sexuality to this Shaw Brothers production
(yes, the same company that produced
the **Black Magic** series and countless
martial arts extravaganzas). It's worth
the price of admission (or tape rental)
just to see Evelyn Kraft run around the
city of Hong Kong in her jungle attire.
Also starring a very young **Danny Lee**
as Kraft's boyfriend.

Incidentally, there exists a European version of this film (*Colossus of
the Congo*) in which Kraft dies at the
end. It also features some brief (but
much appreciated) Evelyn Kraft nudity.

GORY MURDER (1984)
director: **Hwa I-Hung.** Bau Ming·
Cheung Duk Wai·Cheung Suk·Ying
Che ★
A ridiculously disjointed attempt at a
true-crime film, following the procedural work of the Taiwanese police department as they try to retrieve clues
from a mutilated murder victim.

One of the all-time worst—due to
piss-poor editing, claustrophobic cam-

**Rosamund Kwan (L) with Gong Li in
*Great Conqueror's Concubine***

erawork, and a makeshift musical
score.

GRAVESIDE STORY (1988)
director: **Kam Yoo Tu.** ★
The only good thing about this movie
is the title. It's another stupid shot-on-
video waste of time from this loser of a
director who also regurgitated the horrendous **Vampires Live Again** and
the equally terrible **Vampires Strikes**.
Somebody stop this maniac!

GREAT CONQUEROR'S CONCUBINE
(1994)
 aka **KING OF WESTERN CHU**
director: **Stephen Shin.** Ray Liu·
Gong Li·Rosamund Kwan·Wang Lung
Wei·Chang Yi Feng ★★½
After her impressive, award-winning
performance in **Raise the Red
Lantern**, actress **Gong Li** has gone on
to underwhelm audiences with a series of impersonal characterizations
and lackluster roles. Some critics say
it's the result of her breakup with filmmaker **Zhang Yi Mou [Yimou]** (director of *Raise the Red Lantern*), while
others cite poor management as the
culprit.

No matter the reason, this film is
yet another example of Gong Li's recent choice of negligible material. Into
an already bloated marketplace
comes this instantly forgettable tale of
heroism, part costume drama and part
martial arts, positioning the two heroines (Gong Li and **Rosamund Kwan**)

into a peculiar love triangle with Ray Liu.

Director **Stephen Shin** is sorely out of his element here. His former exploitive fare like **Black Cat** (1991) and **Bite of Love** (1990) did not prepare him for the pageantry or scope associated with this type of production. However, on the plus side, he did manage to put Rosamund Kwan and Gong Li together in a bathtub for a memorable scene.

GREATEST LOVER (1988)
director: Clarence Fok Yiu Leung. Chow Yun-Fat·Anita Mui ★★
Take the *My Fair Lady* story (or *Pygmalion* for the highbrow reader; *Opening of Misty Beethoven* for the trash pickers) and twist the genders. **Chow Yun-Fat** stars as an obnoxious nerd transformed into a refined playboy who falls in love with his teacher.

Lesser effort by the **Naked Killer** director.

GREEN SNAKE (1993)
(called **BLUE SNAKE** in Hong Kong) **director: Tsui Hark.** Maggie Cheung· Joey Wang ★★½
Just as some films grow on you with repeat viewing, some also grow *away* from you. While there's much to admire from this entry in the never-ending period fantasy/legend genre,

Maggie Cheung with Joey Wang (R) in Green Snake

the film's many weaknesses ultimately triumph over its too few strengths.

The tale—adapted from a classic Chinese novel about a pair of snake sisters striving to attain human form, seducing both a scholar (successfully) and a monk (not as successfully) in the process—is notably enlivened by a mesmerizing **Maggie Cheung** performance, as she plays the more rambunctious of the sisters.

Regrettably, though, director **Tsui Hark** has chosen to focus on the older sister (**Joey Wang**) and her foppish mate (Wu Kuo Chiu), who fail to deliver a fraction of the chemistry.

Even Tsui's trademark exotic and erotic visuals (which are beginning to border on self-parody here) and his satirically anticlerical stance can't save *Green Snake* from its floundering and dramatically limp episodic narrative, its inept FX (the giant rubber snake is absolutely horrendous), and its messy, chaotic climax.

But on the plus side, any film that has a sequence wherein Joey Wang and Maggie Cheung bathe each other can't be all bad.

GRUDGE OF THE MOON LADY (1980)
director: Kim In Soo. Chin Bong Chin ·Huh Chin ★★½
A medieval love triangle: (1) Man, (2) Poor Girl, and (3) Rich Girl.

Rich Girl tricks Poor Girl into leaving town. Lonely Man marries Rich Girl. Poor Girl is on her way back home when she is caught and held captive in a swamp by an Evil White Cat Spirit. She becomes possessed and returns to the village, where she destroys everything, murders her rival, and is eventually killed by her lover. I guess all's well that ends well.

GUARDIAN AND SHE-GHOST OF SHAOLIN (1984)
director: Yuen Yang. Wu Hsiao Fei· Chiang Pin·Pan Cien Lin ★½

This is a typical dead-girl-gets-revenge-thru-a-ghost story. The only unusual aspect: after taking vengeance, she falls in love with a human. She doesn't want to return to heaven until her boyfriend can join her by killing himself. And he does.

GUNMEN (1988)
director: Wong C. Keung (Kirk Wong). Tony Leung [Chiu Wai]·Adam Cheng·Waise Lee·Carrie Ng·Elizabeth Lee·David Wu ★★
Produced by **Tsui Hark**, in a rather obvious attempt to capitalize on the popularity of the **John Woo**'s **A Better Tomorrow** (also produced by **Hark**), this action period film is a heavy-handed mixture of drama and ultraviolence telling the story of an opium/drug war circa 1926. **Carrie Ng** makes it worth the watch.

GUYS IN GHOST'S HAND (1990)
director: Stanley Wing Siu [Chin Sing Wai]. Alex Fong·Wu Ma·Hui Ying ★★
The ghost of a murdered woman recruits other creatures of the night to join her crusade against the ancestors of the man who killed her. Mindless, low-budget thrill show with vampires, zombies, and ghosts attacking lots of victims. Eventually, the exorcist priests show up and find ways of exterminating the various supernatural entities.
Not as good as **Stanley Wing Siu**'s previous horror film, **Vampire Buster**, but fun for a rainy afternoon.

HAND OF DEATH (1976)
director: John Woo. James Tien· Jackie Chan·Dorian Tan·Samo Hung ★★
An early effort written and directed by **John Woo**, notable for being his only project with **Jackie Chan**. But it's strictly for chop socky fans.
Former Sholin student Chow Sher Fen (James Tien) has betrayed his holy roots and is now a Manchu comman-

der controlling China through fear and oppression. The Buddhist monks order a kung fu fighter named Yun Fe (Dorian Tan) to find and destroy the villain. Yun befriends a long-haired youth (Jackie Chan) for assistance in the project.
The fight sequences are staged by **Samo Hung**, who also costars as an evil sheriff protecting the warlord.

HAPPY GHOST (1982)
director: Clifton Ko Sum. Raymond Wong ·May Lo ★★

HAPPY GHOST 2 (1983)
director: Clifton Ko Sum. Raymond Wong ·May Lo ★

HAPPY GHOST 3 (1984)
director: Tsui Hark (with **Ringo Lam**). Raymond Wong·Maggie Cheung ★½

HAPPY GHOST 4 (1991)
director: Clifton Ko Sum. Raymond Wong ·Pauline Yeung·Wu Ling Chi· Beyond ★★½
Part 1 and Part 2 are intrinsically the same movie, sort of a hybrid *Breakfast Club* meets *Teen Wolf*. Instead of a werewolf helping the team win the ball game, this time it's a ghost.
By the second sequel, this premise was wearing very thin, so there's scarcely any similarity. Part 3 is a meandering, episodic story of five reincarnated spirits and their (mis)adventures back on Earth.
After seven years, someone at Pak Ming Films decided the world needed another episode in the *Happy Ghost* series. Surprisingly, they were right. *Happy Ghost 4* has turned into the biggest hit of the series.
The producers aimed their sights directly at the teen market, first by signing Hong Kong's #1 pop group, Beyond, to costar; and then by using Film Workshop to create some live-action/

animation sequences, à la *Who Framed Roger Rabbit.*

The plot is a throwback to *Happy Ghost* 1 and 2 (1982/1983), combining supernatural happenings in a high school setting. A ghostly ancestor of a teacher helps him out when a ferocious warrior returns from the grave (or, more accurately, from a vivid history lesson).

Filmmaker **Clifton Ko Sum** was responsible for *Happy Ghost* 1 and 2, but not #3, which was directed by **Tsui Hark** and **Ringo Lam**.

HARD-BOILED (1992)
director: John Woo. Chow Yun-Fat·Tony Leung [Chiu Wai]·Anthony Wong·Teresa Mo·Philip Chan ★★★½
Chow Yun-Fat is Tequila, the best marksman on the Hong Kong police force. He's also a cop who is tired of seeing too many fellow officers killed in the line of duty. Tequila believes the old saying "Might Is Right," especially when dealing with the bad guys. He dramatizes his philosophy in the opening scene by waging a full attack against gun traffickers in a crowded dim sum restaurant, proving that he's willing to break the rules and even jeopardize public safety for the sake of his mission. But this violent outburst is really Tequila's brazen message to the gunrunning kingpin (Philip Chen) for him to watch his step. As the film progresses, Tequila tries to nail the big boss but doesn't have enough evidence against him, so he begins dogging one of his gangster bodyguards, a torpedo named Tony (**Tony Leung [Chiu Wai]**). Eventually, Tony confides in Tequila that he is, in fact, an undercover cop. The two join together in an all-out assault on the gang's secret hideout, an arsenal that happens to be located in the basement of a busy hospital.

Many critics have christened this film "the best Hong Kong action/gunplay film ever" and "easily one of the best action films made by any director in the world." It may be a masterpiece, but the movie seems more like an unfinished masterpiece. The first hour tells an intricate story of double-crossings inside the triad mob and undercover agents who can't blow their cover. But during the second part of the film, characterization is compromised for the sake of the action set pieces.

The entire film becomes merely a swirling montage of bad guys versus good guys. And unfortunately, this results in a number of cynical questions. For instance: Why were the gun traffickers hiding their contraband in the basement of a hospital in the first place? And how the hell did so many weapons get secretly shipped in? Or perhaps, more important, how were they going to be transported out? Was all this happening without the hospital's knowledge? Why didn't the staff get suspicious when a virtual gangster convention was congregating 24 hours a day in their basement?

Putting these questions aside, no other Hong Kong movie compares to *Hard-boiled* for sheer bombastic exuberance. It is an amazing example of action theatrics, perhaps even a textbook example. No longer is **John Woo** simply choreographing the spectacular gun fights like a frenzied parade in front of a stationary camera (e.g., *The Killer*). Now his camera is moving with the same intensity as the action he's filming. Never before have so many incredible stunts, wild gun battles, or jarring explosions been accumulated in one package. But, unfortunately, unlike the filmmaker's *A Better Tomorrow, A Bullet in the Head,* or *The Killer,* it's at the expense of the plot.

HARD TO KILL (1992)
director: Phillip Kao. Yukari Oshima·Phillip Kao·Robin Shou·Mark Cheng ★★½

Action is the key word as **Yukari Oshima** plays an Interpol agent sent to Hong Kong on a mission of force against a deadly drug lord (played by director Phillip Kao, the legendary chop socky star, who is married to Oshima in real life).

HAUNTED COP SHOP 1 (1985)
director: Jeff Lau. Jacky Cheung·Hui Gon Ying·Wo Fung·Chan Kai Chia
★½

HAUNTED COP SHOP 2 (1986)
director: Yuen Cheung Yan. Rover K. C. Tang·Alan Tang·Wong Kar Wai
★★★
Vampires have infested a meatpacking plant. The special Monster Police Squad must eradicate them. However, when they botch the job, their division loses face with the police commissioner. They are relegated to menial jobs until the vampires invade the county hospital. Some good and scary FX, but it's mostly just silly.

The sequel is better. It's nonstop action (even before the credits roll) and the ending is . . . well, yes . . . unforgettable. The hero kills the vampire/creature by urinating into a pool, thus completing an electrical circuit and frying the monster. The hero's buddy laments his friend's unfortunate (yet noble) death by saying, "I'll think of him every time I piss."

HAUNTED HOUSE (1986)
director: Ng See Yuen. Linda Chu· Chen Chun ★½
A woman, Tanny (Linda Chu, the porcelain doll lookalike from **Human Skin Lanterns**) is terrorized by the ghost of her dead husband, a gangster executed in prison. Apparently, he's pissed off because his wife is having sex with his attorney.

HAUNTED MADAM (1987)
director: Tony C. K. Lo. Siu Yuk Lung· Bill Pai ★★★
Similar to **Haunted Cop Shop 2** in style and pacing, this film is filled with wonderful, outrageous FX plus astonishing villains (and villainesses), including a ruthless, bloodthirsty superman and a sexy but thoroughly bad sorceress.

It's all tied together with four beautiful policewomen who are told by a reputable fortune-teller that they will all meet the same man at the same time. He is dangerous. He will cause one of you to commit suicide, another to break your head, one of you will be raped, and the last will be killed." Thanks to creative script-writing, each of these prophecies comes true, but with decidedly positive results.

HAUNTED ROMANCE (1990)
director: Kong Yeung. Xuan Chi Hui· Chu Feng ★★
Photographer Fong Cho (Xuan Chi Hui) is sent to the mainland forests on an assignment for a wildlife magazine. While shooting pictures of various animals, he finds a gold locket. The trouble begins when he keeps it, substituting his wife's picture for the one inside the charm. The original owner (is Chu Feng a ghost?) shows up and seduces Fong, cursing him at the same time. Lame plot, saved—ever so slightly—by an abundance of nudity.

HE AND SHE (1994)
director: Cheng Dan Shui. Anita Yuen·Tony Leung [Kar Fai] ★★½
If you've ever wondered (which you probably haven't) what would happen if you mixed *Mystic Pizza* with *Kramer vs Kramer* and then served the whole thing up covered in a Chinese version of the television hit *Friends*—well, this would be your answer.

Here's the story of four friends, picked to live together in an apartment, to see what happens when art starts imitating life imitating art . . . or something like that. And overall, the film is a harmless, entertaining flick and not a bad way to spend 90 minutes of your life. If you don't expect much more than a soap opera, you won't be disappointed.

HE LIVES BY NIGHT (1987)
director: Po Chih Leo [Liang Pu Zhi]. Sillvia Chang·Eddie Chan ★★★
There's an interesting use of fashion and color in this stylishly photographed slasher film, similar to the Italian *giallo* films.

It's the story of a crazed transsexual killer who confesses his crimes to an all-night radio talk-show hostess (Sillvia Chang) until he decides that she, too, must die. Good tension flick.

HE WHO CHASES AFTER THE WIND (1988)
director: Lawrence Lau (Lau Ku Chang). Alex Man·Elizabeth Lee· Stephen Chow ★½
Basically a love story (between detective **Alex Man** and flighty **Elizabeth Lee**) with a prerequisite subplot about a crazed killer trying to avenge his brother. Neither plot is very convincing, and the cop-action stuff seems sorely out of step with the casual pace of the film.

HE WHO'S THE BEST IS THE HIGHEST. See *Best Is the Highest*

HEADHUNTER (1986)
director: Lau Shinghon. Chow Yun-Fat·Rosamund Kwan ★★½
Ex-soldier goes mad after returning from the war. He begins stalking and killing citizens in the city. An early **Chow Yun-Fat** vehicle.

HEART OF THE DRAGON. See *First Mission*

HEARTBEAT 100 (1986)
director: Kent Cheng and **Lo Kin.** Maggie Cheung·Lui Fong ★★
An effective slasher movie in the *Friday the 13th* mold. Graphic horror with some high school humor provided by the teens. Starring a young **Maggie Cheung**.

HEARTY RESPONSE (1988)
director: Law Man. Chow Yun-Fat· Joey Wang ★★½
Chow Yun-Fat plays a cop named Ho Ting Bon. And **Joey Wang [Wong]** is Sun, a homeless shoplifter. After allowing her to stay at his apartment— guess what? They fall in love.

Everythings goes as expected until a former boyfriend discovers Sun's whereabouts. He kidnaps her, rapes her, tattoos her. And when he turns his vengeance on Bon, Sun blows him away.

HEAVEN WIFE, HELL WIFE. See *Loves of the Living Dead*

HEAVENLY SPELL (1987)
director: Man Gon. Lau Siu Kwan· Chung Siu Yen·Bar Lik Kay·Yeung Chuk Lam ★½
The ghost of a girl's dead sister (disguised as a sea serpent) lures people into a swamp. The townsfolk try a variety of spells and curses to cleanse the lake. Eventually a monk succeeds. Don't be fooled for a moment, this one is very bad. The ★½ star rating is for the cheesy rubber dragon in the pond.

HELL HOLE (1989)
aka **ESCAPE FROM HELL HOLE**
director: Maman Firmanstan. Gudhy Sintara·Dicky Zulkarnaen·Siska Widowaty·Leily Sagita ★★
Lots of torture, whippings, and general S&M mayhem in this violent film about a women's prison (which also doubles as a brothel).

As with director **Firmanstan**'s movie *I Want to Get Even*, the main concentration is on a young virgin (Gudhy Sintara) who catches the eye of the evil warden. She'd rather be punished than succumb to his sexual wishes. She's brutalized for most of the film, but eventually she gets her revenge.

HELL RAIDERS
director: **Sisworo Putra**. Barry Prima ·Dicky Zulkarnaen·Jafar Bril·Pudi Purbaya ★★½
The story of the Indonesian fight for freedom against the Dutch in 1945. "What should we do?" ask the townspeople. "Go and fight," replies the holy monk. "You'll be happy if you win—heroes if you lose."
That bit of dialogue represents the kind of sentimentality littering this 2-hour patriotic production. But if you look beyond the knee-jerk propaganda, some of the war scenes are truly epic in scope, charged with the type of bloody realism predominant in Indonesian films. Costarring popular Barry Prima.

HELLO DRACULA (1985)
director: **Henry Leung (Leung Tung Ni)**. Kim To·Lam Kwong Wing·Wong Chun Yu·Puon Sam ★★★
This is perhaps the strangest of the Hong Kong horror films (and that's really saying something!). The rating is based on its flabbergasting quality and not necessarily on continuity. Read on. . . .
Father is dead. Grandpa and three young children are taking his body to the sacred burial ground when their carriage is stopped by a hopping kid vampire who is trying to escape from a Taoist monk.
The vampire child reanimates the dead dad, who becomes Dracula and protects the child by killing the monk. The carriage driver is also killed in the

scrimmage, but grandpa and the kids escape.
When they return to the village and warn the constable that Dad has become Dracula, the official reacts by recruiting vampire hunters from Europe.
Meanwhile (seemingly out of context) the children become friendly with some harmless vampires, apparently not affiliated with Dracula's legion of the undead, and they work out a musical dance number with them. (Mmmmm)
About halfway into this film, the three English-speaking vampire hunters arrive: the boss plus a priest and a nun (who surprisingly gets naked in a shower scene). A meteor leads them to a baseball game played by the kid vampires. The priest sprinkles holy water on a skull (which is doubling as a baseball). When a vampire child touches it, he is electrocuted. This pisses Dracula off. He rises from his grave and kills the three hunters and then attacks the city.
Eventually, Grandpa (a magician in his own right) creates a gang of mercenary bug-child-creatures to fight Dracula and his cohorts. Then, in a particularly downbeat ending, Dad/Dracula is finally killed when one of his real children, wearing a belt of ignited dynamite, runs to his father's open arms. Kaboom!

HER VENGEANCE (1988)
director: **Lan Nai-Tai**. Wang Hsia Feng·Lam Ching Ying·Shing Fui On ★★★
This is a vicious, mean-spirited revenge-for-rape flick, with more than a casual similarity to specialized American exploitation films (e.g., *I Spit on Your Grave*).
Fang Chieh-Ying (Wang Hsia-Feng) is brutally attacked and violated by five ruffians (including perennial HK villain Shing Fui On) after she rejects

their crude advances. The gang rape leaves her severely injured, suffering from an incurable venereal disease. Ying's sister encourages her to seek help from their uncle, Hsuing (*Mr. Vampire's* **Lam Ching Ying**), a former triad boss now confined to a wheelchair.

Initially, he refuses to assist Ying in her mania for retribution, but he does give her a job in his nightclub. She uses the hostess position to lure the low-life attackers into a vengeful web. After Ying begins her deadly one-woman assault, Uncle Hsiung decides to assist her. The conclusion erupts in a barrage of carnage unparalleled in Western cinema.

Besides sleazy segments of gratuitous nudity, the film is loaded with a virtual smorgasbord of blood and gore. The bad guys are skewered with sharp hollow pipes, showered in acid, and sliced up with scissors. Before the movie ends, every major character is dead or dying. They are chopped up or gutted, riddled with bullets or beaten to death.

HERO DEFEATING JAPS (1983) **director: Chang Cheh.** Ti Lung·Shaji Kurata·Chiang Sheng·Lu Feng ★★ There probably weren't many Japanese distribution deals for this film, based on the exploitive title alone. And you won't find a memorial monument built to director **Chang Cheh** in downtown Tokyo. But then, there's never been much love between the Japanese and the Chinese. Or vice versa. This film is just one more nail in the coffin.

For more than ten years, following the success of Chang's kung fu team movies (especially, *Five Masters of Death* [1975] and *Five Deadly Venoms* [1978]), the filmmaker relied extensively on the same group of actors portraying invincible warriors in myriad different conflicts. This time they battle evil Japanese pirates trying to steal the precious book *Summary of Fighting Skills.*

The band of Nippon Ninjas is headed by Shaji Kurata, the man who made a comfortable wage playing nasty Japanese villains in a jillion Chinese films.

HERO OF TOMORROW (1989) **director: Lo Haw-Lo.** Max Mok·Miu Cheng Wei·Blackie Ko ★★ A plodding yet (at times) violent attempt to cash in on the popular *A Better Tomorrow* series, as suggested by the title.

This is the story of a gangster who gets out of prison in Hong Kong, kills his enemies, and goes to Taiwan. There he murders the mob boss and starts a new racket. The conclusion climaxes into the patented gunplay bloodbath; there's a shallowness that permeates the entire production. It lacks the heart and soul of the **John Woo** or **Ringo Lam** productions.

HEROES SHED NO TEARS (1985) **director: John Woo.** Eddie Ko·Lam Ching Ying·Chien Yuet San·Lau Chau Sang ★★★ Here's the film that **John Woo** directed just prior to his mega-hit *A Better Tomorrow.* And perhaps due to the overwhelming popularity of his more accessible gangster epic, this lurid war/action tale is all but forgotten.

It is, however, a good movie about a band of soldiers of fortune (led by **Eddy Ko**) who are hired by the Thai government to capture and bring back a drug-smuggling army general in the Vietnam jungle. Complete with bloodthirsty savages (à la *Man from Deep River*), the film is an ultraviolent and graphically gory adventure. Interestingly, however, the patented Woo melodramatic characterizations are mysteriously missing.

HEROIC FIGHT (1990)
director: Ching Chung Wu. Lin Hsiao Lam·Wu Ma·Dick Wei ★★½
A satire of the triad's involvement in the HK film industry, starring Lin Hsiao Lam (from *Magic of Spell*) as the studio's top action star, Lin-Wang San. There's a funny parody of *The Killer*'s famous cabaret/shoot-em-up scene. Plus an abundance of stunts and demon-paced mayhem, but much of the screwball goofiness is pretty silly.

HEROIC ONES (1982)
aka **INHERITOR OF KUNG FU**
director: Pao Hsieh Lee. Ti Lung· Chang Ling·Kwan Young ★★
This adventure film about a grand tournament in medieval China is included for **Chang Ling** completists (see *Wolf Devil Woman*).
Chang Ling is an expert female fighter who comes to the aid of a swordsman (**Ti Lung**) attacked by bandits while en route to the capital for a martial arts tournament. Eventually they join in the competition but end up exposing a scheme against the emperor. The film has none of the supernatural elements often found in Chang's movies.

HEROIC TRIO (1992)
director: Johnny To [To Ke Fung] and **Ching Siu Tung.** Anita Mui·Maggie Cheung·Michelle Yeoh·Anthony Wong ★★★½

HEROIC TRIO 2: THE EXECUTIONERS (1993)
directors: Johnny To [To Ke Fung] and **Ching Siu Tung.** Maggie Cheung ·Michelle Yeoh·Anita Mui·Anthony Wong·Damian Lau ★★
Three of HK's fighting divas (**Maggie Cheung, Anita Mui,** and **Michelle Yeoh**) unite as Thief Catcher (Cheung), Wonder Woman (Mui), and Invisible Girl (Yeoh) to defeat the Master and his netherworld army.

The cruel villain is kidnapping babies from all over Hong Kong. This inhumane behavior is propelled by his own demented plan for world domination. Specifically, he will train the infants to become superhuman assassins and then choose one of them to become China's future king. All right—it doesn't make much sense. The real reason for watching this action-packed spectacle is the three female stars. And you won't be disappointed.
The sequel propels the viewer into the apocalyptic future, presenting a grim view of life after the Holocaust. A devastating nuclear war has broken out and most of the Earth is dead or dying. Fresh water is the most precious commodity in the world. Maggie Cheung is Chat, a fortune hunter who makes a living by securing and dealing untainted nonradioactive water, but she's constantly attacked by thugs who want to steal it and make their own deal with the black market.
Michelle Yeoh spends most of the film selling her fighting ability to the highest bidder; eventually she joins up with Chat in a battle against a mutant superpower named Evil and a strange Christlike protégé who are using the world problems to create a religious upheaval. Anita Mui, as Wonder Woman, spends most of her time trapped in a jail (at one point she is so hungry that she rips the head from a rat and drinks its blood). But, for the most part, she has little screen time in this sequel.
#2 lacks continuity; it suffers from the underdeveloped story line and lack of a centralized theme. The nononsense approach with darkly ferocious violence is appreciated, but there's not much of a movie here.

HE'S A WOMAN, SHE'S A MAN (1994)
director: Chan Ho Sun [He Fan] aka **Peter Chan Ho Sun.** Leslie Cheung·

Carina Lau in *He's a Woman, She's a Man*

Carina Lau·Anita Yuen·Eric Tsang
★★½
Kim, a young record producer/ songwriter (**Leslie Cheung**) is getting fed up with the Cantonese pop music scene, even though that's what made him the success he is today. Instead, he longs to go to Africa and discover his roots. (Are we supposed to see some similarities here between this character and Paul Simon?)

His girlfriend Rose (**Carina Lau**) is his biggest success story. She's an award-winning vocalist with whom he has fallen in love. But the relationship stifles him, and he decides that the only way to stop falling in love with his discoveries is to take on a male client. Of course this presumes he has no willpower, but that's another story.

Enter Lee (**Anita Yuen**), a young groupie who admires the superstar couple, and hears about producer Kim's open call for male singers. The problem is that Lee is a girl and must pretend to be a man.

But the real problem is that *He's a Woman, She's a Man* starts out as an interesting satire on the music industry (God knows, that's refreshing after years of being fed MTV's crap) but it soon degenerates into a rather lame gender-bending romantic comedy. Most of the originality is gone by 30 minutes into the film.

All that remains is play-out *Tootsie*-style humor, scenes of Lee learning to walk like a man, practicing the art of scratching him/herself, the confusion that ensues when Lee isn't attracted to Rose, etc. Etc. Etc. Certainly, this film is a missed opportunity, suffering from the common production disease of playing it safe.

On the plus side, Leslie Cheung handles the role with a surprising amount of self-effacing good humor and charisma, a far cry from his de- cidedly wooden performances of past. And the film has terrific energy and pace. It also benefits from a true chem- istry between Cheung and Yuen.

So, it's a satire—it's a cheesy ro- mantic comedy—and it's just OK.

HEX (1980)
director: Gui Zhihong [Zhi-Hong]. Linda Chu·Wang Jung·Chen Szu-Chia· Han Kuo Tsai ★
Another man-fakes-death-and-comes- back-as-a-ghost story. Enough already!

HIDDEN HERO (1993)
director: Chang Cheh. Tu Yue Ming· Tung Chi Wah ★★
The legendary king of chop socky, di- rector **Chang Cheh**, is still making films—using the same style, the same techniques and, in this case, the same story. *Hidden Hero* is essentially a re- make of Chang's *Life Gamble* [aka *Life Combat*] (1978). It's the story of a boxer who retires to a quiet life until a gang of thieves force him to take a stand.

The original is better.

Jacky Cheung in *High Risk*

HIGH VOLTAGE (1995)
director: Leung Tung Ni. Donnie Yeh
·Yu Rong Guang ★★
There's some mildly entertaining gun-n-chase action in this predictable cop flick. But the story of a policeman (Donnie Yeh) who follows a criminal to another country after the bad guy murders his wife is nothing new.

And it's done nothing to further **Yu Rong Guang**'s popularity; but insiders are still predicting Yu will be the next **Jackie Chan**.

HIGH RISK (1995)
director: Wong Chin [Jing]. Jet Li·Jacky Cheung·Chingmy Yau·Valerie Chow· Charlie Yoeh (Young)·Billy Chow·Kelvin Wong ★★(★)
Obviously, for director/producer **Wong Ching [Jing]**, nothing is sacred. A few years ago, he was working with **Jackie Chan** in *City Hunter* (1993), patting him on the back and singing his praises. Now **Wong** is viciously lampooning the popular superstar. (Jackie Chan has publicly complained over the cinematic assault in this film.)

About the best thing that can be said about this movie is that, unlike other Wong Ching productions, it

does manage to keep on track; there's continuity and a sense of direction. The movie follows a linear story line, with few sidesteps for slapstick or out-of-character theatrics. But a bigger problem remains; besides the obvious attack against Jackie Chan, there's no reason for the film to exist. Wong Ching's entire purpose is to belittle the world-famous icon in as many ways as possible.

Jacky Cheung plays Jackie (or, rather, he's called Frankie, probably to avoid a lawsuit). Frankie is a mugging, hamming-it-up actor who constantly plants stories in the press about how he always does his own stunts, even though he really doesn't. The death-defying stuff is actually handled by a special team of private stunt doubles. The best is a man named Kit (**Jet Li**), who gravitated to the dangerous occupation after his wife and child were killed by a maniac (Kelvin Wong) in a bus bombing. Kit has worked himself into a superpowered athlete with amazing agility (not unlike Jet Li himself).

On the other hand, Frankie is a jellyfish, a coward who hoodwinked his legion of adoring fans. He uses his unwarranted popularity to become a boorish, arrogant, womanizing creep. In reality, Frankie is a wimp ready to turn tail and run at the first sign of trouble. Then, one day, an ambitious *Hard Copy* television reporter (**Chingmy Yau**) takes pictures of stuntman Kit as he secretly doubles for Frankie. She threatens to expose the scandal on her TV program, destroying the actor's credibility and, thus, his career.

Meanwhile, Frankie and his bodyguards make a public appearance at a snazzy jewelry show. But in typical *Die Hard* fashion, they suddenly find themselves in the middle of a robbery and hostage situation. Frankie freaks out; although he pretends to be in control, it's difficult for him to hide his cowardliness (i.e., Jackie Cheung doing his best Don Knotts imitation). But Kit realizes his nightmare has become a reality; the chief bad guy is the same bastard who killed his wife and kid. This turns the stunt double into a vengeful freedom fighter as he saves the hostages and manages to make Frankie look good at the same time.

HOCUS POCUS (1986)
aka **HOGUS POGUS**
director: **Chien Rue-Sheng.** Lam Ching Ying·Wei Dong·Alice Lau·Lo Ho Kai ★★
The stars of the **Mr. Vampire (Lam Ching Ying** and Wei Dong) series appear in this film about a traveling troupe of actors who perform traditional Chinese horror stories. Stage life and real life blend together when ghosts and spirits start causing trouble.

The choreographed rituals are captivating, but the story is notably weak. However, there's an outrageous subplot about a man urinating on a grave and an insulted ghost seeking revenge.

HOLY VIRGIN VERSUS THE EVIL DEAD (1990)
director: **Wang Zhen-Yi.** Donnie Yen ·Pauline Yeung·Sibelle Hu·Lam Wei Lan ★★★
Pauline Yeung is the Holy Virgin, a Cambodian princess of the High Wind Tribe (she's a mixture of **Wolf Devil Woman** and the cute urchin from **Magic of Spell**). With her magic sword, she confronts a brutal, bloodthirsty creature called the Moon Monster, who has captured explorers from Hong Kong.

HOLY WEAPON (1993)
aka **SEVEN MAIDENS**
director: **Wong Ching (Jing).** Michelle Yeoh·Simon Yam·Maggie Cheung·

Cheung Man·Sandra Ng·Carina Lau· Damian Lau·Do Do Cheng ★★★
After making countess lame-brained slapstick action comedies [namely **Fight Back to School, Royal Tramp**, and **Last Hero in China**], filmmaker **Wong Ching** has made a lame-brained slapstick action comedy that works. Maybe it's because he's not relying on the goofiness of an actor like **Stephen Chow** to keep the story moving.

This time the proceedings more closely resemble the kind of picture **Chu Yen Ping** might direct. Basically, it's far more imaginative. Plus there's a bevy of HK divas doing their best to keep your attention off the slapstick.

Holy Weapon (Damian Lau) is ready to marry Mon Ching Sze (**Michelle Yeoh**), but he's challenged to a duel by a deadly Japanese warrior, Super Sword (convincingly played by **Simon Yam**). The wedding is put on hold.

Desperate for super fighting skills, Holy Weapon takes a magic potion and defeats Super Sword. But the drug has altered his brain, and he's now a raging mad killer. Eventually he goes into hiding.

Three years later, evil Jap Super Sword returns with a vengeance. Mon Ching Sze seeks out her ex-fiancé and joins forces with him and a pack of strange characters (including **Maggie Cheung** as a runaway princess and **Cheung Man**, a female ninja who can transform into a black widow spider) to defeat the ferocious warrior.

HOME FOR AN INTIMATE GHOST (1990)
director: **Lam Yee Hon.** Charlie Cho· Go Mei Han·Lam Min Yuen·Miyuki Shoji ★½
Even the gratuitous nudity can't help this tediously slow sex comedy about the adulterous liaisons among the

members of an aristocratic family in ancient China.

Master Mandy (Charlie Cho) is trying to bump off his bitchy wife so he can marry a servant girl. He even tries to kill her by hiring a man with the world's hardest penis to fuck her to death. But she has a few tricks up her sleeve, too. Interestingly, none of them (nor anything else in this turkey) has anything to do with a ghost.

HONG KONG BUTCHER (1985)
director: Jeff Lau. ★
A maniac on the loose-type movie, but don't expect a Dr. Lamb. Mostly it's a police procedural film with occasional glimpses into the motivation of the killer. Despite the title, it's a decidedly bloodless adventure.

HONG KONG EVA (1992)
director: Wu Kuo Ren. Agnes Chan·Wong Oi Mei·Bill Tung ★★
Don't expect anyone named Eva in this sex/action romp featuring Bill Tung as a gentle ex-con who befriends a group of women and restores their faith in men. He helps them with their problems and beats up a lot of guys who assault them. Eventually he falls in love with Ann (Agnes Chan), after his daughter plays matchmaker.

It's all very low-key with moments of erotica when the story starts to drag too much. In a surprise ending, all the women are killed by a vicious gangster and our hero goes bonkers.

HONG KONG GODFATHER (1990)
director: Lo Lieh. Andy Lau·Alan Tang·Tommy Wong·Roy Cheung ★★★
Following a police raid on a dope factory, undercover narc Sam Lam (director **Lo Lieh**) is killed by a Triad icepick to the brain. The cops subsequently blame Mr. Koo, elderly godfather of the powerful Hung Ling Society, forcing him to flee HK.

In his absence, Koo's son Mark is appointed as new leader, but his position is jeopardized by the unstable antics of his hot-tempered brother, Mike (Tommy Wong). After all, as a gangster stated eloquently in **Ringo Lam**'s **Full Contact**: "Business is like shitting . . . smoothness is important."

Friction soon develops between the Hung Ling Society and another branch of the Triad network, the Hoi Lung Society, run by the devious Fred (Alan Tang), who by eliminating all opposition wishes to promote himself to wholesaler instead of merely a retailer in the lucrative local drug cartel. When Mark is murdered by Fred's men, his brother York (**Andy Lau**) is elected his successor in the Hung Ling empire, and all-out war threatens to erupt among the Triads.

Happily, *Hong Kong Godfather* contains not one shred of goofball humor. Scenes of brutality are often accompanied by soaring choral harmonies and hymnlike chanting. Extra poetry is gained with stylish but simple photography (e.g., hundreds of white prayer sheets fluttering in the wind at a mountaintop funeral; a spent cigarette tumbling slo-mo to the ground while emitting a cascade of delicate ash).

As with **John Woo**'s work, brutality is offset in perfect balance by inoffensive sentimentality. The film aptly ends on an ominous closeup of a flapping Mainland Chinese flag, illustrating how free enterprise in Hong Kong could be jeopardized by the Communist "corporate merger" of 1997.

HORRIBLE GHOST OF THE OLD HOUSE.
See *Tale of a Female Ghost*

HORROR INN (1986)
director: Yao Feng Pan. Cheung Sui Yuk·Yui Chung Yee ★
The owner of an out-of-the-way hotel is hiding his crazy wife in the basement.

His secret is discovered when one of the guests mysteriously disappears. Pretty terrible.

HOST FOR A GHOST (1988)
    aka **MOST FOR A GHOST**
director: Ding Shan-Yu. Danny Chan ·Pauline Wong·Kenny Bee ★
Here's a movie about a spirit who escapes the pain of Hell by agreeing to return among the living. The majority of the film concerns itself with the ghost's search for a perfect body to possess. Lots of lame and very tedious sight humor and slapstick.

HOT HOT AND POM POM (1992)
director: Joseph Cheung. Lam Ching Ying·Jacky Cheung·Bonnie Yu·Tung Wei ★★★
Here's a kick-ass, detonation-maximum gun-action fest camouflaged behind a terrible title. **Jackie Cheung** isn't as irritating as he tends to be. And **Lam Ching Ying** (the popular priest from **Mr. Vampire**) absolutely steals the show in his hard-nosed *Dirty Harry* supercop role.
    The final half-hour is among the best examples of bullet-frenzied may-

Jacky Cheung (middle) with Tung Wei and Bonnie Yu in *Hot Hot and Pom Pom*

hem ever captured on film. Bonnie Fu is knock-down sexy, in the same slutty way as she was in **Full Contact** (also 1992) as Virgin.

HOUSE OF THE LUTE (1979)
director: Lau Shinghon. Yum Tat Wah ·Kwan Koi Sham·Lok Bec Kay·Chan Lap Pun ★★
An elderly man marries a young woman and moves to the country. She gets sexually involved with the houseboy; together, they kill the old man. But he returns as a ghost. Atmospheric and cautious. Lots of time is spent waiting for things to happen.

HUMAN SKIN LANTERNS (1982)
    aka **HUMAN LANTERNS**
director: Sun Chung. Lo Lieh·Linda Chu· Lui Yung·Chen Kuan Tai·Lo Meng ★★★
A demented artist (played by martial arts star **Lo Lieh**, future director of **Black Magic with Butchery** and **Summons to Death**) kills young girls and skins them. He pours mercury into an incision on their foreheads, which allows the epidermis to peel more easily. The skins, in turn, are used to create beautiful, ornamental lanterns in the shape of the dead girls.
    This period horror tale is written by I Kuang, author of many "dark" Asian horror films, including **Black Magic 2: Revenge of the Zombies** and **Seventh Curse**. It also stars Linda Chu as the porcelain lady.

HYPOCRITE (1986)
director: Lo Wan Shing. Ha Suk Ling ·Chung Pui·Lau Wai Man·Cheng May Mei ★★
An abundance of subplots makes this film very difficult to follow; however, visually it is quite striking. Through a zealous use of light and shadowing, it is also very grotesque, especially the segments about a sadist (Chung Pui) and his captive coed.

I LOVE MARIA.
See *Roboforce*

I WANT TO GET EVEN (1988)
director: **Maman Firmanstan.** Eva
Arnez· Cliff Sangra·Dicky Zulkarnaen
·Wenna Roiser ★★½
Another violent Indonesian film, this
time dealing with a young virgin (Eva
Arnez) who is tricked into joining a
prostitution/slavery racket. After loads
of torture and sordid sex, she escapes
and (as the title indicates) gets revenge.
    Director **Firmanstan** made a simi-
lar S&M motion picture called **Hell
Hole.**

ICEMAN COMETH (1991)
    aka **TIME WARRIORS**
director: **Clarence Fok Yiu Leung.**
Yuen Biao·Maggie Cheung·Yuen
Wah ★★★★
An Asian mixture of *Time After Time* with
Iceman as frozen bodies (from the Ming
Dynasty) are found in the Himalaya
Mountains. After being whisked to
Hong Kong for examination, they are
thawed and rejuvenated.
    One of the icemen is a Royal
Guard policeman (Yuen Biao); the
other is an archvillain named San
(Yuen Wah) who had raped and mur-
dered his way across ancient China.
Their chase, once cut short by a
mishap in the mountains (hundreds of
years earlier), now continues in Hong
Kong.
    Along the way, the hero is be-
friended by Polla **(Maggie Cheung),** a
prostitute who suddenly finds herself in
the middle of the perilous situation.
She adds a level of charm to the
breakneck action.

IMP (1981)
director: **Dennis Yu.** Charlie Chin·
Dorthy Yu·Yue Hua·Kent Cheng ★★½
Graphically detailed surgery, zombies, and gory deaths in another *Rose-*

mary's Baby-type story. Familiar plot;   **105**
unique approach.

IMPETUS FIRE (1988)
director: **Hwa Hu [Mok Hung].** Dong
Hoi·Choi Fun·Sui Lee·Ding Ho Dui
★★½
The rating is given with reservations.
Not everyone will be amused (or entertained) by this controversial Filipino/
Chinese production. However, director
Hwa Hu's excessive disregard for con-
ventions (the opening scene in a dance
hall grinds on relentlessly for 10 excru-
ciatingly boring minutes in a demented
vision of *American Bandstand*) plus an
unsuspected ultraviolent conclusion put
this film in a class by itself.
    Girls returning home from a high
school dance find themselves involved
in perverse sexual games, first with
each other and then with the yearbook
photographer **(Dong Hoi).** As they slip
deeper into peer-pressure depravity,
their behavior becomes more and more
psychotic, until Choi Fun takes a decidedly vicious revenge. Very X-rated,
sleazy but grudgingly fascinating.

IMPETUS FIRE 2 (1990)
director: **Hwa Hu (Ken Leung).** Sha
Ky· Sui Man·Yeung Jing·Yen Shing Yin
*a rating is insignificant; insert your
own*
If you're a fan of **Impetus Fire,** then
you have an idea of what to expect
this time around. Likewise, if you
hated *Impetus Fire,* you know to avoid
this one.
    Similar to #1, the plot is wafer-
thin. In fact, an argument could be
made for the complete absence of
plot. Two guys and two girls get together and visit an erotic entertainer,
who performs for them in her living
room. The show makes them hot. They
fondle one another and eventually en-
gage in some very uninteresting sex.
Graphic hard-core sex, but still uninteresting.

Enough of the niceties . . . the real reason this film has become a cult fave is the "show" itself. If you want to see an attractive woman do outlandish things (unprintable things) with her genitalia, don't even think twice. This is the show of shows. (The film is also known as *A Beautiful Woman and Her 18 Tricks*.)

IN BETWEEN LOVES (1990)
director: Chuen Yium San. Alfred Cheung ·Maggie Cheung ★½
A taxi driver becomes obsessed with a female TV news reporter in this low-key Asian version of *The Fan*.

IN THE BLOOD (1988)
director: Andy Lau. Andy Lau·Wu Ma·Corey Yuen· Chin Sui Ho ★
Actor **Andy Lau** directs this slow wanna-be-an-action-film about an accident-prone policeman. His friend **Samo Hung** plays a waiter in a cameo part. But nothing seems to click.

IN THE LINE OF DUTY 1 (1986)
aka **ROYAL WARRIORS**
director: David Chung. Michelle Khan· Hiriyuki (Henry) Sanada· Michael Wong·Chan Wai Man ★★★★

IN THE LINE OF DUTY 2 (1987)
aka **MIDDLE MAN**
director: Cha Chuen Yee [Cha Fu-Yi]. Cynthia Khan·David Wu·Billy Chow· Chris Lee ★★★

IN THE LINE OF DUTY 3 (1988)
aka **FORCE OF THE DRAGON**
director: Arthur Wong/Brandy Yuen. Cynthia Khan·Hiroshi Fujioka·Dick Wei·Michiko Nishiwaki ★★★★

IN THE LINE OF DUTY 4 (1989)
aka **WITNESS**
director: Yuen Woo Ping. Cynthia Khan·Donnie Yen·Michael Wong·Michael Woods ★★★½

IN THE LINE OF DUTY 5: A BEGINNING
aka **QUEENS HIGH** (1991)
director: Chris Lee. Cynthia Khan· Simon Yam·Ricky Hung·Ken Tsang· Billy Chow ★★★
It's easy to see why this series continues to be one of the most popular among the stiff competition of Hong Kong action flicks. It gives the audience exactly what it wants.

The saga showcases two actresses, **Michelle Khan [Yeoh Chu Kheng]** (in the first) and **Cynthia Khan [Yang Li Chiang]** (in the remaining installments); both ladies consistently prove that it's possible to kick some kung fu ass and look cute at the same time. This series is blatantly straightforward regarding its sledge-hammer intention. Pure and simple, this is exploitation. Action for action's sake. The plot is little more than an excuse for the mayhem.

Interestingly, despite the traditional animosity between Japan and China, two of the films (#1 and #3) feature Japanese characters in pivotal roles. In both cases, as male detectives. Hiriyuki [Henry] Sanada costars in #1 as Peter Yamamoto, a policeman who retires to Hong Kong with his wife and child, only to have his family killed by a fanatical terrorist. In #3, similar to *Black Rain*, Hiroshi Fujioka plays a Jap cop who arrives in Hong Kong to avenge the death of his partner.

Although the 1990 version (*In the Line of Duty 5: The Beginning* aka *Queens High*) is an extravagant heroic bloodshed flick, it's a sequel in name only. Cynthia Khan (looking great in a very kinky outfit, complete with thigh-high boots) takes over the family organization after her father and husband, two notorious gangsters, are killed.

There is much confusion over this series—specifically, regarding which films are (and are not) part of it. Some of this is caused by title changes in various international markets (e.g., Bo Ho Films has rereleased #2, also called *Middle Man* in some Asian countries) under the *In the Line of Duty #5* banner.

The situation is further complicated by the existence of a similar series called **Yes! Madam** that at various times also stars both Michelle Khan (**Yes! Madam 1**) and Cynthia Khan (**Yes, Madam '92: A Serious Shock**). Plus, using the above-mentioned *Middle Man* example, in some countries this film is known as *Yes! Madam #5*. It also appears that *In the Line of Duty 4* has been released some places as *Yes! Madam #4*. And some sources claim *Yes! Madam 1* (aka Police Assassin) is actually *In the Line of Duty 1* with *Royal Warriors (#1)* becoming the second in this series. But it should be mentioned that the international English-language print viewed for the purpose of this book clearly credits *Royal Warriors* as *In the Line of Duty 1*.

For the record: Cynthia Khan's *Forbidden Arsenal* was released throughout Europe as *In the Line of Duty 6*. And Hong Kong-based Sil-Metropole Organization has announced the release of future *In the Line of Duty* films, but to avoid legal problems, they plan to call it *In Line of Duty*.

INCORRUPTIBLE (1992)
director: Raymond Leung. Simon Yam·Anita Yuen·Alan Tang·Carrie Ng
★★★½
Big-budget production based on the true story of police inspector Charles Lee (Alan Tang) and his special anti-triad branch of the Hong Kong Force (established in 1956). **Anita Yuen** plays his wife. And **Simon Yam** once again shines as the gangster kingpin.

1992 was a good year for Simon Yam. Besides this film he also made *Dr. Lamb, Full Contact,* and *Run and Kill.*

INFRA-MAN (1976)
aka SUPER INFRA-MAN
director: Hua Shan. Danny Lee· Wang Shieh·Yuen Man Tzu·Terry Liu
★★
Obviously inspired by the Japanese *Ultraman* (1966), this HK solar-powered superhero **(Danny Lee)** defends the world from an army of kung fu fighting aliens led by the Dragon Princess (Terry Liu). Inoffensive fun, in a Saturday morning sort of way.

INHERITOR OF KUNG FU.
See *Heroic Ones*

INNOCENT NYMPHS.
See *Blood of an Indian Fetish Cult*

INSANITY (1993)
director: Leung Siu Hung. Simon Yam·Cathy Chow·Raymond Wong
★★½
Take a moment and imagine this. You're a woman, alone in your new suburban house—waiting for your husband to come home from work. A thunderstorm is raging outside. You feel uneasy. You can't fight a dreadful feeling. It's like something awful is going to happen. This afternoon you found out that you're pregnant. Maybe that's why you're on edge. Perhaps everything is really okay. But yet. . . .

Suddenly, a psychotic killer breaks into your house. He has just killed your husband and tracked you down from the ID in the wallet. He thinks you're his cheating wife. He wants to kill you. And he's got all night to do it.

You just imagined the plot of *Insanity,* another entry in the growing list of new wave roughies coming out of Hong Kong. It stars **Simon Yam,** currently making quite a name for himself in one twisted flick after another (from

Dr. Lamb to **Full Contact** to **Run and Kill)**. **Cathy Chow** is incredible as the trapped housewife. And producer/writer Raymond Wong plays her husband.

Add an extra star to the rating if you're a fan of sadistic horror cinema. They made this one for you.

INSPECTOR WEARS A SKIRT (1988)
aka **TOP SQUAD**
director: **Wellson Chin (Jackie Chan)**. Sibelle Hu·Cynthia Rothrock·Billy Lau·Ann Bridgewater·Regina Kent·Sandra Ng·Bill. Tung·Hui Ying Hung ★★½

INSPECTOR WEARS A SKIRT 2 (1989)
aka **TOP SQUAD 2**
director: **Wellson Chin (Jackie Chan)**. Sibelle Hu·Amy Yip·Billy Lau·Ann Bridgewater·Jeff Falcon ★★★
Jackie Chan produced (and reportedly directed) both of these girls-with-guns action flicks starring **Sibelle Hu** as a no-nonsense commander of a female S.W.A.T team. The lethal ladies in her charge include Cynthia Rothrock, Anne Bridgewater, Regina Kent, Sandra Ng, and (in #2) busty Amy Yip.

The plot for #1 centers around a police tournament between the male and female members of the special forces teams (the girls win) and the capture of a notorious gang of thieves.

In #2, Sibelle falls in love with Kan (Billy Lau), the leader of the male S.W.A.T. unit. But the real action comes when the thieves break out of jail, with Sibelle and her battling babes in hot pursuit.

Many critics consider these as lesser films, merely female versions of Chan's **Project A** movies. Stylistically, they are very similar, and Jackie used the same *Project A* sets for most of the action scenes. But, if you like girls-n-guns action, don't miss 'em.

INTO THE FIRE (1989)
director: **Lo Kien**. Chin Siu Hao·Ngai Sing ★
A very tired story of two buddies on the lam after being wrongly accused of killing some cops. Lackluster direction and the absence of the patented HK hyperaction make this film a chore to plow through.

INTO THE NIGHT (1989)
director: **Lu Jian Ming**. Dick Wei·Ao Cai Ling·Wu Ma ★★½
This is another man-comes-back-from-the-grave-to-seek-revenge tale, gone haywire. It starts out as a simple story. Man (Dick Wei) comes home and finds his wife, (Ao Cai Ling) in bed with a friend; the two lovers kill him and bury his body in the garden. But he returns as a ghost.

Now here's where it gets complicated. The wife and boyfriend rent the house to another girl; meanwhile, the ghost enters the body of a house-painter, who freaks out and kills his partner. He is arrested for the murder, but manages to get away from the policeman. He returns to the house, which is now occupied by the new girl. They fall in love, but their romance is interrupted by the vengeful policeman (also now possessed!), who is angry that his prisoner had escaped.

The whole thing escalates into a gory bloodbath wherein everybody (the wife, the lover, the killer, the cop; but not the girl) is killed.

INVINCIBLE (1984)
aka **GENERAL INVINCIBLE**
director: **Chang Ling**. Chang Ling·Adam Cheng·Ting Feng ★★½
An action/adventure movie with fantasy overtones from alluring **Chang Ling** (alias **Pearl Cheong**). Great sets and impressive sword play. Plus Chang!

INVINCIBLE (1993)
director: **Luo Shun Chuan** and **Lin Shing Lu.** Wang Jie·Ke Shou-Liang·Cheung Man·Billy Banks ★★
The night before the Gulf War in 1991, unified forces of France and Hong Kong sent Foreign Legion troops to attack Iraq. Their goal was to save the royal family of Kuwait. This is the story (told mostly in flashback) of the HK criminals who became mercenary heroes in the Middle East. Unnecessarily long and labored.

IRON ANGELS.
See *Angel*

IRON ANGELS 2.
See *Angel 2*

IRON MONKEY (1993)
director: **Yuen Woo Ping.** Donnie Yen·Yu Rong Kwong·Jean Wang·Tsang Sze Man ★★½
Another historical adventure/fantasy produced by **Tsui Hark,** this time dealing with unrest in Chekiang during the Ding Dynasty. Donnie Yen is Wong Kai Ying, an innocent fighter forced to capture the revolutionary Robin Hood bandit, Iron Monkey, who is hiding behind the mask of a doctor **(Yu Rong-Guang).**
Stylish kung fu and amazing wire stunts orchestrated by veteran Yuen Woo Ping (best remembered for directing **Jackie Chan's** *Drunken Master* [1978]), but, overall, this one is suggested for fans of the genre. Also starring Tsang Sze Man and Jean Wang (from *Once upon a Time in China #4* and *Swordsman 3*).

ISLAND OF FIRE (1991)
director: **Chu Yin Ping.** Jackie Chan·Tony Leung [Chiu Wai]·Samo Hung·Andy Lau·Wang Yu·Tuo Chung Hua·Kao Hsiung ★★★★
A top-notch cast **(Jackie Chan, Tony Leung [Chiu Wai], Samo Hung,**

Andy Lau, and **Wang Yu)** add additional firepower to this contemporary prison-cum-heroic-bloodshed film directed by veteran filmmaker **Chi Yin Ping** (of *Golden Queen Commando* fame).
With similarities to the Japanese movie *Death Shadows,* this one tells the story of a warden who fakes death certificates of condemned convicts, recruiting them into an army of secret assassins against untouchable criminals.
The crackerjack ending finds Jackie, Samo, and Andy in an ultraviolent war against a drug lord's militia, John Woo fashion. Very different for Jackie Chan. . . .

ISLAND WARRIORS (1984)
director: **Chu Yin Ping.** Linda Young·Yun Chung·Yu Feng·Wong Tao ★★★
There's an island populated only by women; it is invaded by pirates but the females remain victorious. The women take captives. Some of the men are experimented on (castrations, etc.) and some are experimented with (copulation, etc.). The whole thing ends, after a major conflict, with the two sexes living together in harmony. By the way, there are musical numbers (!?!).

ISLE OF FANTASY (1984)
director: **Chien Yueh Chuen.** Raymond Wong·Loletta Lee ★½
A silly film about a group of Girl Scouts trapped on a desert island, with drug smugglers and a giant ape.

JAILHOUSE EROS (1989)
director: **Wong Ching (Jing)** with **Ha Sau Hin.** Amy Yip · Richard Ng · Loletta Lee ·Fong Tsui Feng ★★½
All the usual babes-behind-bars perils are in this film, plus (thanks to a Devil-worshipping cellmate) there are ghosts and *jiangshi* (hopping zombies) along for the ride.

JIANG-HU [RIVER-LAKE]: BETWEEN LOVE AND GLORY.
See *Bride with the White Hair*

JULY SPIRIT (1986)
director: Wang Chung Kuan. Yien Ping Chun·Woo Yan Man·Shek Fung· Tien Ping Chun ★
A young couple visits a house haunted by the ghost [vampire] of a criminal (Yien Ping Chun) freshly executed in prison. It's a horrendous script, made even more unbearable by the sloppy camera-work.

JUMPING ASH (1983)
director: Ronnie Yu. Siao Fong Fong ·Chen Hui Min·Chen Sing ★★
Grinning Tiger (Siao Fong Fong) leaves his gangland home in Amsterdam. He goes to Hong Kong to fight the powerful drug-trafficking cartel responsible for his brother's death. Here's an early example of a HK gun movie from one of the genre's best directors. Interestingly, Ronnie Yu later shot *China White* (1989) in Amsterdam's Chinatown.

Yuen Biao in *Kickboxer*

JUST HEROES (1989)
director: John Woo. Danny Lee· Stephen Chow·John Chiang·Chan Koon Tai· Kelly Cho·Wu Ma·David Chaing ★★
Similar to the other **John Woo** gangster films, but this one suffers from the absence of strong characters, coupled with a very contrived script. There are wagonloads of "cool" macho posturing, plus typical melodramatic tirades about loyalty, but most of it seems like lip service.
The barren plot (about the Hong Kong Mafia in shambles after the mysterious slaying of its leader) has more than the usual amount of excessive gunplay. But, unfortunately, the ignition spark is missing.

JUSTICE WOMEN.
See *Midnight Angel*

KICKBOXER (1993)
director: Wu Ma. Yuen Biao·Lu Hsiu Ling·Wu Ma·Yen Shi Kwan·Yuen Wah ★★½
A contemporary variation on the he-insulted-our-school motif, as **Yuen Biao** (charming, as always) fights to save his reputation and the good name of the Wong Fei Hong school after officials discover opium in his baggage.

KICKBOXER TEARS (1992)
director: William Su. Moon Lee· Yukari Oshima·Billy Chow·Mark Cheng ★
An attempt to recapture the flavor of the early chop socky flicks, but seriously marred by amateur direction and a ramshackled plot. Even **Moon Lee** and **Yukari Oshima** (yes, pitted against each other again) can't save this film about a kickboxing school facing foreclosure.

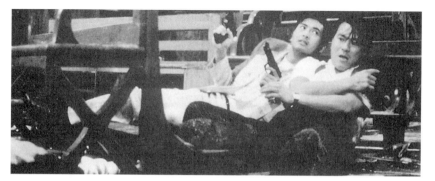

Danny Lee (R) with Chow Yun-Fat in *The Killer*

THE KILLER (1989)
director: John Woo. Chow Yun-Fat·
Danny Lee·Sally Yeh (Yip)·Chu Kong·
Shing Fui On ★★★★
Hong Kong's #1 action director, **John Woo** (now making films in the United States) delivers his most famous movie, an explosive no-holds-barred story about an impossible triangle involving a tough cop **(Danny Lee)**, a blind cabaret singer **(Sally Yeh [Yip])**, and a professional hitman, Jeff **(Chow Yun-Fat).**

This is a very violent film. It is extraordinarily brutal, a constant swirl of gun blasts and bloody mayhem within a bittersweet tale of love and loyalty. Most HK fans have already seen this film, probably numerous times. At the risk of being redundant, the plot deals with Jeff's plight after he accidentally blinds a nightclub singer during a particularly nasty gun battle. He vows to take one more job (the killing of a corrupt business tycoon) so he can amass enough money for an operation to restore the girl's sight. But the triad who hired him has a different idea. Since he's planning to get out of the business, they decide to kill him instead of pay him. Meanwhile, a hard-nosed cop is on Jeff's trail and everything culminates with an explosive showdown inside a church.

Initially, the film ran 142 minutes, 35 minutes longer than the current

commercial version. Woo himself made the edits shortly after the film opened theatrically in Hong Kong. The original version contained more footage dealing with a complicated subplot surrounding another hitman **(Chu Kong),** Jeff's closest friend, working for the same triad. Most of that performance is missing from the finished print.

Publicly, John Woo has praised French filmmaker Jean-Pierre Melville, crediting the director as the one who influenced him the most. Woo has also mentioned that Melville's movie *Le Samurai* (1978) is the primary inspiration for *The Killer.* Amazingly, *The Killer* is a virtual clone of that film, with Chow Yun-Fat copying Alain Delon's mannerisms (double-fisted gun action) and even his wardrobe (including the white gloves). The plot, also dealing with a hitman who accidentally blinds a nightclub singer, is close enough to be considered a remake rather than an inspiration.

KILLER AND THE COP (1992)
director: Pierre Yau. Wai Tin Chi·
Sheh Sau·Y. H.Chan ★½
Shot-on-video crap masquerading as a film. UK cop, Ho To Wang (Wai Tin Chi), is on the trail of a counterfeiting ring run by a printing tycoon in Hong Kong.

KILLER ANGELS (1989)
director: Lui Jun-Gu. Moon Lee·Lau Jia Hui ★★★½
An excellent *Angel* rip-off as these three "Blue Angels" (including tremendous **Moon Lee [Lee Choi Fung]***;* don't miss her great nightclub scene) wipe out the entire Mafia gang when they take on a mission protecting a former mob member (Lau Jia Hui) who is ready to turn state's evidence.

At least 60 bad guys dance the blood ballet during an incredible final half-hour of nonstop gunplay and ka-boom explosions.

KILLER LADY (1993)
director: Cheung Ren Jie. Sylvia Chang· Lin Wei·Shia Kuang Li· Charles Cao ★★
A young girl, Show Show **(Sylvia Chang),** sees her parents accidentally killed at the hands of an inexperienced cop. Fifteen years later, she masterminds a sting against a greedy triad boss (Lin Wei). Show Show plans to use the money to level an assault against the police.

Besides being overly melodramatic, the film suffers from confused characterizations dealing with hidden identities and improbable coincidences. As it turns out, the cop who killed Show Show's parents is the father of her best friend, Cheng-May (Shia Kuang Li)—and she is, secretly, an undercover policewoman.

Gibberish nonsense with moments of kick-ass chop socky action. Also starring Charles Cao as Show Show's newspaper reporter friend.

KILLER SNAKES
director: Kuei Chin Hung. Kan Kuo-Liang· Li Lin Lin·Chen Chun ★★★
Chi Long (Kan Kuo Liang) has a miserable life. He's a loner, a society misfit. He's constantly the butt of a bully's jokes. The boy is always getting beaten up, harassed, and robbed. Women despise him; employers take advantage of him. No one cares about Chi Long.

He has two obsessions—fantasizing about women being tortured and spending time with his only friends, snakes. Soon he discovers that he can combine both activities and live very happily.

A disturbing, mean-spirited film from the Shaw Brothers with graphic violence, sleazy S&M sex, and wagonloads of slithery serpents. Also starring Li Lin Lin and Chen Chun; written by HK horror veteran I Kuang [**Seventh Curse, Black Magic,** and **Human Skin Lanterns**]. Director Kuei Chin Hung is also responsible for the depraved **Bamboo House of Dolls.**

KILLER'S BLUES (1990)
director: Raymond Lee. Ti Lung· Olivia Cheng·Kwan Hoi Sang·Fennie Yuen ★★★
More than anything else, this film is a tremendous vehicle for **Ti Lung,** perhaps one of HK's most underrated actors. He brings a worldly charisma to his role of Ming Lo, an aging gangster torn between two warring factions within the same mob. Ming is a high-ranking hitman who goes to prison in 1975 after killing an informant. Before serving time, he arranges for his girlfriend, Wai **(Olivia Cheng),** to adopt the victim's 4-year-old daughter, Shuet.

Upon his release in 1989, Ming finds himself at odds with the younger factions of the triad as he assumes the right-hand position to the elderly boss (Kwan Hoi Sang). Further, he is constantly reminded of his bloody past by the presence of the now 18-year-old Shuet (Fennie Yuen). Ming decides to retire from the triad and marry Wai. But, in a nasty-edged, downbeat ending, the boss is murdered and Ming finds that history has a peculiar way of repeating itself.

Written by successful Golden Harvest boss, Raymond Chow, this film is an impressive heroic bloodshed pic with an effective bittersweet tone.

KILLER'S LOVE (1992)
director: Jamie Luk. Simon Yam·Do Do Cheng ★★

What happens when a studio hires a romantic comedy director to make a heroic bloodshed movie?

If you're really curious, see this film. Director **Jamie Luk,** best known for films like **My Will . . . I Will** (1986), has made a movie that vacillates wildly from lighthearted romance to bloody carnage, often without the conviction of either genre.

Do Do Cheng is a country schoolteacher who takes in a mysterious boarder **(Simon Yam).** Of course, they fall in love. And, of course, he's hiding a dangerous secret. This handsome Romeo is actually a former hitman trying to retire from his life of crime. But, there's a vengeance-seeking psycho on his trail. And, well, it doesn't take much to figure out what happens next. Does it?

KILLERS MUST DIE (1990)
director: Cheng Siu Keung. Siu Yu Fei·Mak Tak Lo·Chow Chuan Yumi ★½

A shabby attempt to capitalize on the slick Hong Kong gangster films. But the movie lacks style. And a budget.

A Mafia hitman, Chi Fei (Siu Yu Fei) avenges the death of his godfather boss. During the execution, he meets (and falls in love with) a Japanese bohemian artist named Yin Lian (Chow Chuan Yumi), who helps him escape from the clutches of the mob.

Just don't make me sit through it again. . . .

KILLER'S ROMANCE (1990)
director: Philip Kao (Kao Li). Simon Yam·Joey Wang·Luk Cheung ★★★
Simon Yam (from **A Bullet in the Head, Dr. Lamb,** and **Run and Kill**) is

Nidaine, the son of a Japanese underworld kingpin. When his father is killed by a rival Chinese gang, Nidaine takes revenge. Like **Dragon from Russia,** the story is loosely based on the popular Japanese comic book, *Crying Freeman.*

Also starring sexy **Joey Wang [Wong]** as the girl who witnesses one of Nidaine's deadly hits and finds herself in a compromising position.

KING OF BEGGARS (1993)
director: Gordon Chan Kar Sheng. Stephen Cow·Ng Man Tat ★★★

If you're a **Stephen Chow** fan, then consider this a 4-star film, because without a doubt it's the best thing he's ever done. Chan (Stephen Chiauo [Chiau Sing Chi]) gets involved in a martial arts tournament for the wrong reason. Not for honor or sport, but because a pretty rebel girl has promised to share her bed with him if he wins.

Well, he wins, but then he loses on a technicality, and he's banished from the town (because the corrupt bosses have been looking for an opportunity to get rid of him and his meddlesome father). Then he befriends the beggars living in squalor outside the city. Soon Chan finds himself appointed their leader and they all rally against the town bosses.

Ultimately, this is a comedy. But unlike Chow's other films, here is a comedy that's funny because it's both intelligent and satirical—not because it relies on pratfalls and food fights.

KING OF WESTERN CHU.
See *Great Conqueror's Concubine*

KUNG FU CULT MASTER (1993)
director: Wong Ching [Jing]. Jet Li·Chingamy Yau·Samo Hung ★★★

Perhaps, director **Wong Ching**'s best film to date. It's still flawed, but compared to the crap he's usually churning out, this one is a masterpiece.

Martial arts master **Jet Li** plays a young man who is torn between avenging the death of his parents and helping the killers in a battle against a far greater enemy. A fantasy (with horrific overtones) chop socky actioner with enough kinky subplots to gain cult status.

KUNG FU VAMPIRE BUSTER.
See *Mr. Vampire: New Mr. Vampire*

KUNG FU WONDER CHILD (1989)
director: Lee Tso Nam. Lin Hsiao Lan
·Yukari Oshima·Jack Long·Chang Shan ★★½
You'll find everything in this film! Magic spells, zombies, human skin masks, barbaric magicians, flying kung fu action, irreverent humor. Yes, you'll find everything that puts an Asian fantasy movie in a class by itself. Plus, as a bonus, this frenzied motion picture features two popular divas: the sumptuously sexy **Yukari Oshima** (star of dozens of fighting-female-flicks like **Midnight Angel, Final Run, Death Triangle,** et al.) and frolicsome Lin Hsiao Lan (see **Magic of Spell, Heroic Fight,** and **Magic Warriors**). But the problem with the film, and others of the same ilk, is it tends to be insultingly juvenile with more than its fair share of sophomoric bathroom gags and goofy silliness.

KUNG FU ZOMBIE (1983)
director: Hwa I Hung. Billy Chong· Kwon Young Moon·Chaing Tao·Cheng Kay Ying ★★
There's lots of great stuff in this movie. Unfortunately, it all takes place in either the first ten minutes or in the last half-hour. Forget the middle (take a nap), but don't miss the zenith, over-the-top fight scene between **Billy Chong** and the ferocious zombie.

LABORATORY OF THE DEVIL.
See *Man Behind the Sun 2: Laboratory of The Devil*

LADY AVENGER.
See *Revenge for a Rape*

LADY GHOST AND THE CANNIBAL GIRL (1988)
director: Htuhan So. ★
Terrible. Another unwatchable bore from Thailand. There's not even a touch of nudity to save it; strangely, the heroine even wears her clothes while taking a bath!
Aulhe decides to attend a festival with her friends instead of taking care of her sick mother. When she returns, her mom is dead. Aulhe is cursed, her spirit possessed, and eventually she has to fight the "cannibal girl" to become part of the human race again.

LADY IN BLACK (1986)
director: Sun Chung. Lin Ching Hsia· Tony Leung [Chiu Wai] ★★★
A quality melodramatic tale of deception and betrayal with a vicious conclusion, directed by **Sun Chung** (best known for **Human Skin Lanterns**).
Lin Ching Hsia is May Fung, a woman who embezzles $500,000 (Hong Kong money; $35,000 USA) from her job and gives it to her husband Chan Sang **(Tony Leung),** who claims to have an opportunity to invest in a no-risk, get-rich-quick scheme. In reality, he owes the money in gambling debts and has no intention of paying back his wife. Instead, he tosses her into the ocean and reports it as a suicide. He feigns innocence when the police investigate. But May survives. She is rescued by a Vietnamese refugee boat. And, in a style similar to the HK ghost/revenge stories, May seeks and finds her vengeance.

LADY SUPER COP.
See *Supercop: Female*

LADY TIGER (1989)

director: Ry-Man. ★½ or ★★★

Depending on your reasons for liking Asian cinema, you will find this film either intolerable or incredible. So pick your own rating.

As it turns out, the new neighbors, a brother and sister, are capable of turning into tigers when they get sexually excited or are physically threatened.

No, they don't become real tigers. They grow fangs and claws. And they growl a lot. But they keep their general appearance (except at the end, when the girl, Tucan Tia, becomes a genuine tiger and is shipped to a zoo).

However, they are vicious. And they graphically kill a lot of people during the film, including the doctor's wife. Eventually, Doc falls in love with Tucan and tries to protect her from the pissed-off villagers. He rescues the girl from a crucifixion and (as already mentioned) has her committed to a zoo, which he visits lethargically daily.

LADY WOLF (1991)

director: Richard X. C. Tung. Joey Wang·Wu Ma ★★★

Similar in look and style to the Jean Rollin vampire films, this Asian opus tells the story of three beautiful female werewolves (led by **Joey Wang [Wong]**) and their vengeance against Hsi Wei, a fur merchant and his ancestors. Prolific character actor Wu Ma (Ng Ma Wu) makes an appearance as a relentless hunter who has spent years tracking down the creatures, but never quite catching them.

Certainly, these are not werewolves in the traditional Western sense. Rather, they are gorgeous seductresses who transform into white-haired, fanged creatures (with tails) at the moment of attack. Usually during sex. You'll never think of farts the same way after viewing this film.

LASER MAN (1986)

director: Peter Wang (with Tsui Hark). Tony Leung [Chiu Wai]·Sally Yeh (Yip)·Maryanne Urbano·Marc Itayshi ★★★½

When is a Hong Kong movie not a Hong Kong movie? This film is certainly an enigma.

It was shot in New York and lensed by Ernest Dickerson (the talented cameraman-turned-director who rose to notoriety as Spike Lee's cinematographer and later found fame as an action director [i.e. *Nowhere to Run, Tales from the Crypt*]).

The music is performed by Japanese composer Ryuichi Sakamoto. **Peter Wang** is the writer and director (with producer **Tsui Hark**). And it features a collection of international actors including Maryanne Urbano and Joan Copeland, plus HK faves **Tony Leung [Chiu Wai]** and **Sally Yeh** not to mention Marc Itayshi, a Japanese actor who plays a Chinese scientist named Arthur Weiss.

The entire production has a mixed pedigree for sure. But the result is a very entertaining black comedy with a tongue-in-cheek philosophy: "Modern technology kills." Those words are prophetically uttered by police Lieutenant Lu (played by director Peter Wang) while he investigates an accidental laboratory death.

Arthur Weiss's assistant (Willie Reale) had been killed instantly during a disastrous laser experiment (all that remains is the man's penis!) Of course, Arthur loses his job. But then, it appears his luck has changed when he's hired by a mysterious businessman who seems more than casually interested in the laser experiments. . . .

LAST BLOOD

aka **12 HOURS OF TERROR** (1991)

director: **Wong Ching (Jing)**. Alan Tam·Andy Lau·Eric Tsang·Leung Kar Yan ★★½

An ultraviolent crime tale as a fascist Japanese Mafia group tries to take over in Hong Kong. First it's massacre time between the two underworld gangs. And then with the Hong Kong police, led by popular **Andy Lau.** The biggest problem is filmmaker **Wong Ching (Jing).** His everything-but-the-kitchen-sink approach is, at the very least, distracting.

LAST BREATH (1989)
director: Lee He (He Chi Chiang). Wo Chen Chu·Chung Han·Chen San ·Woo Wai ★★½
It's 1972 in Vietnam. The movie opens with Vietnamese men applying for positions in the United States Army, followed by a brief look at their boot-camp experiences. Quickly, they find themselves on a tour of duty. After an exploitive experience with Saigon whores, the men are captured by the Viet Cong. For the remainder of the film, this special unit is viciously tortured at the hands of the demented leader, Master Kong (Wo Chen Chu).

LAST DUEL (1989)
director: Fan Tsui Fen [Tommy Fan]. Alex Man·Rosamund Kwan ★★
Does the end justify the means? Suen (played by Alex Man) seems to think so. He's imprisoned after being framed by a corrupt policeman. When Suen gets out of prison, he decides to take revenge on the cop, now a high-ranking detective, by tormenting and raping the policeman's girlfriend. Soon he's burning down the cop's house. And then, he cold-bloodedly kills a street criminal, and plants evidence implicating the detective. It all ends in a bloody free-for-all, with no one left to tell tales in the morning. If there's a point to be made by director **Fan,** it's difficult to find it in the murky story line.

LAST HERO IN CHINA (1993)
director: Wong Ching (Jing). Jet Li· Gordon Liu·Cheung Man·Lau Kar Fei ★★½
Jet Li left **Tsui Hark**'s *Once upon a Time in China* series, taking the Wong Fei Hong character with him to a rival studio.
This story, void of the political baggage that weighs down the **Once upon a Time in China** saga, finds hero Wong Fei Hong moving his school (he can't pay the escalating rent) to another region in China. But soon he butts heads with a corrupt police chief (chop socky kingpin Gorden Liu [Liu Chia Hui]) when he discovers a female slavery ring operating under his nose. **Cheung Man** plays a girl looking for her missing sister.
Most of the action is played straight, but director **Wong Ching** [*Fight Back to School, City Hunter, Royal Tramp*, etc.] can't seem to resist the goofy stuff. Wong Fei Hong dressed like a chicken, clucking up a storm during the final conflict, is downright embarrassing.

LAST HURRAH FOR CHIVALRY (1982)
director: John Woo. Wei Pai·Liv Sung Ren·Lee Hoi San ★★
Few people would bother with this martial arts, chop socky flick if it weren't for **John Woo**'s name in the credits. It's better than some of his other early attempts (e.g., *Plain Jane to the Rescue* and *Hand of Death*), but the stone-faced hero, **Wei Pai,** doesn't spark any charisma. And some of the eccentric kung fu sequences (Wei Pai's match with the Sleeping Wizard, a master who fights while asleep) are below par.

LEE ROCK (1991)
director: Larry Lau [Lau Ku Chang]. Andy Lau·Cheung Man ★½
Another **Andy Lau** police action/drama. And it's as nondescript as Lau himself (quite a disappointment from

director **Larry Lau,** who shined with **Gangs** and Cageman).

A *Prince of the City* opus dealing with corruption in the police force, as witnessed by vice detective Lee Rock (Andy Lau). It's difficult to understand why this straight-arrow cop marries the daughter of a Mafia boss in the first place, except she's great-looking **Cheung Man.** But, anyway, that's when his problems start.

Simply, the film is talky and pretentious. Plus there's an irritating cliff-hanger ending that would indicate a Part 2 is coming, whether we want it or not.

LEECH GIRL (1969)
director: Jin Weng/Lin Yixiu. Ma Shayue·Jin Luhua·Wang Kunseng ★★
An early Hong Kong film that suffers from poor filming techniques and off-camera action. The title comes from the fact that a magician force-feeds poisonous leeches to the heroine in hopes of driving her insane, thus keeping her from marrying the chief's son.

Don't expect **Centipede Horror.** The FX are implied, not seen.

LEGACY OF RAGE (1987)
director: Ronnie Yu. Brandon Lee· Michael Wong·Regina Kent·Mang Hoi ★★★

This is the only made-in-Hong Kong movie with Brandon Lee. Reportedly, Brandon was reluctant to make HK movies because he was afraid of critical comparison between himself and his superhero father, **Bruce Lee.**

But filmmaker **Ronnie Yu** (cult director of *Bride with the White Hair*) created a perfect vehicle for Brandon by mixing heroic bloodshed and chop socky action with a vicious vengeance theme. Brandon plays a poor bastard imprisoned for murder after being framed by his best friend. While he's in jail, his friend is busy raping his girlfriend and, simultaneously, rising to Mafia kingpin. But when Brandon gets out of jail, all hell breaks loose.

LEGAL INNOCENCE (1993)
director: Cha Fu Yi [Cha Chuen Yee]. Anthony Wong·Wu Chen Yu·Cecilia Yip· Yeung Si Min ★★★
Another entry in the growing list of contemporary category III films [the new wave of HK brutal violence and sex movies restricted to adults only]. This one opens with the grisly discovery of a decomposed body in a suburban house. Lovers Patrick Wong (Wu Chen Yu) and Kitty Yueng (Yeung Si Min) are arrested, convicted, and sentenced to death. Kitty commits suicide in prison,

117

Brandon Lee in *Legacy of Rage*

THE FILMS

but Patrick hires a female lawyer, Shirley Tsang **(Cecilia Yip)**, to reopen the case. She eventually succeeds in proving Patrick's innocence. However, after marrying him, Shirley soon discovers the truth is sometimes more twisted than anyone dares imagine.

Also starring **Anthony Wong** as a persistent cop who gets to the bottom of things. A fierce cinematic assault loosely based on a true occurrence, beautifully filmed by Cha Fu Yi with an exceptional musical score. Upon its release, the film received criticism for playing loose with the facts. Another version, seemingly more accurate **(Remains of a Woman)**, was released later in the year amid much more positive accolades.

LEGEND OF A DRUNKEN TIGER (1992)
director: Robert Tai. Alexander Lo Rei ·Hui Ying Hung·Hso Tung ★★
The '90s will become known as the renaissance or the ruin of Hong Kong cinema, depending on whether you're a fan of martial arts films or not. The technology of FX filmmaking has improved dramatically over the past 20 years, so perhaps it's natural for chop socky producers to rework the genre in current state-of-the-art fashion. But for many film buffs, these movies are one-trick ponies, and after you've seen a couple of them, you're ready for something else.

Unfortunately, this film brings nothing new to the genre, except more elaborate fighting techniques. This will be enough for some of you, but it falls short of my minimum expectations.

The plot (Drunken Tiger's quest to rid the Chinese countryside of foreign thieves) is little more than an excuse for boxer Alexander Lo Rei to kick some ass for about an hour and a half.

Li Kin Sang's *Legend of Emperor Yan*

LEGEND OF EMPEROR YAN (1995)
director: Li Kin Sang. Tian Shao Jun· Li Ming ★★★
A sprawling, big-budget rendering of Emperor Yan, the first ruler of China. The lavish sets put this film in a class by itself. But the story of strife and honor within this primitive society is amazingly alien, bordering on the fantastic instead of historic accuracy.

Yet the battles are incredibly reenacted, painting scenes of intense hand-to-hand savagery (obviously before the advent of gunpowder) against the breathtaking expansive wilderness. Enchanting cinematography adds a further dimension to this story of the two warring emperors, Yan (Tian Shao Jun) and Huang (Li Ming).

LEGEND OF THE LIVING CORPSE (1980)
director: Chang Chen. Carter Wong· Chin Han ★
Usually you can depend on actor **Carter Wong** for (at the very least) a

sleazy good time, but this anemic ghost tale is just plain boring. Don't fall for it.

LEGEND OF THE MOUNTAIN (1979) **director: King Hu.** Hsu Feng·Sylvia Chang·Tien Feng·Shih Chun ★★½
A long (110 minutes) fantasy film about a man and his quest for nirvana. There are a few interesting FX (especially the flying, flute-playing good witch), but most of it is tedious going, regardless of its "classic" status. Filmed in Korea.

LEGEND OF WISELY (1986) **director: Tang Chi-Li.** Sam Hui·Ti Lung ·Eva Cobode Gracia·Teddy Robin Kwan· Heidi Makinen ★★★★
Perhaps the most underrated of all the Hong Kong action flicks, it stars pop singer Sam Hui (of *Aces Go Places* fame) as an *Indiana Jones*-type scifi writer/adventurer who is searching for a mystical Buddhist pearl (*i.e.*, Lost Ark of the Covenant). But there are bad guys looking for it, too. Especially eccentric Howard Hope (Hughes?) and his beautiful assistant (Eva Cobode Gracia, the blonde firecracker in *Armour of God 2*). They plan to use it as an unusual bartering tool with UFOs!
A loosely based sequel, *Bury Me High,* came a few years later from the same director.

LETHAL CONTACT (1989) **director: Kent Cheng [Cheng Jui Si]** and **Ricky (Billy) Lau [Lau Chang Wei].** Kent Cheng·Ricky Lau·Amy Yip ·Jeffrey Falcon·Sibelle Hu ★★★
Two cops, code names Penguin and Polar Bear (Fatty **Kent Cheng** and **Ricky Lau**), are ordered to assist a visiting policeman from Borneo, Lo Raimy (Wilson Lam). When their incompetence results in Raimy's death during a gun battle with drug traffickers, they are temporarily suspended. Penguin and Polar Bear decide to make amends by joining with Lo's wife

(Jaclyn Chan) to find the killers. As it turns out, she not really Lo's wife at all, but part of the gang behind the whole thing. Eventually police supervisor Nut Ying **(Sibelle Hu)** gets involved in the case, and—after being kidnapped—is rescued by Penguin and Polar Bear.
It's irritating to watch a film self-destruct before your eyes. The make-it-up-as-you-go story line hopelessly gyrates between well-choreographed action sequences and ridiculous stooge humor. The end result is most unsatisfying, indeed.
Amy Yip (called **Amp Ip** in the credits) costars as a prostitute sharing the apartment with the cops. But sadly, she has little to do. Some of the patter between Cheng and Lau is legitimately funny. And perhaps the film is notable for its transvestite villain. Jeffrey Falcon does have nice legs.

LETHAL PANTHER (1990) **director: Godfrey Ho.** Yoko Miyamoto· Sibelle Hu ★★ or ★★★
Director **Godfrey Ho** (under various pseudonyms) has spent the better part of his career creating movies from bits and pieces of unfinished or unreleased projects, usually for the Joseph Lai Company. In the mid-'80s, he reached international notoriety when he hired American/Italian movie star Richard Harrison for [supposedly] one HK film; after all the editing was finished, a minimum of 20 movies surfaced (composite junk, with titles like *Ninja Showdown, Hitman the Cobra, Ninja Thunderbolt, Scorpion Thunderbolt, Ninja the Protector,* etc.).
It seems Ho is so comfortable with this mix-and-match style that when he's given the opportunity to direct a full-fledged production, it still resembles a composite. And that's the problem with this film, thus the mixed rating. If continuity is an important part of your movie enjoyment, bypass this film.

Taken out of context, much of *Lethal Panther* is exciting, if not brilliant. Yoko Miyamoto is an incredibly captivating presence on the screen. And **Benny (*Magic Crane*) Chan**'s camerawork adds to her dominant stature. She plays Ling, a top Japanese hitwoman—cold, calculating, and beautiful. She seems equally at ease in the midst of an explosive gun battle or in the heat of passionate lovemaking. Quite simply, she owns every scene she's in.

Unfortunately, the rest of the film doesn't fare as well. And the segments dealing with a Filipino gang of counterfeiters are sorely underdeveloped. **Sibelle Hu** (as CIA agent Betty Lee) tries hard to keep the action moving, but she has little to do within the structure of the film.

LEWD LIZARD (1985)
director: Wang Yung Ling/Norman Chu. Norman Chu·Xiao Hua·Jiang Shan ★★½
This one is very nasty by Western standards. A young suitor (Norman Chu) loses his girlfriend (Xiao Hua) to a wealthy businessman. At first he's angry. Then, in a fit of depression, he goes to the seashore where he finds (what else?) lizards.

Immediately the man puts the lizards into a bag and takes them home. At this point, the plot turns very strange: for no apparent reason, the man becomes obsessed with ladies' dirty underwear (!?!) (actually sniffing the panties to make sure!), and he steals six or seven "tainted" ones from public rest rooms and brothels.

But why? Well, here's where the plot turns repulsive: he mixes the juices from the underwear with a special "aggressive compound" and then injects the fluid into the lizards. These little reptiles (now hooked on "love jizz") become soldiers in his personal battle against females.

"I hate women!" he screams, hold-

ing the helpless victim's legs apart, allowing the little creatures to gain entrance. Lots of women die, driven mad with sexual ecstasy and (of course) pain, while the misogynist psycho howls with laughter.

In a particularly tasteless segment, he meets a girl he really likes (Jiang Shan). The sound track bursts into a sappy love song as the two flirt, kiss, walk, run, and kiss again. But while boating, she finds the jar of lizards ("What cute things!" she says. "Don't touch them," he responds protectively. "Don't be silly," she answers, pushing him away) and promptly opens the jar and drops the lizards down her bikini trunks (!!!). "I love the fe-e-l-l . . . O God! No!" she cries in delirious agony. Too bad. True love never runs smoothly.

LICENSE TO STEAL (1991)
director: Samo Hung. Joyce Godenzi·Anges Aurelio·Yuen Biao·Richard Ng·Samo Hung·Yang Tsing Tsing ★★½
Two cat-burglar sisters (Joyce Godenzi and Agnes Aurelio) risk getting caught when the "good girl" (Joyce, of course) falls in love with the nephew **(Yuen Biao)** of the detective on the case. Not one of **Samo Hung**'s best films, but the action is swift and excellently choreographed.

LIFE AFTER LIFE (1981)
director: Peter Yung. George Lam·Fora Cheung ★
Puppets come to life and wreak havoc in feudal China. Don't you have something better to do?

LIFE'S GAMBLE 23.
See *Bloodbath 23*

LIQUID SWORD (1992)
director: Wong Ching [Jing]. Aaron Kwok·Tsui Sui Keung·Liu Chia Hui·Chingmy Yau (cameo) ★
Now this time I'm very serious. We need to get organized. Perhaps letters

to the Hong Kong consulate, maybe a telethon, or perhaps even a ninja hit squad . . . whatever it takes. But **Wong Chin [Jing]** must be stopped before he single-handedly destroys HK cinema with his obscenely prolific output of garbage.

In this one, pop singer-turned-actor **Aaron Kwok** stars as Chu, a lightning-fast swordsman, in search of the ultimate fight with a monk named Flowerless. This film is no more than a series of silly vignettes detailing the hero's wacky journey and the various goofballs he encounters along the way. Remember how awful you thought Wong Ching's **Royal Tramp** was? This one's even worse.

LONG ARM OF THE LAW (1984)
director: **Johnny Mak [Mak Don Hung]**. Lam Wai·Wong Kien ★★★★

LONG ARM OF THE LAW 2 (1987)
director: **Michael Mak [Mak Dong Kit]**. Alex Man·Wong Siu Fung ★★★★

LONG ARM OF THE LAW 3: ESCAPE FROM HONG KONG (1989)
director: **Michael Mak [Mak Dong Kit]**. Andy Lau·Max Mok Siu Chung· Elizabeth Lee·Hsu Chin Kang ★★★
Currently **Michael Mak [Mak Dong Kit]** is best known for his artistic sex films (e.g., **Sex and Zen**), but not so many years ago he and his brother were critically heralded for this impressive series, known as the "Big Circle" films.

While not truly sequels, these three movies are similar in theme. Basically, gangs from China [Guangdong] are slipping into Hong Kong to pull off robberies and then escape back across the border to safety (thus, the Big Circle moniker).

The Mak brothers were criticized for perpetuating the popular HK prejudice against the mainland Chinese by painting them as heathen criminals with no sense of morality. But the films more correctly show the strong code of honor among the gangsters (not unlike the bond cementing the characters in Coppola's *Godfather* series).

#1 is generally considered the first of the HK heroic bloodshed films, released two years before **A Better Tomorrow.** Its cast is a collection of unknowns, handpicked by director Johnny Mak [Mak Don Hung] after interviewing hundreds of mainland Chinese. The result is a true-life creation, resembling an ultraviolent documentary. #2 and #3 are a bit more polished, starring Alex Man and **Andy Lau,** respectively.

LOVE AND THE CITY (1995)
director: **Jeff Lau.** Leon Lai·Wu Chien Lien ★½
Heavy-handed story of a boy who grows up hating his father for being a "timid mouse" and a girl (Wu Chien Lien) who falls in love with the kid's brooding personality. It stars pop-singer-turned-actor **Leon Lai** in yet another hammy performance as the pained, misunderstood delinquent. Not all singers have what it takes for the silver screen. Perhaps Leon should reconsider his career options before continuing this charade any further.

Director **Jeff Lau** tries hard, but too many bad movies have killed his creative spirit. He's learned to be complacent, wallowing about knee-deep in sappy melodramatics. After the mess he made with **Eagle Shooting Heroes** (1993), it's astonishing he's still making films at all.

Even the basic story of a street kid who tries to escape an unfair murder charge is uninspired, to say the least. Dull, to say a bit more.

LOVE IN THE TIME OF TWILIGHT (1995)
director: **Tsui Hark.** Nicky Wu·Charlie Yeoh [Young] ★½

121

If **The Lovers** (1994) was **Tsui Hark**'s comeback film, this one must be considered a major stumble on the rocky road back. Seemingly, without fully understanding why *Lovers* was a hit, filmmaker Tsui was anxious to repeat the success. He rehired the same two leads (pop stars **Charlie Yeoh** and Nicky Wu) and had them play lovers once again, this time in a half-baked *Back to the Future* rip-off.

It all has something to do with Nicky playing a character who inadvertently gets mixed up in a bank robbery. But when things get harried, he and Yan Yan (Charlie Yeoh) are sucked into an alternative dimension (through a lamp post), and there they eventually fall in love.

It's difficult to believe this is the brainchild of the same director who gave such classics as **Zu Warriors from Magic Mountain** (1983) and **Once Upon a Time in China** (1991) to the world.

LOVE ME VAMPIRE (1987)
director: Irene Wang [Kao Wei Lau]. Chang Xiao Hai·Lin Xiao Ni ★½
The Oriental answer to America's *Fright Night* (1985), but there's more concentration on the high school motif similar to the Hong Kong **Happy Ghost** series.

It's cute. What the hell. . . .

LOVE ON DELIVERY (1994)
director: Lee Han Chang. Stephen Chow [Chiau Sing Chi]·Christy Chung ·Ng Man ★★½
It was inevitable. After two intelligent films (**From Beijing with Love** [1994] and **King of Beggars** [1993]), **Stephen Chow [Chiau Sing Chi]** really had no choice but to go back and star in something silly for his fans. They must've felt betrayed by his recent excursion into class productions with scripts that didn't rely on food fights and pratfalls.

This film works as a diversion, a minor nod to the comic roots that made him Hong Kong's #1 box office draw. But it's not the return of Stephen Chow the buffoon; here is Stephen Chow the clown.

He plays a downtrodden delivery boy who suddenly has a chance to date a beauty like Christy Chung. And the humor, as goofy as it may be, is a logical extension from that premise.

When he dresses like Garfield the Cat and fights Christy's pushy boyfriend, it makes sense within the structure of the story. It's not merely a vignette concocted to get laughs.

It could be worse.

God knows, it used to be.

LOVE TO KILL (1993)
director: Kirk Wong. Anthony Wong· Elizabeth Lee ★★★½
This is a very odd entry in **Kirk Wong**'s distinguished list of films. He's the current uncrowned King of HK crime films with such projects as **Rock 'n' Roll Cop, Organized Crime and Triad Bureau, Jackie Chan's Crime Story,** and **True Colors** in his credits.

And then there's this movie.

It's an amazingly distasteful horror film about domestic violence, starring **Anthony Wong** in a role similar to his award-winning performance in **Untold Story.** Here, he plays Sam Wong, an embittered brute of a man who enjoys making life miserable for his wife (Elizabeth Lee) and their young son. She is subjected to countless perverse sex-n-torture games that eventually propel Wong into a completely psychotic state.

If you had a hard time with the family slaughter scenes in **Untold Story,** avoid this film. The bloodbath created here manages to eclipse even them. But if you want to see the new extremes of HK depravity, it's here.

LOVE WITH A GHOST IN LUSHAN (1975)

director: Buo Fong. Fong Peng·Wu King Ping·Yu Fay ★★

A medieval, fantasy ghost film with some outrageous moments, but mostly it's the familiar man-in-love-with-a-ghost theme.

THE LOVERS (1994)

director: Tsui Hark. Nicky Wu·Charlie Yeoh [Young] ★★★

This one is being touted as **Tsui Hark**'s comeback after a series of box office failures. But it must be somewhat unnerving for the prolific filmmaker, since this variation of the *Romeo and Juliet* theme doesn't particularly cover any new ground.

Of course, it's visually stunning. But all of Tsui's films are stunning. It's a costume fantasy, but so was **Magic Crane.** It's a tragic love story, but ditto for **Green Snake.** Seemingly, for some reason, this one clicked, and the others didn't.

Perhaps the Hong Kong audiences were impressed by the grand spectacle of the film. But many critics have cited the "overproduction" as a quality that took the tenderness away from the heart of the film. If Tsui had been more concerned with the chemistry between the two leads—and less concerned with thunder and lightning—*The Lovers* might have been one of his greatest films, instead of merely a very good one.

LOVER'S TEAR (1992)

director: Cheng Chi-Liang. Ni Shing· Samo Hung·Lam Ching Ying·Yukari Oshima ★★½

Chung Ao (Ni Shing), a rookie cop from HK's anti-smuggling unit, goes to mainland China to retrieve confiscated merchandise. But, secretly, his true goal is to arrest Lin Wei, the gangster boss behind the traffickers. Although the Chinese Commissioner, Kong **(Samo Hung),** warns him of the international diplomacy problems, Chung quickly throws caution to the wind and befriends one of the gang members **(Lam Ching Ying).** Chung's position is compromised when he becomes infatuated with the boss's daughter (Ni Shing), resulting in an effective, bittersweet ending.

You'll find loads of rip-snorting action, complemented by stylish camerawork and a good score by John Sands. Also starring **Yukari Oshima** in a cameo as a Chinese cop.

LOVES OF THE LIVING DEAD (1986)

aka **HEAVEN WIFE, HELL WIFE**

director: Peter Mak. Annie Bai·Peter Mak ★★½

An outrageous zombie movie filled with blood and gore and a beautiful queen vampire (Annie Bai) in a short red dress. Also starring director **Peter Mak** as the hero.

LUCKY STARS.

See *My Lucky Stars*

LUNATIC FROG WOMEN (1989)

director: Yang Chin Bong. Chen Wan Yuan·Ting Shann Hsu ★★(★)

Six female prisoners-of-war lead an escape from a North Vietnamese women's detention camp. The survivors join the rebel forces and plan a counterattack on the enemy. The film culminates in the assault, giving way to lots of fighting, brutal hand-to-hand, and some terrific gun stuff.

Maybe standard uniform attire for fighting female soldiers is a midstomach pullover, camouflage T-shirt and matching short shorts, but I kinda doubt it. If that doesn't bother you, then see this one. Great-looking babes taking themselves very seriously while they really kick butt.

It also has one of the coolest titles of all time.

LUNATICS (1986)
director: Derek Yee Tung Sing. Fung Shui Feng·Deanie Yip·Paul Chun Pui· Chow Yun-Fat·Ma Sze Chen·John Shum ★★

Since the success of director **Yee**'s *C'est la Vie, Mon Cheri* (1993), some of his earlier films have been dusted off and rediscovered. This one, while not a masterpiece, is a well-meaning study of mental illness in Hong Kong's underground. The emphasis is on Doctor Tsui (Fung Shui Feng), a free-clinic shrink who spends his time helping hapless street clients. A newspaper reporter, Tina Lau (Deanie Yip), accompanies the social worker for a week as he introduces her to his shadow world.

Some critics have complained that the movie would've been more accessible if the filmmaker hadn't purposely created such an unlikable group of clients with overtly violent lives (e.g., **Chow Yun-Fat**'s character is a hopeless derelict who buried his son alive after he contracted hepatitis; Paul Chun Pui is a psycho who spends most of his life tearing heads off chickens, until he goes on a frenzied rampage against a grade school).

MAD MISSION series.
See *Aces Go Places* series

MAGIC AMETHYST (1990)
director: Cheng Jui Si (Kent Cheng). Sibelle Hu·Kent Cheng ★★½
Here's a fast-paced action comedy about a young couple who, inadvertently, are the target of a blood cult from India when a dying Hindu priest entrusts them with a sacred statue.

Lady Hai from Bombay **(Sibelle Hu),** dressed in a gold Superwoman costume, chases the reluctant heroes through the streets of Hong Kong as they try to find Prince Cayle and the Sha Jan Temple. After the amethyst is returned, the film becomes a crackling, blood-splattering gun fest as even Lady Hai is destroyed by her own gang.

MAGIC COP (1989)
aka **MR. VAMPIRE 5**
director: David Lai [Lai Da Wei]. Lam Ching Ying·Billy Chow·Wilson Lam· Michiko Nishiwaki ★★½
Uncle Feng (**Lam Ching Ying,** the priest from the *Mr. Vampire* series) is a former police detective who rejoins

Anita Mui in *Magic Crane*

the force to investigate a drug trafficking case involving ghosts and vampires. The conclusion is a lot of fun, visually.

There's also some valuable supernatural folklore offered: If a cursed body stiffens, it's a vampire; if it doesn't stiffen, it's an ogre. Now you know.

MAGIC CRANE (1993)
director: **Benny Chan.** Tony Leung [Chiu Wai]·Rosamund Kwan·Lawrence Ng·Anita Mui ★★½

Here's yet another **Tsui Hark**-produced historical fantasy/adventure epic. School against school, temple against temple, empire against empire. The Shaolins from Shun Mountain versus the Ten Chong School. Does anybody really care about the particulars?

I guess even Hark realizes all this is becoming tedious. That's why he's added a giant crane (which, by the way, looks great in long shots, but rather silly close up) and a valley of giant turtles, **Gamera** fashion.

Forget the plot and watch the FX. With **Tony Leung [Chiu Wai], Rosamund Kwan,** Lawrence Ng, and crane-riding **Anita Mui.**

MAGIC CRYSTAL (1986)
director: **Wong Ching [Jing].** Cynthia Rothrock·Yuen Biao·Andy Lau·Max Mok·Richard Norton·Chen Pai-Hsiang ★★½

Exhilarating but nonsensical martial arts sci-fi. The magic crystal is an outer space gemstone with extraordinary powers (it gives super strength to its owner), and it waddles around like a turtle when it gets lonely. Everybody is after the magic crystal, from the KGB to the HK police. The whole thing culminates in a secret chamber underneath the Acropolis Theater in Greece, where a UFO is discovered. The crystal, it seems, is an important part of the spaceship's computer system. The extraterrestrials can't activate the

rocket without it. But, before the final liftoff, the crystal (apparently pregnant) reproduces a miniature offspring for the team of good guys (Cynthia, Yuen, and Andy).

MAGIC NEEDLES (1989)
aka **MIRACLE NEEDLES**
director: **Lee Leung.** ★★

This is a medieval melodrama with a very obvious (and biased) political message. Dr. Nip and his magical acupuncture (the practice of piercing parts of the body with needles to treat disease) cures the Emperor's son after the regular doctors fail. It's acupuncture versus medical science in this slow-paced oddity.

MAGIC OF SPELL (1986)
director: **Ching Chung Wu.** Lin Hsiao Lan·Cheng Pei Pei·Law Yoi ★★★

Tim Paxton wrote about this film in his magazine *Monster:* "It's a 'this-is-so-cool-I-don't-want-to-blink-or-I'll-miss-something' experience."

I'm not sure anybody could say it better. This movie is loaded with a virtual parade of eye-popping, mind-blowing, utterly flabbergasting segments. And these segments are so demented, so crazed, that the viewer will be dumbstruck by their sheer vitality. Where else can you see a heroine chased by a giant boulder with teeth while an evil magician bathes in a pool of blood?

Impishly cute Lin Hsiao Lan continues her mischievous yet heroic character from **Kung Fu Wonder Child.**

MAGIC STORY (1986)
aka **YOUNG MASTER VAMPIRE**
director: **Ricky Lau.** Sun Kim Chu· Don Bil·Wong Shi Kit ★★

Lots of slapstick antics as a priest goes through the rituals designed to control an army of zombies, but the actual plot has to do with a boy who tries to win the respect of his girlfriend's father by becoming a vampire-hunting ghost buster. However, after visiting the magical netherworld, he decides to recruit supernatural aid in his quest for the girl.

A seemingly important piece of Oriental zombie control information is revealed in this film: you can become invisible to a vampire, ghost, or zombie if you hold your nose when they're around. Good to know, right?

MAGIC SWORD (1993)
director: Ting Shan Si. Lee Chi Kay·Emily Chu ★★½
The director of *Beheaded 1000* is at it again, but this time he's aided by state-of-the-art special effects. The film, a fantasy/adventure set in ancient China, deals with a swordsman who creates the ultimate blade (thanks to a bizarre suicide by his wife) and an evil warlord who tries to steal the magic sword.

MAGIC WARRIORS (1991)
director: Lee Tso Nam. Lin Hsiao Lan·Law Yoi·Sham Sam ★★½
The production team behind *Magic of Spell* return with the star, Lin Hsiao Lan, for more zany mayhem. Using many of the same sets (and production values), this film features even more outlandish fantasy, including gill monsters, flying swordsmen, acid pits, tree creatures, evil warlocks, and magic spells.

MAGICIAN WARS (1987)
director: Tam Leung Xen. ★
The story relies mostly on FX or sight gags, primarily limited to flying objects (sort of like the bedroom scene in *Poltergeist,* but not nearly as effective).

There is no consistent plot in this paltry film, only a recurring thread of a story line about two magicians who are trying to impress the same girl. One of the worst.

MALEVOLENT MATE (1993)
director: Lin Chin Wei. Wong Kwong Leung·Fu Yuk Ching ★½
The beginning will catch your attention, but you'll be asleep by the end.

It starts with a remarkably brutal murder and dismemberment (obviously the reason for the Category III rating), but quickly degenerates into a talky police procedural opus. For some odd reason, the film is shot like a who-dun-it even though the killer is obvious from the beginning. For those who manage to stay awake, there is a plot twist about 75 minutes in. But it's not worth the wait.

MAN BEHIND THE SUN (1990)
director: He Chi Chiang [T. F. Mous]. Wong Kong·Wong Ying Git·Cheung Kwok Man ★★★½

MAN BEHIND THE SUN 2: LABORATORY OF THE DEVIL (1991)
director: He Chi Chiang. Wong Kong·Iwanbeo Leung·Wan Man Ying·Andrew Yu ★★

MAN BEHIND THE SUN 3: NARROW ESCAPE (1992)
director: He Chi Chiang. Wong Kong·Wan Man Ying ★★
#1 is an uncompromising (well-filmed but repulsive) movie that vividly shows the atrocities committed by the Japanese against the Chinese inside the walls of the "scientific research oriented" Concentration Camp 731 during World War II, run by a stern commandant (Wong Kong).

The camera doesn't stray from the horrendous images; rather, it uses those scenes [e.g., a young blind boy's chest is cut open and his heart is removed "just to see what it looks like"] to emphasize the incredible lack of inhumanity by the oppressing Japanese. Sobering and powerful.

Part 2: Laboratory of the Devil initially ran into heavy censorship problems (the original Hong Kong version was cut by the censors to 47 minutes!), but it's difficult to see what the furor was all about. Apparently, the offensive material was more political in nature, due to a growing social awareness between China and Japan. Aside from some unsettling experimentation dealing with embryos, it's tame by Western standards. The lion's share of the film deals with placement of blame and historical documentation. The strong story stagnates.

The third installment, *Narrow Escape*, drops the exploitive edge of #1 completely. The year is 1945, and the Japanese are beginning to lose their foothold in China. The Russian army is marching through Asia, freeing the cities under Japan's domination. The officers at Torture Camp 731 are under strict orders to destroy all evidence of the inhumane experiments and escape before the Russians invade the base and discover the clinic's horrible secrets. Some of the scenes of mass annihilation are disturbing, but, overall, the once-powerful saga has become diluted.

Also see **Comfort Women** [directed by **Wong Kong,** the actor who played the commandant in this series] for a loosely based sequel dealing with prostitution and venereal disease at Camp 731.

MAN FROM HONG KONG (1974)
director: Brian Trechard-Smith and **Jimmy Wang Yu.** George Lazenby· Jimmy Wang Yu·Samo Hung·Susan Leitch ★★½
Not to be confused with the later George Lazenby Hong Kong spy film **Stoner** (1980), this one features chop socky superstar **Jimmy Wang Yu** in the heroic role. Lazenby, recovering from his disastrous attempt at playing James Bond in *On Her*

The transsexual evil emperor Jade Face Pope in *Man of Nasty Spirit*

Majesty's Secret Service (1969), is the archvillain attempting to rule the world from his headquarters in Sydney, Australia.

Jimmy Wang Yu (formerly called **Wang Yu,** named Jimmy for this film, and the moniker stuck) had the dubious distinction of being the first actor advertised internationally as "the New Bruce Lee."

The irony, of course, is that Wang Yu made at least ten movies before **Bruce Lee** made one, and he is generally considered the first chop socky superstar. The crass Western promotion for this film was an embarrassment.

MAN OF NASTY SPIRIT (1993)
director: Chung Leung. Bijon Wajut· Lee Chung Ti ★★½
More wacky mayhem from the director of **Dragon Pearl** (1989) and **Thrilling Bloody Sword** (1986). This time, the big difference is the addition of Category III sex.

Besides the bizarre fight sequences with fireballs, flying fingernails, flipping zombies, power-fisted wizards, nasty vampires, and the like, there are huge portions of nudity and surprisingly graphic soft-core gyrations with characters like Jade Face Pope, a cruel transsexual emperor.

The plot, as insignificant as it may be, deals with the theft of an ancient book of spells by the nasty Pope, and the efforts of Princess Bao to retrieve it.

MANY FACED WOMAN (1989)
director: Wang Hsiung [Wang Yung Ling]. Norman Chu·Emily Chow ★
Norman Chu (the star of **Lewd Lizard**) is a tormented artist specializing in psychedelic body painting. He is one of three men unknowingly sharing the same woman. Eventually, she blackmails each of them and becomes rich. Try to stay awake.

MARTIAL ARTS MASTER: WONG FEI HUNG (1992)
director: Hwang Hang Lee. Chin Kar Lok·Lam Ching Ying ★★
Yet another version of the Wong Fei Hung legend, this time concentrating on the popular fighter's early years. Don't watch it hoping for a history lesson; the producers have admitted most of the information is fictional.

But Chin Kar Lok is a skilled fighter who doesn't rely on wire stunts to impress a jaded audience. If chop socky is your bag, don't miss this actioner dealing with bad opium traffickers and Wong Fei Hung's mission to stop them.

MASTER (1990; released in 1992)
aka **WONG FEI HUNG**
director: Tsui Hark. Jet Li·Yuen Wah· Crystal Kwok·To Wai Woo·Lam Ping Hong ★★½
Initially shot in '90, this film was shelved for two years. Many skeptics refer to this shot-in-America flick as **Tsui Hark**'s white elephant. But it isn't as bad as the delayed release might suggest, and certainly better than many of Hark's later films from the mid-'90s.

Although the plot is predictable, it remains an interesting showcase for the incredible martial arts talents of **Jet Li [Li Lian Ji]**. The story resembles the **Bruce Lee** legend, as a young man arrives in San Francisco and a couple Latino hoodlums rob him (soon they become his first students). After the mandatory stranger-in-a-strange-land acclamation, Jet discovers his master was the victim of an attack by a nasty kung fu gang. At the film's conclusion he gets revenge by defeating the bad guys' teacher, a snotty, bad-ass fighter named Johnny.

Full of racist clichés and simplistic solutions, this film is best viewed as contemporary chop socky, no more and no less.

MASTER OF ZEN: TAMO MONK (1992)
director: Yuen Cheung Yeung. Er Tung Sheng·Wu Ma·Fan Siu Wong·Yuen Chun Yeung ★★
Grandiose martial arts production telling the story of Bhodidharma, the Indian monk who created kung fu.

Cast of thousands and painstakingly documented, but the whole thing seems more like religious propaganda than bonafide entertainment.

Director **Yuen Cheung Yeung** initially gained notoriety as an actor in the popular chop socky/monster opus **Miracle Fighter** (1982). He also directed a few, including goofy cult fave **Shaolin Invincibles** (1977), which featured kung fu fighting gorillas.
(See Roots/Martial Arts section)

MASTER'S NECKLACE (1992)
director: William Oscar Sun. Ray Lui ·Tsui Po Fung·Lee Kwok Lun ★★½

Significant for its nonchalant attitude toward the supernatural—as if curses and ghosts are part of everyday life. This eccentricity shrouds the film with an interesting combination of stark realism and childish naïveté. The result is a twisted contemporary fantasy (not unlike a Grimm's fairy tale for adults).

A woman (Tsui Po-Fung) uses black magic to kill off her rich husband, Lee Chan-Fu (Lee Kwok Lun). She arranges to have his body buried face-down to keep him from returning to haunt her. The cemetery gravekeeper, who is secretly running a skeletal supply center for universities, retrieves the body. And in doing so, he unleashes Lee's ghost.

Unfortunately, the story becomes ridiculously convoluted when the spirit befriends a cop (Ray Lui) and convinces him to help in a revenge plot.

MATCHING ESCORT.
See *Wolf Devil Woman 2*

MEN BEHIND THE SUN.
See *Man Behind the Sun*

MERMAID GOT MARRIED (1994) **director: Kent Cheng.** Christy Chung·Cheng Yee Kin·Kent Cheng·Yuen King Tan ★½

Here's a light romantic comedy, obviously influenced by the American film *Splash*. Perky Christy Chung is the mermaid. She saves the life of a drowning teacher (Cheng Yee Kin) by slipping him an oxygen pearl. After following him to the city (apparently she wants the pearl back), the mermaid masquerades as a real girl and becomes a student in his class. As expected, they eventually fall in love but soon start experiencing compatibility problems.

This is below-average entertainment. The obvious gag wears thin quickly, and there seems to be nowhere for the plot to go. Much of the acting is exaggerated and downright goofy, almost as though the performers are trying to compensate for

Christy Chung in **Mermaid Got Married**

the weakness in the script. **Kent Cheng** has directed some fun fluff in the past, but this one is less than memorable. Unless you're a Christy Chung fan. And you just want to stare.

MIDDLE MAN.
See *In the Line of Duty 2*

MIDNIGHT ANGEL (1988)
aka **JUSTICE WOMEN**
director: **Yee Chik-Ki.** Yukari Oshima ·May Law·Mark Cheng·Miu Ki Wai ★★½
If all the silliness were shaved away (especially the goofy stuff with the police captain), an exceptionally good parody would surface. Long before **Heroic Trio** (1992) appeared, filmmaker **Yee Chik Ki** directed this similar tale involving caped-crusader beauties and a very frightening villain.

Three sisters become vigilantes when a cop boyfriend is murdered by the brutal drug lord. Besides the anticipated ultraviolent ending, the film is interspersed with scenes of the masked superwomen avenging various street crimes. For example, the girls take a moment to kick some butt when they encounter a husband beating his pregnant wife on the street corner; and ditto when they run into a two-bit thief robbing a blind man.

Yukari Oshima is particularly wonderful. At this point in her career she was still bursting with enthusiasm. Unfortunately, the '90s brought nothing but a string of same old parts to her; she lost her spark midway through the decade.

MIGHTY PEKING MAN.
See *Goliathon*

MILLION DOLLAR HEIRESS.
See *Wheels on Meals*

MILLIONAIRE'S EXPRESS.
See *Shanghai Express*

MIND FUCK (1990)
director: **Tu Mah Wu.** Yuen Lui·Clare Chan ★★
Certainly, it's the best of the Chinese hard-core (XXX) films reviewed for this book. But, then, that's not really saying much. In this one, an unfaithful man poisons his wife so he can join the black wizard and his trampy girlfriend. The wife returns from the grave and stalks her assassins.

She has the ability to kill by placing her hands on a person's head. This scrambles their brain, making eyeballs roll around in the sockets and smoke swirl from their ears. The process is called a mind fuck.

MING GHOST (1991)
director: **Raymond Xen-Tu [Xu Tian-Rong** and **Chen Ni].** Joey Wang·Alex Man· Jenny Yen·Choi Tin Wing ★★★
Obviously inspired by the success of the **Chinese Ghost Story** series, this film is much starker and more simplistic. The style closely resembles the Euro art films of the '60s, relying on posturing and symbolism instead of the slam-bam action typical of most Hong Kong movies.

The story centers on the ghostly return of a woman (**Joey Wang [Wong]**) who was cursed and tortured for being a whore.

MIRACLE NEEDLES.
See *Magic Needles*

MIRACULOUS FLOWER (1984)
aka **PHOENIX: WOLF NINJA**
director: **Sze Ma Peng.** Chang Ling· Ho Ling Yen·Rose Kuei·Chung Hua ★★★
This is the third in **Chang Ling's Wolf Devil Woman** trilogy (loosely and distantly related). There are evil warlords and witches, magic spells and swords

in this film about a beautiful female warrior and her journey through ancient China as she searches for White-Haired Fairy (Rose Kuei).

MISS BUTTERFLY (1993)
director: Lin Hui-Huang. Law Wai Keung·Tung Ai Ling·Wilson Lam ★★
Here's a slow film about a fast subject. Cat (Law Wai Keung) is a professional car thief. She is the best in the business and very attractive, too. Everyone makes passes at her. That is, everyone except the boss at her legitimate cover job. No matter how hard she tries, no matter how big a bitch she is, poor Cat can't seem to drag Ben (Wilson Lam) away from his snooty girlfriend, Elder (Tung Ai-Ling).

MISS O (1980)
director: Cheung Sung with **Li Tzu Hsing.** Chow Yun-Fat·Sarina Sai ★★½
A very young **Chow Yun-Fat** (using the name **Aman Chow Yun**) is the star of this obscure erotic thriller. Sporting shoulder-length hair and psychedelic bellbottoms, he meets Miss O (Sarina Sai) and marries her. But he soon begins to realize that she isn't quite right.
Miss O suffers from a sleeping disorder. At unexpected moments she simply conks out. All this leads to an unlikely and ludicrous kidnapping. Of course, Chow comes to the rescue.

MISSION KILL (1990)
director: Lee Chu. Moon Lee·Simon Yam·Max Mok Siu Chung·Eddie Kao ★★
Moon Lee is probably sick of playing the same role over and over. Once again she's a kick-ass detective who foils vicious drug trafficking gangsters. They hire professional hitman **Simon Yam** (also destined to play the same villainous part repeatedly) to wipe her out. Loads of action, but instantly forgettable.

MISSION OF JUSTICE (1992)
director: Wong Chung. Moon Lee· Yukari Oshima·Carrie Ng·Yu Wok ★★½
More of the same. But better than most. **Moon Lee** and **Yukari Oshima** are two federal Agents on a suicide mission. They have 10 days to infiltrate and destroy the drug-trafficking operation in Thailand's Golden Triangle jungle.
Also starring **Carrie Ng** in a thankless role. She has little to do but look sexy. Fortunately, she was able to survive this kind of miscasting and, within a few years, became one of HK's most prestigious actresses.

MISTRESS OF THE THUNDERBOLT (1984)
director: Chang Cheuh. Jimmy Wang Yu·Cheng Pei Pei ★★★
Silver Roc **(Wang Yu)** is an enemy of the corrupt governor; a writ of execution is issued against him. He joins forces with his old classmate and lover, Golden Swallow (Cheng Pei-Pei). Together, with their furious swordplay concatenation, they conquer all the bad guys.
Another classy adventure from the Shaw Brothers.

MIXED UP (1985)
director: Henry S. K. Chow. Agnes Chan·Deborah Moore·Fanny Cheung ·Lo Ho Gai ★★
An okay kids-in-peril horror comedy with a vampire and something that looks like the Frankenstein monster. The final creature confrontation on a pleasure yacht (similar to **Eddie Romero**'s *Beast of Blood* segment) is the standout.

MOMENT OF ROMANCE (1990)
director: Benny Chan. Andy Lau·Wu Chien Lien·Ng Man Tat ★★★★

Andy Lau with Wu Chien Lien in *Moment of Romance*

MOMENT OF ROMANCE 2 (1993) **director: Benny Chan.** Aaron Kwok· Anthony Wong·Wu Chien Lien ★★★½ If you only see one **Andy Lau** film, this is the one to choose. Perhaps he's played this type of character so many times he's finally got it down. But, regardless, this is a flawless performance. And, on top of that, the movie clicks by offering a well-written script, alive with a menacing sense of danger.

Andy Lau is a two-bit gangster "wheel" man, Wah Dee, who suddenly finds himself in the middle of a robbery gone bad. Due to creative driving, Wah is able to save himself and the other gang members. But there's a problem: What are they going to do with the hostage, an innocent girl named Jojo (Wu Chien Lien).

Wah defies the other members when they decide to kill her. He rescues Jojo and escapes, with the gang in pursuit. Soon, the two fugitives realize they must stop running and take an aggressive stand against the gangsters.

Officially the movie is directed by **Benny Chan,** but rumors still persist that much of the action was shot by the film's producer, **Ringo Lam.**

Obviously *Moment of Romance 2* isn't a direct sequel. The plot is similar, i.e., a boy and a girl get mixed up with the mob and are forced to take vengeance into their own hands.

Wu Chien Lien (she also starred in #1) is impressive as Celia, an illegal immigrant from mainland China who becomes a prostitute in Hong Kong and unluckily witnesses the murder of a triad kingpin. **Aaron Kwok** is the knight in shining armor who rescues her from the ambitious gangster who killed his boss. It's superb entertainment, but not as good as the first one.

MONKEY WAR (1985) **director: Chan Chun Liang (Chang Ling).** Lau Sham Him·Cho Skek Lam· Bon Wong·Chuen Yet Lone ★★★ Originally released as a two-part film and then reedited into one feature, this one tells the story of the Buddhist Monkey King and his rise to power in medieval China. The main emphasis is on fantasy. The comic book action probably made it very popular with kid audiences. But there's lots of visual delights for older genre fans. The standout is when the giant spiders transform into beautiful, evil witches.

Fun filmmaking from Chang Ling, the female actor/director best known for **Wolf Devil Woman** (1982).

MOON LEGEND.
See *Chinese Legend*

MOON WARRIORS (1992)
director: Ching Siu Tung. Andy Lau·Maggie Cheung·Anita Mui·Kenny Bee ★★½
Obviously inspired by the '90s historical fantasy rage in Hong Kong cinema, this one benefits from a strong cast: **Andy Lau** (finally in a serious role again), **Maggie Cheung** and **Anita Mui.** Another plus is the classy direction of **Ching Siu Tung,** who too often is underrated.

There's lots of action, swordplay, and kung fu stunts. But the film suffers from the lack of a strong, centralized villain. However, there is a cool scene when a killer whale saves the day.

MORTUARY BLUES (1990)
director: Jeff Lau. Yuen Fui·Sandra Ng ★
The talented director of **Haunted Cop Shop** and **Operation Pink Squad** pulls a boner here. No matter how hard he tries to duplicate the charm of his earlier films, **Jeff Lau** emerges as merely a desperate filmmaker.

Slapstick replaces horror in this tale of female zombies energized by the moon. But even their pasty presence can't give credence to wacky shenanigans of the possessed cops.

MOST FOR A GHOST.
See *Host for a Ghost*

MOST WANTED (1994)
director: Wong Kam Tin. Lau Ching Wan·Kent Cheng ★★
A routine police thriller about an undercover Hong Kong cop who is branded a wanted criminal, closely recalling **Ringo Lam**'s *City on Fire* and, of course, Quentin Tarantino's Lam-inspired *Reservoir Dogs*.

In *City On Fire*, **Chow Yun-Fat** played the undercover cop torn between the camaraderie of a robbery gang and duty to indifferent police superiors. Chow is such an accomplished actor that the audience strongly feels the torment of his dual existence and his attraction to the robbery gang. However, in this one, the stylistic mannerisms of **Lau Ching Wan** (usually seen in tearjerkers like *C'est la Vie, Mon Cheri* [1993] and *Tears and Triumph* [1994]) fails to draw the audience into his out-of-character character. While his taut features, intense looks, and short, burly frame may suit him well for playing brooding personalities, his one-note expression is limited to a kind of fixed, dazed mugging, with a cigarette constantly hanging from his mouth. We never know what he's thinking, or what he wants. By the time he makes his final stand at police HQ, we no longer care enough about him to experience the full impact of his dilemma.

On the other hand, **Wong Kam Tin**'s direction boasts a gritty quality, making excellent use of nighttime Hong Kong and a variety of dramatic city locations, particularly a sprawling abandoned beach-house that serves as the gang's hideout. The jewel robbery and subsequent police chase/shootout are competently done, although lacking the flair of a **John Woo,** Ringo Lam or **Yuen Kwei.** Most of the cast, turns in unremarkable performances, with the notable exception of the rotund, always watchable **Kent Cheng.**

MOUNTAIN WARRIORS (1990)
director: Eddie Lam. Eddy Ko·Waise Lee·Carrie Ng ★★½
Sort of like a remake of *Heroes Shed No Tears,* with Eddy Ko (the unsung hero of that film, playing the vicious villain in this one) and Waise Lee as an ex-soldier recruited for a special assignment called Operation Earthworm. Lee and his band of mercenaries (including feisty **Carrie Ng**) go into the Vietnam jungles in search of an anti-American terrorist training camp.

If you're looking for war action, with lots of blood and bullet-riddled bodies—look no further.

MR. CANTON AND LADY ROSE (1989)
aka **MIRACLE**
aka **BLACK DRAGON**
director: Jackie Chan. Jackie Chan· Anita Mui·Richard Ng·Bill Tung·Lo Lieh·Jackie Cheung·Yuen Biao·Gloria Yip ★★★
A mixed bag. And very unusual for **Jackie Chan.** Perhaps as a direct response to the critics who chastise him for the "mindless, nonexistent plots" in his films, Jackie has created a good-looking movie that relies more on characterization than stunts. And while some of the film seems overtly ostentatious, much of it works very well.

Jackie Chan, acting as both star and director, tells the story of a poor Chinese immigrant who makes good in corrupt Hong Kong circa 1940.

MR. POSSESSED (1988)
director: Wong Ying. Kenny Bee·Do Do Cheng (Carol Cheng) ★★½
Whenever he becomes sexually excited, a shy boy (Kenny Bee) is possessed by an evil spirit. While under the influence of the demon, he says things like "Go up on the roof and

streak" (!?!) and "Fuck a duck" (!?!?!). All this is happening because his family is cursed with an end-of-a-bloodline spell.

There is also an unexpected subplot about a friend who turns into a vampire sort of werewolf and crashes the girls' slumber party. The two plots don't appear to be related in any way.

MR. VAMPIRE (1984)
director: Lau Chang Wei (Ricky Lau). Lam Ching Ying·Moon Lee·Ricky Hui·Lu Nan-Chuang·Wu Ma ★★★★
The first and most impressive in this popular series. Don't be put off by the title. The movie has all the unique elements that distinguish Oriental horror films from those of other countries. In fact, this film is probably one of the best introductions to this genre.

There's lots of action and thrills, plus a young, incredible-looking Moon Lee. In addition, Lu Nan Chuang is the monk's apprentice, and there's a tremendous performance from **Lam Ching Ying** as the chief vampire buster, also known as the "one eyebrow priest." Incidentally, **Lam**'s career is deeply rooted in chop socky flicks. He was the martial arts choreographer for most of the **Bruce Lee** films and he has a costarring role in *Fists of Fury.*

Perhaps one of the more surprising aspects of this series is the true identity of the director, **Lau Chang Wei.** He's best known today under his Anglo pseudonym, **Ricky Lau**—the popular character actor-turned-director. Interestingly, he never starred in any of the *Mr. Vampire* films, but he did direct and appear in a cloned series called *Spooky Family* with his friend and collaborator **Kent Cheng.**

Others in this series:

MR. VAMPIRE 2 (1985)
director: Lau Chang Wei. Moon Lee·
Lam Ching Ying·Lu Nan-Chung·Yuen
Biao ★★★

MR. VAMPIRE 3 (1986)
director: Lau Chang Wei. Lam Ching
Ying · Yuen Biao · Richard Ng · Samo
Hung (cameo) ★★½

MR. VAMPIRE 4 (1987)
director: Lau Chang Wei. Wu Ma·
Anthony Chan·Loletta Lee ★★

NEW MR. VAMPIRE (1988)
  aka **KUNG FU VAMPIRE BUSTER**
director: Chung Leung. Xiao Lao
Chang·Lu Fang·Hung Wa ★★

NEW MR. VAMPIRE 2 (1989)
  aka **ONE-EYEBROW PRIEST**
director: Mason Ching. Lam Ching
Ying·Xia Feng Wang ★★

MR. VAMPIRE 5.
  See *Magic Cop*

MR. VAMPIRE 1992 (1992)
director: Ricky Lau [Lau Wei Chang].
Lam Ching Ying·Ricky Hui ★½
Lam Ching Ying returns as the one-
eyebrowed priest in this much anticipated, but sadly disappointing, sequel
to the popular series. This time the villainous vampires are ghosts of
aborted fetuses (called holy babies)
who hate the human world for taking
away their opportunity to continue the
reincarnation chain. It's a unique idea,
but not substantial enough to carry the
film.
  Plus the characters are disturbingly
listless and one-dimensional. Too many
sight gags bog down the middle of the
film; even the climax fails to ignite. Try
Wizard's Curse or *Ultimate Vampire*
instead.

MURDER (1993)
director: Lawrence Cheng. Carol
Cheng·Lawrence Cheng ★★★
There are more twists and curves here
than you'll find in a bowl of Chinese
noodles. That isn't necessarily a good
thing, and the number of coincidences
in the plot may be more than the casual viewer would care to endure. But
Lawrence Cheng fares much better
with this tense thriller than he did with
Finale in Blood (1991).
  Jessica and Lung Lau (Carol
Cheng and Lawrence Cheng) are having marital problems. She's an asser-
tive, bitchy lawyer who will do anything,
including suppress evidence, to protect
her wealthy clients; he masquerades as
an investment broker but is really laun-
dering dirty Thai drug money for the
mob. They should be perfect for each
other, except they can't trust one another.
  When Lung lies to his wife about
an investment, she steals and hides his
briefcase full of money earmarked for
a U.S. Mafia client. In a fit of rage, he
shoots Jessica. Thinking she's dead,
Lung concocts a story about a break-in
and calls the police. However, his wife
isn't dead. She's hospitalized and
eventually comes out of a coma, but
now she's suffering from amnesia.
Lung still needs to know where she hid
the money, so he befriends her. And
he starts eliminating any friends who
could blow his cover.
  As a director, Lawrence Cheng is
surprisingly accomplished. His story,
although needlessly convoluted at
times, is crisp and intriguing. Even
though he relies on many tired con-
trivances, there are enough fresh
ideas to make this one work.

MURDER OF MURDERS (1982)
director: Sun Chung. Lo Lieh · Linda
Chu·Yo Hua ★★½
The incredibly valuable Six Gems
are stolen from a fortresslike jewelry

establishment in medieval China. The plot thickens when the #1 suspect, Pan Chen Feng (played with sinister glee by **Lo Lieh**) is mysteriously poisoned in this unique Asian who-dun-it murder mystery.

Probably shot in tandem with *Human Skin Lanterns,* this one features the same cast and same director.

MY BETTER HALF (1993)
director: **Lee Han Chang.** Lee Chung Ning·Yip Sin Yee ★★★
This film is something of a rarity in Hong Kong cinema. The omnibus technique: a collection of different short stories tied together by one similar theme. With *My Better Half,* director **Lee** has woven three tales of eroticism into a tapestry of terror, unified by peculiar relationships between husbands and wives.

The first story of the trilogy is about a dead man who is given a second chance at life if he can figure out and perform some complicated sexual positions with his living wife before dawn. Next, it's a tale of a wife who is forced into prostitution to pay for her husband's operation, but when he recovers from the surgery he's none too happy. And the third story (always the best one in an omnibus film) is about a woman confessing to the chainsaw slaughter of her husband and then discussing his tastiest parts after cooking him.

Black humor, scary visuals, clever script and good performances.

MY COUSIN, THE GHOST (1986)
director: **Wu Ma.** Richard Ng·Kenny Bee·Mui Wen Se·Alam Tam·Wu Ma ★★★
A man (Richard Ng) sells his restaurant in the UK and returns to share the profits with his cousins in Hong Kong. There's lots of forced humor (dealing mostly with cramped living quarters and bad food) until someone discovers that the man is actually a zombie.

Simon Yam (L) in *My Crazy Love for You*

The final half-hour is filled with good FX (especially when a female ghost removes her head) and features music liberally lifted from *Ghostbusters.*

MY CRAZY LOVE FOR YOU (1993) aka **DON'T STOP MY CRAZY LOVE FOR YOU**
director: **Tao Ten Hong.** Simon Yam· Michelle Wong ★★★
Okay, here's another misleading title—but the movie is worth the watch. Favorite psycho **Simon Yam** is back again doing what he does best: being crazy. This time he's a computer nerd who becomes hopelessly obsessed with a TV news anchorwoman (Michelle Wong). He stalks her for a while and then breaks into her house. For the last half of the film he tortures and sexually brutalizes the poor girl until she finally has the opportunity to take revenge. This vengeance leads to one of the most surprising lines of dialogue in Chinese cinema, as Simon screams: "I can't believe you shot my dickie!"

MY DREAM IS YOURS (1988)
director: **Derek W Cheung Chang.** Joey Wang·Jacky Cheung·Yueh Wah ·Ellen Chan·David Wu ★★

It's a rather tough premise. A group of people get together to steal a treasure and defeat the evil gangsters protecting it. Sounds somewhat plausible, right? Except the caper they're planning will take place in a dream. Supposedly, if you really want something bad enough you can snatch it in a dream and bring it back into the real world. Or something like that.

It's fun as escapist entertainment. And **Joey Wang** is totally knock-down beautiful in this one.

Samo Hung (R) with Helen Lio in *My Flying Wife*

MY FATHER IS A HERO (1995)
director: Corey Yuen [Yuen Kwei]. Jet Li·Yu Rong Guang·Anita Mui·Tsu Miu·Blackie Ko ★★★

Celebrated action director **Corey Yuen** has done something very unusual here. He's created a film that contains more character development than action. This is especially peculiar since it also stars kung fu kingpin **Jet Li.** And odder yet, because it was co-scripted by **Wong Ching [Jing].**

But *My Father Is a Hero* is a three-dimensional study of an undercover cop, Kung Wei (Jet Li), as he longs for a normal family life (especially after he learns that his wife has become seriously ill) but finds himself relegated to the secret world of crime (he's on the trail of a maniac killer **[Yu Rong Guang]**).

Anita Mui is exceptional as a cop who helps Kung when the going gets tough. She's also the one who becomes babysitter for his kid when Kung's wife dies.

Don't be put off by the obvious sentimentality in this script. That's only one aspect of the film. There's also a good amount of gun-n-fu action (don't forget, action is Corey Yuen's forte).

But the movie also suffers from some unfortunate scenes of slapstick and stupid sight gags. Perhaps that's to be expected from the pen of Wong Ching. At least Corey Yuen's tight direction has kept those lapses to a minimum.

MY FLYING WIFE (1990)
director: O Sing Pui (suspected pseudonym for **Chang Peng Yu).** Helen Lio ·Samo Hung·Yu Li·Fok Shu Wah· Shing Fui On ★★½

Je-e-e-z-z! What the hell is going on here? If nothing else, this mean-spirited comedy vividly shows the chasm separating East and West sensibilities.

Because of mounting gambling debts owed to a gang of loan sharks, Helen Lio wants to kill herself by jumping off a building. Two ghosts (a mom and her little boy) are waiting at the bottom, where they plan to suck the pearl of life [soul?] from Helen's body and begin their reincarnation process. But Siu Hung, one of the gang members, rescues the hapless girl in the nick of time. The ghosts are really pissed off and retaliate against the triad. Meanwhile, gang boss Chan Yu Qun **(Samo Hung)** orders Helen Lio to pay off her debt by becoming a one woman brothel for a few months, granting a series of freebies to him and his men. Eventually, Boss Chang makes peace with the mom ghost when he discovers that she was his lover in a former lifetime, and her ghost son is actually his child.

Good-looking production; tasteless story.

MY LUCKY STARS (1985)
director: Samo Hung. Samo Hung · Jackie Chan · Sibelle Hu · Lam Ching Ying · Richard Ng · Andy Lau ★★★

MY LUCKY STARS 2: TWINKLE TWIN-KLE LUCKY STARS
aka **TARGET** (1985)
director: Samo Hung. Jackie Chan · Samo Hung · Yuen Biao · Andy Lau · Richard Ng · John Sham · Fung Shui Fan ★★★
Mindless fun laced with loads of thrilling stunts and exceptional fight sequences. Muscles **(Jackie Chan)** and Ricky **(Yuen Biao)** are two Hong Kong policemen sent to Japan to capture fleeing Blackhead (Eric Tsang). He's a crooked HK cop taking asylum in Tokyo with an embezzled fortune in diamonds. After a frenzied fight in an amusement park between the good guys and the bad guys (Blackhead plus a gang of Jap ninjas), Ricky is captured. Muscles solicits help from his chief. Knowing he can't use Hong Kong cops for backup ["They'd be recognized for sure"], he requests assistance from his old orphanage buddies, the Lucky Stars, a bunch of flim-flam criminals headed by Fastbuck **(Samo Hung).**

From this point, the lion's share of the film concentrates on the zany escapades of the Lucky Stars as they prepare their assault on the villain's stronghold. Remarkably, Jackie Chan's role is reduced to cameo status; he isn't even involved in the final slam-bam fight sequence. But on the brighter side, the Stars (Richard Ng, Fung Shui Fan, Charlie Ching, **Andy Lau, Sibelle Hu,** plus, of course, **Samo Hung**) are so entertaining, he's barely missed.

Incidentally, although the locale of the film is supposed to be Japan, most of the scenes are actually shot in Hong Kong. The hotel used for the stunt-n-action stuff is, in reality, the Hong Kong Omni Plaza.

The same cast returns for *Twinkle Twinkle Lucky Stars* with the addition of a new pack of villains, featuring **Lam Ching Ying** and Dick Wei plus the ferocious Japanese female fighter, Michiko Nishiwaki. And, happily, Jackie Chan has a meatier role.

MY PRETTY COMPANION (1992)
director: Len Tsu-Chow. Chiu Yu Ri · Ti Lung · Tang Chen Ye ★★
The mob kills a model's boyfriend and she goes to the police for protection. A spunky female cop and her two partners investigate. Tons of HK-style ultra-violence, especially in the gun department. But the film is mostly significant due to an extraordinary amount of sex and nudity. Sort of a Hong Kong variation of an Andy Sidaris film.

Starring Chiu Yu Ri (as the girl cop) and Tang Chen Ye and Tung Li (as her partners).

MY WIFE'S LOVER (1992)
director: Kevin Chu. Maria Mok · Noel Chik ★★★
Director **Kevin Chu** brings his TV commercial/music video technique to this wildly erotic tale of lesbian lovers. There's lots of nudity and deliberately paced, sensuous lovemaking scenes (shot in David Hamilton soft-focus style) throughout this story of a professional-photographer husband who gets turned on while filming his wife in the arms of her female partner.

MY WILL . . . I WILL (1986)
director: Jamie Luk. Chow Yun-Fat · Olivia Cheng · Raymond Chen ★★½
Hollywood used to call this type of film a screwball adult comedy. Instead of Rock Hudson and Doris Day, we've got **Chow Yun-Fat** and **Olivia Cheng.**

After almost dying in a freakish accident, wealthy widow Wang Kam (Olivia Cheng) decides she needs a will. But unfortunately she doesn't have any heirs. With the aid of her attorney (an unscrupulous lawyer played by Raymond Chen), she draws a contract for a male who will help her father a child. Even though she currently has no mating prospects, she is deluged with a variety of candidates, including an oblivious private investigator, Alex Fung (Chow Yun-Fat).

Harmless, but cleverly written, fluff.

MYSTICS IN BALI (1989)
director: H. Tjuit Djalili. Ilona Agathe Bastion · Yos Santo · Sofia Wo · W. D. Mochtar ★★★

Indonesian horror films tend to be the most graphically gory of all the Southeast Asian entries. And this one probably leads the pack.

Popular exploitation director **Djalili** (best known for the second installment in **The Warrior** series) creates an excessive black magic tale complete with snake transformations, ugly warlocks, cackling witches, and the legendary Leać blood cult.

A female writer from the States visits India, hoping to learn more about the most powerful magic in the world. Soon, she is taking lessons from the Mystic Witch of the anagogic Leać sect. But, secretly, she is being used to secure certain juices needed for eternal life.

The witch dislocates the trainee's head. And in a sequence that will astonish even the most jaded horror enthusiast, she sends her on a mission to a nearby house where a woman is about to give birth, ordering the head to devour the baby upon delivery.

NAKED COMES THE HUNTRESS (1985)
director: Hwang Feng. Li Ying Ying · Chen Hsing ★

Carrie Ng as a hitwoman in *Naked Killer*

Cool title. Bad movie. A fantasy film about three hunters who fall in love with a forest nymph (Li Ying Ying) living in the snowy mountains. Also starring Chen Hsuing as the surviving hunter.

NAKED KILLER (1992)
director: Clarence Fok Yiu Leung. Chingmy Yau · Simon Yam · Carrie Ng ★★★★

NAKED KILLER 2:
RAPED BY AN ANGEL (1993)
director: Lau Chang Wei (Ricky Lau). Chingmy Yau · Simon Yam · Mark Cheng ★★★

Perhaps *Naked Killer* is the perfect asian cult cinema film! The story is of a beautiful hitwoman, Kitty **(Chingmy Yau)**, seeking vengeance for her mentor's death. The murdering culprit is a lesbian bitch named Princess (played to the sleazy hilt by **Carrie Ng**) who has a romantic interest in Kitty. The plot is further complicated by the emergence of an impotent police detective **(Simon Yam)** who is also infatuated with Kitty.

Chingmy Yau assaulted by a killer clown in *Naked Killer 2: Raped by an Angel*

This film is part of the new wave of roughies coming out of Hong Kong, filled with nudity, lesbian sex, ultraviolence, and gore. They are called Category III movies.

The sequel has little to do with the first one, yet all of the original cast members are back, with the addition of Mark Cheng (of **Peking Opera Blues**) as the devious villain. Director **Lau Wei Chang**'s plot is a distinctive departure from #1 (Chingmy Yau is stalked by a lecherous lawyer), featuring an absolutely tasteless conclusion.

NARROW ESCAPE.
See *Man Behind the Sun 3: Narrow Escape*

NEIGHBORS ARE PHANTOMS.
See *Our Neighbors Are Phantoms*

NEW KIDS IN TOWN (1985)
director: **Lau Kar Yung (Leung).**
Moon Lee·Chin Siu Hao·Lee Ka Sing· Liu Chia Liang ★½
For **Moon Lee** enthusiasts. Two brothers go to Hong Kong to live with their uncle, and study kung fu. They learn about modern life from their cousin, Siu Fung **(Moon Lee [Lee Choi Fung])**, but soon find themselves mixed up in a battle with vicious criminals.

NEW LEGEND OF SHAOLIN (1994)
director: **Wong Ching [Jing]** and **Yuen Kwei [Corey Yuen].** Jet Li· Chingamy Yau·Tsu Miu·Wang Lung Wei·Hui Miao ★★½
Regardless of the title, it's not a new legend at all. It's a new version of the old Hung Shi Kwan legend, but in typical **Wong Ching [Jing]** fashion the most creative elements are cloned from another medium. This film more closely resembles the Japanese *Baby Cart (Lone Wolf and Child)* series than the Shaolin folk hero legend.

Dad Hung **(Jet Li)** and his son Wen Ting (Tsu Miu, a precocious kid bordering on obnoxious) attempt to escort four Shaolin monks to a temple in Nui. These monks hold valuable information as to the whereabouts of a sacred treasure (in fact, individual sections of a map are tattooed on each of their backs).

There's lots of martial arts mayhem (directed by action wizard **Yuen Kwei, [Corey Yuen]**) and breathtaking fighting (many critics say Jet Li has never been better), but filmmaker Wong Ching can't resist loading the rest of the story with stupid pratfalls and ridiculous outbursts of slapstick. The incongruity cheapens the entire adventure.

NIGHT CALLER (1987)
director: **Philip Chan.** Pauline Wong· Melvin Wong·Phillip Chan·Pat Ha ★★★½
This is a tough, no-nonsense thriller with amazingly exploitive overtones. A lesbian relationship gone sour is the catalyst for this film, which features graphically convincing, slasher-type knife killings plus highly disturbing, decadently psychotic behavior from the villainess.

There are also tender, bittersweet moments in the midst of the absolute madness. Impressive camerawork, fast-paced direction, solid acting, and an offbeat ending put this film in a class by itself.

NIGHT EVIL SOUL (1988)
director: George Leung. Lee Chu Ying·Lin Ke Ming ★★★
Similar to (but better than) *Grudge of the Moon Lady,* this one successfully combines elements of horror and fantasy into one exuberant package.

As the legend goes, a beautiful witch named Ko (Le Chu Ying) had controlled the whole region through the spirit of her black cat. When some of the townsmen turned up dead, both she and her cat were executed. However, they return from the grave and, with an army of crazed felines, they wipe out the entire community.

100 years later Chin Hisuing (Lin Ke Ming) and his financée, Kim, are convorting around the Pond of the Black Cat when he becomes hopelessly infatuated with a mysterious woman (obviously the evil Ko). In order to save the relationship, Kim must go into battle against cat/creature Ko.

NIGHT OF OBSESSION (1994)
director: Wang Yung Ling [Hsiung]. Lian Wei Jin·Wu Mia·Steven Poon·Xu Zhi Yan ★★
Wang Yung Ling, the demented director of *Lewd Lizard* (1985), is still making movies. But don't expect *Lewd Lizard* madness here. This one is a by-the-book sex drama.

Lian Wei Jan is a pretty, hardworking career girl with a drinking problem. Steven Poon (from *Snake Devil)* is a boyfriend who only wants to get laid and couldn't care less about her alcohol dependency.

NINE DEMONS (1983)
director: Chang Cheh. Sun Chien·Chien Tien Chi·Lu Feng·Chiang Sheng·Wang Li ★★½
A youthful warrior sells his soul to the Devil in exchange for power and fighting skills. He is protected by a necklace consisting of nine miniature skulls.

Lian Wei Jan in *Night of Obsession*

When in battle, these skulls become demon children who cannibalize the opponent in a bloody frenzy. Soon the warrior finds that he cannot control the heightening mad lust of the children. This leads to a final and unsatisfying confrontation.

NINJA HOLOCAUST (1985)
    aka **108 GOLDEN KILLERS**
    director: **Shen Liu Li.** Casanova Wong·Chan Wei Man ★
Bad. Bad. Bad. An uneven mixture of martial arts and sex, featuring a cast that should have known better. Put together by a director who probably doesn't.

Everybody's looking for a missing pearl necklace because, for some unknown reason, the combination for a swiss bank account is inscribed on it.

Times are tough when an accomplished chop socky actor like Casanova Wong [Ka Sa Fa] is in junk like this.

NINJA IN ANCIENT CHINA (1993)
    director: **Chang Cheh.** Tung Chi Hwa ·Tu Yu Ming ★½
A throwback to the chop socky films of yesteryear by one of the genre's most prolific and celebrated directors, **Chang Cheh.** But sadly, there's little to recommend in this ineffective adventure yarn, as students take revenge when a general kills their teacher.

NINJA'S FINAL DUEL (1986)
    director: **Robert Tai.** Alexander Lo Rei · Lee Hai Shing · William Yen · Lee Yi Min ★★★
Director **Robert Tai** should get points for having the sheer stamina to create an eight-hour fantasy/adventure film. Of course, not all of it works, and Hsien Shen Films wisely reedited the opus for video (to date they have released two 90-minute versions from the original feature extravaganza).

After the success of Tai's **Mafia vs.**

Ninja (1983) (see Roots section of this book), he secured the budget necessary to begin work on this chop socky chronicle.

The story vacillates between traditional martial arts action and innovative bewitching concoctions (e.g., ninjas riding gigantic spiders as they attack the Shaolin monastery). It also offers wonderfully hammy, melodramatic performances as Alexander Lo Rei plays a Japanese priest bound for the Shaolin Temple in China. He's on a solemn mission to warn the monks of a pending Ninja attack against the monastery.

NINJA VAMPIRE BUSTER.
    See *Vampire Buster*

NOBODY'S HERO (1991)
    director: **Ko Shou Liang.** Liu Wai Hung·Fong Kang ★★½
Lung (**Liu Wai Hung**) is pissed off at the world. Especially the gangster world of flashy clothes and big cars. Why? His girlfriend left him for a wiseguy. He hates gangsters so much, he decides to become a cop. But he fails the police exam. Instead, Lung becomes a security guard. The mob wants to pull a heist in his building, so they try to scare him off by brutalizing his new girlfriend. Obviously, this doesn't work. Instead, Lung goes berserk and retaliates against the Triad.

Goofy plot made palatable by good performances and gritty camerawork.

NOCTURNAL DEMON (1991)
    aka **DEMON INTRUDER**
    director: **Ricky Lau [Lau Chang-Wei].** Moon Lee·Yuen Wah·Tsui Sui Ming·Yuen Kwai ★★ or ★★★
Ignore **Moon Lee**'s goofy haircut (why, Moon, why?). Forget all the nonsense in the middle of this film dealing with

Amy Kwok with Yi Tang Ming (R) in
No Fear for Loving

her dumb-as-a-rock cousin. And concentrate on the real plot.

The Nocturnal Demon is a brutal
killer, slashing his way through countless ladies, cutting out their tongues
and feeding the gristle to his pet fish.
After killing her best friend, he focuses
his bloodthirsty assault on Lee and her
family.

From the director of the *Mr. Vampire* series and *Naked Killer 2:
Raped by an Angel.*

NO FEAR FOR LOVING (1994)
director: Fred Tan [Tan Hua Xiong].
Yi Tang Ming · Kwok Ai Ming [Amy]
★★★
Finally, here's a HK film that takes the
AIDS virus seriously. After many years
of AIDS jokes in Hong Kong cinema,
this is the first movie to approach the
subject with sensitivity. Yi Tang Ming is
surprisingly good as the decent family
man who contracted the deadly disease. And **Amy Kwok [Kwok Ai
Ming]** is convincing as his wife, who
goes from shock, to outrage, to suici-
dal after learning the truth.

NOMAD (1980)
director: Wilson Tong. Leslie Cheung
· Yip Tong · Pat Ha ★★
Marks the acting debut of pop singer
Leslie Cheung, but the film is little

more than a pretentious version of   **143**
Frank Perry's *Last Summer* (1969). A
teenager learns about love and death
during a hot HK summer.

NO REGRET, NO RETURN (1994)
director: Lan Nai Kai. Mok Siu
Chung · Vivian Chow · Tsui Bo Hwa ·
Tsang Kong ★★★
If genre films prove anything, it's that
an enormous amount of money doesn't
have to be spent to produce a successful movie. Here's another example
of a small, but ambitious, film delivering the goods. Action. And more action.

After a string of big budget epics
(especially *Assassin* [1993] and *Fire
Dragon* [1994]), **Max Mok [Mok Siu
Chung]** returns to his roots in this
bloody gangster tale directed by his
friend **Lan Nai Kai** (of *Erotic Ghost
Story* and *Rikki O* fame).

The plot is an exercise in simplicity, with more than a casual nod to **The
Killer.** Hitman Victor **(Mok)** is fingered
by the mob after pulling a job for
them. Victor suddenly finds himself in
a tight situation. He must trust and depend on two hostages (an innocent
motorist [played by director Tsui Bo
Hwa] and a TV newswoman [perky
Vivian Chow]) while he attempts to
take on the vicious triad gang.

NO WAY BACK (1990)
director: Lee King Chu. Mok Siu
Chung · Danny Lee · Lam Wai · Ti Wei ·
Lung Fong ★★
Another in the flood of gangster pics
to flow out of Hong Kong after the success of *The Killer.* This one offers nothing new, including the same basic
themes of police corruption, drug-
trafficking criminals, and foiled deals
in Thailand.

Danny Lee, as always, is the cool
police captain. But, as in most of his
'90s films, he has little to do. **Max
Mok [Mok Siu Chung]** is adequate as

the policeman who quits his job and joins the triads to discover what happened to an undercover cop. However, he's much better in **No Regret, No Return** (1994), where he's given the opportunity to act instead of pose.

NUTTY KICKBOX COPS.
See *Skinny Tiger & Fatty Dragon*

OBSESSED (1983)
director: Henry Chan. Eddie Chan · Anna Ho · Alexander Wong · Rainbow Ching ★★
A fireman is possessed by the spirit of a dead burned woman after he unsuccessfully tries to rescue her from a burning house. Thus begins a series of loosely related vignettes, as his normal macho life is disrupted by an emerging feminine persona.

The lead character is played with an idiosyncratic flare by notorious Hong Kong transvestite Eddie Chan. This tailor-made role tends to be overly clichéd, often slipping into stereotypical mannerisms for the sake of fleeting cinematic jokes.

OCCUPANT (1986)
director: Ronny Yu. Chow Yun-Fat · Sally Yeh (Yip) · Raymond Wong ★★★
The spirit of a dead singer takes over another girl's body in order to solve the murder. Good FX and camerawork elevate this one above other Oriental fare with a similar theme.

Primarily, it's significant for the superb acting of **Sally Yeh** in a pivotal role. **Chow Yun-Fat** stars as her boyfriend (they would later be reunited in 1989's **The Killer**). Cameraman/filmmaker Raymond Wong makes a rare screen appearance as a nerdy realtor also in love with Sally.

ON THE RUN (1988)
director: Corey Yuen. Yuen Biao · Lo Lieh · Yo Hua · Yuen Wah · Charlie Chin ★★★
Yuen Biao is a cop. His wife is murdered by a hitwoman (Yo Hua) from Thailand. But when she is betrayed by her gangster employer, the murderess joins forces with Biao to bring the triad to its knees.

Cherie Cheung (L) Leslie Cheung (C) Chow Yun-Fat (R) in *Once a Thief*

Jet Li (second from left) and Tsui Hark (second from right) with production crew from Once Upon a Time in China

Huge helpings of action fill the gaping holes in the plot. In fact, it's so much fun to watch, you don't mind incidentals like the ludicrous story line.

ONCE A THIEF (1991)
director: John Woo. Chow Yun-Fat • Leslie Cheung • Cherie Cheung • Kent Tsang Kong ★★★½
Although **John Woo** directed this movie after establishing his ultraviolent reputation (with the epics like **The Killer, A Better Tomorrow, A Bullet in the Head,** etc.), this production more closely resembles his earlier, light-comedy entries. Except for an explosive, gun-cracking conclusion, there are no other compromises to his current habitude of action-oriented filmmaking.

Apparently the title Once A Thief was lifted from a 1965 Ralph Nelson film that starred Alain Delon (long-time fave actor of John Woo). But the story has none of the gritty quality of that American crime-noir opus. Rather, this tale of charming thieves operating out of the French Riviera could easily be the bastard stepchild of similar Alfred Hitchcock romantic thrillers from the mid-'50s (To Catch a Thief [1955]).

A good cast (including **Chow Yun-Fat, Leslie Cheung,** and **Cherie Cheung**) helps the time pass quickly. Popular bad guy Kent Tsang Kong once again plays a villain.

In the United States, Fox Television contracted director Woo to produce a weekly TV series, called Once a Thief, based on this successful film.

ONCE UPON A TIME: A HERO IN CHINA (1992)
director: Tang Chi Li. Alan Tam • Carol Cheng ★
This unwelcome parody of **Tsui Hark**'s epic series falls miserably short, telling the remarkably unfunny story of a cook (Alan Tam) who tries to stop an opium ring in ancient China.

A misguided project from the director of **Butterfly and Sword** and **Legend of Wisely.**

Zao Wen Zhiou (L) with Hung Yan Yan in *Once Upon a Time in China 5*

ONCE UPON A TIME IN CHINA (1991)
director: Tsui Hark. Jet Li · Yuen Biao · Rosamund Kwan · Kent Cheng · Jacky Cheung ★★★★

ONCE UPON A TIME IN CHINA 2
(1992)
director: Tsui Hark. Jet Li · Rosamund Kwan · Donnie Yen · Max Mok · David Chiang ★★★½

ONCE UPON A TIME IN CHINA 3
(1993)
director: Tsui Hark. Jet Li · Rosamund Kwan · Max Mok · Lau Shun ★★★

ONCE UPON A TIME IN CHINA 4
(1993)
director: Yuen Bun. Lao Wen Zhiou · Jean Wang · Max Mok · Lau Shun ★★½

ONCE UPON A TIME IN CHINA 5
(1994)
director: Tsui Hark. Lao Wen Zhiou · Rosamund Kwan · Kent Cheng · Mok Siu Chung · Elaine Lui ★★
A sprawling epic series of love and romance, chivalry and betrayal (plus some piracy on the high seas and rip-snorting kung fu action) as famed director **Tsui Hark** re-creates a convincing portrayal of turn-of-the-century China and vividly chronicles the country's advance into the 20th century.

His two lead characters symbolize the turmoil of China itself. On one hand, there's the uneducated but intelligent, self-employed Wong Fey Hung (played with charming innocence by mainland kung fu star **Jet Li [Li Lian Ji]**) and then, on the other hand, there's his fiery lover **(Rosamund Kwan)**, a worldly, foreign-groomed aristocrat. Their union is central to the film, and represents the country's ongoing political struggle.

The other notable stars, **Jacky Cheung, Kent Cheng,** and **Yeun Biao,** did not return to the series after #1, but martial arts kingpin Jet Li continues in the lead role. The plot of #2 isn't as intricately constructed as the first installment, but the action scenes are more plentiful and breathtaking. The story revolves around apolitical Wong Fey Hung as he fights the corrupt White Lotus Society, as prejudiced organization bent on eliminating foreign influences in China. It seems Wong isn't motivated by cultural ramifications, but rather, a simplistic (humane?) desire to assist the underdog.

#3 concentrates more on the continued rise of nationalism in China, and it becomes bogged down in despair and propaganda. The only high spots are the well-choreographed fight sequences and the intrinsic charm of Li.

Jet Li does not return for #4. And Tsui Hark, apparently tiring from the directing chores, remains the producer but passes the directorial reins to **Yuen Bun.** Although it's filled with impressive wire tricks and amazing kung fu stunts, the sprawling scope of the series is reduced to footnote status. With

Lao Wen Zhiou (as Wong Fei Hong) and Jean Wang replacing Rosamund Kwan (as Aunt Yee).

Jet Li took the Wong Fei Hong character to a competing motion picture company (Win's Movie Ltd.), where a sequel of sorts, called **Last Hero in China,** was directed by Wong Ching.

By 1995, the producers of this series probably were asking themselves if anybody really cares about any more sequels. Especially after the lukewarm reception #5 got from critics and audiences alike.

Even director Tsui Hark seems to be out of ideas for driving this series forward. The fifth one is a throwback to the first two. But it's just not as good as #1 and #2.

Much of the original cast is reassembled here. **Kent Cheng** returns as Porky Lang, **Max Mok [Mok Siu Chung]** is Su, and Hung Yan Yan plays Clubfoot again. Even Rosamund Kwan is back as Aunt Yee (replacing Jean Wong who played the love-struck Aunt in #4). But Jet Li, the original Wong Fei Hong, seems to have left Tsui Hark's stable permanently (amid some nasty rumors), and Lao Wen Zhiou continues in the boxer's vacated role.

Despite the formidable cast, this film is surprisingly bland. The sweeping historical impact is gone, replaced by a weak love story (Aunt Yee is still determined to marry Wong Fei Hong) and uninspired pirate action (these sequences pale when compared to the original feature).

Recluse actress Elaine Lui (remembered for her **Angel** days) almost steals the show as an ass-kicking pirate. But then, there's really not much show to steal. Even for a pirate.

The biggest problem with this series (by Western standards, anyway) is its underlining expectation. Unfortunately, there's an assumption that the viewer already has some detailed knowledge of Chinese history. Thus many of the intricacies in this lengthy production are lost on the casual viewer.

ONE EYEBROW PRIEST.
See *Mr. Vampire: New Mr. Vampire 2*

OPERATION CONDOR.
See *Armour of God 2: Operation Condor*

OPERATION PINK SQUAD (1986) **director: Jeff Lau.** Cheung Man · Wu Jun Ru · Annie Bai ★★

OPERATION PINK SQUAD 2: THE HAUNTED TOWER (1989) **director: Jeff Lau.** Cheung Man · Luo Nan Kuang · Annie Bai · Wu Jun Ru ★★★

Obviously influenced by **Angel,** also released in 1986, the original *Operation Pink Squad* is a fast-paced action/adventure film, featuring beautiful girls with machine guns. But unfortunately the plot is merely routine stuff.

For the sequel, director **Jeff Lau** takes the girls, puts them into a horror motif, and adds a touch of humor. The result is outlandishly bizarre.

Especially noteworthy is an awesome villainess (Luo Nan Kuang) who has the power to disjoin her head from her body. As her body continues to chase Pink Squad (Wu Jun Ru, Annie Bai, and **Cheung Man**) through the corridors of the haunted castle, her head zooms at breakneck (pardon the pun) speed, chomping, biting and nipping at everything in its path. The Squad then uses miniature helicopters to chase it and (in scenes reminiscent of the ball in *Phantasm*) the copters eventually surround the head; however, she chooses to self-destruct in an explosion of blood and gore. The FX are so good that one almost believes it all.

There's lots more, including legions of Living Dead-type zombies and four kung fu mystics who arrive through a door to heaven. These priests, armed only with the power of musical instruments, go into battle against the creatures and (like an MTV video gone bonkers) kill them with music.

OPERATION SCORPIO (1991)
director: Liu Chia Liang. Chin Gar Lok·Yuan Jeung·Liu Chia Liang ★★
Chop socky films aren't dead. And here's the proof. It's a contemporary version of the classic martial arts films, directed with gusto by Liu Chia Liang, veteran kung fu filmmaker (**Legendary Weapons of China, Eight Diagram Pole Fighter**, et al.).

Fei Yu Shu (Chin Gar Lok) takes revenge when Master Li's noodle shop is destroyed by a vicious kung fu gang, helmed by Sunny the Scorpion. Produced by Samo Hung.

OPIUM AND THE KUNG FU MASTER (1984)
director: Tang Chi Li. Ti Lung·Chen Kuan Tai·Tang Chi Li ★★½
Somewhat of a sequel to **Chang Cheh**'s chop socky actioner **Ten Tigers of Kwantung** (1979). In this one, **Ti Lung** returns as the superhero leader of the powerful Kwantung clan.

But he's got a problem. There's a monkey on his back. This isn't some kind of fighting technique like the drunken monkey. Nope. This is an opium monkey. Lung is hopelessly addicted.

As a result, all hell has broken out. The bad guys have taken over. They've killed the master's students, raped the women, and in general have become a real nuisance. **Tang Chi Li** (yes, the film's director) plays the blind master who cures our hero and nurtures him back to health just in time for the final conflict.

Anthony Wong and Cecilia Yip in Organized Crime and Triad Bureau

Also starring former kung fu superstar Kuan Tai [*Dynasty of Blood*].

ORGANIZED CRIME AND TRIAD BUREAU (1993)
director: Kirk Wong. Anthony Wong·Danny Lee·Cecilia Yip ★★★
Despite the title, director **Kirk Wong** concentrates more on the workings of organized crime and HK triads (personified by veteran heavy **Anthony Wong**) than on the Bureau (led by **Danny Lee,** Chinese movie cop incarnate). This film fuses **Big Heat**'s (1988) interdepartmental police tensions with inverted **To Be #1** (1991) gangster thrills as it chronicles a manhunt for fleeing gangsters.

Anthony Wong delivers a relatively restrained performance, especially in light of his award-winning **Untold Story** rantings. But in typical Wong fashion, his trafficking activities seem less dramatic than his domestic problems. They involve a variety of peculiar mistresses, including shotgun-toting **Cecilia Yip.**

OUIJA SEXORCISM (1988)
director: T. Q. X. Lam. Loy Yum Chen
·Wu Chi Chi·Cheung Ti ★
Utterly tasteless. A household is possessed by the sex spirit of a ouija board in this shot-on-video atrocity. The ultimate shock scene features a woman being violated by a snake. In reality, it's an obvious rubber snake, and the FX people have a devil of a time getting it inside the poor struggling actress. You'd get more enjoyment from banging your head on the table.

OUR NEIGHBORS ARE PHANTOMS
(1989)
director: William Chang. Danny Chan·Cheung Man·Amy Yip·Sandra Ng·Wu Ma ★★½
Obviously, this one was inspired by the lukewarm USA hit, The 'Burbs. But, regardless of its cloned ancestry, this film is much more satisfying than the American counterpart.

After being trapped inside a photograph for 60 years, an evil ghost family finally escapes. They take over a house in the suburbs, and use it as their headquarters (while they collect the souls of 49 humans, in an attempt to regain eternal life). A brave, but inept, off-duty cop (Danny Chan) gets suspicious and rallies the neighborhood.

The cast and crew are similar to **Ghostly Vixen,** probably shot simultaneously. Watch for gorgeous **Cheung Man** and busty beauty **Amy Yip** in costarring roles.

OUTLAW BROTHERS (1988)
director: Frankie Chan. Frankie Chan·Yukari Oshima·Michiko Nishiwaki·Max Mok·Jeff Falcon ★★★
Another action pic from martial arts master **Frankie Chan,** starring **Yukari Oshima** (also see **Burning Ambition**). This time she's a kung fu cop, deeply undercover as a health spa worker try-

ing to get a lead on an oppressive triad gang. As with most Chan films, the plot isn't as important as the fight sequences. And Yukari gets to match wits with another Japanese female fighter, Michiko Nishiwaki.

OWL VS BUMBO (1985)
director: Samo Hung. Samo Hung· George Lam·Michelle Yeoh ★
The gun is loaded, but it's only shooting blanks. The comedy sketches fall flat and the action is forced in this pitifully routine film.

Too bad. Usually you can depend on **Samo Hung** for high quality, but not this time. The story deals with two small-time criminals (Owl and Bumbo, **Samo Hung** and George Lam) who get bamboozled into helping a police captain clear his name after a catastrophic misunderstanding.

PAINTED FACES (1988)
director: Alex Law. Samo Hung·Lam Ching Ying·Cheng Pei-Pei·Wu Ma ★★★½
It's a fascinating docu-drama on the Peking Opera youth school and its most famous trio of students: **Jackie Chan, Samo Hung,** and **Yuen Biao.** Some of the exercise techniques are amazing, and the strict disciplinary tactics are most shocking. But it offers an explanation for the incredible stunts these actors later were able to endure and incorporate into their successful careers.

Starring **Lam Ching Ying [Mr. Vampire]** and Samo Hung (in an award-winning role) as the tough instructors. Also with female chop socky star Cheng Pei Pei [**Mistress of the Thunderbolt**].

PAINTED SKIN (1992)
director: King Hu. Joey Wang·Yin Yang King·Samo Hung ★★★
Classic HK director **King Hu (Legend of the Mountain,** Touch of Zen, Fate

of *Lee Khan, Swordsman*) creates a whimsical tale of a ghost (**Joey Wang [Wong]**) who can't enter the afterlife because her soul has been stolen by archvillain, Yin Yang King. She must resort to painting her skin (thus the title) in order to live among humans. Also starring **Samo Hung** as a selfish priest who tries to take advantage of the situation.

A film with more similarities to *Chinese Ghost Story* than the current run of kinetic sword-and-fantasy tales. Somewhat refreshing because of its slower, more thoughtful pace.

PANTYHOSE HEROES (1989)
director: **Raymond Sen (Samo Hung).** Samo Hung·Alan Tam·James Tien·Liu Chai Yung ★

First, there was William Friedkin's *Cruising* (1980), a vicious film about a straight cop (Al Pacino) who pretends to be gay so that he might catch a sick homosexual serial killer. This controversial film was reworked as a parody in James Burrow's *Partners* (1982), a tasteless bomb starring John Hurt and Ryan O'Neal. Then, for some reason, the Chinese decided to remake it again in 1989 with **Samo Hung** and Alan Tam. And this time it's even more homophobic than the *Partners* abortion. Unless you think fag jokes are funny, fast-forward through the dialogue and watch Samo Hung's stimulating fight sequences. He's never looked better.

PAPER MARRIAGE (1988)
director: **Samo Hung.** Samo Hung· Maggie Cheung·Joyce Godenzi·Billy Chow·Dick Wei ★ (or, if you prefer, ★★)

If you thought Peter Weir's *Green Card* (1990) was terrific, then perhaps this one's for you. But there seems to be a serious case of miscasting going on here. **Maggie Cheung** is trying to find a husband so she can se-

cure Canadian citizenship. She bribes a broke Chinese fighter (**Samo Hung**) to marry her. Does anyone else have trouble with this picture?

The only highlight in this barren romantic comedy is, at one point, Maggie Cheung is reduced to professional mud wrestling to put food on the table. It's worth sitting through 90 minutes to see beautiful Ms. Cheung catfighting her way to success.

Joyce Godenzi, one of the standouts in *Eastern Condors,* is relegated to a costarring role here. Interestingly, she became Mrs. Samo Hung in 1995.

PASSION 1995 (1995)
director: **Clarence Fok Yiu Leung.** Simon Yam·Christy Chung·Yuen King Dan·David Wu·Do Do Cheng (in a cameo) ★½

Here is a flawed example of HK's new self-consciously hip cinema, where everyone has an attitude and no character seems more than an arm's length away from a new Jean-Paul Gaultier outfit. It's a wanna-be cool film that will lose its luster long before other international *Pulp Fiction* clones leave the editing board.

This is tired cinema, made even more tired by lackluster performances from the two leads, **Simon Yam** (looking lost in his black beret) and Christy Chung (hopelessly miscast as Gucci, the worldly street girl).

PASSIONATE KILLING IN A DREAM (1992)
director: **Wong Kuo Chu (Parkman Wong).** Michiko Nikyo·Lin Pin Jun ★★★

It's a frightening thriller about a pretty artist named Sha Sha Lee (Japanese actress Michiko Nikyo) who *sees* graphic murders in her dreams. The crimes are, in fact, being committed by a demented serial killer (Lin Pin Jun). He was a professional boxer, demoralized in the ring. The defeat caused severe physical and emotional damage. Now he stalks the streets looking for women he can brutalize. This Asian variation of *Eyes of Laura Mars* (1978) is greatly enhanced by an exceptional musical score and Yu Dong Ching's brilliant photography. Another entry in the new wave of HK roughies, featuring nudity and ultraviolence unmatched in contemporary Western cinema.

Director Parkman Wong is better known as a HK producer (e.g., *Dr. Lamb* and *Untold Story*).

PEACE HOTEL (1995)
director: Wai Ka Fai. producer: John Woo. Chow Yun-Fat·Cecilia Yip·Chin Ho·Lawrence Ng ★★★★
After two heavily promoted, yet disastrous, films (*God of Gamblers Returns* [1994] and *Treasure Hunt* [1994]), **Chow Yun-Fat** returns in one of his very best features. Reportedly, he had been so concerned about getting back on the right track, Chow wrote the story himself. He wanted **John Woo** to direct, but settled for the popular filmmaker's taking an overseeing position as the movie's producer.

Of course, rumors persist that Woo did much more than oversee the production. And, truthfully, some of the film smacks of Wooisms, the patented dove shots, the slo-mo gun action, the melancholy ballad before the final blowout, and the melodramatic machismo. But much of the film is *not* Woo. Certainly, never before has a John Woo film featured such a bold female character. **Cecilia Yip** as the mysterious Lam Ling is one of the film's strongest features.

The movie opens in 1920 Shanghai, at a country villa. A frenzied madman (Chow Yun-Fat) is on a slaughtering spree. Apparently, he is wiping out his gang due to an attempted double-cross, and because a few of

them made the mistake of raping his woman. He's not checking on who's innocent or who's guilty. He's killing everybody. This massacre marks the birth of the Peace Hotel.

This man, known, hereafter as The Killer, turns the villa into a hotel sanctuary for fugitives. As the film gets under way, he has operated this place for 10 years, on the premise that if a criminal makes it to the boundaries of the hotel, he will be able to live there in peace. But a new and vicious county leader (Lawrence Ng) challenges the Killer's safe haven when shelter is given to a girl who killed a triad boss.

The most striking thing about *Peace Hotel* is how much it wants to be a spaghetti Western. Cagne Wong's soundtrack could easily pass for the composions of Ennio Morricone. And, regardless of how intricate the plot may be, it's still a variation on Sergio Corbucci's *Django*, right down to the Killer's machine gun attack on the Grand Hall men. Not to mention the film's central dilemma—should this girl, whom nobody likes much anyway, be sacrificed to save all the others, or should the hero fight for principles symbolized by the girl? The answer may surprise even a jaded HK fan.

PEACOCK KING (1988)
aka **PEACOCK PRINCE**
director: Lan Nai Kai. Yuen Biao · Pauline Wong · Hiroshi Mikami · Narumi Yasuda·Gloria Yip·Liu Chia Hui ★★★
Unexpected things constantly happen (a high compliment indeed) in this story about Hell Virgin (Pauline Wong) and her attempts to take over the world. There's hi-tech stop-motion animation, plus dragons, black magic, bitch queens, zooming fireballs, and the hero Peacock King **(Yuen Biao).** It's a bewitching delight. For the sequel, see *Saga of the Phoenix.*

PEACOCK PRINCESS (1985)
director: Zeng Xio. Li Xiuming · Zu Jing Ming ★★
Bearing no relationship to the popular *Peacock King* series, this oddity comes from mainland China, the People's Republic of China, to be more exact. It tells the story of a corrupt emperor, his bigoted philosophies, and the princess (Li Xiuming) who convinces him to change his cruel ways.

The high point of the film is the well-choreographed traditional dance sequences. They're worth the watch.

PEARL OF THE ORIENT (1993)
director: Chen Ching Lo. Tang Chen Yie · Chen Feng Chi · Da Yu Li Nai · McLauren Lu ★★
When things get hot in America for gangster Tony Hwang (Tang Chen Yie), he migrates to Hong Kong. There he befriends little rich girl, Sandy (Chen Feng Chi). But his real target becomes Sandy's mother (Da Yu Li Nai), and her horse-training farm.

Typical HK action pic played with all the subtlety of a soap opera. Also starring McLauren Lu as Sandy's friend, Annie.

PEDICAB DRIVER (1990)
director: Samo Hung. Samo Hung · Billy Chow · Liu Chia Liang · Lowell Lo · Max Mok · John Shum · Mang Hoi · Lam Ching Ying ★★★½
A big-hearted kung fu movie dealing with the lives and loves of two pedicab drivers, Fatty Tung **(Samo Hung)** and Malted Candy **(Max Mok).** These two coolie buggy-cyclists find themselves in one mess after another, from work-n-wage disputes to puerile girl problems, street wars with competing pedicab agencies to vengefully jealous boyfriends. Samo Hung is in top form; incredibly agile for his large bulk, he's the very description of a gentle giant. Meanwhile, Max Mok as a shy, love-struck simpleton manages

to spark more charm than he has in many roles.

Ultimately, this slice of life tale is generally considered Samo Hung's masterpiece. It successfully combines martial arts with nonstop breathtaking action sequences populated with very likable characters. Also starring Billy Chow as the villain, and popular chop socky director/actor **Liu Chia Liang** as a gambling den owner.

However, some genre fans may not be amused by some of the tasteless jokes, especially as Samo, plus an insanely obsessive pimp (John Shum) and a lecherous bakery owner (Lowell Lo) all chase after a voluptuous, big-breasted pancake maker (Nina Li Chi).

PEKING OPERA BLUES (1986)
director: Tsui Hark. Lin Ching Hsia · Cherie Chung · Sally Yeh (Yip) · Mark Cheng · Ku Feng · Li Hai Sheng ★★★★
Generally considered the best **Tsui Hark** film, this one certainly deserves its reputation as one of the modern classics of the Hong Kong cinema.

It's the story of three women **(Lin Ching Hsia [Venus Lin], Cherie Chung,** and **Sally Yeh** [aka **Sally Yip**]), who come from diverse backgrounds but unite to expose a government conspiracy in historic Peking. Lin Ching Hsia steals the spotlight from her two costars. She's a dutiful daughter, torn between her political conscience and devotion to her father.

Despite the obvious artistic merits of the film, Tsui Hark isn't afraid to mix elements of grim depravity into the adventure. Case in point—there's a disturbing whip and torture sequence wherein the tormenter halts the lashing to wipe blood from the whip, then resumes beating the heroine with hearty enthusiasm.

PEOPLE'S HERO (1987)
director: Derek Yee Tung Sing. Ti Lung · Tony Leung [Chiu Wai] · Elaine Jin ★★½

When an inexperienced robber **(Tony Leung [Chiu Wai])** holds up a bank, he gets more than he bargained for. One of the hostages turns out to be a gangland boss **(Ti Lung)** who isn't amused by the embarrassingly botched job. The godfather reveals his true identity to the kid, and they begin working together on a plan to save the foiled operation.

Ti Lung found himself in a similar story two years later with *Run, Don't Walk* (1989).

PHANTOM KILLER (1985)
director: **Feng Tsui Fan.** Kao Hsiung·Wei Pai·Li Yuan Hua·Shaw Yin Yin ★
Nothing unusual here. It's a standard police thriller about a murderer who never leaves any clues except petals from a flower. Bloodless. Shockless. Comatose stuff.

PHANTOM LOVER (1995)
director: **Ronnie Yu.** Leslie Cheung·Wu Chien Lien·Huang Lei·Liu Lin ★★½
This was a highly anticipated production from **Ronnie Yu,** but unfortunately it doesn't come close to the magic of his previous *Bride with the White Hair* (1993). The story is a retelling of *Phantom of the Opera.* And, make no mistake, the familiar Yu trademarks are in full force. The film is loaded with Yu's talent for visual artistry, his unique picture blocking, coupled with his ability of capturing light and shadows in ways that make his filmmaking peers jealous.

But the fatal flaw lies in the listless characterizations, punctuated by **Leslie Cheung**'s uninspired performance as the phantom. He seems to misunderstand the role, playing Song Dan Ping as a deformed soul who hides his face behind a mask for vanity reasons, out of embarrassment for his deformity, rather than because of the tragic situation dealing with his undying love for Du Yu Yan (Wu Chien

Lien). Director Yu should have paid more attention to the runaway performances and the inherent weaknesses in the script. Unfortunately, the end result is a great looking, but highly unsatisfying, film.

PHANTOM WAR (1991)
director: **Phillip Kao** and **Simon Yeung.** Alex Man·Ng Ngai Cheun·Phillip Kao ★★★
After the war, a Vietnamese couple (Alex Man and Ng Ngai Cheun) moves to England, where they learn to fight a new battle against racism, poverty, and (ultimately) the Chinatown Mafia.

PHOENIX THE RAIDER (1985)
director: **Ulysses Yueng (Chu Yen Ping).** Lin Ching Hsia·Elsa Yeung·Eagle Lee·Jaguar Lee ★★
The two lead stars from *Golden Queen Commando/Pink Force Commando,* **Lin Ching Hsia** (aka **Venus Lin**) and Elsa Yeung, are together again, this time in a more typical Hong Kong police/action thriller. Despite the on-screen dynamics of the two leading beauties, the result is a decidedly routine and highly predictable story of two friends on the opposite sides of the law.

PHOENIX: WOLF NINJA.
See *Miraculous Flower*

PHYSICAL WEAPON.
See *Underground Banker*

PICTURE OF A NYMPH.
See *Portrait of a Nymph*

PINK FORCE COMMANDO (1985)
director: **Lawrence Full [Chu Yin Ping].** Lin Ching Hsia·Elsa Yeung·Sally Yeh (Yip) ★★★½
This sort of a sequel to *Golden Queen Commando* finds all the original cast members (including **Venus Lin [Lin**

154   **Ching Hsia],** Elsa Yeung, and **Sally Yeh**) in a new plot.

Venus betrays her gang (for a man, no less!). She regains their respect by chopping off her arm, replacing it with a Gatling gun. The action is swift and (like *Golden Queen Commando*) very reminiscent of the violent Italian spaghetti Westerns. This strange hybrid even has a mysterious dressed-in-black bounty hunter who helps the girls during their final assault against an overwhelming attacking army (in an obvious parallel to America's *Alamo* legend). Also see **Fantasy Mission Force** from the same director, made the same year.

PINK LADY (1991)
director: Otto Chan. Yip Lang Hung · Li Mei Kee ★★★

Can a movie be both poignant and exploitive at the same time? Or maybe the better question: Should it be?

Pink Lady is perhaps the ultimate Asian lesbian movie. Granted, it doesn't have much competition. There's **My Wife's Lover** and **The Cruel Kind** (see separate reviews), and lesbianism is a topic whispered about in various other productions. But that's the point, isn't it? In this film, Jenny (Yip Lang Hung) and Michelle (Li Mei Kee) lament over the very same thing. They are constantly asking each other why "their kind" isn't talked about. And why they aren't accepted.

Of course, there are no answers. And besides being an honest, forthright drama, this movie is an effective love story. But it's wildly prurient as well.

Director **Chan** misses no opportunity to capture these two beauties in the nude as they caress one another. Plus the ending is both melodramatic and unnecessarily bloody.

PLAIN JANE TO THE RESCUE (1984)
director: John Woo. Ricky Hui · Siao Fong Fong ★

No question about it, this movie is an abortion. It's an embarrassing skeleton in filmmaker **John Woo**'s closet, probably causing him to break out in a cold sweat at the mention of its title.

This is the worst sort of creature: a comedy without laughs. It's the meandering story of a girl (Siao Fong Fong) and her attempt to keep an old man from losing his company and from being committed to an asylum by his wicked son (Ricky Hui). Interestingly, though, this film remains **Woo**'s only try (to date) at featuring a woman in a pivotal role.

POINT OF NO RETURN (1991)
director: Lai Guo Jian [Guy Lai]. Jacky Cheung · Joey Wang ★

A family that slays together stays together. Or then, maybe not.

Dad and his two sons are hitmen, but friction erupts in the family when one of the siblings falls in love with his intended victim. More silliness masquerading as heroic bloodshed, this time from lightweight director **Guy Lai** (**Detective in the Shadow** [1991] and **Ghost for Sale** [1987]).

POLICE ASSASSIN.
See *Yes! Madam*

POLICE STORY 1 (1985)
aka **JACKIE CHAN'S POLICE FORCE**
director: Jackie Chan. Jackie Chan · Maggie Cheung · Bill Tung · Lin Ching Hsia ★★★½

POLICE STORY 2 (1987)
director: Jackie Chan. Jackie Chan · Maggie Cheung · Benny Lai · Bill Tung ★★★★

POLICE STORY 3: SUPERCOP (1991)
director: Stanley Tong. Jackie Chan ·

Michelle Yeoh · Yuen Wah · Kelvin Wong·Maggie Cheung ★★★
In #1, Jackie is a cop assigned to protect beautiful **Lin Ching Hsia** (this time using the **Brigette Lin** pseudonym). She's the prosecution's key witness in a gangland trial, but she's also a reluctant and ungrateful ward. (How many times have we seen this plot device used?) The story may be worn, but the stunts are great. Plus, there's lots of action, especially in the final 15 minutes when **Jackie Chan** eliminates all the gangsters and destroys a shopping mall, too.

#2 emerges as (perhaps) his best action movie. The plot is almost nonexistent (something about gangsters manufacturing explosives), but it's a nonstop roller-coaster ride, featuring some of the most amazing stunt and action sequences ever put on film. This one is a great introduction to the Jackie Chan genre.

#3 is a disappointing departure, perhaps because Jackie gave directing reins to **Stanley Tong** (of *Stone Age Warriors* fame). The result more closely resembles a James Bond spoof than a sequel to the *Police Story* saga. But Jackie plays it fairly straight, and the inclusion of **Michelle Khan** as his spitfire partner makes it above-average action fun.

Maggie Cheung plays Jackie's girlfriend May throughout the series, although she has little to do in #3.

POLICE STORY: SUPERCOP 2.
See *Project S*

POM POM (1984)
director: Joseph Cheung. Samo Hung·John Shum·Richard Ng·Jackie Chan·Dick Wei·Philip Chan ★★½

RETURN OF POM POM (1985)
director: Joseph Cheung. Samo Hung·John Shum·Richard Ng ★★

POM POM STRIKES BACK (1986)
director: Ip Wing Cho. John Shum · Richard Ng·Philip Chan·May Lo ★★
A precursor to the *My Lucky Star* movies (probably **Samo Hung**'s inspiration for those far better films) featuring the madcap misadventures of two Hong Kong detectives, Beethoven (John Shum) and Ah Chow (Richard Ng). Most of the humor deals with the animosity between the two bumbling cops and their bewildered supervisor, Inspector Chan (Philip Chan). The plots focus on procedural foul ups (#1), mistaken identities (#2), and protective custody mishaps (#3).

Jackie Chan has a cameo as a motorcycle cop in #1. **Samo Hung** produced and costarred in *#1* and *#2*. Series director Joseph Cheung also made the distantly related *Hot Hot and Pom Pom* in 1992 (see separate review). For that one, there is a character named Pom Pom, but not for these.

PORTRAIT IN CRYSTAL (1982)
director: Lin Shew Hua. Tang Chia · Lung Tien Hsia ★½
The plot is almost incoherent, switching from the creation of living crystal statues to a supernatural conflict on Spirit Island. Certainly this is a lesser, desperate attempt by Shaw Brothers to capitalize on the budding horror genre to keep their doors open.

The story is nonsensical, a collection of cheesy special effects and multicolored fog, flying skulls, and vomiting maidens.

PORTRAIT OF A NYMPH (1988)
aka **PICTURE OF A NYMPH**
director: Wu Ma. Joey Wang·Yuen Biao ★★
Okay. Okay. Stop me if you've heard this before. All right. It's a romantic action film. The setting is ancient China. And there's this guy who's kinda shy, but he really knows martial arts, and

he falls in love with a beautiful ghost played by **Joey Wang.**

Obviously inspired by *Chinese Ghost Story* (1987), this one is recommended only for those die-hard Joey Wang fans who haven't seen her play a beautiful ghost in a movie so far this week.

PORTRAIT OF A SERIAL RAPIST (1994) **director: Parkman Wong.** Danny Lee •Parkman Wong•Fan Siu Wong ★½ Don't confuse this film with the much better, similarly titled *Diary of a Serial Rapist* (see review). This is quickie exploitation junk made by a group of people who should have known better (**Danny Lee** and director/producer **Parkman Wong**). It features essentially the same gang of cops from *Untold Story.*

The story opens with a series of rapes and murders. Before long, a suspect is arrested. And, in similar fashion to all the other HK true-crime films, the cops beat the hell out of him during questioning while he continues to swear his innocence. This time the cops not only hit and pound on him, but they also make him strip so they can humiliate him emotionally.

As it turns out, they've arrested the wrong man. And the real serial rapist continues to attack women. The police finally crack the case and discover the true rapist. It turns out he's a pervert with a stash of pornography and a wife who had no idea about his extracurricular activities.

Danny Lee could have phoned in his performance. His screen time is limited to approximately 15 minutes, during which time he does relatively nothing except look stern.

The entire cast assembles for yet another similar B-feature, *Shoot to Kill* (see review), which was probably made in tandem with this project.

POSSESSED (1985) **director: David Lai (Lai Dai Wai).** Lau Siu Ming • Siu Yuk Long • Sue Chan • Irene Wan•Wen Bixia ★★ An inner city motif mixed with folk superstitions plus old dark house stuff. Sort of fun.

POSSESSED 2 (1990) **director: David Lai (Lai Dai Wai).** Wong Siu Fung•Kong Mei Pooh•Sui Yuk Long•Chung Wong ★★★ Not truly a sequel. This one really delivers with lots of action and grisly monsters. One of the better Hong Kong horror films. Don't ignore it because of the Part #2 status.

POSTMAN STRIKES BACK (1982) **director: Ronny Yu.** Liang Cha Jen • Chow Yun-Fat•Yuen Yat Chor•Cherrie Chung ★½ This film is a far cry from *Bride with the White Hair,* but director **Ronny Yu** was responsible for both. To call *Postman Strikes Back* a lesser work would be a gross understatement. It's better described as a misfire.

Four professionals are hired to escort a secret shipment to Lo Yang Pass. En route they discover their cargo is actually contraband weapons earmarked for a political enemy, so they switch from mercenaries to zealots and plan an attack against their employer.

It's fun to see **Cherie Chung** in her debut role, although she doesn't do anything memorable. And **Chow Yun-Fat** appears to be hopelessly miscast as a kung fu boxing rogue. This is especially noticeable when compared to the fighting skills of his costar, boxer Liang Cha Jen [sometimes translated as Leung Kai Yen].

POWERFUL FOUR (1991) **director: David Lam.** Danny Lee • Simon Yam•Kent Cheng•Lee Chi Hung ★★★★

The film opens as friends and colleagues of Hong Kong ex-police commissioner Luk Kong (Lee Chi Hung) are attending his funeral in Singapore. Despite the fact that the commander was under investigation for corruption by the current members of the HK secret service, his three former associates **(Danny Lee, Simon Yam,** and **Kent Cheng [Cheng Chuen Yan])** come out of hiding to attend the service—even though they know it will surely result in their arrest.

Through an extended flashback, the film examines the allegedly illegal activities of the four policemen and their relationships with the underworld and the community. A poignant story that unflinchingly explores the thin line between criminal and cop, and ultimately asks the question: Does the end justify the means?

The conclusion sports a thrilling gun-and-action climax that rivals the best of the **John Woo** ultraviolence spectaculars. Exceptional filmmaking by underrated producer-turned-director **David Lam.**

Incidentally, this movie marks the beginning of the **Danny Lee/Simon Yam/ Kent Cheng** triumvirate that will continue (in various groundbreaking projects, e.g., **Dr. Lamb** and **Run and Kill**) for a number of years.

PREGNANT BY A GHOST (1975)
director: Rom Bunnag. Lo Lieh·Fang Ye·Rung Iawan·Scripati Makul ★★
Rosemary's Baby rip-off, notable only because of rather explicit sex scenes depicting the demonic impregnation.

PRETTY WOMAN (1995)
director: Norman Chan. Veronica Yip·Russell Wong ★★½
Lots of nudity and general soft-core erotica, including some very sexy gymnastics in an exercise room. This is the ultimate "Veronica Yip gets naked flick" with truckloads of gratuitous

Veronica Yip in *Pretty Woman*

flesh featuring an 11-minute shower/ masturbation scene.

The story itself starts out strong but quickly becomes (as the title blatantly suggests) just another clone of the Richard Gere/Julia Roberts hit.

In this one, prostitute Nama **(Veronica Yip)** is hired to deliver a resignation letter to the personnel department of an investment company. Why? Well, one of the workers had accidentally killed a female employee while raping her on the desktop late one night (talk about on-the-job harassment!), and he hires Nama to impersonate the dead girl.

But after Nama goes through the motions, she finds herself attracted to a handsome young man in the office and decides to stay on the job.

PRETTY WOMEN AT WAR (1990)
director: Yang Chin Bong. Wai Ying Hung·Yip Kai Ling·Mo See Wak·Bok Ying ★★½
Four Hong Kong beauties are forced into prostitution after being arrested and put into the custody of a rich

politician. They are tortured (similar to *Yang's Searching for Love*) but manage to escape. They take refuge in the home of a female freedom fighter who teaches them urban warfare. This all sounds much better than it really is, but the girls (especially Wai Ying Hung) look great.

PRIMITIVES (1988)
director: Sisworo Gautama. Barry Prima·Jenny Haryono ★★½
Here's proof the Italians don't have a corner of the cannibal film genre. Although, if this film is any indication, Ruggero Deodato doesn't need to worry about his *Cannibal Holocaust* legacy.

Roland (Barry Prima) and Rita (Jenny Haryono) are two students who journey into the New Guinea jungles to conduct research on the Hundru tribes. As expected, their trip soon becomes a nightmare of survival.

Loaded with sequences of savage animal mutilation and graphic blood-n-gore.

PRINCE OF THE SUN (1990)
director: Hwa I Hung. Lam Ching Ying·Cynthia Rothrock·Conan Lee·Sheila Chan·Jeff Falcon ★★
Lam Ching Ying, the *Mr. Vampire* hero, is Kentum, a monk trying to protect the Young Chieftain (the reincarnated spirit of the Living Buddha).

The beginning and end are loaded with exciting, fantasy-oriented action sequences. But the entire middle is snail-racing time.

PRINCESS MADAM (1988/90)
aka **UNDER POLICE PROTECTION**
director: Godfrey Ho. Moon Lee·Michiko Nishiwaki·Yang Pan Pan·Tsang Kong ★★½
Mix-and-match specialist **Godfrey Ho** creates another film from remnants. This time the result is more successful

than usual, since the majority of *Under Police Protection* [*Princess Madam*, original Hong Kong title] is culled from an unfinished project with **Moon Lee** and Michiko Nishiwaki.

He spices up this tired story [two female cops protecting a key witness ready to testify in a mob trial] with unrelated footage about HK's cocaine racket and the hapless prostitutes who get sucked into it.

PRISON ON FIRE (1987)
director: Ringo Lam. Chow Yun-Fat·Tony Leung [Chiu Wai]·Hon Kwan·Roy Cheung ★★½

PRISON ON FIRE 2 (1991)
director: Ringo Lam. Chow Yun-Fat·Chang Chung Yung·Victor Hon Kwun·Yu Li ★★★

Chow Yun-Fat in *Prison on Fire 2*

During the four years between these two films, director **Ringo Lam** grew as a filmmaker. His pacing became swifter, his stories less clichéd, and his camera more probing. Although **Chow Yun-Fat** plays the same character in both films, it's not until #2 that we really get to know much about him. And that's mostly due to Lam's secure attitude toward the persona behind the facade.

Although #1 is a good prison drama (with **Tony Leung [Chiu Wai]** shining in a sympathetic role) the plot remains a routine potboiler about evil wardens, cruel gangs, and cowardly stool pigeons. #2 adds unique personalities and complicated ethics to an intense, battle-scarred story. This film marks the beginning of Ringo Lam's metamorphosis into one of Hong Kong's best directors.

PROJECT A (1984)
director: Jackie Chan. Jackie Chan · Samo Hung · Yuen Biao · Dick Wei
★★★½

PROJECT A 2 (1987)
director: Jackie Chan. Jackie Chan · Lam Ching Ying · Maggie Cheung · Carina Lau · Rosamund Kwan ★★★
Turn-of-the-century pirate films, written and directed by **Jackie Chan,** who also stars as [Dragon] Mi Yong, a brave and wisecracking Coast Guard officer. Lots of stunts, kung fu fighting, food fights, toilet humor, and goofy sight gags.

Much of #1 deals with the temporary disbanding of the Coast Guard due to political dissention among various incompetent government officials. It especially concentrates on training exercises and police orientation—that is, until the coastline is threatened by deadly pirates (led by Dick Wei). Eventually Dragon joins forces with a gambling rogue, Fei **(Samo Hung),** to fight the bad guys.

#2 continues the adventure with the addition of **Lam Ching Ying** as the new pirate leader, with **Maggie Cheung** and **Carina Lau** as two revolutionary spies who get Jackie into a lot of trouble. However, both Samo Hung and **Yuen Biao** are missing, reportedly due to a personal quarrel between them and **Jackie Chan;** officially, their publicist insists that they couldn't make the film due to previous commitments, namely, Samo Hung's feature *Eastern Condors,* which was under production. Perhaps because of their nonparticipation, Jackie changed the concept of the film from #1's martial arts extravaganza to a more stunt-oriented opus. Many critics have cited this film as containing Chan's best action-oriented stunts. Plotwise, in this one he is no longer a member of the Coast Guard; now he's one of the Dock Police Patrol. But the enemy is still the same, the pirates assisting trafficking gangsters in the China Sea.

Both films are fun actioners, particularly if you're a Jackie Chan fan. Many enthusiasts will insist these are Chan's best films, especially with regard to his unique directorial ability. These movies introduced a new and wildly successful blend of slam-bam action with genuinely funny scenes of broad humor.

Most Chan fans already know the story of Jackie's brush with death during *Project A's* filming. In one of his stunts (falling from a tower), he anticipated that his dive would be broken by a series of awnings. Unfortunately, the canopies didn't hold and he ended up smashing against the ground, head-first (watch the outtakes during the closing credits for a play-by-play). Luckily, he wasn't injured seriously and continued shooting the film after a short recuperation.

159

Michelle Yeoh fights Yu Rong Guang in *Project S (Supercop 2)*

PROJECT S (1994)
aka **SUPERCOP 2**
director: **Tong Kwai Lai [Stanley Tong]**. Michelle Yeoh [Khan] · Jackie Chan · Yu Rong Guang · Yukari Oshima · Dick Wei · Fan Sui Wong ★★★
Sure it's good! **Michelle Yeoh** kicks ass and she looks better than ever. The plot is a bit of a stretch. She's a cop who discovers that her former boyfriend (the rogue **Yu Rong Guang**) is planning a major caper, the robbery of Hong Kong's most impenetrable bank.

The weakest link of the film is **Jackie Chan**'s cameo, played entirely in drag. His campy performance is gratuitous and hopelessly out of place in this otherwise dynamic motion picture.

PROTECTOR (1985)
director: **James Glickenhaus**, additional footage by **Jackie Chan.** Jackie Chan · Danny Aiello · Roy Chiao · Moon Lee · Bill Wallace ★★ (★★★ HK version)
The same tired plot you've seen hundreds of times before: a cop, wrongly accused by his superiors, is demoted; through the humiliating experience he stumbles across necessary information to clear his name and stop the bad guys (in this case, drug traffickers).

This film was another failed attempt to introduce **Jackie Chan** to the American market in the '80s (also see *Battle Creek Brawl*). It's constantly a mystery as to why Hollywood always seems to screw around with success. More specifically, why would a movie studio hire stuntman extraordinaire/contemporary king of martial arts Jackie Chan and then make a movie without stunts? without martial arts?

Chan got into an ugly dispute with director Glickenhaus over this very question. In fact, Chan was so unhappy with the film, he returned to Hong Kong and reshot the second half. He eliminated the nudity and the low-key ending, adding car chases and chop socky action. The Asian version includes 30+ minutes of new footage not in the American print.

QUEEN OF BLACK MAGIC.
See *Black Magic 3*

QUEENS HIGH.
See *In the Line of Duty 5: A Beginning*

RAGING THUNDER (1990)
director: **Corey Yuen.** Cynthia Rothrock·Max Thayer·Loren Avedon ★★
HK action director **Corey Yuen**'s attempt at an Americanized adventure pic. A mostly Anglo cast (including Cynthia Rothrock, Loren Avedon, and Max Thayer) perform lots of tae kwon do fighting in a tale of an ex-soldier who recruits an army of Vietnam War buddies to find his kidnapped girlfriend in Bangkok.

THE RAID (1991)
director: **Tsui Hark** with **Ching Siu Tung.** Dean Shek·Jacky Cheung·Joyce Godenzi · Tony Leung [Chiu Wai] · Corey Yuen ★★
An attempt to transfer comic book action to the screen. But **Tsui Hark** quickly betrays his own project by concentrating too heavily on listless characterizations, relegating the action to a secondary role (the same criticism was leveled against Tsui for his handling of *A Better Tomorrow 3*). Many of the scenes are nicely intermeshed with watercolored pulp illustrations, but those drawings remain the most interesting thing about this film.
Intended as a *Magnificent 7* meets *Eastern Condors* extravaganza, the film tells the story of a retired soldier (Dean Shek) who recruits his own army to fight the dreaded Manchurians. Nice idea, but it withers on the vine.

RAIDERS OF THE DOOMED KINGDOM (1988)
director: **Sumat Saichur.** Sorpang Chatri·Peter Ramwa ★★

A grim and bloody war film dealing with the exploits of a gallant special forces unit on a final assignment in the jungles of North Vietnam. The war is officially over. America has pulled troops out of Saigon, but the CIA gives a secret assignment to a Vietnamese officer, Cobra (Sorpang Chatri). He and his band must rescue General Chu (Peter Ramwa) from the Viet Cong and find an incriminating microfilm before it falls into the hands of the Thailand government. Prepare yourself for a particularly unsettling ending dealing with a double-cross by the ugly Americans.

RAINING NIGHT'S KILLER (1986)
director: **Lau Kar Leung.** ★★
A good suspense story about a serial killer **(Chu Yan Rong)** loose in the city, but he strikes only when it rains. Graphic and chilling, but unfortunately very slow.

RAISE THE RED LANTERN (1991)
director: **Zhang Yimou [Zhang Yi Mu].** Gong Li·Ma Jingwu·He Chaifei·Cao Cuifeng·Kong Lin ★★★★
The award-winning Chinese/Hong Kong art film that thrust **Gong Li** into international prominence. An argument could be made that this movie is too highbrow for inclusion in a book called *Asian Cult Cinema,* but its exclusion would be a grave disservice indeed.
This is the majestic story of sex and loyalty in China's 1920s, told with striking perception by a young concubine (Gong Li) who joins a rich nobleman's extensive harem. Despite the seemingly chauvinistic subject matter, *Raise the Red Lantern* emerges as one of the greatest, most starkly honest, depictions of female bonding ever presented on the screen.

THE RAPE AFTER (1986)
director: Ho Meng Hua [Ho Menga].
Chang Ching Yu·Tsui Sui ★★★½
After all is said and done, this one remains one of Hong Kong's best horror films. It's bursting with enough chills and imaginative scares to fill a dozen traditional fright flicks (a similar accolade could also be applied to the same director's **Black Magic.**)

One of the best things about this film is the complete lack of slapstick humor that too often mars the consistency of HK horror. Rather—from the opening moments, when Shu Ya **(Chang Ching Yu)** visits her retarded, deformed brother (a victim of syphilis, a disease passed on by his adulterous father), this motion picture creates an atmosphere of dark tension, creeping evil, and a foreboding sense of gloom.

As the story unfolds, we see a rotting corpse in a maggot-infested closet; a woman who chops her finger off with a meat cleaver; an abortion interrupted by an angry, vicious ghost; a priest whose ears are ripped off by a gang of zombies—plus magic spells, a killer fetus, severed heads, and rats erupting into fiery fur balls!

RAPE AND DIE (1987)
director: Lionel Ko Cheung. Chow Shu Lan·Lu Leung Wei·Wu Menga Da
★
Exploitive title, but not much of a movie. A girl (Chow Shu Lan) runs away from home after her mother's pimp of a boyfriend tries to rape her. There's also an interwoven alternate story (a unique multiple-choice approach to filmmaking) about the mob and a missing suitcase of jewels.

Also starring Lu Leung Wei and Wu Menga Da in thankless roles.

RAPED BY AN ANGEL
See *Naked Killer 2: Raped By an Angel*

RECORD OF BLOOD (1986)
director: Tsang Chung Chiang. ★
This Hong Kong equivalent of *Death Faces* (you know, the horrible American let's-make-a-quick-buck *Faces of Death* rip-off) is a "shockumentary" filled with out-of-focus newsreels of executions and war crimes, plus a wretched feature about drug trafficking through Thailand that encompasses most of the film's running time. Don't get suckered.

RED AND BLACK (1986)
director: Andrew Kam Yuen Wah.
Joey Wang·Eric Tsang·Leung Chia-Hui·Wu Ma·Lam Ching Ying ★★½
Here's an unusual (and unlikely) amalgamation of a parasite-vampire motif in a politically motivated war saga, deeply saturated with propaganda overtones.

In 1941, during the Japanese occupation of mainland China, a man is infected by a Nippon vampire soldier. He manages to climb into an underground cavern, where he impales himself on a wooden stake. 25 years later, after the Mao Communist revolution, he's inadvertently resurrected by his unsuspecting son (Leung Chia-Hui) and returns to life long enough to infect the People's leader.

RED SHIELD (1992)
director: Parkman Wong [Wong Kuo-Chu]. Danny Lee·Leung Ka Yan ★½
It's all been seen before. Cops are trying to capture gun traffickers (this time it's the dreaded Ma An Mountain Triad), but the law is too lenient and the crooks are too cagey. Detective Lui Ti-Ken **(Danny Lee)** becomes suspicious when a nondescript officer

Danny Lee in *Red Shield*

(Leung Ka Yan) succeeds in shooting one of the bad guys.

Everybody seems to be sleepwalking through the scenes. Even Phil Chen's sound track is lackluster. A disappointment.

RED SPELL SPELLS RED (1983)
director: He Yong Lin (Titus Ho). Tony Chun Yip·Leung Chi Hong ★★
Mayhem in Borneo! Exorcism! Possessed natives! Explorers discover images of devils on film when they return from the jungles, so they go back to take a closer look. The ending pays off. But similar to the Italian *Cannibal* films, there's lots of "mondo" footage in this gross-out flick.

RED TO KILL (1994)
director: Billy Tang [Tang Hin Sing]. Chung Suk Wai·Lo Man Yee·Ng Ai Cheung ★★★
Another rough ride in Hong Kong sleaze from the notorious director **Billy Tang,** the man responsible for both *Dr. Lamb* (1992) and *Run and Kill*

(1993). In the first 10 minutes of this entry, a psycho necrophile kills a woman and rapes her; at the same time, the film intercuts to a mentally disturbed woman who jumps from a high rise building with her young child, his head exploding like a ripe watermelon when they hit the ground—then the film gets really violent.

As it turns out, the action is set in a hospital for retarded young patients. There's a dedicated lady social worker and her favorite patient Ming-Ming (Lo Man Yee), a gorgeous 21-year-old ballet dancer with the mind of a 10-year-old girl. There's also a wacko doctor named Chan (Chung Suk Wai), who goes around sexually assaulting and killing a bunch of women, presumably because they're wearing red (thus the title).

However, Chan is basically a romantic guy; he may be a rapist, a necrophile, and a murderer, but he does have a heart. He falls in love with Ming-Ming after seeing her dance in a gorgeous red dress. Naturally Chan forces Ming-Ming to satisfy his carnal desires, but he doesn't kill her. In fact, he wants them to live happily ever after.

This is problematic for Ming-Ming, who is not quite used to this behavior. Presumably, even a gal with the mind of a 10-year-old doesn't like being brutally raped. After the ordeal, she proceeds to mutilate her "violated, soiled regions" with a straight blade. The social worker finds her, still sitting in the bathtub, clogging up the drain. The girl confides in her and they take Chan to court. Presumably because this is a movie, the case is thrown out of court. Then the girls prepare a trap for Chan, but he surprises everybody (including the audience) by taking a straight razor and slashing his way to infamy.

Red to Kill is excessively grim, salacious, vile, offensive, and sleazy. The rapes and murders are filmed in cold, clinical ice-blue hues (similar to Tang's work in *Dr. Lamb*). They are excessively graphic, as is much of the nudity. The acting is surprisingly good, and in many instances understated.

REINCARNATION OF GOLDEN LOTUS (1989)
director: Clara Law. Joey Wang·Eric Tsang ★★½
This is a good-looking reincarnation flick, suggesting that nothing ever changes and everything is predestined, no matter how many times a soul comes back.

It begins with Golden Lotus **(Joey Wang)** in the afterlife. She is complaining about how awful her life was and how she wants revenge for the death of her lover. Golden Lotus is reborn in mainland China, where she is miserable. She becomes the victim of rape and mistreatment, and is eventually labeled as a traitor. But a wealthy businessman (Eric Tsang) rescues Golden Lotus and takes her to Hong Kong, where they marry. Soon she meets and falls in love with her destined soulmate (nobody seems too concerned about her husband). After some bouts with drugs and sex, she is once again responsible for her lover's death.

Director **Clara Law** was very vocal about her disdain for this film, complaining that the Hong Kong audiences were stupid for supporting it. In actuality, she was probably more upset because they *hadn't* supported her ambitious art films (e.g., *Farewell China*). Unfortunately, over the next few years, things became worse for the frustrated director. Clara even got roped into making the mindless juvenile comedy *Fruit Bowl,* with **Leon Lai** and **Vivian Chow.**

REMAINS OF A WOMAN (1993)
director: Clarence Fok Yiu Leung. Carrie Ng·James Pak·Loletta Lee ★★★
A drug raid nabs Billy Chan (James Pak) and Judy Yu **(Carrie Ng,** in the haunting role that won her top industry awards) on murder charges after acid-scarred human remains are found stewing in a metal trunk. The bubbling slop is Lisa, part of this cocaine-addicted lust triangle gone awry. So Billy and Judy wind up in jail.

While the prosecutor continues to investigate, a Bible study member, Annie Cheung **(Loletta Lee)** acts as a liaison between imprisoned Billy and Judy. Annie is unaware that by sharing information with the two accused killers, she is actually helping them corroborate their alibi.

The subsequent courtroom dramatics are spiced up with catfights, kinky drug-induced sex and climactic gore. Plus a surprise ending. The whole thing is loosely based on a true story, the infamous Patrick Wong case. This was also the basis for another Cate-

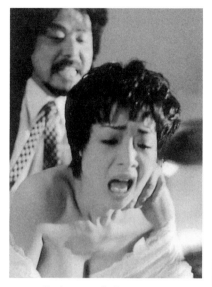

Amy Yip in *Requital*

gory III thriller, ***Legal Innocence,*** made earlier in '93.

REQUITAL (1992)
director: Chu Yin Ping. Alan Tang · Amy Yip · Jimmy Wang Yu · Lo Lieh ★★★

Director **Chu Yin Ping** remains one of the most underrated, wildly eccentric of all HK filmmakers. For more than a decade he's been churning out a collection of cockeyed classics, from ***Golden Queen Commando*** to ***Fantasy Mission Force,*** from ***My Flying Wife*** to ***Slave of the Sword.*** Certainly, director Chu has mellowed somewhat over the years, but he still brings an unparalleled enthusiasm to his projects, resulting in distinctively fresh interpretations within the rigid structures of each genre he chooses to tackle.

With this movie, Chu continues his excursion into heroic bloodshed following the success of his ***Island of Fire*** (1991). This brutal homage to American gangster classics, complete

with a sepiatone prologue, tells the story of Tung (Alan Tang) and his rise to power within a Taiwanese triad.

At first he's portrayed as a cold-blooded killer, but slowly he learns to operate within the unique code of the underworld. Ironically, his humanistic approach to gangland control is eventually responsible for his downfall.

Visually, this film draws not only from American crime noir but also from the Japanese *Baby Cart* series. Case in point: when violence erupts, the result is spurting geysers of blood. The killings resemble extreme moments from a gory horror film more than the typical gangster flick.

And did we mention **Amy Yip**? Once again she turns in a terrific performance, similar to her work in **To Be #1.** It's too bad her early roles, based on sophomoric sex jokes pertaining to her bust size, have kept Amy from being taken seriously as an actress.

This film also benefits from casting former chop socky kingpin **Jimmy Wang Yu** as the weathered triad boss.

RETREAT OF THE GODFATHER (1990)
director: Chen Chi Hwa. Wu Ma · Ke Jing Xiong · Lam Wai ★★

Kwong (prolific Wu Ma) is a Mafia king. When a rival gang steals a rare Chinese artifact from him, he blames his two bagmen and he threatens to "cut their life" if they don't recover the treasure. They do. But then they double-cross him in a bloody gunbattle at the film's predictable conclusion.

Even though it seems that Wu Ma appears in two out of three Hong Kong films, it's difficult to take him as a serious villain. He's been the butt of too many jokes in too many comedies; he simply isn't threatening enough to play a Mafia boss. He has the same problem in **John Woo's Just Heroes.**

RETURN ENGAGEMENT (1991)
director: **Cheung Ren-Jie (Joe Cheung).** Alan Tang • Simon Yam • Andy Lau•Chingmy Yau ★½
Yet another **John Woo** wanna-be film. But unfortunately this director forgot to include likable characters. Much of the running time is hopelessly lost on a Mafia boss (Andy Lau) trying to find his missing son. The final shoot-out is bloody but boring. It's time for something new.

RETURN OF THE DEMON (1985)
director: **Wong Ching (Jing).** Shing Fui On•Dick Wei ★★½
An early effort from actor-turned-director Wong Ching [Jing] effectively mixing terror and comedy, reminiscent of *Abbott And Costello Meet Frankenstein* in style, if not concept. Shing Fui On is the dimwitted hero tricked into releasing a supermonster trapped inside a Buddhist statue. This results in a collection of horror parodies featuring zombies (with spikes in their heads, similar to those in **Black Magic 2**), beautiful female ghosts who want to immortalize their souls through physical communion, a priest who transforms into a dog (which leads to some sophomoric jokes about drinking dog piss). It's not great filmmaking, but a guilty pleasure from a director who later lost his ability to distinguish between humor and silliness (e.g., **Fight Back to School, Royal Tramp,** et al.).

RETURN OF THE EVIL FOX (1989)
director: **George Leung.** Wu Kwan Yu • Chan Kai Ling • Wu Kong • Woo Fung ★★★
Evil Fox is a beautiful villainess with powerful claws and matching super powers. She has journeyed through time and is ready for vengeance against the Maosan family for their generations of past heroics against her clan.
    With a look and style similar to his

Night Evil Soul, director George Leung makes his meager budget sparkle like a million dollars. Plus, there's a cast of likable characters and some innovative scare sequences.

RETURN OF IRON ANGELS.
See *Angel 3*

RETURN TO A BETTER TOMORROW (1994)
director: **Wong Ching [Jing].** Lau Chin Wan•Chang Yee Kin ★★
By calling this film *Return to a Better Tomorrow,* it sets itself up for comparison with **John Woo's** classic films. But then, that was the idea. Right? Director/producer **Wong Ching [Jing]** is not known for subtlety, and he has no shame when it comes to making a buck.
    There's lots of action here, shot with a Ringo Lam rock-n-roll style (while not an original technique, it's better than the slapstick vignettes usually associated with Wong Ching productions). But the story is tired, yet another variation of the young-gangster-climbing-up-the-ranks-to-become-boss theme. Wong tries to beef it up by including some quirky characters (à la *Pulp Fiction*), but he forgets to make them interesting.
    And his real-life girlfriend, **Chingmy Yau,** should sue his ass for felonious assault on a career. Her role of a drug-addicted mom, locking her four-year-old daughter in a cage between abusive torture sessions, is a new low—even for filmmaker Wong.

RETURNING (1995)
director: **Cheung Siu Keung.** Tony Leung [Chiu Wai]•Wu Chien Lien•Sandra Ng•Bill Olive ★★★½
An excellent offbeat ghost story from **Assassin** director **Jacob Cheung [Cheng Siu Keung],** giving a horrific twist to the Ruin Ling Yu legend (see **Center Stage** [1992]).

In this one, **Tony Leung [Chiu Wai]** is an aspiring writer who becomes obsessed with the memory of celebrated actress Sui Mei, victim of an unusual suicide. He finds more than he bargained for when he and his wife (Sandra Ng) investigate her abandoned house, rumored to be haunted.

Chills derived from a well-written, beautifully photographed, production. No cheap thrills here. This is classy adult shock stuff.

REVENGE FOR A RAPE
aka **LADY AVENGER** (1987)
director: Yang Chin Bong. Lu Shiao-Fen · Hua Lun · Kao Nian Kuo · Chu Shiao Ling ★★★
Imagine the plot of *Lipstick* (1976) with the sleaziness of *Ms. 45* (1981), and the result is this movie.

Lu Shiao-Fen is a fashion model who becomes the wrathful lady avenger as she retaliates against the man who raped her. Initially, she tries to put him away legally through court proceedings, but her case fails when he proves that her provocative photos are purposely inciting. Then she takes the law into her own hands.

REVENGE OF ANGEL (1991)
director: Corey Yuen. Moon Lee · Wu Ma · Corey Yuen ★★½
Moon [Mona] Lee, the actress who became popular by starring in the action-oriented *Angel* series, this time plays a turn-of-the-century ghost bent on revenge named Angel.

Early in the film, she is killed during a scuffle caused by a belligerent suitor. Twenty years later her spirit returns and convinces a young man to avenge her death.

The plot is nothing new, but director **Yuen** delivers stunning visuals and extraordinary cinematography. And of course Moon Lee is always entertaining.

REVENGE OF THE GHOST (1981)
director: Lee Yoo Sub. ★★½
Combination mad plastic surgeon and vengeful ghost story, plus a Jack the Ripper-type killer. None of it fits together very well, but it's fun to watch.

REVENGE OF THE NINJA (1988)
director: Ratno Timoer. Barry Prima · Dana Christina · Advent Bangun ★★½
Ignore the misleading title. This is a good, contemporary action/horror film starring Barry Prima (from *The Warrior* series), with lots of over-the-top Indonesian blood and gore.

Twice, beating hearts are ripped from hapless victims. Plus, this movie also features a legion of living dead (Lucio Fulci style).

The ghost of a powerful kung fu master takes possession of a young woman named Mya. He forces her to wear a sacred red necklace. A renegade motorcycle gang tries to steal the necklace, but Mya's boyfriend Ricky (Barry Prima) protects her. Eventually the *Mad Max*-esque gang recruits an evil magician to help them. He does everything he can do, including reanimating the dead.

REVENGE OF THE ZOMBIES.
See *Black Magic 2*

RICH AND FAMOUS (1986)
director: Wong Tai Loy [Taylor Wong]. Chow Yun-Fat · Andy Lau · Danny Lee · Alex Man · Pauline Wong · Alan Tam ★★½
Standard gangster fare, instantly forgettable. There's not much to recommend, with the exception of another charismatic performance by **Chow Yun-Fat.** He plays Mafia boss Chai who befriends a pretty girl (Wong Siu Fong) after her brother is kidnapped and beaten by a rival gang.

Most of the film is a meandering journey through machismo. Lots of posturing, tough talk, and hammy melodramatics. The conclusion, a tense assassination attempt against Chai at his own wedding, is easily the best part of an otherwise dull cinematic excursion.

A sequel, *Tragic Hero,* exists.

RIGHTING WRONGS (1987)
    aka **ABOVE THE LAW**
director: Corey Yuen (Yuen Kwei).
Yuen Biao · Cynthia Rothrock · Melvin Wong · Roy Chiao · Karen Sheperd
★★★
From the very beginning, when the hero **(Yuen Biao)** belligerently shoots a car's gas tank while the bad guys are desperately trying to claw their way out, there's no doubt that this guy really means business.

Yes, it takes an unconventional hero to catch today's uncompromising, hard-boiled criminals. And this movie is filled with nasty villains who do terrible things, like dynamiting a room full of children. However the unique (and yes, surprising) aspect of the film is that this vengeance-seeking, gun-wielding hero is a lawyer! Definitely, he has an intractable way of settling out of court.

RIKKI O (1991)
    aka **STORY OF RICKY**
director: Lan Nai Kai. Fan Siu Wang · Jean Pol · Yukari Oshima · Frankie Chin
★★★★
Based on a Japanese comic *(Riki Oh),* this film gives new meaning to the term "over the top."

It's the story of mild-mannered Rikki (Fan Siu Wang), who freaks out when his girlfriend is killed by drug-dealing gangsters. He gets revenge by using a special type of kung fu (taught to him by his uncle). But he also goes to prison for his efforts.

This isn't just any old prison—this is a maximum-security penitentiary of the future (apparently by the year 2001, the government is no longer

able to afford the escalating price of prison reform, so the job is franchised to the private business sector). But, heroic Rikki can't turn a blind eye to the brutality and the persecution going on around him. After eliminating a prison-guard bully (Jean Pol, from *Operation Scorpio*), Rikki becomes a saint to the lowly prisoners. The administrators, fearing revolt, try to squelch him without elevating him to martyr status. Rikki retaliates by setting fire to a secret opium stash in the prison's greenhouse.

However, the secret of the film's success is that it's not afraid to be completely and totally outrageous. For example: during Rikki's fight with Jean Pol, the villain commits hara-kiri and then tries to strangle our hero with his own intestines! But Rikki whacks him on the back of the head with such strength, that Pol's eyeball pops out and quickly becomes dinner for a pack of birds. Yet that's not all—in the same fight sequence, Rikki's arm is slashed; his muscle is cut, rendering his hand useless. But this minor inconvenience doesn't stop him. With his good hand, he digs into his sliced arm, pulls out the tendons, knots them, and continues the fight!

Remember all this happens in just one of many similar scenes. It would be impossible in this limited space to list every gory wonder. But if ultra-violence is your mania, don't miss this extraordinary pic from filmmaker **Lan Nai Kai** (director of **Erotic Ghost Story, Her Vengeance, Peacock King,** et al.). Interestingly, this movie was a Hong Kong/Japan coproduction and there are considerable differences between the versions released in the prospective countries. The HK edit is considerably less offensive, with most of the extreme gore scissored from the print, whereas the Japanese version appears to be complete.

ROBOFORCE
aka I LOVE MARIA (1988)
director: **Wong Che Keung** with **Tsui Hark.** Sally Yeh (Yip) · Tony Leung [Chiu Wai]·John Sham·Tsui Hark·Lam Ching Ying ★★★★
An early film from **Benny Wong (Wong Che Keung)**, who later directed girls-n-gun flicks (e.g., **Angel Force** and **Dreaming the Reality**) plus the cult hit **Robotrix.** This time he delivers a non-stop SF action masterwork with giant robots and a very sinister villainess named Maria (**Sally Yeh [Yip]** in a dual role). The film is also significant for the second-unit direction by **Ching Siu Tung** (future **Chinese Ghost Story** filmmaker).

The story deals with an evil band of gangsters, called the Hero Gang, who take over the city with their giant robots, smashing banks and destroying the police units in the process. A secret government agent man and a former gang member **Tsui Hark** (John Sham) try to stop the powerful triad by activating their own female cyborg against the gang's Pioneer 1.

The camerawork is extraordinary in this rare mixture of horror, scifi and humor. The well-written characters are complemented by an infectious musical sound track that adds an unexpected luster to the film (unfortunately, in the English version, the original sound track is replaced with a terrible, bland electronic score).

ROBOTRIX (1991)
director: **Simon Yun Ching.** Hui Hui Tan·Aoyama Chikako·Amy Yip·David Ng·Billy Chow·Ken Goodman ★★★½
"Combining human thoughts with a robot's computer program," a scientist muses, "that could have serious repercussions."

"Why?" a reporter asks.

"Because you can't control a robot with a human brain." And so with that bit of obvious foreshadowing, the film begins. Since thoughts can be transferred only at the moment of death (gosh, everybody knows that, right?), the master Japanese criminal Ryuichi kills himself and becomes immortalized inside his robotic creation. Meanwhile, in Robocop fashion, after a policewoman is fatally wounded, her brain is drained into a fighting female robot shell. She and other female cyborgs help the police as they try to find a playboy sheik kidnapped by Ryuichi.

There's lots of action, nudity, and soft-core sex (especially when a sexy humanoid played by busty **Amy Yip** volunteers to go undercover as a prostitute). Many HK video prints are missing a brutal rape sequence that was featured in the theatrical version.

ROCK 'N' ROLL COP (1994)
director: **Kirk Wong.** Anthony Wong ·Carrie Ng·Yu Rong Guang·Wu Xing Guo ★★★
Anthony Wong is the rock 'n' roll cop, Inspector Hung of the Hong Kong Police Organized Crime and Triad Bureau (it's interesting that one year earlier he was a bad-guy trafficker chased by the same squad in Kirk Wong's **Organized Crime and Triad Bureau** [1993]). Besides being a computer whiz and a guitar player, Inspector Wong owns a secondhand record store on Ap Liu Street in Kowloon.

His prized possession is the original vinyl pressing of Deep Purple's Live in Osaka (1972), which unfortunately is destroyed in a shoot-out with the Red Scarf, a gang of brutal mainland criminals using grenades and AK-47s. He is sent to Shenzhen to track down the leader of the gang, Shum Hung (**Yu Rong Guang**) with the help of Captain Wong Run (Wu Xing Guo) of the Shenzen Police Force. Things get complicated when Wong Kun discovers that Shum Hung's girlfriend, Hou Yee, (**Carrie Ng**), is his ex-lover.

Rock 'n' Roll Cop has an excellent cast. Anthony Wong and Carrie Ng were Hong Kong's top award-winning actor and actress the previous year (he for *Untold Story,* she for *Remains of a Woman*). And Wu Xing Guo won the best newcomer award. Plus, HK insiders are predicting Yu Rong Guang will be the next **Jackie Chan.**

Unfortunately, the movie is marred by melodramatics, especially the Wong Kun and Hou Yee subplot. Kirk Wong does not add anything new to this story of a Hong Kong cop meeting mainland police. It's been done to death over the past ten years. As for Anthony Wong, he is only repeating his portrayal of the cool cop from the 1990 TV movie *Iron Butterfly* right down to mustache and mannerisms.

But despite these distractions, many critics are calling it *The New Hard-boiled.* Frankly, the shoot-out scenes are incredible. If you like gun-mayhem, don't even think twice. You *need* to see this movie. You won't even notice the feeble plot.

ROMANCE OF THE VAMPIRES (1994) **director: Ricky Lau [Lau Chang Wei].** Yung Hung·Ching Fung·Usang Yeong Fang·Lin Go Bin ★★½

A woman (nomadic beauty Usang Yeong Fang, from *Beauty Evil Rose*) grieves over her husband's corpse at rest in a glass coffin. The estate lawyer makes the mistake of accepting a date with the flirtatious widow. After some frenetic sex in an alleyway, she plunges her fangs into his neck and drinks heartily.

Switch to Rainbow (Yung Hung, new starlet introduced in **Chinese Torture Chamber Story**), a blind beauty who turns the occasional trick for an escort company where her mother works as a phone-sex operator. Her goal is to save up for a retina operation.

Usang Yeong Fang in *Romance of the Vampires*

Meanwhile, the (un)dead hubby (Ching Fung) is now awake and feeds from his wife's fresh supply of people juice. Apparently not satisfied after making love in the crystal casket, Fung visits a call-girl's house and notices a picture on her night table. Could it be? The woman in the picture, the blind Rainbow, is identical to his lost love from a decade past. Thus begins an interesting love triangle, with horrific overtones.

Although this film is directed by **Ricky Lau [Lau Chang Wei],** it doesn't have the immediate impact of his ground-breaking cult hit **Mr. Vampire** (1984). But the movie has the right attitude, and unlike many other Hong Kong horror pics, it doesn't lose sight of its mission. This is a vampire film, not a comedy.

ROSE
aka **BLUE VALENTINE** (1992) **director: Samson Chiu.** Maggie Cheung·Roy Cheong·Veronica Yip ★★½

Anita Mui in *Rouge*

A rather nondescript piece of fluff love story, with jarring moments of sudden violence. **Maggie Cheung** and Roy Cheong play the lovers plagued by his association with the triads.

ROUGE (1987)
director: Stanley Kwan. Anita Mui·Leslie Cheung·Alex Man·Emily Chu·Lui Chia Yung ★★★
Here's a contemporary ghost story with historically romantic overtones.
It's a stunning, well-written story of a ghostly beauty **(Anita Mui)** who, after many years of searching, reunites with her love mate **(Leslie Cheung).**
Basically it's a bittersweet story, reminiscent of **Dream Lovers,** with a movie-within-a-movie theme.
Produced by **Jackie Chan.**

ROYAL TRAMP (1992)
director: Wong Ching (Jing). Stephen Chow · Cheung Man · Kong Yu · Wu Man Dat ★★

ROYAL TRAMP 2 (1992)   171
director: Wong Ching (Jing). Stephen Chow·Lin Chin Hsia·Cheung Man ★
Stephen Chow (Stephen Chiauo Sing Chi) is perhaps Hong Kong's most popular male star, but beneath his GQ good looks is Jerry Lewis. And his films resemble a collection of frantic slapstick sketches with little regard for story line. They are simply vehicles for Chow's broad and goofy brand of humor, this time choreographed in a period adventure setting.
Fortunately, he's popular enough to attract top-line female costars. If it weren't for **Cheung Man** (in #1) and **Lin Ching Hsia** (in #2), viewing these two films about a swordfighting roque would be as enjoyable as a trip to the dentist.

ROYAL WARRIORS.
See *In the Line of Duty 1*

RUMBLE IN THE BRONX (1995)
director: Stanley Tong. Jackie Chan·Anita Mui·Karyn Cross ★½
Jackie Chan is finally basking in long-overdue recognition stateside. Even the casual American moviegoer has become aware of him through numerous cinematic references to his stuntwork and fighting ability (e.g., Sylvester Stallone's character in *Demolition Man* claimed to learn his skills by watching Jackie Chan movies).
And, in a surprise move, MTV gave its top acting trophy (Lifetime Achievement Award) to Jackie Chan on the 1995 MTV Movie Awards Show.
Plus, Jackie Chan has finally constructed a distribution deal in the United States (apparently with a variety of different companies, including New Line Pictures). Starting with *Rumble in the Bronx,* his films are officially released in America.
But the damnable shame is—the first Jackie Chan film most Americans

will see is arguably his worst movie. At least, it's his worst movie in 15 years (not counting *City Hunter* [1993]).

Rumble in the Bronx is so bad, it can't even be saved by Chan's frenzied stuntwork. This movie has no heart. It has no soul. And the germ of a plot changes direction so many times, it might as well not be there either.

Jackie plays a HK cop vacationing in New York (for some reason, all references to his occupation were cut out of the American release). He learns that his uncle has sold a market to a woman **(Anita Mui)** who is being terrorized by a street gang. The two quickly fall in love and he decides to help her out. After kicking a little butt, Jackie loses interest—seemingly, in both the story line and Anita Mui. In the edited American version, there isn't much of the Chan/Mui relationship anyway. Most of her performance is left on the cutting room floor.

A second plot dealing with diamond thieves is introduced, allowing Jackie the opportunity to kick some more ass (there are definitely a lot of fight scenes in this movie). He also has plenty of time to do a bunch of stunts and then chase the bad guys around New York in a souped-up tank. In the meantime, Jackie has the opportunity to woo another girl, a blonde biker with a heart of gold (Karyn Cross).

Jackie Chan also sings the theme song during the closing credits for the original HK version. His song is missing from the American print.

The movie was released on February 23, 1996, in the States and instantly found recognition as an unqualified hit, opening on 1,826 screens in the continental USA and Puerto Rico, grossing over $10 million during its first seven days. It was the top-grossing film of the week. Although most critics and fans agree this is not a very good film, it was exciting to see Jackie on the big screen. And for many Americans this was the first time they had ever seen the incredible Jackie Chan stunts. The movie may suck, but Jackie Chan's undeniable charm and personality manage to shine through.

RUN (1994)
director: Derek Chang [Man Gon].
Leon Lai·Veronica Yip ★★

This is a Hong Kong version of Robert Rodriguez's cult hit *El Mariachi* (1993). Not an "inspired by" version (e.g., *Black Cat*, based on *La Femme Nikita*), this is an actual clone. First-time director **Derek Chang** (celebrated music-video craftsman in HK) has duplicated exact scenes, imitating Rodriguez's camera style and directing technique.

If there's a difference between this production and that of the more popular *El Mariachi*, it's in the level of violence. Director Chang has toned down the story's savage intensity to match pretty boy **Leon Lai**'s popish personality.

But, otherwise, it's the same. A young musician (this time, Fai from Hong Kong) is vacationing in Mexico, trying to forget a love gone bad, when he is mistaken for a fiendish killer. At that point bandits chase Fai all over the Mexican countryside until he meets Ying (**Veronica Yip**), who gives him sanctuary in her bar. These two become lovers and eventually hunt down the real killer to avenge the death of her brother.

Aside from the obvious reasons (Leon Lai and Veronica Yip fans stand and be counted), it's difficult to imagine why anyone would waste their time with this facsimile when the original is so much better.

RUN AND KILL (1993)
director: Tang Ji Ming (Billy Tang). Simon Yam · Kent Cheng · Danny Lee · Melvin Wong ★★★★

Fatty Cheung (**Kent Cheng**) finds out his wife is cheating on him, so he goes to his favorite bar and gets plastered. There, he meets a guy who is willing to listen to his complaints about the whore wife. Inadvertently, Fatty says he wishes the woman were dead; without knowing it, he has just made a deal to have her knocked off. After his wife is brutally murdered, Fatty is pressed for some big bucks by the hitman, but he refuses to pay. He's beaten and his business is burned to the ground. An old gangster friend offers to help him get revenge against the mob, but he's killed in the process. As it happens, the friend has a brother named Fung (**Simon Yam**), who becomes Fatty's worst nightmare.

Fung is really pissed off over his brother's death. He kills Fatty's grandmother and then torments his young daughter. In a particularly gross segment, Fung turns the little girl into a bonfire while her father is forced to watch the incineration. This repulsive scene accelerates into excruciating bad taste as Fung takes the charred corpse and puts it at Fatty's feet, all the while imitating the girl's voice: "Daddy, I'm all dark. Don't you recognize me?" Eventually, Fatty snaps and takes revenge against Fung and his gang.

No question about it, this is a very rough film. Don't be fooled by the leisurely paced opening 20 minutes. It develops into a cinematic endurance test. The movie is just one more reason why director **Billy Tang** is considered HK's most dangerous filmmaker (also see *Dr. Lamb* [1992] and *Red to Kill* [1994]).

RUN, DON'T WALK (1989)
director: Wong Chung. Ti Lung · Law Ching Ho · Kent Cheng · Richard Ng ★★½

Don't be put off by the nondescript title. Here is a HK action comedy that really works, enhanced by a clever script (which relies on well-drawn characters and humorous plot twists instead of the usual slapstick pratfalls) plus an excellent cast.

Ti Lung is Lok Pui, a convicted felon just released from a four-year prison sentence. As he's taking his first breath of freedom, Lok is approached by Big Boss Sing (Law Ching Ho), who tries to reel him back into the old gang. Determined to go straight, he rejects the offer. But the police, especially two determined undercover cops (fatty **Kent Cheng** and Chan Chuen-Yan), don't believe it and put him under constant surveillance.

Unfortunately, Lok picks the wrong time to visit his neighborhood bank. As he's trying to withdraw a few dollars from his account, a novice gunman (Richard Ng) robs the place. When the jittery thief botches the job, mayhem erupts. He grabs Lok as a hostage. In the confusion, the police mistake Lok for the robber, and he suddenly finds himself on the lam in a stolen car with a panicked partner. Ti Lung made a film with a similar plot two years earlier, *People's Hero* (1987).

RUN TIGER RUN (1984)
director: John Woo. Bin Bin · Teddy Robin · Tsui Hark · Pan Yin-Tze ★

It's difficult to imagine a worse film. It's even more difficult to believe this atrocity came from director **John Woo**.

This is the story of a misunderstood brat (Bin Bin) who finds it impossible to adjust to life when he's adopted by his rich grandfather (**Tsui Hark**) after the death of his parents. A *Mary Poppins*-ish nanny teaches him the joys of a happy childhood.

Of historic note, *Run Tiger Run* marks the first screen relationship between

173

John Woo and his future producer **Tsui Hark.** The two would eventually join as the production team behind the trend-setting *A Better Tomorrow* (1986).

SAGA OF THE PHOENIX (1990)
director: Nam Nai Choi. Yuen Biao·Gloria Yip Wong·Sui Fung·Shintaro Katsu·Li Lai Chen ★★
Yuen Biao is back as Peacock (see *Peacock King* for Part 1). But this time, he is frozen in an ice cage by the Hell Queen during the early part of the film and not thawed out until the final reel. In between, the movie seriously gets off track.

The lion's share is wasted on the juvenile exploits of Genie, a furry creature who carries the midportion of the story.

Lots of money down the drain this time. Watch the original instead.

SAM THE IRON BRIDGE: CHAMPION OF MARTIAL ARTS (1993)
director: Fung Pak Yuen. Too Siu Chun·Yu Hai·Lilly Li ★★

SAM THE IRON BRIDGE 2: ONE ARMED HERO (1993)
director: Wai Hon To. Too Siu Chun·Lilly Li·Fennie Yu ★★★
Let's see, why don't we make a movie? It can't be that hard. Don't worry about being creative. All the good ideas have been used anyway, right? Just take a little bit of that, and mix it with a bit of this, and throw in some of that over there—and po-o-of, we've got a brand-new flick. The people will love it. After all, it's just like all the other ones.

Sam The Iron Bridge 1 and *2* aren't bad movies, they just offer nothing new. In #1, Sam Liang (Too Siu Chun) enters a martial arts contest so he can win the money to pay for his upcoming wedding. Of course, he emerges victorious and is subsequently offered a constable position. But soon he finds himself at odds with an opium trafficker named Prince Mu.

In #2, the better of the two, Too Siu Chun continues in the role of Sam Liang. Now, he's married, and he has become the town's top law enforcer. His arch enemy, Prince Mu, is out for vengeance and a trap is set for Sam. The hero loses both his arm and his wife; he spends the remainder of the film on a frenzied blood mission. Same old, same old.

SATIN STEEL (1994)
director: Clifton Ko Sum. Jade Leung·Lee Yuen Weh·Russell Wong ★★
Jade Leung plays Sergeant Jade Leung of the HK Royal Police Force. She and her partner Ellen (Lee Yuen Weh) are on a cross-country chase through Indochina for an illegal arms trafficker and his criminal gang.

Here's raw action, but the characteristics that tend to make it palatable are missing. Director **Clifton Ko Sum** doesn't have the flare for quick cuts, fancy camera angles, or machine gun edits; instead he expects the action to carry itself.

Perhaps it could, if the star were **Jackie Chan** or **Jet Li,** but model-turned-actress Jade Leung doesn't have the fighting expertise necessary to carry a scene on her own. And this time she doesn't have **Stephen Shin** (the director who made her look so great in *Black Cat* [1991]) to help compensate for her inadequacies; instead, she's got Clifton Ko Sum, whose major claim to fame is the *Happy Ghost* series (1982-1991). Perhaps that's why some of the fight scenes are bogged down with goofy slapstick. And maybe it also explains why one of the villains turns out to have a bionic arm.

SATYR MONKS (1994)
director: Shek Ping. Wong Kwan·Yeung Ching Ching ★★ *(if you're look-*

ing for sex, add a (*) star and go directly to the last paragraph)
A group of monks operate a temple. They appear to be holy priests, but secretly they worship carnality and the desires of the flesh. The boss monk is dedicated to a mission of deflowering 108 virgins. This, of course, means lots of screen time is dedicated to naked bodies and softcore gyrations.

The film also features a mysterious female superhero who beats up the monks. And a dastardly villain named Steel Palm who beats up a good guy trying to protect the women. There's also a master called Double Kick who teaches the good guy how to beat up Steel Palm.

So there's a lot of beating up and beating off. None of it fits together very well. I'd suspect it's really a mix-n-match production, created from various bits and pieces of unfinished or unreleased movies. There's no proof for this suspicion, except the film makes no sense otherwise.

However, for HK voyeurs—don't be swayed by the incongruous plotline. This film offers an abundance of gratuitous nudity and some very steamy lesbian scenes.

SAVIOR (1984)
director: Ronny Yu. Wong Suk · Bak Ying · Wu Man Hong ★★★
A *Dirty Harry* clone directed with style and vigor by filmmaker **Ronny Yu**, celebrated director of **Bride with the White Hair**. Inspector Tom Chu (Wong Suk) is a maverick cop looking for a psycho sex slayer, a pervert who enjoys slicing up prostitutes.

It seems young Paul Kwoh had watched as his mother slit her throat with a razor blade. Her last words to him were "Women are tramps. Tramps took your daddy. And now tramps killed your mummy." Years later, with his brain twisted in complete madness,

Aaron Kwok in *Saviour of Souls*

Paul Kwoh is on the streets chopping up the ladies of the night.

And Inspector Tom loses a partner trying to stop him.

SAVIOUR OF SOULS (1992)
aka **TERRIBLE ANGEL**
director: Corey Yuen (with **David Lai**). Aaron Kwok · Anita Mui · Andy Lau · Kenny Bee · Gloria Yip ★★★

SAVIOUR OF SOULS 2 (1993)
director: Corey Yuen. Andy Lau · Rosamund Kwan · Yuen Kwai · Richard Ng ★★
The action sequences in *Savior of Souls #1* are among the best you'll ever see, but the silly love story is absolutely excruciating. Perhaps this comes as no surprise since director **Cory Yuen** is best known for his frantic, demon-paced action films (**Righting Wrongs, She Shoots Straight**, and the **Yes, Madam!** series).

It's the story of an evil hitman, Silver Fox (**Aaron Kwok**), and his relentless search for a female revolutionary named May Yiu (**Anita Mui**). You'll find unique fantasy elements at work here, including sidekick Ching-Lan's (**Andy Lau**) encounter with the Madame of the Pets in a female stronghold, plus lots of magic spells and swift swordplay in contemporary Hong Kong.

Only Andy Lau returns for the sequel. He's joined by **Rosamund Kwan** (who almost arrives too late for a starring position) and Richard Ng, hamming it up in a villainous role as the Devil King. Silly comedy sketches and overly long sight gags keep this one from being taken seriously, but the scenery (mostly snowy mountains, photographed in Canada) is quite refreshing and provides a nice backdrop for the much-anticipated action sequences.

SCARE THE LIVING (1991)
director: Lee Leung. Hui Ying Hong · Ku Fun ★★★
In ancient China, a young woman is beheaded for practicing sorcery. Years later her mummified torso is unearthed during an excavation project. Mystically, she is reanimated and begins a search for her missing head. Surprisingly, it's not as stupid as it sounds.

Anyway, the head has taken possession of an attractive girl (Hui Ying Hong), who is eliminating ancestors of the men who initially convicted her. Also starring Ku Fun as the cop on Hui's trail.

SCARED STIFF (1988)
director: Donny Yu. Eric Tsang · Anita Mui · Chow Yun-Fat ★
This film tries to touch all the bases, with elements of horror, fantasy, comedy, action, suspense, and even some dramatic moments. The result is an unsettling hodge-podge that resembles peanut butter on a pizza. Even **Chow Yun-Fat** in a small role as the sadistic cop-villain can't save it.

SCHEMING WONDERS (1991)
director: Norman Law. Shing Fui On · Lee Yuan Ba ★★½
A comedy with people getting shot in the back and blown up by bombs? Once again, here's a film that shows the big difference between Eastern and Western cinema. Essentially, this is a strange mixture of lighthearted comedy and ultraviolence [somehow mixing the *Lethal Weapon* cop/buddy formula with *Police Academy* gags], but the charisma between the two cops (tough Shing Fui On and flatfoot Lee Yuan Ba) makes it an enjoyable excursion.

SCHOOL ON FIRE (1988)
director: Ringo Lam. Lee Lai Yui · Lau Chun Yan · Yuen Kit Ying · Lam Ching Ying ★★★
This earlier effort by **Ringo Lam** is a mean-spirited, ultraviolent look at triads and their youth gangs. Although not as strong as director Lam's later powerhouse films (**Full Contact** is still his masterpiece), this is a terrific exploitation film with an exceptional cast.

Don't expect namby pamby *To Sir with Love* sentimentality. And this film wasn't made to educate an adult audience (e.g., **Larry Lau**'s *Gangs*). Ringo Lam was interested only in making a violent action film. And on that level he succeeded.

The movie follows Chu Yuen Fong (Lee Lai Yui) as she unwillingly gets sucked into the gang underworld. After watching some triad students beat up another student, she makes the mistake of fingering them to the cops. This doesn't please the head boss, who is shaping these kids into mean, fighting triad machines. He makes her pay hard cash for squealing.

But when she can't pay, Yuen Fong ends up whoring herself for the money. This pisses off her father, who tries to rescue her from this sordid life. But when he bites it, she has to take revenge into her own hands.

SEA WOLVES (1990)
director: Cheng Siu Keung. Cynthia Khan · Simon Yam · Gary Chow ★★★

A cop/action movie that benefits from an unusually intelligent script, somewhat of a rarity in HK ultraviolent films. Plus, it features two of Asia's biggest stars: **Simon Yam** (fresh from his career-making role in **Bullet in the Head**) and fiery beauty **Cynthia Khan** (best known for her sumptuously excessive series **In the Line of Duty**).

Drug smugglers are using refugee ships from Vietnam to transport their illegal shipments. A band of modern-day pirates intercept the boats, robbing and killing everyone. The HK Royal Police try to stop it all.

SEARCHING FOR LOVE (1987)
director: Yang Chin Bong. Chuan Chi Hui·Tang Chen Yie ★★
It's sleazy. It's rough.

A woman, Maria Jo (Chuan Chi Hui) is looking for her long-lost father (Tang Chen Yie). She eventually finds him. But first, she is kidnapped, inducted into a slavery ring, tortured and raped . . . yes, she finally does find Daddy. It turns out that he is the madman running the slave-smuggling racket!

SEEDING OF A GHOST (1986)
director: Yang Chuan. Phillip Ko · Chuan Chi Hui ★★★★
This film was originally designed as the third entry in the **Shaw Brothers' Black Magic** trilogy, but censorship problems plagued the production, resulting in a less-than-enthusiastic distribution. However, the uncut version of this film in many ways surpasses its predecessors, especially on the gross-out level. And in the gratuitous nudity department.

A taxi driver is suspected of murdering his unfaithful wife, Irene. But actually she'd been raped and killed by a pair of delinquent psychos, who attacked her as she was returning home from an adulterous affair with her lover. Frustrated, the husband (Philip Ko [Kao Fei]) contacts a warlock, who agrees to level a lethal curse against everybody remotely responsible for Irene's death.

The result is a relentless barrage of vengeance, graphically administered. Victims upchuck worms. Body parts explode. In short, there's an absolutely amazing amount of blood spilled, sprayed, and splattered . . . making this movie the zenith, the apex, the very top in the Asian gore category. Also starring Chu Shao-Chiang and Chuan Chi Hui (the tormented star from **Searching for Love**).

SERIOUS CRIMES SQUAD.
See *Crime Story*

SEVEN COFFINS (1987)
director: Ting Shan Si. Kwan Shan · San San·Lee Ying ★★
A feeble attempt to combine the budding HK lenience toward nudity and sex with a haunted house tale.

There's a whorehouse next to an old, haunted inn. When one of the prostitutes won't perform her duties, she's locked inside the adjoining building. "Men just take your body," Madam Chiao (Kwan Shan) warns the disobedient whore, "but ghosts take your life."

Meanwhile, Wang Ching-Feng (San San), the legitimate owner of the inn, arrives. She wants to rid the house of the seven ghosts, restless spirits who supposedly lost their lives at the hand of a Manchu rebel. After an extensive plan involving her husband (Lee Ying) masquerading as a Taoist priest, the mistress of the whorehouse is exposed for killing Wang's parents and stealing their fortune. The ghosts leave the inn when karma is balanced.

SEVEN MAIDENS.
See *Holy Weapon*

SEVEN WARRIORS (1989)
director: Terry Tong. Adam Cheng·
Teresa Mo·Jacky Cheung·Tony Leung
[Chiu Wai] · Lo Lieh · Wu Ma · Samo
Hung·Max Mok·Kuo Chui ★★★
In 1954, the legendary Japanese director Akira Kurosawa made *Seven Samurai*, the film about poor farmers who hire professional mercenaries to protect their feudal village from bandits. This plot served as the foundation for the John Sturges American Western classic, *The Magnificent Seven* (1960), wherein gunslingers are paid to guard a Mexican town from a vicious gang of thieves.

Seven Warriors is a Hong Kong remake that more closely resembles the style of the Sturges adaptation, as a besieged community hires seven rogue fighters to stop a marauding pack of revolutionary bandits. Each of the heroes are social misfits who eventually become humanized by the strife. However, the broad characterizations are mere cornerstones for the final confrontation that bestows freedom to the village, but deals death to most of the warriors.

This version benefits from a fine cast, including Adam Cheng as the noble leader, plus **Tony Leung [Chiu Wai]**, **Jacky Cheung** (wearing a stylish long coat, spaghetti Western fashion), Teresa Mo, Shing Fui On, **Max Mok,** Ben Lam, and—Wu Ma as Ghost, a retired military officer who (similar to the Robert Vaughn character in the Sturges version) is convinced that the whole conflict was really over a hidden treasure.

The film also features a brief cameo by **Samo Hung** (rumored to be the codirector with **Terry Tong**) as the village patriarch slain in the opening sequence.

SEVENTH CURSE (1986)
director: Lan Dei Tsa. Andy Lau·Dick Wei·Maggie Cheung·Chow Yun-Fat·
Lin Chi Shin·Yasuaki Kurata·Joyce Godenzi ★★★
While a group of explorers are on an expedition in the jungles of Thailand, an anthropologist (Andy Lau) stumbles upon the bizarre ritualistic ceremony of the Worm tribe. A beautiful girl (Lin Chi-Shin) is tied to an altar and is being sacrificed to a creature that looks like *Alien*.

The explorer saves her, only to be captured himself by the witch doctor. Helplessly, the unfortunate anthropologist watches as a friend is annointed with a strange gunk that causes his body to convulse and explode in a shower of worms and other slithering creatures. Then the witch doctor snatches up the eyeball of the ruined friend and forces it down the throat of the explorer.

Immediately, the hero's body is infected with erupting painful blood boils. However, he does manage to escape, and his physical malfunction is reversed when the girl cuts off her nipple (!) and feeds it to him. All this takes place in the first half hour!

Next, it's one incredible scene after another. There are magic spells using blood of black dogs and black sheep, and others using the blood of freshly slaughtered children from a nearby tribe! There are small *Alien* creatures that burrow into the victim's chest and out the other side plus a large *Alien* creature (called Old Ancestor) that rips the head off the victim and drinks blood from the stump!

Also, as an extra bonus, this movie features **Chow Yun-Fat** in one of his early roles, as he blows the hell out of the creature with a rocket launcher.

SEX AND ZEN (1991)
director: Michael Mak. Lawrence Ng·Amy Yip·Kent Cheng·Lo Lieh·Carrie Ng·Isabella Chow ★★★½

An excellent attempt to merge erotic literature with film. Based on a famous Chinese book [*Carnal Praying Mat*] by Chao Meng Fu, written in the 17th century, this movie delivers a collection of tales dealing with the joy (and in some instances, the pain) of sex.

Refreshingly graphic without becoming hard-core. Generally, a most intelligent journey into sleaze and eroticism with Lawrence Ng, **Kent Cheng**, Lo Lieh, **Carrie Ng**, Isabella Chow, and **Amy Yip** (in her only nude scene to date).

SEX OF THE IMPERIAL (1991)
director: Woo Ka Chi. Wong Ten Ying·Hung Po Wu ★½
A ruler in ancient China is anxious to have a male son, but so far he's had no luck. Six consecutive wives have failed to conceive a baby. But his newest wife, figuring the problem has to do with the king's potency rather than the wife's fertility, decides to secretly sleep with many men in order to insure her pregnancy.

It's not a bad idea for a soft-core sex romp. However, since the production is so sloppy and cheap, only skin fans are apt enjoy it.

SHANGHAI EXPRESS (1987)
director: Samo Hung. Samo Hung· Yuen Biao·Eric Tsang·Olivia Chang· Rosemary Kwan · Cynthia Rothrock · Yukari Oshima·Dick Wei ★★½
A nice blend of Chinese slapstick comedy and martial arts mayhem, brewed by filmmaker **Samo Hung**. It boasts a star-studded cast of Samo's buddies (**Jackie Chan** is conspicuous in his absence), plus it marks HK acting debuts for Cynthia Rothrock and **Yukari Oshima**.

In the tradition of movies like *Grand Hotel*, this one is little more than a number of vignettes tied together by the fact that everyone is aboard the maiden run of the Shanghai Express.

SHANGHAI SHANGHAI (1990)
director: Teddy Robin Kwan. Samo Hung·Yuen Biao·Anita Mui·Lo Lieh· George Lam·Sandy Lam ★★½
A terrific cast in a rather lackluster production. There are some great sets and cinematography (the Shanghai of 1930 looks surprisingly authentic), but the story is uninspired. A country rube (**Yuen Biao**) goes to Shanghai to find his brother but instead winds up in the middle of a war between two gangs (**Samo Hung** and Lo Lieh are the two rival triad kingpins).

Anita Mui is caught between the two warring families. George Lam plays the long-lost brother who is now working undercover for the military police. His position is compromised because he's infatuated by a goddaughter (Anita Mui) of one of the gangster leaders. Realistically, Anita has little to do except look pretty. But she's trapped in a ridiculous subplot about her involvement with a band of revolutionary patriots.

SHAOLIN POPPY.
See *China Dragon*

SHE SHOOTS STRAIGHT (1991)
director: Corey Yuen. Joyce Godenzi ·Yuen Wah·Tony Leung [Chiu Wai]· Samo Hung·Carina Lau ★★★
This film is little more than a showcase for action star Joyce Godenzi (the Anglo/ Chinese kickboxer from *Eastern Condors*). And, as such, it's loads of fun. The incidental plot deals with a female cop (Godenzi) and her fight against the Mafia Triad (headed by *Iceman Cometh* villain Yuen Wah) while she tries to keep her marriage intact. **Tony Leung [Chiu Wai]** stars as her enervated cop husband. **Samo Hung** produced the film and stars as the chief of police. In real life, he married Joyce Godenzi in 1995.

SHOCKING! (1987)
director: **Ho Fong.** ★
An old-dark-house motif with *Amityville Horror* cloned theme, as a reporter and his family move to a haunted house in the country. The ending is a major disappointment. You'll feel cheated.

SHOGUN AND LITTLE KITCHEN (1991)
director: **Ronny Yu.** Yueu Biao·Wu Ma·Leon Lai·Monica Chan ★
It's sad to see a talented, veteran filmmaker like **Ronny Yu** stoop to this type of drivel. **Yuen Biao** is a martial arts fighter who becomes a cook in his uncle's outdoor shelter for the homeless.

What happened to this director? Avoid this one and see his **Bride with the White Hair** (1993) instead.

SHOOT TO KILL (1994)
director: **Wong Kam Tin (Parkman Wong).** Danny Lee·Parkman Wong· Cheung Kar Fai ★½
Another quickie exploitation feature (probably shot in tandem to the similar **Portrait of a Serial Rapist**) produced by **Danny Lee**'s Magnum Productions and directed by **Parkman Wong**. It's the story of 18-year-old Lo (Cheung Kar Fei), who gets out of prison and promptly becomes a raving psycho killer, attacking his old gang with a machete; then he kills a hostage during a robbery.

After the ruckus, the film's attention shifts to Danny Lee and his gang of cops (the same ones from **Untold Story**). Eventually, they catch the rotten kid and, in typical fashion for this kind of film, they beat the hell out of him in a police interrogation. Lu finally confesses, and everybody walks away satisfied. Everybody except the audience.

SISTERS OF THE WORLD, UNITE (1991)
director: **Maisy Choi.** Sally Yeh (Yip)· Silvia Chang ★½
An unintentional kick in the head to the Women's Lib movement. The only sisters who will unite for this film are the ones protesting its lightweight depiction of a woman's strife in a man's world.

Sally Yeh and **Silvia Chang** compromise their powerful screen presence in this fluffy tale of contemporary male/female love relationships.

SKETCH OF A PSYCHO (1990)
director: **Dennis Yu.** Wu Choi Fan· Fung Sui Fang ★★½
The director of **Evil Cat** and **Imp** creates a scary, killer-on-the-roam, slasher movie punctuated by the unnerving, extreme close-ups (similar in style to many of the great Italian thrillers).

SKINNED GIRL (1993)
aka **NEW HUMAN SKIN LANTERN**
director: **Lau Chang Wei [Ricky Lau].** Tony Leung [Kar Fai]·Chingmy Yau ★★
Poor **Ricky Lau**. His filmmaking career was riding high with truly wonderful films like **Mr. Vampire** and **Spooky Family**, and then he began making movies for HK's biggest hack, producer/ director **Wong Ching [Jing]**. Now he's directing mediocrity like *Skinned Girl*.

It's not actually a terrible movie; it's just not very good. Certainly not on par with his earlier films.

In this one, **Tony Leung [Kar Fai]** is searching for a skin lantern. Apparently it was created hundreds of years ago, from the skin of his girlfriend in a former life. Her soul can't be released to heaven as long as the skin is stretched over the lantern, so he must find the lamp and free the girl's spirit.

Karl Maka (L) with Samo Hung in *Skinny Tiger and Fatty Dragon*

This leads to some interesting supernatural thrills and chills since the lantern is being kept by a sadistic psycho monk who is willing to stop at nothing to keep his hands on it.

SKINNY TIGER & FATTY DRAGON
aka **NUTTY KICKBOX COPS** (1990)
director: Lao Kar Wing. Karl Maka · Samo Hung · Wanda Jessica Yeng · Ngai Hong ★½
A major disappointment from director **Lau Kar Wing** (*Tiger on the Beat*) relying too much on the tired buddy/cop relationship between Skinny Tiger (baldy **Karl Maka**) and Fatty Dragon (**Samo Hung**). The good cop/bad cop routine quickly wears thin in this episodic action comedy.

These two unconventional policemen get into trouble when they "search" a beautiful robbery suspect, Sally (**Wanda Jessica Yeng**). She brings charges against them. Their supervisor uses it as an opportunity to assign them undercover, secretly on the trail of jewel thieves, Sally and her transvestite partner, Eddie (**Ngai Hong**).

SKIN-STRIPPER (1991)
aka **SKINNED GHOST**
director: Chan Chi Hwa. Lam Ching Ying · Chen Ying Chi · Lau Nan Kuang
★★★
What a nasty-edged film this is!

Movie producer Mr. Lau (Lau Nan Kuang) wants to build an entertainment amusement park (similar to Universal Studios), but he can't get the proper zoning clearance from the city. He bribes the police captain with money *and* the promise of bedding the studio's leading actress, Chi Chi Chiang (Chen Ying Chi). But the starlet is tired of being Mr. Lau's private whore. . . .

While she sulks on the producer's balcony, lightning strikes a power generator and live wires tumble onto her. Chi Chi's body is burned beyond recognition.

Doctors shake their heads and plastic surgeons reel with disgust. No one can help her. Finally Mr. Lau contacts a black magic priest who agrees to perform a "change spirit ritual" on the girl. This involves the kidnapping of another female, skinning her, and attaching the flesh to Chi Chi's burned body. After the ceremony, the victim's corpse is buried along the sandy shoreline.

At this point, the gory skin-graft horror tale takes an unexpected twist. Three teenage couples go camping at the beach. After one of the boys pisses on the grave, the skinned ghost is resurrected and possesses Chi Chi's body. She proceeds to skin her enemies until the entire bloody mess is stopped by a good-wizard recluse (**Mr. Vampire's Lam Ching Ying**).

This horror movie, admittedly not exceptional filmmaking, benefits from top-notch gory FX and wildly perverse sex scenes. The savage love-making between Chi Chi and Captain Yong, culminating with his bloody skinning, is among HK exploitation cinema's most gratuitous moments.

SLAUGHTER IN XIAN (1989)
director: Chang Cheh. Tung Chi Hwa · Hsu Shao Jien · Tu Yu Ming · Chow Lung ★★
Director **Chang Cheh** has been making movies for more than two decades. But, seemingly, his innovations are gone, replaced by tired plots and repetitive chop socky action. This time, a policeman takes law into his own hands when he discovers all his colleagues are corrupt.

SLAVE OF THE SWORD (1993)
director: Chu Yin Ping. Pauline Chan · Max Mok · Rene Murakami ★★½
It's good to see Asia's cockeyed visionary **Chu Yin Ping** still hard at work after a decade of demented productions. While this film isn't as good as **Golden Queen Commando** or even **Fantasy Mission Force** (both 1984), it still shines when compared to other pitiful low-budget fare. Plus it's quite a showcase for sexy Pauline Chan.

She plays Wu Nien, an unfortunate girl kidnapped and sold to a brothel during the brutal days of the

Ming Dynasty. The madam, Sister Hon (Rene Murakami), takes an immediate liking to her and they become lovers. But Madam Hon's brother, a swordsman named Yun (**Max Mok**), is attracted to young Wu. This results in a battle between the two siblings, ultimately causing both of their deaths. As it turns out, that was precisely Wu's plan from the beginning. The whole thing was part of a vengeance pact Wu made on behalf of her father.

Incidentally, you'll recognize some of the sets, stolen from **Butterfly and Sword** in true exploitation fashion.

SLEAZY DIZZY (1991)
director: Raymond Sen. Tien Niu · Roy Cheung · Lung Fong ★
It's the **Angel** motif played mostly for laughs. Despite an ultraviolent beginning and end, this story of a female cop and her two less-than-honest friends is mostly a collection of unremarkable sight gags.

SLICKERS VS. KILLERS (1992)
director: Samo Hung. Samo Hung · Joyce Godenzi · Lu Li · Jacky Cheung · Lam Ching Ying ★★★½
An enjoyable action/comedy about a high-powered telephone salesman (**Samo Hung**) who suddenly finds him-

Samo Hung (L) with Do Do Chen in Slickers Vs. Killers

self in the middle of a murder plot with the killers on his tail.

Lots of good action sequences and a clever script. Plus a tremendous cast, including Lu Li and Joyce Godenzi as the women in Hung's life; **Jacky Cheung** is a snotty cop, and **Lam Ching Ying** is the vicious killer. One of Samo Hung's best performances of recent years (perhaps he needs to direct himself more often), plus this time, he gets the opportunity to kick some major ass.

SNAKE DEVIL (1995)
director: Antonio Yu with **Delio Hung** and **Jarin Phomrangsai.** Steven Poon · Lim Mei Mei · Ho Ka Kui · Well Tiraj ★★

Snake Devil

The advertising campaign promoted **183** this one as "an exceptional joint production between Hong Kong, Thailand and Taiwan." And it truly is a joint production, with three different directors (**Antonio Yu**, Taiwan; Delio Hung, HK; Jarin Phomrangsai, Thailand). And three equally diverse leading stars (Steven Poon, HK; Lim Mei Mei (Taiwan); Well Tiraj (Thailand). However, this "exceptional joint production" is not exceptional at all. Or perhaps they meant it's exceptional if you're smoking a joint.

In reality, *Snake Devil* is a jungle girl film, slightly better than **Women of the Jungle** and slightly worse than **Snake Girl Drops In**. Steven Poon is the hunter who finds and falls in love with the jungle girl (Lim Mei Mei) but later discovers her terrible secret. She is the queen of a snake cult and transforms into a medusa during the full moon ceremonies.

SNAKE GIRL DROPS IN (1986)
director: Huoy King. Dy Savet · Roy Chua · Chang Kong Chu · Tong Kwong · Dyna ★★½
An Oriental jungle girl movie, features beautiful snake girl (Dy Savet) who wears a Tina Turner wig to cover a nest of live snakes (!?!); whether these snakes are actually part of her scalp is never explained. Anyway, she freely joins a group of explorers and returns with them to civilization (which, by the way, appears to be only a few miles away).

Some incredible moments (eating a live frog, watering her "snake" hair in a men's room urinal), but mostly it's scantily clad snake girl against the evil gangsters.

Isn't that enough?

SOUTH SEAS BLOOD LETTER (1984)
director: Tsai Ku with **Chou Ming Hung.** Ko Chun Hsiung · Wang Pao Yu ★★★

The Vietnam War is over. A group of persecuted Vietnamese refugees manages to evade the military police and escape the country via a small shipping vessel destined for Hong Kong. Before long, they are lost in the ocean. And soon they run out of food and water. Some die, but others survive by drinking urine, until they shipwreck on a deserted island.

Their total existence is reduced to a simple, basic craving for food. For example, when they find a snake, the group goes wild in a feeding frenzy, tearing the serpent apart and devouring the still-moving pieces.

Eventually, their blood mania escalates into a crazed cannibalistic delirium culminating with consumption of a young child, followed by mass suicide. An unsettling film, due mostly to its relentless trek into absolute gross-out bleakness. How far should a film go? An old question. But in light of viewing this movie, it's a poignant question.

Difficult to recommend; impossible to forget.

SPIRIT OF LOVE (1993)
director: Tong Ky Ming. Loletta Lee · Lam Wai·Che Yen Ping ★★½
Lu (**Loletta Lee**) is protected by a talisman that contains the spirit of her dead baby. Now, why or how her dead baby's spirit came to exist inside a talisman is a very good question.

Apparently, while pregnant, Lu walked in on her husband as he was banging his mistress. Lu went bonkers and got pushed down the stairs by hubby, causing a miscarriage. A necromancer conjured up the fetus's soul and inserted it into a medallion for good luck. But the talisman is accidentally broken and the spirit escapes. The soul becomes an invisible kid. Only Lu can see him, but after the media does a story on the tyke, he be-

comes the target for gangsters who want to use him for illegal gains.

The plot is cute in an eccentric sort of way; however, the main reason for watching is Loletta Lee, who seems to really enjoy getting naked.

SPIRIT VS. ZOMBIE (1989)
director: Yao Fenpan. ★★
This should actually be called "The Priest Vs. the Vampire" because there are no spirits or zombies in the film. Instead, it's the story of a vampire father and young son who are resurrected in modern Taiwan.

Mostly, the film plays on sympathy as these two strangers in a strange land are separated from each other (à la *American Tail* sentimentality). Regardless of the otherwise maudlin script, the ending comes as a complete surprise when the father is blown to smithereens and the shocked, forlorn young child walks off into the fog. Alone.

SPIRITUAL LOVE (1985)
director: David Lai [Li Da Wei]. Chow Yun-Fat·Cherie Chung ★★
The title does not refer to platonic love. Rather, this is a fairly interesting tale of a triangle between a man, his wife, and the ghost of his dead girlfriend. Unfortunately, this plot has already been done and redone countless times.

SPIRITUAL MARTIAL (1979)
director: Chu Chi Hung. narrated by Lo Kwok Hung ★★
A Southeast Asian/Malaysian mondo shockumentary depicting the various aspects of SM (in this case "SM" means spiritual martial arts, but it could easily stand for sado/masochism), concentrating mostly on beatings, whippings, self-flagellation, and various other pain endurance

tests. For about a half hour, it's interesting.

SPLIT OF THE SPIRIT (1987)
director: Fred Tan. Pauline Wong · Hsa Shu Yuang·Wu Hsao Ging·Koo Kwan Chung ★★★½
Pretty Pauline Wong is a famous choreographer possessed by the avenging spirit of a dead woman, killed by her playboy lover. There are some imaginative slayings as Pauline stalks and eliminates everybody connected with the cursed death.

The name *Split of the Spirit* comes from the title of Pauline's play, which is about a tormented girl with a split personality. The tie between real life and stage life results in an interesting twist during the surprise conclusion.

SPOOKY FAMILY (1989)
director: Ricky Lau with **Kent Cheng.** Kent Cheng·Lay Sze·Wong Sil Fong· Wu Kwan Yu·Ricky Lau ★★★

SPOOKY FAMILY 2 (1991)
director: Ricky Lau. Kent Cheng·Lam Ching Ying·Lay Sze ★★½
In the tradition of the **Mr. Vampire** series from the director of the same (actor Ricky Lau [Lau Chuen Wei]), this one is filled with nonstop horror action, some of it deeply rooted in Chinese ghost mythology, thus strange by Anglo standards. A combination of gross terror with eye-popping FX, silly slapstick, and even some dirty humor make the film a balls-to-the-wall fun time. Plus there's even an *Addams Family* rip-off theme song.

A band of unscrupulous magicians revive the Copper Vampire (the most evil creature to ever live) by mixing their tainted blood with that of the creature. Master Chu Kar (fatty **Kent Cheng**), ghost hunter extraordinaire, is hired to fight the monster. He is aided by his odd family, plus a ghost

servant and the spirit of his former girlfriend.

Chief magician, **Lam Ching Ying** (one-eyebrow priest from the **Mr. Vampire** series), joins the cast for zany horrific activities in #2. But it's almost overkill.

SPOOKY! SPOOKY! (1986)
director: Lo Weng-Tung with Samo Hung. Joyce Godenzi·Wu Ma·Jacob Cheung·Richard Ng·Corey Yuan·Billy Lau ★★★
The beach is closed. "Oh No!" cry the teenagers. But even worse: some disobedient swimmers are turning up dead. "Is it red tide?" the teens ask. Has the Blue Monster returned?

No. It all has to do with an ancient curse, and now the lake is haunted. When a pretty girl is sucked into the water, she returns from Hell as a superpowerful sex ghost (Joyce Godenzi). There are further exploits involving skeletons in quicksand, electrically charged fish creatures, zombies, plus attacks by severed heads *and* severed hands.

In a highly controversial segment the severed hand crawls into the police chief's pants and masturbates him.

SPY GAMES (1989)
director: David Wu with **Tsui Hark.** Kenny Bee·Joey Wang·Noriko Izumoto ★½
An unsuccessful attempt at a screwball comedy, mixing romance, pop music, and espionage. A Japanese singer (Noriko Izumoto) believes her father has been kidnapped, so she goes to Hong Kong to find him. Quickly she finds herself emeshed in the problems of an idiot news reporter (Kenny Bee), further complicated by a sexy policewoman (**Joey Wang [Wong]**) and a conflict with Russian spies.

Elaine Lui (L) in *Stone Age Warriors*

STEEL HORSE.
See *Dead End of Besiegers*

STONE AGE WARRIORS (1990)
director: Stanley Tong. Elaine Lui ·
Nina Li Chi · Fan Siu Wong · Devi
Sabah ★★★½
Similar to the Italian-made jungle
movies, this one tells the story of beautiful Eko Lee (Elaine Lui, striking recluse
star of *Angel 1* and *2*), who journeys
into the New Guinea jungles to find
her missing father.
    Joined by an equally gorgeous in-
surance investigator, Lucy (Nina Li Chi
from *Tiger on the Beat*) and a guide,
Abdula (Devi Sabah), Carey goes
deep into the Emerald Forests. The result is a violent, breathtaking adventure that ranks as one of the best Asian
exploitation films.

STONER (1980)
director: Huang Feng. George
Lazenby · Angela Mao · Samo Hung ·
Betty Ting · Huang In Sik ★★★
The supervillain Mr. Sinn (Huang In

Sik) has manufactured a new habit-
forming drug, an aphrodisiac called
the Happy Pill. He hopes it will lull the
world into a blissful stupor, allowing
him the opportunity to take control. Initially, Sinn ships the drug to Australia,
where the sister of Federal Agent
Joshua Stoner (George Lazenby) becomes hopelessly addicted. Stoner
joins forces with an American FBI
agent (played by legendary kickboxer
Angela Mao) to stop the crazed mega-
lomaniac. Together they invade Sinn's
island fortress off the coast of Hong
Kong. After lots of kung fu action, they
are captured and subjected to a variety of carnal tortures in the Temple of
Ultimate Bliss.
    Obviously this film was inspired by
the James Bond tale *Dr. No* (1962).
But the strange mix of perverse sexuality and martial mayhem distin-
guishes it from the countless other
clones. Try to pick up the Hong Kong
version. It runs 25 minutes longer (112
minutes) than the Anglo edit, and features more Angela Mao footage, not
to mention nudity and extended fight
sequences.

STORY OF A GUN (1991)
director: Wong Che Keung. Ng Man
Tat · Charles Heung ★★
It probably seemed like a good idea
on paper. But as a movie, this story of
gun trafficking from China is hopelessly clichéd. The only saving grace is
the rousing conclusion.

STORY OF RICKY.
See *Rikki O*

STORY OF ROSE (1986)
director: Yuen Chein Feng. Chow
Yun-Fat · Maggie Cheung ★★★
In less enlightened times—before the
Women's Lib movement—this kind of
flick would've been called a woman's
film. It's a romantic, bittersweet drama
about the loves that bloom and wither

in Rose Wong's life, from her teen years thru adulthood. And as such, *The Story of Rose* is an engaging tearjerker.

Chow Yun-Fat plays a dual role (initially as her older brother; then later, as Ka Ming, a boyfriend who rescues Rose from depression following a loveless marriage, only to be hit by a motorist while en route to their wedding). But the real star of this film is beautiful **Maggie Cheung**, who sparkles as a teenager and radiates as an adult. Her range of emotion is extraordinary, foreshadowing the wide variety of roles she would later play in films as diverse as *The Actress* and **Heroic Trio**.

STRANGE DEAD BODIES (1981)
director: Kang Bum Koo. Kang Myung·Yoo Kwang Ok ★★★
An Oriental version of Jorge Grav's *Living Dead at Manchester Morgue* (1974): an insecticide brings the dead back to life, plus it causes premature childbirth. The scenes of the deformed babies being born are very shocking (because it's real), but the zombies aren't as memorable due to rather poor makeup.

STRANGE RAPE CASE OF SUNKAM HILLSIDE (1993)
aka **UNKNOWN MYSTERY**
director: Li Yuen Ching. Danny Cheung·Charles Wan ★(★★)
Why do you watch HK films? Did you gravitate to Asian movies in hopes of sexual and violent excess no longer generated by the American movie machine? Or were you intrigued by the cultural differences, enamored of the cinematic freshness? There is no correct answer. Valid arguments can be made for either reason.

However, with regard to this film, if you're looking for sheer exploitation—this is it. If your standards tend to be more lofty, don't bother with this one.

In style and concept it's a clone of *Dr. Lamb* (1992). But that's like comparing steak to hamburger. It's not as poorly made as **Unpublicized Case** (1993), but there's nothing artistic about this film. It exists as a true crime chronicle, eager to exploit the very atrocity it condemns.

As the film opens, Kang (Danny Cheung) is arrested for a violent rape/murder. For the next 90 minutes his life story unravels. It's filled with the usual clichés—including his unhappy childhood and his reckless life with a gang. In the flashback, Kang meets a girl, dates her, and becomes serious about her. One day, while they are making out in the park, two foreigners (probably British, based on their accent) beat the shit out of Kang and rape/kill his girlfriend.

From this point on, Kang hates all foreigners. So when the opportunity arises for him and his gang to beat the shit out of a foreigner and rape the Anglo girlfriend, they snatch it. Kang goes completely nuts with the blood frenzy, and he bites off the girl's nipple, mutilates her vagina, and smashes in her face.

If there's a point beyond the true detective pulp mentality, it's lost on me. Is it a good movie? That depends on why you watch HK movies in the first place.

SUMMONS TO DEATH (1984)
director: Lo Lieh. Tang Ching·Lo Wei ·Fei Jin ★★★
This is one of the coolest of all the HK films. Cool in the James Bond sense. And made even cooler with a great jazz score by Wang Foo-Ling.

It's an odd mixture of espionage, adventure, and melodrama—similar to the Euro rip-offs of the British spy films, but with a decidedly Asian flare, thanks to very stylish direction from actor/writer **Lo Lieh**.

A charming rogue, Teng Lei (Tang Ching), gets mixed up with gangsters and modern pirates when he becomes involved with the crime boss's daughter (Fei Jin). She convinces him to help locate a buried treasure on a remote (and supposedly uninhabited) island).

This Shaw Brothers caper more than casually resembles the *Dr. No* adventure.

SUPERCOP: FEMALE (1993)
aka LADY SUPER COP
director: Lai Guo Jian. Carina Lau · Waise Lee · Teresa Ho · Eric Tsang · Chan Wai Man ★★

A predictable girl/cop action flick. Chang Mi-Hua (**Carina Lau**) returns from Canada to take over an incompetent unit of the HK police force. She is at first amused by their lack of discipline. But when the inevitable disaster strikes, Chang decides it's time to whip them into shape.

Some good girl-with-guns stuff spread sparingly throughout the film with nice ultraviolent touches, including an over-the-top torture sequence with dental instruments (remember *Marathon Man*?), but most of the time it's slow going.

SUPER LADY COP (1992)
director: Yuen Chun Man. Cynthia Khan · Alex Man ★★½

This isn't great filmmaking (unconvincing stunts and substandard comedy severely cripple the futuristic punch), but it's still worth a look.

Cynthia Khan is a cyborg cop on the trail of three nasty criminals (also cyborgs). She's aided by goofy Alex Man (who should've been written out of the script).·

Video game enthusiasts will cheer when Khan transforms herself into Chun Lee of *Streetfighter* fame. She's certainly more convincing than **Jackie Chan**, who attempted the same gag in *City Hunter*.

The most irritating thing about this movie is the director's constant reliance on fast motion. This type of Keystone Cops filmmaking is no longer funny or unique. It's just irritating. And it tends to cheapen the entire production, adding an unintentional air of camp to Khan's martial arts prowess.

SUPER NINJAS.
See *Five Element Ninja*

SWORD OF MANY LOVES (1994)
director: Mak Dong Kit [Michael Mak]. Leon Lai · Michelle Lee · Cheung Man · Li Kar Yang ★½

A Johnny Mak-produced adaptation of Jin Yong's *Adventures of Young Flying Fox* sounds promising. But *Sword of Many Loves* is the worst adaptation ever of a Jin Yong's novel. Well, unless you count **Wong Jing/Stephen Chow's** rock-bottom *Royal Tramp* (1992).

It's a pity because *Adventures of Young Flying Fox* is one of Jin Yong's most powerful stories. Putting the kung fu fighting aside for a moment, other Yong adaptations like *Heavenly Sword and Dragon Sabre* and *The Brave Archer* are great because of the characterization and the intense emotional rage of the plot.

In this one, we have the story of a young pugilist, Hu Rei (**Leon Lai**), learning about the treacheries of the martial world and about the loves won or lost in the process. In the novel, Jin Yong gave these clichés new interpretations, alive with well-drawn characters. Both of these elements are missing from this film.

The powerful triangular relationship between Hu Fei, Cheng (**Michelle Lee**), and Yuan (**Cheung Man**) is gone. Instead, only a facade remains, nothing more than comic melodrama clichés. When Cheng sacrifices her life for Hu Fei in the novel, it's one of the most powerful enactments of the sacrifice of love in Chinese literature. Here Leon Lai and Michelle Lee are merely going through the motions, repeating their lackluster "chemistry spark" from **Wicked City** with no respect for the source material.

SWORD STAINED WITH ROYAL BLOOD (1993)

director: Brandy Yuen. Yuen Biao · Danny Lee · Elizabeth Lee · Cheung Man ★½

Don't bother with this one unless you're suffering from severe withdrawal symptoms and you need a sword movie real bad. Or unless you want to see **Danny Lee** play something besides a cop. Remake of the **Chang Cheh** 1980 film.

SWORDSMAN (1990)

directors: Tsui Hark, Ching Siu Tung, Hu King, Ann Hui, Wah A. Kam Yuen. Jacky Cheung · Sam Hui · Lam

Jet Li in *Swordsman 2*

Ching Ying · Yuen Wah · Cheung Man · Cecilia Yip ★★½

SWORDSMAN 2 (1992)

director: Ching Siu-Tung. Jet Li · Lin Ching Hsia · Rosamund Kwan ★★★½

SWORDSMAN 3: EAST IS RED (1993)

director: Ching Siu-Tung. Lin Ching Hsia · Joey Wong · Yu Rong Kwong ★★★

Regarding *Swordsman #1*, a valid argument can be made that too many cooks (or, in this case, directors) spoil the soup. Parts of this film are extraordinary, but too much of it is needlessly confusing. Overall, this wanna-be epic (based on the classic 2000-page Chinese novel, *The Wandering Swordsman*) suffers from far too many inconsistencies in what should have been a simple straightforward adventure tale about a young swordsman, Ling (Sam Hui), and his search for a stolen scroll. However, there is some interesting comic book violence and a few beautiful women with swords (especially **Cheung Man**) to perk your interest from time to time.

The significant difference between #1 and #2 is the cast. Virtually everyone from the first episode is replaced! Now, swordsman Ling is played by **Jet Li [Li Lian Ji]**, the current favorite flavor of kung fu enthusiasts. And his sidekick is voluptuous **Rosamund Kwan** (one of the few Hong Kong actresses who could give **Amy Yip** competition in the big-breast category).

Overall, *Swordsman #2* is much more accessible to the casual viewer. The story is a return to the basics. A sinister dictator has gained control of the sacred volume (which was stolen in #1). The document bestows supreme supernatural power on the owner—but only if the owner castrates himself, which he does. Slowly, through the process of the film, he is turning into a female (played with wicked sexual charisma by **Lin Ching Hsia** [more recently known as **Brigitte Lin**]).

Lin's performance is so perversely unique (quite a departure from her *Peking Opera Blues* days) that she steals the limelight. *Swordsman 3* concentrates exclusively on her character and her insatiable quest for villainous domination.

SWORDSMAN IN DOUBLE FLAG (1991)
director: He Ping. Gao Wei · Zhao Man ★★★
There's some interesting controversy surrounding this mainland China production, and already it has gained somewhat of a cult following. It's been called a symbolic martial arts film, and a popular European critic labeled it "The Asian *El Topo*." Some people have interpreted the film as a thinly veiled religious allegory mixing Christian and Buddhist mythology, while others claim it's really a metaphorical plea to China for caution in the 1997 Hong Kong takeover.

All this speculation proves one thing, *Swordsman in Double Flag* does something that few chop socky films have ever attempted. This motion picture breaks tradition. It has aspirations of being more than a genre actioner.

It's the story of a teenage swordsman (Gao Wei) who goes to the desert town of Double Flag to find and marry his betrothed wife, 12-year-old Good Sister (Zhao Mana). The townspeople hate him immediately because he's a foreigner, and they hate him even more after he pisses off a notorious bandit who takes revenge on the city.

TAI CHI MASTER (1993)
director: Yuen Woo Ping. Jet Li · Michelle Yeoh [Khan] · Chin Sui Hao (Johnny Chin) · Samo Hung ★★★½
Basically, *Tai Chi Master* is a state-of-

the-art chop socky film, directed with style and heroics by **Yuen Woo Ping**, one of the best genre filmmakers in the business. Over the years, he's been responsible for a series of the most striking, most distinguished martial arts films, ranging from **Buddhist Fist** (1980) to **Miracle Fighter** (1982). He was even the man behind **Jackie Chan**'s two most popular fist flicks, **Drunken Master** and **Snake in the Eagle's Shadow** (both 1978). Is it any wonder that director Yuen has created one of **Jet Li**'s best films? This is especially noteworthy in light of the awful **Wong Ching [Jing]**/Jet Li collaborations like **Last Hero in China** (incidentally, made the same year).

In this one, Jet Li and Chin Sui Hao are constantly at odds with each other. Even though they are best friends, they always seem to find themselves on opposing sides (but clearly, Jet is always the good guy).

Michelle Yeoh plays the leader of a rebel group opposed to the king. Don't expect much from her; the best scenes are given to the two male leads.

TAKES TWO TO MINGLE (1992)
director: Cao Jian Nan. Danny Lee · Yuan Di Ying · Wu Ma ★★½
A tough-as-nails cop, Wong Lee (Danny Lee), becomes irate when he learns that his sister (Yuan Di Ying) is dating the son of a powerful triad leader. There's loads of over-the-top action in this enjoyable variation of the HK ultraviolent action film.

TALE OF A FEMALE GHOST (1987)
aka **HORRIBLE GHOST OF THE OLD HOUSE**
director: Shin Ren. ★
When her coffin is disturbed by grave robbers, a ghost princess (Lee Chian Chian) returns to get revenge. But she seems more preoccupied with getting laid.

X-rated sex action with some of the ugliest people ever put on screen in fornicating positions. A good argument for abstinence.

TALE OF EROS.
See *Erotic Ghost Story 3*

TARGET.
See *My Lucky Stars 2: Twinkle Twinkle Lucky Stars*

TASTE OF KILLING AND ROMANCE (1994)
director: **Veronica Chan.** Andy Lau · Anita Yuen·Waise Lee·Mark Cheng ★
More killing and less romance would have been nice, especially since the two leads (**Andy Lau** and **Anita Yuen**) are so goddamn boring, incapable of generating anything closely resembling a spark between them.

They play two hitmen (hitpeople?) whose paths cross during a shoot-out. Ko and Yu Feng are immediately attracted to each other. They quickly fall in love and then into bed. For the sake of the audience, these two self-important misfits should've kept their mouths shut. The deep, meaningful conversations are ludicrous at best, and embarrassing at worst. Most of us gravitated to Asian cinema to avoid this very type of film.

TAXI HUNTER (1993)
director: **Herman Yau.** Anthony Wong·Lawrence Ng·Yu Wing Kwong ·Lai Hoi Shan ★★★
Anthony Wong, with his demented everyman persona, manages to turn mediocre roles into works of art. This time, his performance adds a satirical dimension to this grim study of a serial killer. He plays a mild-mannered man who takes revenge against taxi drivers after his wife's death is caused by one.

It's directed by **Herman Yau**, the TV director/producer who rose to fame when he assisted **Danny Lee** in the making of **Untold Story** (1992), which also starred Anthony Wong.

TEARS AND TRIUMPH (1994)
director: **David Lam [Lam Tak Luk].**
Anita Yuen·Lau Ching Wan·Lam Man Lung ★
Another HK genre director bites the big one. **David Lam**, after directing **Powerful Four** and **First Shot**, sells out to the hanky crowd in this highly improbable soap-opera drama dealing with high finance and cheap affairs.

Anita Yuen (steppin' strong since her acclaimed performance in **C'est la Vie, Mon Cheri** [1993] and finally canonized by winning the 1995 HK Best Actress award for **He's a Woman, She's a Man**) is back again, this time as an unwed mom climbing the corporate ladder.

Then one day the heel (Lam Man Lung) who fathered her child comes back into her life. It seems that he has since wedded right by marrying the boss's daughter and is now the manager of the conglomerate that has bought the company where our long-suffering heroine works.

He convinces her to become his mistress, but meanwhile she falls in love with the illegitimate stepson of the company's CEO. . . .

Is it necessary to go on? You must get the picture.

TEENAGE TRAP (1986)
director: **Billy and China Chung.**
Tommy Chung · Connie Yik · Frankie Chan ★★
Two teenagers arrive in Hong Kong from Guang Zhou, hoping to find money and prosperity. They wave good-bye at the train station and go separate directions. Ah-Man (Tommy Chung) becomes an auto mechanic; Lin (Connie Yik) works on an assembly line.

After being drugged and raped by her boss, Lin leaves the job and

192 becomes a call girl. She meets a small-time hood named Wing (Frankie Chan, using the pseudonym Mandingo). When Ah-Man loses his position at the garage, Lin convinces Wing to bring him into the mob.

Shot like a Japanese pink movie, this film features an abundance of nudity and gritty sleaze, but it suffers from a tired script. Future action filmmaker Frankie Chan [**Burning Ambition, Outlaw Brothers**, and **Armour of God 2**] serves as both the kung fu director and the cinematographer for this project.

TERRA COTTA WARRIOR (1990)
director: Ching Siu Tung. Gong Li · Zhang Yi Mou ★★★½
A sprawling, partially historic, action-oriented drama from director **Ching Siu Tung** (**Chinese Ghost Story, Swordsman**, and **Witch from Nepal**) telling the story of the emperor's personal swordsman, his loss of innocence, and quest for power. But ultimately it's about reincarnation and true, undying love spanning time.

When the swordsman's girlfriend is executed for sorcery (burned at the stake à la Spanish Inquisition), he travels into the twentieth century to find her wandering spirit.

Epic in scope. Cast of thousands. The two lead actors have become Hong Kong's most celebrated entertainers (director Zhang Yi Mou and his mistress, **Gong Li**, both of whom created the award-winning art film **Raise the Red Lantern**). The exceptional camerawork is orchestrated by Peter Pau (of **Bride with the White Hair** fame).

TERRIBLE ANGEL.
See *Saviour of Souls*

TERROR IN A WOMAN'S PRISON.
See *Anger*

THAT'S MONEY (1990)
director: Wong Che Keung [Benny Wong]. Wu Meng Ta·Mok Siu Chung·Hui Ying Hung ★★½
Here's a lightweight action/comedy from director **Wong Che Keung** (listed in the credits as **Benny C.Y. Wong**), that preceded his cult hit, **Robotrix**, by a year.

That's Money deals with a naive officeworker named Paul (**Max Mok [Mok Siu Chung]**). He and his friends gain possession of $1 million (U.S.) in syndicate drug money stolen after a big morphine deal. Needless to say, nasty mob boss Jimmy Wong wants the cash back, and he orders his strong-arm boys to retrieve it.

Sophomoric jokes about erections and lesbians are prominent, ensuring an overall goofy tone, but violence becomes progressively harder-edged, and the finale spirals to a frenzied gun-n-boxing denouement.

One of the heroines (there are actually three high-kicking kung fu kittens, including Hui Ying Hung) stakes a guy, using a sharp fence picket. Somebody else does a face-flop through a glass coffee table. A vast explosion with stuntmen leaping from upper-story windows ahead of erupting flames provides the adrenalized climax.

As with so many HK action flicks, it's the dynamism of the editing that makes this one click. Of course, the effortless aerobatics of the three supple she-cats also helps.

THEY CAME TO ROB HONG KONG (1989)
director: Clarence Fok Yiu Leung. Dean Shek·Chiugmy Yau·Eric Tsang·Cheung Yiu Yeung ★
The only one robbed will be you. Don't fall for this poorly written giant bore of a movie. A dark day for director **Fok**. See His **Naked Killer** instead.

Lau Cheung Wan and Joyce Jiang in *Thou Shalt Not Swear*

THOU SHALT NOT SWEAR (1992)
director: **Stanley Wing Siu [Chin Sing Wai].** Lau Cheung Wan·Lai Yin San ★★½
Okay. This one opens as a murder mystery. Inspector Chou (**Lai Yin San**) investigates a double killing. It seems someone shot through a window, hitting a hook holding a ceiling fan. The fan dropped and dismembered two people while they were having sex in the bed below. A closer inspection proves the crime wasn't committed with a bullet, but rather with a squash. And Inspector Chou realizes he must be dealing with a criminal of superhuman strength to be able to throw a vegetable through a window and break a chain. A good assumption, eh?

Of course, he's really dealing with a demon resurrected, unknowingly, by five girls who chanted a blood oath to prove their friendship. Chou joins up

with Ti (a thinner and younger looking **Lau Cheung Wan** who found fame a few years later in *C'est la Vie, Mon Cheri* [1993]) to solve the crime and help the girls, who have become possessed.

One of **Stanley Wing Siu**'s better efforts that vacillates smoothly between dark comedy and gross-out horror.

THREE AGAINST THE WORLD (1989)
director: **Brandy Yuen.** Andy Lau· Rosamund Kwan ★½
A pretty bad movie from the director of *In the Line of Duty 3*. It's a caper film about thieves who are attempting to break into a museum and snatch a valuable artifact. Purposely shot in Keystone Cop fashion, complete with sepia-tone flicker. **Andy Lau** plays the chief of security, and he can't decide if he's starring in a comedy or an action flick. We're not sure either.

THRILLING BLOODY SWORD (1986) **director: Chung Leung.** Lau Shun Him ·Fong Fong Fong·Hai Ling Ling·Chung Yik ★★½

An Oriental retelling of the *Snow White* story with a cyclops monster, a couple dragons, an evil warlock, and monkey men thrown in for good measure. It's fun and there's never a dull moment.

THUNDERBOLT (1995) **director: Gordon Chan.** Jackie Chan· Anita Yuen·Michael Wong·Lo Wai Kwong ★★

Well—this story of **Jackie Chan** and his car is better than the previous one of Jackie Chan and his tank (**Rumble in the Bronx**), but it's a far cry from his epic movies like **Drunken Master 2, Dragons Forever, Police Story**, or **Project A**. This is truly pale filmmaking, offering nothing more than various levels of mindless action with absolutely no concern for characterization, continuity, or common sense. Jackie Chan plays a character named Jackie Chan, who works as a mechanic for his father's garage and junkyard. But he finds time to train with the Mitsubishi racing team in

Jackie Chan in *Thunderbolt*

Japan, and he works undercover for the HK Police in their crusade against illegal drag racing.

This is one busy guy!

Plus he has attracted the attention of a crack TV news reporter named Amy Yip (!), played by **Anita Yuen**. She accompanies Jackie one evening as he chases and captures a hot-rod thrill driver named Cougar (Lo Wai Kwong). It turns out that Cougar is an internationally wanted criminal, and he is incarcerated in the HK jail.

So, Jackie becomes a hero. Amy Yip gets her big story. And they fall in love (but amazingly these two superstars are listless partners, merely going through the motions, reciting their lines without a spark of electricity between them). Meanwhile, Cougar's gang rescues the bad guy from jail. The vengeful gangster boss masterminds an attack on Jackie's house, destroying it, injuring daddy, and kidnapping his baby sisters in the process. Apparently the girls were snatched because Cougar wants to challenge and beat Jackie Chan on the drag strip. He's trying to lure the top driver to Japan for a big stock-car race.

It's not clear why Cougar is allowed to participate in the Japanese competition at all, especially since he's one of Interpol's ten most wanted convicts. But the whole thing escalates into a massive race and then an even bigger brawl with Jackie and Cougar pitted against each other inside a Japanese pachinko gambling palace.

1996 saw the release of another Hong Kong car movie, **Full Throttle** with **Andy Lau** (see review). Jackie Chan's next film would be **First Strike: Police Story 4** (1996).

TIGER CAGE (1988) **director: Yuen Woo Ping.** Jacky Cheung·Donnie Yen·Simon Yam·Do Do Cheng ★★½

TIGER CAGE 2 (1990)
director: Yuen Woo Ping. Donnie Yen · Cynthia Khan · Rosamund Kwan · David Wu · Robin Shou · Michael Woods ★★★

TIGER CAGE 3 (1992)
director: Yuen Woo Ping. Cheung Kwok Leung · Cheung Man · Michael Wong · Wong Kam Kong ★★
Accomplished chop socky filmmaker **Yuen Woo Ping** (*Iron Monkey, Snake in the Eagle's Shadow, Drunken Master*, et al.) directs all three of these gun-fu cop movies. There's lots of action, both hand-to-hand fights and extensive gunplay. #1 deals with corrupt, drug-trafficking police officials who are exposed after a notorious triad gang is brought to its knees by an aggressive Narcotics Squad helmed by Donnie Yen (who is killed halfway through the film) and his trusted officers, played by **Jacky Cheung** and Do Do Cheng.

Donnie Yen is back in the lineup for #2, but he's a different character. This time Donnie is an undercover cop searching for a suitcase of dirty money. **Cynthia Khan** and **Rosamund Kwan** are on hand to give assistance when the fighting gets frenetic. The main emphasis is on the martial arts action sequences; Cynthia was made for these kinds of roles.

#3 doesn't fare very well. The plot is not developed beyond the basics; it merely serves as an excuse for some bone-crushing martial arts action. Kung fu boxer Cheung Kwok Leung heads the cast. He's a high-powered secret agent on the trail of a powerful HK businessman (Wong Kam Kong) suspected of criminal activities. Cheung is aided by Michael Wong and **Cheung Man,** who plays his girlfriend.

These three films are quite popular with chop socky fans. But some more demanding critics have complained over the simplistic story lines and the predictability of the projects.

TIGER ON THE BEAT (1988)
director: Lau Kar Leung. Chow Yun-Fat · Conan Lee · Ti Lung · Nina Li Chih ★★★½

TIGER ON THE BEAT 2 (1990)
director: Lau Kar Leung. Danny Lee · Conan Lee · Ellen Chan · Roy Cheung ★★★
Chow Yun-Fat and martial arts boxer Conan Lee star as partners in this police thriller. The plot has to do with the search for a drug lord's killer, but the real reason to watch is the charismatic relationship between the cop buddies. There's also a breathtaking chainsaw battle at the film's finale. Plus busty Nina Li Chih.

In #2, there's lots of action, car chases, and kung fu as Conan Lee returns. But Chow Yung-Fat does not. A buddy picture without buddies is a sad thing.

Danny Lee tries to take Chow's place, but the real excitement is a character called Sweet Dream (Ellen Chan). This girl drips (perhaps the wrong choice of word) with sex appeal, and she wields a wicked gun.

TIGERS (1990)
director: Eric Tsang. Andy Lau · Wong Yat Wah · Tony Leung [Kar Fai] ★★
This one's best described as a police drama. It's a theatrical version of a popular Hong Kong television show, with all the leading stars reviving their original small-screen characters.

Five policemen accept dirty money from a notorious gangster. Most of the film spends time examining each cop's motive for taking the bribe. Unexpectedly, the ending shifts gears by abandoning the ethical questions raised by the first part of the film in favor of a more traditional, yet bloody, shoot-out.

TIL DEATH DO WE SCARE (1985)
director: Lau Kar Wing. Eric Tsang·
Olivia Cheng ★★
Here's a horror comedy, as the ghosts
of three deceased husbands play
cupid with the widow.

The film is directed by **Lau Kar
Wing**, brother of popular director **Lau
Kar Leung**. The conclusion FX are orchestrated by American makeup wizard Tom Savini.

TIME WARRIORS.
See *Iceman Cometh*

TIME YOU NEED A FRIEND (1984)
director: John Woo. Ku Ren·Shen
Bien ★★★
Easily the best of **John Woo**'s early
films (pre-***Heroes Shed No Tears***). It's
a HK variation of Neil Simon's *Sunshine Boys* (1975), the hit play-cum-
movie with George Burns and Walter
Matthau as two ex-vaudeville partners
who get roped into making a TV special.

In this Woo version, Ku Ren and
Shen Bien are a former comedy team
who, after not talking to each other
since their breakup 14 years prior,
suddenly find themselves hosting a
telethon fund-raiser. As expected, they
begin as wary enemies but wind up as
friends. The conclusion, particularly
downbeat, finds Shen dying of a heart
attack on stage while the audience ap-
plauds for more.

There's a particularly bewildering
segment worthy of mention. Initially
when Ku and Shen practice their
comeback routine before a live studio
audience, they are performing the type
of slapstick goofiness that supposedly
made them famous [pie-throwing, pratfalls, etc., not unlike the kind of silliness found in most of the other John
Woo comedies]. The audience is so
unimpressed by the broad humor that
many of them are falling asleep, and
some walk out, shaking their heads in

disappointment. This forces the comedy team to revamp their show. The result is a slick disco extravaganza of
singing and dancing that brings the
house down. Now exactly what is the
message here? If a show biz team
reunites after years of separation,
wouldn't the audience prefer seeing a
reenactment of their heyday? And not
some bastardized *Flashdance* routine?
What does this say about contemporary perception of classic performers?
If Dean Martin and Jerry Lewis [or
even Cheech and Chong] had reunited, would the audience truly enjoy
seeing them do it to a rap song?

TO BE #1 (1991)
director: Poon Man Kit. Ray Lui·Amy
Yip·Cheng Chak·Cecilia Yip·Waise
Lee·Tsang Kong ★★★★
An ambitious rendering of Hong
Kong's true-life Scarface, Ying Ho
(played with exceptional gusto by Ray
Lui). Like life itself, characters filter in
and out of his world, to be used and
abused—and ultimately forgotten—as
Ho scratches and claws his way to the
top of the vicious underworld.

Amy Yip disappears after turning
in one of her best performances as the
gangster's girlfriend; and Waise Lee,
playing the loyal friend Kit, is around
only when Ho needs a shoulder to
lean on. The true dynamics of the film
lie squarely on Ray Lui's performance.
And succeed it does! His character
matures and then self-destructs before
our eyes.

A thinking man's shoot-em-up, stylishly directed by Poon and beautifully
lensed by Peter Pau. Certain to keep
your attention throughout its 150+
minutes.

TO HELL WITH THE DEVIL (1983)
director: John Woo. Michael Hui·
John Woo ★½
In this variation of the Faust legend,
there's an unholy scrimmage between

the spirit of a defrocked priest and a disciple of Satan. They are both fighting over the soul of a mortal who wants to be a pop singer. Certainly not one of **John Woo**'s best. Reportedly, he has said, "The special effects were great, but the drama was hopeless." At least he was half right.

TONGS (1987)
director: Phillip Chan. Simon Yam · Lawrence Tan ★
Two brothers escape the ravages of Communist China only to find themselves victims of heartless capitalism in the United States. **Simon Yam** becomes a drug dealer; Lawrence Tan joins a gang.
   This one is overly preachy and made on a shoestring, with little concern about continuity. Too many unintentionally funny scenes make *Tongs* impossible to take seriously.

TOOTHLESS VAMPIRES (1987)
director: Lu Wong-Tu. Che Bao Luo · Chan Yi Xin ★★½
Here's a comedy horror film that works, because much of the humor is very hip.
   The story itself is about a family of vampires that, due to a genetic imbalance, don't have fangs. Their harebrained schemes for getting blood are both shocking and funny.

TOUCH OF EVIL (1994)
director: Tony Au. Tony Leung [Kar Fai]·Rosamund Kwan·Michael Wong· Elizabeth Lee ★★★
It's a very ugly world, filled with more than just a touch of evil. That's the message behind this great-looking but exasperating film. It's not so much a movie as a collision course. Once these characters are set into motion, like crash-test dummies, they serve only one purpose: to get smashed up.
   Detective Leung (**Tony Leung [Kar Fai]**, sporting decidedly nonregulation shoulder-length hair) is a crazed narcotics cop dedicated to the destruction of a drug-trafficking cartel run by Boss Quiao. Leung will stop at nothing to get the mission done. He is undisciplined, loud, egotistical, and utterly savage in his assault against anyone who gets in the way, including his girlfriend (Elizabeth Lee), a fellow cop who's tired of keeping quiet about Leung's brutal procedural methods.
   As the film opens, the detective bullies a pretty suspect, Coco (**Rosamund Kwan**), into betraying her gangster boyfriend, King (Michael Wong). But then, later, she becomes uneasy about the treachery and tries to save King by convincing him to sever his mob ties. Soon, Big Boss Quiao suspects a security breach, and he decides King must be eliminated. The whole thing escalates into a blood-n-guts gun finale, as popularized by **John Woo** and seen in countless HK flicks since *A Better Tomorrow*.
   This one is better than many of its predecessors. Rosamund Kwan brings a sense of respectability to the entire lurid affair. But it's a harsh movie with an unusually high threshold for screaming and crying. And when people aren't yelling at each other, they're shooting guns, blowing things up, and smacking each other around. Director Au has perfected the baseball bat approach to filmmaking.

TOUCHES OF LOVE (1994)
director: Alan Yuen. Maggie Shaw · Wong Hei·Anna Lau ★½
Isn't there enough product out there without having to release this shot-on-video crap?
   Here's an omnibus dealing with stories of love shared by customers in a neighborhood bar. Maggie Shaw is pretty, and she tries. Maybe, someday, she'll be in a real movie.

TRAGIC HERO (1986)
director: Taylor Wong. Chow Yun-Fat
·Andy Lau·Alex Man ★★½
A sequel to the humdrum *Rich and Famous*.

It's the story of two brothers (**Andy Lau** and Alex Man), members of rival triads, and their personal struggle with the gangster lifestyle. Like the first film, most of the action doesn't come until the end. But the conclusion does offer an impressive two-man assault on the triad boss' house. Significantly, a similar suicide mission conclusion was used the following year for *A Better Tomorrow 2*.

TRAIL (1983)
director: Ronny Yu. Ricky Hui·Chang Seshi·Cheung Fat·Miao Tian ★★½
Smugglers use zombies to transport opium, but the authorities begin to investigate. They trace the zombie trail back to a pagoda, where they discover a vampire running the entire operation.

Veteran filmmaker **Ronny Yu** has created not only a peculiar tale (written with producer Michael Hui) but also a movie with classic good looks. Obviously, much time was invested in this production to re-create the compelling mystical atmosphere. Even though the film is outrageous in plot, director Yu never compromises tradition.

TRANSMIGRATION ROMANCE (1991)
director: Wong Shee Tong. Cynthia Khan ★
I guess it's good to see **Cynthia Khan** in something besides a female-cop actioner, but if this is the only alternative—let's go back to the basics. A make-it-up-as-you-go supernatural thriller about a guy in love with a ghost (where have we seen that before?). Khan plays his spiritually conscious sister who rescues him from a half-baked

reincarnation plot. Transmigration? Indeed. . . .

TREASURE HUNT (1994)
aka **AMERICAN SHAOLIN**
director: Lau Chang Wei [Ricky Lau]. Chow Yun-Fat·Wu Chien Lien·Roy Chiao·Michael Wong ★½
A major disappointment from **Chow Yun-Fat**. There's no denying it, this movie is a real mess. It tries too hard to be everything to everybody and, as a result, has nothing to offer anyone. This supernatural romantic action/ adventure martial arts comedy is a certifiable dud.

Chow plays an American secret agent on assignment in China. He goes undercover inside the Shaolin Temple to capture a band of antique smugglers, but soon falls in love with Mei (Wu Chien Lien), a holy woman sporting psychic powers. Eventually Chow has to fight the bad guys, but first he has a chance to teach the monks about Western culture (i.e., baseball, video games, and french fried potatoes). It's not funny. It's just trite.

TRIAD SAVAGES.
See *Code of Honor*

TRIADS: THE INSIDE STORY (1986)
directed by: Raymond Leung. Chow Yun-Fat·Roy Cheung·Chan Wai Man· Wong Chi Cheung ★★½
An early **Chow Yun-Fat** action/crime melodrama, telling the story of a man who takes over his father's organized crime business.

TROUBLE COUPLE (1990)
director: Ranwood Chen. Olivia Cheng·Bok Yuen ★
The only thing worse than a shot-on-video horror film is a shot-on-video action film. You don't need this in your life. None of us do.

TRUE COLORS (1986)
director: Kirk Wong. Ti Lung · Raymond Wong · Lin Ching Hsia ★
Bad stuff. A hopelessly inept attempt to remake a '40s Hollywood gangster film. (In fact, critic Richard Akiyama insightfully recognized the film's similarity to the James Cagney/Humphrey Bogart vehicle *Angels with Dirty Faces*.)

It's the story of two childhood buddies who take opposing paths in their adult life. One becomes a gangster (**Ti Lung**) and the other is a minister (Raymond Wong) running a home for wayward boys (I know, it's just to-o-o melodramatic for serious consideration!). Even **Lin Ching Hsia** can't save this mess.

TWELVE ANIMALS (1991)
director: Ching Chung Wu. Lu Su Ling · Lee Hsi Ki · Yeung Hong · On On
multiple choice rating:
(mark the correct box with a ✓)
☐ *A:* ★★★★
☐ *B:* ★★★
☐ *C:* ★★
☐ *D:* ★

From the director of *Magic of Spell* (1986), this one is either utterly flabbergasting or terminally juvenile, based on your own criteria.

For fans of Asian fairy-tale fantasy, *Twelve Animals* is well-made, filled with eye-popping mayhem and outlandish dementia.

Plotwise: times are tough for Buddha. His kingdom is being threatened by the Hell God and a beautiful vampire blood queen named Evil She. A dying monk sends Princess Bai Ma (child actress Lu Su Ling) to Devil Island to recruit help from the 12 mythical animals of the zodiac to fight Evil She.

If you've never seen this kind of fantasy pic (peculiar to the Chinese culture), here's a good place to start. If

you hate it, bypass the rest; if you love it, go find **Wolf Devil Woman** (1982).

TWILIGHT SIREN (1990)
director: Lau Chang Wei (Ricky Lau). Ku Fun · Du Kui Hua · Shu Wen Huai ★★
It begins as a rather traditional horror story (with an especially good opening sequence showing motorcyclists being torn apart by a creature or creatures unknown).

Wendy and Jay (Ku Fun and Du Kui Hua), while searching for buried artifacts, uncover a skull and sacred tablet from the Ming Dynasty. Soon, a ghost emerges from the skull and solicits their help in finding the rest of her body so that she might become reincarnated. However, the "protector of the gate" (a ferociously powerful female spirit and, apparently, the creature from the opening segment) tries to stop them.

Unfortunately, the entire middle section of this film is ruined with a ridiculously embarrassing subplot about a dimwitted student of mystical arts named Tao (Shu Wen-Huai) and his lusty pursuit of Wendy.

TWIN DRAGONS (1992)
director: Tsui Hark with **Ringo Lam.** Jackie Chan · Maggie Cheung · Teddy Robbin · Nina Li Chi ★★★
This film answers the burning question: Are two **Jackie Chan**s better than one? Obviously inspired by Jean Claude van Damme's *Double Impact* (1991), this one tells the story of twin babies separated at birth. One of them becomes a world-famous concert pianist, Ma Yu (played by Jackie) and the other is an auto mechanic who studies kung fu, Wan Ming (also Jackie). Of course, their paths eventually cross in a madcap adventure dealing with gangsters and a beautiful heroine (**Maggie Cheung**).

The second half of the film is a barrage of stunts and action sequences.

The conclusion in an auto-testing garage delivers the spectacular type of frenzied Jackie Chan entertainment we've come to expect, providing him an array of props and obstacles to flip in and out of.

But, too often, the pace of the rest of the film is stalled with tired sight gags and anticipated humor dealing with mixed identities. Many fans expected something more, given the expertise of two accomplished directors like **Tsui Hark** and **Ringo Lam,** but the film remains escapist entertainment—quick to satisfy but easy to forget.

TWIST (1995)
director: Danny Lee. Simon Yam · Danny Lee · Kwan Sau Mei · Shing Fui On ★★★★
For those who thought **Danny Lee**'s *Dr. Lamb* was a fluke, think again. This film is equally effective, equally well made, and equally definitive. While *Dr. Lamb* is one of the best examples around of vicious HK cinema (see review), this one is the definitive police-procedural HK film. It is a textbook account, detailing the investigation of a multimillion-dollar heist at the hands of a sophisticated ring of bank robbers.

The actor Danny Lee has been so average in films recently, a masterwork like this comes as a surprise. His characters are fresh even though the subject matter isn't. These people say things and do things that real people say and do. They are alive.

Simon Yam gives a refined, confident performance, reminiscent of his work in *Bullet in the Head* (1990). Danny Lee as Captain Lee Tit Kin is once again heroic, not pompous (e.g., *Untold Story* [1992]).

Even though this is Lee's first film as a solo director (**Billy Tang** assisted with *Dr. Lamb*; **Herman Yau**, with *Untold Story*), his camerawork is astonishingly good. He has a natural eye for blocking and framing that few of his peers seem to understand.

TWO WOMEN FROM NETHERWORLD (1982)
director: Park Yoon Kyo. Kim Ki Joo · Huh Jin ★★
A raped girl kills herself and returns (with a ghost friend) to take revenge. With Kim Ki Joo and Huh Jin.

ULTIMATE VAMPIRE (1991)
director: Ricky Lau [Lau Chang Wei]. Lam Ching Ying · Chin Siu Ho ★★★
Basically, this is an unofficial sequel to the popular *Mr. Vampire* series. **Lam Ching Ying** returns as the one eyebrow priest. This time he rescues his loyal student Hsi (Chin Siu Ho), a young man who has fallen in love with a beautiful vampire.

UNDECLARED WAR (1990)
director: Ringo Lam. Olivia Hussey · Vernon G. Wells · Danny Lee · Rosamund Kwan ★½
This one was planned as an international project, with high-hopes of attracting a Western audience (thus the inclusion of Anglo/Euro actors, Olivia Hussey and Vernon G. Wells). But it chooses to ignore everything extraordinary about modern Asian cinema. No stunts! No martial arts! And no gunplay! Instead, there's only a routine spy plot about a terrorist hitman.

It's a shame Cinema City Production Company put such heavy restrictions on director **Ringo Lam**. But then maybe his *Full Contact* masterpiece is a direct result of freedom from those very shackles.

UNDERGROUND BANKER (1994)
aka PHYSICAL WEAPON
director: Lam Hing Lung [Bosco Lam]. Anthony Wong · Lawrence Ng · Ho Gar Koi · Ching Mei ★★½
Anthony Wong plays a conscientious man who is trying to find a nice apart-

ment for his family. When a woman mysteriously falls from a window to her death, her place becomes available (shades of Roman Polanski's *The Tenant* [1976]).

The Wong family moves in only to discover their next-door neighbor is Dr. Lamb! Lawrence Ng plays the notorious killer this time around, with a calmness that would make **Simon Yam** proud.

But the real plot deals with Wong's wife (Ching Mei). She gets shafted in an investment scam by a local gang leader. When her financial problems get worse, she secretly goes to a loan shark (the "underground banker") and ends up owing even more.

Well, into the gutter now. She is raped, forced into prostitution, and gang-banged on video. Wong goes to the banker to plead on his wife's behalf, but he's beaten and humiliated. His apartment is destroyed, the gang kills his wife and disfigures his kid. There's only one thing to do. . . .

Go get help from his neighbor, Dr. Lamb. The doctor is anxious to get back into killing again, so he joins Wong and his sister in an attack against the gangsters.

If all this seems stupid, that's because it is. Some critics have suggested it's supposed to be a satire on the Category III genre, while others have simply dismissed it as another **Wong Ching (Jing)** script gone haywire.

UNKNOWN MYSTERY.
See *Strange Rape Case of Sunkam Hillside*

UNMATCHABLE MATCH (1992)
director: Parkman Wong. Stephen Chow·Chan Wai Man·Vivian Chow· Shing Fui On ★★
A fizzled attempt for **Stephen Chow [Chiau Sing Chi]** to shed his goofball image and enter the more lucrative (in-

Singer Vivian Chow in *Unmatchable Match*

ternationally speaking) action film genre. In the previous few years, Stephen had become Hong Kong's #1 box office draw, but he remained unknown in the world marketplace. With this film he attempted to break through the glass ceiling.

But unfortunately he had two things working against him. First, the cop-buddy script wasn't very good; and second, his fans weren't willing to let him lose his clown persona.

Luckily, he was not derailed by this film's lukewarm reception. He went on to star in the more successful productions **King of Beggars** (1993) and **From Beijing with Love** (1994).

Nonetheless, this film will be remembered as Stephen Chow's transition movie.

UNPUBLICIZED CASE: HUMAN SAUSAGES (1994)
director: Chow Lo Wen. Ng Choi Lai ·Man Su ★½

A call girl on the run from her pimp is killed late one night. Across town, a butcher, deep in debt, kills his roommate for calling him a cripple. He decides to turn the dead fellow into sausages rather than risk the body being discovered. Prostitutes continue to turn up dead as the crazed pimp, Kayo, refuses to allow any of them to leave. Bodies appear; people disappear. The cops have their hands full trying to solve both cases. The two killers are finally discovered and justice is served.

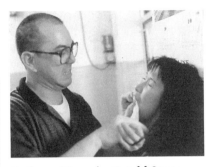

Anthony Wong in *Untold Story*

Now, it certainly doesn't take a rocket scientist to know there's something fishy going on here. It seems obvious that, in a rush to capitalize on the current wave of Hong Kong true crime films (e.g., **Dr. Lamb, Unknown Mystery, Untold Story**, etc.), a producer has resurrected two unfinished shelved films, spliced them together with an unconvincing wraparound and [with all the finesse of a used car salesman] is selling what initially looks like the real thing, but in actuality is merely a sham.

The visual techniques of the two story lines are so dissimilar in style and competence there's no way they could have come from the same director. While this isn't a new concept in Hong Kong cinema (**Godfrey Ho**, to name one offender, made a pile of money with patchwork projects), it is a disconcerting experience for even the most forgiving exploitation enthusiast.

Sadly, the footage revolving around the butcher and his homemade human sausages is quite good. But not good enough to recommend the rest of the film.

UNTOLD STORY (1992)
aka **BUNMAN**
director: **Herman Yau** with **Danny Lee**. Anthony Wong·Danny Lee·Parkman Wong·Sing Fui An ★★★½
This is the film that catapulted An-

thony Wong from costarring roles to headliner. And especially surprising, due to the grim subject matter, this is the film that won him the Golden Horse Award for Best Actor in 1993 (a prestigious Asian Academy Award-type salute). This is also actor **Danny Lee**'s second movie as a codirector (his first was **Dr. Lamb** [1992] with **Billy Tang**), plus filmmaker **Parkman Wong**'s debut as an actor. And, on top of everything else, this film is quite good.

It's based on a factual event, the crime of Wong Chi Hang. Wong was a man who claimed he bought a restaurant from the previous owner, Cheng Lam. But in reality he had slaughtered Lam and his entire family with a meat cleaver and proceeded to feed their bodies to unsuspecting patrons. The scenes showing the actual massacre, including small children, are the most brutal you're likely to see.

But the structure of the film is, perhaps, too close to *Dr. Lamb* for its own good. The narrative follows the same exact path. First, the bodies are discovered, then police investigate and arrest probable suspect Wong. When he refuses to confess, the cops torture him and eventually lock him in a cell with the vengeful brother of the dead Lam. Finally, Wong admits to the crime and describes in complete detail how it was committed.

A good case can be made justifying the similarities, especially since Danny Lee was the filmmaker for both. And it is true that because of the technique, this film seems to capture the grittiness of crime. Codirector **Herman Yau**'s handheld camerawork during the flashback scenes gives a documentary feel to the segments, making the entire production more chilling (obviously a technique he learned while producing news and television programs for Hong Kong's TV networks).

Oddly, the weakest element is Danny Lee the actor. He tries to develop a Casanova Cop character, but he comes off as a buffoon. In every one of his scenes, whether in the police station or on location, he has a different beautiful woman (call girl?) hanging on his arm. This causes a numbing amount of tongue-hanging-out remarks from the jealous cops in his command. Perhaps Danny Lee has created this Romeo character to counter the recent gossip in the HK tabloids about his own sexual preference. But it appears he doth protest too much.

VAMPIRE BUSTER (1989)
director: Norman Law/Stanley Wing Siu. Jacky Cheung · Kent Cheng · Danny Chan·Fung Shui Fan ★★½
Here's a thinly veiled allegory disguised as a horror comedy. It tells the story of a cursed Chinese vase from the Communist mainland that falls into the hands of a HK capitalist. Inside the vase is the spirit of a vampire which possesses the rich industrialist, causing him to attack and destroy everyone who trusts him.

Besides the obvious ramifications of the politically charged plot [especially with regard to China's takeover], this film is significant due to an outstanding cast of popular HK actors, including Fung Shui Fan (as the businessman Kay), **Jacky Cheung**, fatty **Kent Cheng**, goofy Danny Chan, plus **Shie Min-Chi** and Liang Yun-Shin as the pretty girlfriends.

VAMPIRE CHILD (1987)
director: Wang Chung Kuan. Chuan Chuan·Wang Chiang·Chai Yu-Niang ★★
Silly fun in the **Magic of Spell** vein, as a beautiful good witch gives the vampires a chance to know Buddhism and change their ways. She seems to have met her match when she challenges the King of Evil. But a vampire kid, Chuan Chuan, and his family save the day.

VAMPIRE FAMILY (1993)
director: Eric Tsang. Eric Tsang·Jimmy Lin·Cheung Man·Chan Hi Lung ★★½
Here's one in the tradition of HK horror comedies like **Spooky Family** (1989) and **Toothless Vampires** (1987), with more slapstick and lowbrow humor than chills.

It seems that a vampire couple must wait 1000 years to produce a child. The parents in this film have two children, Jimmy and Linda Vamp (Jimmy Lin and **Cheung Man**), so they have been together for at least 2000 years. In fact, they claim their "best friend of old" was none other than

Cheung Man (L) and Chan Hi Lung in Vampire Family

Jesus Christ, who personally officiated at their marriage (the dates are a bit off, but mom claims she was pregnant when she walked down the aisle).

Even though there are moments of brilliance, the story isn't cohesive. Director **Tsang** prefers sketches to plot. If he had expanded any one of the many ideas (Jimmy Vamp's job at the hospital, his parents rediscovery of their lust for blood, Linda's longing for companionship, the problems of a thinning bloodline causing children to age faster than their parents, etc.), there would have been a better film here.

VAMPIRE VS. VAMPIRE (1991)
director: Lam Ching Ying. Lam Ching Ying·Chion Siu Hou·Lui Fong·Billy Lau·Maria Cordero ★½
Lam Ching Ying has starred in so many of these films, playing the same role without variation since establishing the prototype in *Mr. Vampire* (1984), who would be better to direct one of them? At least, the concept must've looked good on paper. But, sadly, the one-eyebrowed priest has made a mess of things here.

As usual, Lam plays an exorcist priest. So far, so good.

But unfortunately, this time, he has a vampire-kid sidekick who is constantly mugging for the camera. These two unlikely partners go about their ghost-busting business in a series of unrelated vignettes; thus the film lacks the continuity of a cohesive full-length feature. Plus, for the first time, Lam Ching Ying looks like he's not having fun anymore. He probably isn't.

VAMPIRE'S BREAKFAST (1986)
director: Wong Chung. Kent Cheng·Emily Chu·Wong PakMan·Ng Ma ★★
An okay story about a newspaper reporter (**Kent Cheng**) who stumbles upon a nest of vampires living in contemporary Hong Kong. The police

don't believe him (of course), so he sets out to get proof to back his story. The movie is a comedy-horror blend with mediocre FX.

VAMPIRES LIVE AGAIN (1987)
director: Kam Yoo Tu. Bok Yuen·Loretta Ying ★

VAMPIRES SETTLE ON THE POLICE CAMP (1991)
director: Chan Chi Hwa. Go Hong·Woo Fung·Lo Hoi Pang·Chu Sui Wai ★½
Another **Haunted Cop Shop** clone that relies more on humor than on horror. Even though it's not as bad as *Ghost Mansion*, the plot is remarkably similar.

Teenagers studying to become cops eventually save the day when the vampires attack.

VAMPIRES STRIKE BACK (1988)
director: Kam Yoo Tu. Bok Yuen·Cheung Yu ★
These two movies are among the very worst Oriental horror films. They are shot-on-video messes that vacillate between lame terror sequences and embarrassing comedy bits. Somebody should take away **Kam Yoo Tu**'s video camera. The world would be a better place.

VENDETTA (1993)
director: Leung Siu Hung. Ray Lui·Veronica Yip·Tommy Wong·Kent Cheng ★★★
Another solid terror film from *Insanity* director **Leung Siu Hung**.

This time he creates a similar good-people-tormented-by-a-psycho thriller, as Detective Chan (Ray Lui) is stalked by a wacko criminal who wants revenge against the cop for the deaths of his brother and sister. It's also about the possibility that Detective Chan's newborn twins may (or may not) be possessed by the spirits of the two dead thieves.

If there's a fault in this film, it's the same one that clutters the conclusion of *Insanity*. Leung appears to be a director who lacks confidence in his rudimentary story. He tries to spice it up with a supernatural twist. In the case of both films, he should've left well enough alone. The movie was working just fine. The freaky villain was evil enough. Ghosts (no matter what the reason) weren't necessary.

VENGEANCE IS MINE (1988)
director: Tang Hin Sing (Billy Tang). Rosamund Kwan·Yip Tung Shing ★★★
A drug-crazed gang of delinquents attacks and rapes a nurse (**Rosamund Kwan**) as she is walking home from her hospital. These crazies continue to torment her and her friends (for the entire film) until she finally takes justice into her own hands.

The conclusion is an explosion of violence and carnage. From the future director of **Dr. Lamb** and **Run and Kill**.

VENGEANCE OF SNOW MAIDEN (1982)
director: Ng See Yuen. Yen Chen·Cho Ken·Mo Ka Kay·Yeh Sui ★
Cool title; lame story with "ice princess" overtones about a girl raised in the wilderness by a witch.

VENGEFUL VAMPIRE GIRL (1980)
director: Kim In Soo [Kim Si Hyo]. ★★
A raped woman kills herself during the vicious sex attack by biting off her tongue, thus bleeding to death. Ten years later she returns as a ghostly vampire to seek revenge.

VENUS: WOLF NINJA.
See *Wolf Devil Woman 2*

VIOLENCE SUPREME.
See *I Want To Get Even*

VISA TO HELL (1990)
director: Dick Wei. Dick Wei·Ching Sui Ho·Lam Wei·Chu Bo Yee ★★½
A team of cops go undercover to catch a triad kingpin. He retaliates by invading the home of Officer Cheong, killing his family. A battle ensues. Both the cop and the bad guy fall to their deaths from the top of a building.

The remaining cops, with the help of a Buddhist monk, leave the human world, and join Cheong for the ultimate fight in Hell. Creative effects, clever idea. Dick Wei is both the director and the star.

WAR OF THE WIZARDS (1980)
director: Richard Cann (Sadamasa Arikawa). Charles Lang·Richard Kiel ·Betty Nununi ★★ *or* ★★★
I have mixed feelings about this motion picture. The first half is painfully slow and cumbersome. But the second part is adventurous. Thus the double rating.

It tells the story of a dreamer named Ty (Charles Lang) who discovers a magic dish capable of granting him any wish. For the final 40 minutes, he is inadvertently transported (via a giant phoenix) to the island lair of an evil, but beautiful, witch (Betty Nununi), where Ty also meets her bodyguard giant (played by Richard "Jaws" Kiel) and engages in a well-choreographed fight sequence.

WAR VICTIMS (1987)
director: Jon Bierium. Marissa Hague·Roy Tiraych·Nenna Roiser·Dicky Zulkarnaen ★★½
Similar to the Italian Nazi atrocity/women concentration camp films, this one relies totally on gritty brutality and sado behavior. "Beat me until I'm dead, but I'm not going to tell you anything!" screams Marissa Haque, a

female Malaysian captive of the Japanese army. Those words pretty much sum up the entire motion picture.

WARRIOR (1985)
director: Sisworo Putra. Barry Prima · W. D. Mochtar · Dana Christina · Eva Arnez ★★½

WARRIOR 2 (1987)
director: H Tjut Djalili. Barry Prima · Eva Arnez · Nenna Roiser ★★★

WARRIOR 3 (1988)
aka **WARRIOR AND BLIND WARRIOR**
director: Worod Suma. Enny Beatrice · Barry Prima · Rudy Pusba · Siska Widowaty · Leily Sagita ★★
Barry Prima is Jaka Sembung. These three fantasy/adventure films tell the story of his exploits against the evil Dutch dictators. The movies are competently filmed and fun to watch, but their major contribution is their balls-to-the-wall approach. In these kung fu fights, people bleed. Gore flows. Lots of it.
The best example is in *Warrior 2*, when the villainess gets her face ripped off. Unfortunately, in #3 he is joined by Barta the Blind Warrior (Enny Beatrice), probably the most *un*interesting hero in Asian cinema.

WARRIOR'S TRAGEDY 1 (1993)
director: Frankie Chan. Ti Lung · Frankie Chan ★★★

WARRIOR'S TRAGEDY 2 (1993)
director: Frankie Chan. Ti Lung · Frankie Chan ★★★
Warrior's Tragedy is based on a Gu Long swordfighting novel. Most of the action takes place in a desert town that is destroyed in the end, similar to so many spaghetti Western movies. And similar to Clint Eastwood's stranger character in *Fistful of Dollars*, the stranger here is **Ti Lung** as Fu.

Fu is a nihilistic fighter, avenging the massacre of his family 20 years previous, sowing destruction wherever he goes. Ti Lung is superb in this mysterious, but brutal, killer role. Recently, Ti has returned to his kung fu roots with movies like *Blade of Fury*, *Young Hero* and, of course, *Drunken Master 2*. His stoic expression brings a touch of class back to the genre.
However, the same cannot be said for filmmaker **Frankie Chan**, who plays Yip, the detective hero of the movie. In the original story, Gu Long created the lighthearted character of Yip as a foil against the bleakness of Fu. But Frankie Chan is, quite simply, too influenced by his own lighthearted comedies (*Outlaw Brothers*, *Fun and Fury*, etc.). Chan's street-level humor is quite jarring, especially when it deflates the solemn mood created by Ti Lung. It's a shame a project of this magnitude was relegated to such an ineffective filmmaker.
But *Warrior's Tragedy* still has something going for it: a gripping story—which remains intact. Beyond all else, this is a murder mystery, almost a blueprint for the genre. But remember, Gu Long is famous for unexpected twists in his stories, and this is no exception.

WATCH OUT! (1988)
director: Tony Leung. Ng Choi Fan · Yun Wei Fo ★★★
This is a very strange "comedy" that breaks many cultural taboos. Two ghosts fight for possession of the same body. Eventually an agreement is made: Ghost #1 will occupy the body only until he sires a baby; then Ghost #2 will kill him and take over. #1 adopts a homosexual lifestyle to protect himself, but soon he falls in love with (and marries) his maid. When she becomes pregnant, he tells her about the sad eventuality. This leads to completely tasteless segments, wherein

the wife tries to "lose" the baby. First, she attempts an abortion, and then tries to trip and fall. She hoodwinks robbers into beating her, and finally pays a judo master to hit her in the stomach. But each time Ghost #2 intervenes. An amazingly repulsive plot line, right?

The Tony Leung credited as director is not either of the actors of that name.

WE ARE GOING TO EAT YOU (1983)
director: Tsui Hark. Tsui Siu Keung · Gao Hung · Wong Kam Seng ★★★
Tsui Hark, perhaps Hong Kong's best-known director, made this black comedy in 1983 (some sources claim 1980). It tells the story of a federal agent named 999 who travels to China to capture a notorious bandit. En route he befriends a petty thief who is also heading to the city of Rolex. Neither man is aware that the town is completely populated with cannibals.

Lots of blood and gore, plus a strange mixture of horror and sexual humor (especially in the scenes where a town transvestite wants to play with 999 and eat him in the process).

WEAKNESS OF MAN (1991)
director: Raymond Leung. Cecilia Yip · Mui Kiu Wai · Carrie Ng · Wong Tun Ling ★½
It's supposed to be a naughty sex comedy/drama having to do with a married guy who can't have kids, but his wife thinks he's been bopping somebody else because a woman, six months pregnant, came knocking. So the wife has an affair with another guy, but then finds out he's married to her best friend, who's having an affair with her uncle.

Toward the end of the movie Mui Kiu Wai says: "Let's forget the whole thing, it's too complicated." I think he was speaking for all of us.

WEDDING DRESS OF THE GHOST (1981)
director: Park Yoon Kyo. Chung Se Hyuk · Sunwoo Eun Sook ★
A man kills a hitchhiker. A month later, while driving home, he runs over her again. Or was it a ghost? Who cares?

WHEELS ON MEALS (1984)
aka MEALS ON WHEELS
aka MILLION DOLLAR HEIRESS
director: Samo Hung. Jackie Chan · Yuen Biao · Samo Hung · Lola Forner · Herb Edelman · Richard Ng ★★★★
An evil count (Herb Edelman) kidnaps a beautiful heiress (Lola Forner) to siphon her inheritance. **Samo Hung** is a private eye hired to find her. **Jackie Chan** plays a street merchant in love with the girl. And **Yuen Biao** is his faithful sidekick.

It'd be a toss-up between this film and *Dragons Forever* for best honors during Jackie's transitional period (from chop socky to crime story flicks). Featuring cameos by Richard Ng, John Shum, and Wu Ma.

WHITE HAIR DEVIL LADY (1985)
director: Chu Yuan [Cheung Xin-Yan]. Ling Xue Hua · Chang Shan ★
Based on the 1954 Leung Yu-Sang novel, *Jiang-Hu* (River-Lake), which also inspired the much better *Wolf Devil Woman* (1982) and, later, *Bride with the White Hair* (1993), this film doesn't deserve to be mentioned in the same breath.

It's a poorly made, disjointed fantasy flick with Ling Xue-Hua as the white-haired wonderwoman.

WHORE AND THE POLICEWOMAN (1993)
director: Wong Kwok Chu. Michiko Nishiwaki · Cheng Yin Lai ★★ *add another ★ if you like sado/sex violence*
This is a surprising, graphic crime and gun-fu thriller. A high-ranking government official (Kao Tien Chien) is se-

cretly obsessed with whip-and-bondage games. When Kao kills a prostitute during a particularly nasty session, he blackmails the prosecutor (Yin Li Shi) into taking the investigation elsewhere.

The police arrest the girl's roommate, May Lin, as the killer, but soon an ass-kicking female cop named Chiang (Nishiwaki Michiko) comes to her rescue and concocts a plan to expose the real culprit. Aside from the graphic S&M stuff, it goes as you'd expect.

WHO'S THE GHOST IN SLEEPY HOLLOW (1989)
director: Hsu Hsia [Hsu Wen-Hsieh].
Viv Chih-Rung·Sung Kang Ling·Wang Dao Yu ★
A young delivery man survives his encounter with spooks in Sleepy Hollow. However, the ghosts, under the power of a phony spiritualist, invade the city. Cheaply made and very talky.

WHO'S (THE) KILLER (1992)
aka **BLOOD ISLAND**
director: Wu Kuo-Ren. Luo Sai-Li·Shing Fui On ★★
A group of HK students with their archeology teacher, Ms. Feng (nomadic Luo Sai-Li), visit an island for a research project. The inhabitants are a weird group of society rejects (including Shing Fui-On as a mentally retarded psychopath).

Apparently, 20 years before, there was a witch who lived in the village. And on September 28 she decided to end her life, but first she took an axe to most of the other townspeople. The remaining survivors went insane.

With the arrival of the students [conveniently on the 28th of September], the curse is revitalized. Bodies are cut in half. Heads severed. Limbs chopped off. It's a gruesome body count horror film, offbeat in execution, as if written by an Oriental Richard

Jacky Cheung is attacked by a rapter in *Wicked City.*

Laymon. Too bad it doesn't make more sense.

WICKED CITY (1992)
director: Mak Tai Kit (with Tsui Hark). Jacky Cheung·Leon Lai·Michelle Lee·Tatsuya Nakadai·Yuen Woo Ping·Roy Cheung ★★★
Adapted from the Japanese adult animation feature *Supernatural Beastie City*, this ambitious project is quite a departure from the glut of Hong Kong gun-n-gangster and/or sprawling epic flicks. Starring **Jacky Cheung, Leon Lai**, and **Michelle Lee**, it tells the futuristic story of life among the Rapters. Cheung and Lai are two undercover HK agents on a frantic mission to defeat an alternate society of creatures who live off human blood.

Similar to George Romero's *Night of the Living Dead*, no explanation is given for the deadly Rapters' existence; instead, the film's only concern is with stopping them. In fact, there is little time spent on anything except the breakneck pace, the nonstop conflict between the humans and the creatures.

The thread of plot deals with Shudo, the son of the king Rapter, who wants to nullify his father's decision to live in harmony with humans. He and his followers are bent on world domination through complete and utter annihilation. This, of course, gives the film ample excuse for the frenzied carnage and bloody madness that follows. The result is a sensory overload of shape-shifting, exploding body parts, and absolutely staggering special effects.

WIDOW WARRIORS (1989)
director: Wang Lung Wei. Elizabeth Lee·Michiko Nishiwaki·Tien Niu·Wei Ying Hung ★★★
Here's somewhat of a rarity in the realm of HK girls-with-guns flicks. This one also has an intelligent plot with three-dimensional characters. Don't misunderstand, it's definitely an action pic, as three women take on the triad gang responsible for the deaths of their husbands.

Director **Wang** has dabbled in a variety of genres since his early chop socky film debut, **Crazy Guy with Super Kung Fu,** but cult fans still say **Escape from the Brothel** is his best.

WILD PARTY (1992)
director: Wong Pak Tse. Yang Siu Lu ·Vincent Lim·Chim Bang Hei·Pauline Chan ★★
Szeto Tak runs a partner-swapping club called the Happy Pal Club. However, most of the clients are anything but happy. Sure, they have all the sex they can handle, but the noncommittal atmosphere only adds to their already frustrated lives.

The film concentrates on four major players. A young secretary (Yang Siu Lu) is forced by her psychia-

trist boss (Vincent Lim) to have sex with all the men at the party. Keung (Chim Bang Hei), a lonely taxi driver, is secretly attracted to the poor girl, and Susan (Pauline Chan) helps him rescue the girl from the ugly situation.

WILD SEARCH (1990)
director: Ringo Lam. Chow Yun-Fat· Cherie Chung·Roy Cheung·Wong Kwong Leung ★★★
Chow Yun-Fat is a cop who confronts a gang of violent triad psychos. He also finds time to rescue a little girl and fall in love with her aunt (**Cherie Chung**).

It's a good-looking film from vet **Ringo Lam,** best known for **City on Fire, Esprit d'Amour,** and the incredible **Full Contact.**

WILL OF IRON (1990)
director: John Cheong. Maggie Cheung·Michael Wong·Jacky Cheung· Crystal Lee Kwok ★★
What the hell is **Maggie Cheung** doing in junk like this? She brings too much class to such a transparent production. However, on the other hand, we've come to expect these kinds of tedious projects from **Jacky Cheung**.

Two couples, Michael and Maggie (conveniently named after the

Maggie Cheung (R) with Crystal Lee Kwok in Will of Iron

leading players, Michael Wong and **Maggie Cheung**) and Jacky and Carol (**Jacky Cheung** and Crystal Lee Kwok; is this really **Amy Kwok**?) get involved with ruthless gangsters due to Jacky's dependency on drugs. It seems that he owes the mob a lot of money for purchasing too much nose candy. His friends, Michael and Maggie, help him raise the money and kick the habit.

But it's too late; the young gangster leader, Sam, is pissed because Maggie had told him to "fuck off" in front of his boss. The whole thing weaves its way to the inevitable gun-fu bad-ass conclusion, in which all the mob guys are killed, Michael bites the dust (but he takes 10 bullets first) and Carol has a miscarriage.

The message? Just say no.

WIND, FOREST, FIRE, MOUNTAIN (1983)
      aka **FISTFUL OF TALONS**
director: Sun Chung. Billy Chong · Wang Ing Sik ★★★
There's no question about it, this is **Billy Chong**'s best motion picture, probably because he's finally working with a skilled filmmaker. Too many movies with hack directors (like **Hwa I Hung**) almost took their toll on this martial arts boxer.

Sun Chung has the reputation of an eccentric. Even his friends call him a recluse. Over the past 20 years, he's made only a handful of films, but those few are considered genre classics, especially his **Avenging Eagle** (1979) with **Ti Lung** and Alexander Fu Sheng. It's little wonder Billy Chong jumped at the opportunity of working with this master after being trapped in so many humdrum chop socky B grinders.

The combination worked, resulting in a smart, action-packed story of an overly confident boxer who loves to fight, and takes every opportunity to prove it.

Incidentally, Billy Chong was born **Willy Dohzan**, and before finding success as a Hong Kong genre star in **Crystal Fist** (1979), he was a pop singer in Indonesia.

WING CHUN (1994)
director: Yuen Woo Ping. Michelle Yeoh [Khan] · Donnie Yen · Waise Lee · Tsui Siu Keung · Michael Chow ★½
For the first time, legendary director **Yuen Woo Ping** puts a female in the lead role for one of his films. The project must have looked promising to the investors—powerhouse diva **Michelle Yeoh** in the story of Shaolin Temple's only woman disciple and her special style of kung fu fighting, known as Wing Chung Fists.

How could it miss? Especially in the hands of the genre's most acclaimed chop socky filmmaker, on the heels of his highly successful **Tai Chi Master** (1993). Yet, the effort falls flat. For some misguided reason, director Yuen purposely tones down the action sequences, and soft-sells Yip Wing Chun's contribution to the world of martial arts; then he adds insult to injury by including huge helpings of (un)funny vignettes and embarrassingly awkward sexual humor.

WINNERS AND SINNERS (1983)
director: Samo Hung. Jackie Chan · Samo Hung · Yuen Biao · John Sham · James Tien ★★
Not in the same league as **Dragons Forever** or **Wheels on Meals**, this **Jackie Chan** film more closely resembles his **My Lucky Stars** films.

Five small-time crooks go into a legitimate business together when they get out of jail, but quickly they find themselves caught between two triad gangs. Lightweight fun with **Yuen Biao**, John Sham, James Tien, and of course Jackie and **Samo Hung**.

WITCH FROM NEPAL (1987)
director: **Ching Siu Tung.** Chow Yun-Fat·Cherie Chung·Dick Wei·Chu Bao Yi ★★★
A terrific 1987 wham/slam horror story with fantasy overtones from competent **Ching Siu Tung** (director of **Swordsman, Terra Cotta Warrior,** and the **Chinese Ghost Story** series).

Sheila, the good witch from Nepal (played by **Cherie Chung**), convinces Joe Wong (**Chow Yun-Fat** in another fervid role) to confront the Devil incarnate, an evil catlike creature with superhuman strength. Great FX and lots of action. Plus, there's a very erotic love scene in the rain between Chow Yun-Fat and the witch. Sizzling fun.

WITCH WITH THE FLYING HEAD (1979)
director: **Woo Lian Sing.** Tsang Yin·Fariney Chang ★★½
Okay, the film is dated and the special effects are cheesy. But *Witch with the Flying Head* demands respect due to its sheer zeal and gross-out aspirations. Make no mistake, it's gory.

And, as the title suggests, there's a flying head. Not just a cleanly chopped flying head, but one with the internal organs attached! Remember, this was 10 years before **Mystics in Bali** (1989) featured the same thing.

WITNESS (1993)
director: **Cha Fu Yi [Cha Chuen Yee].** Mok Siu Chung·Gi Gi ★★
This is another true crime story by director **Cha Fu Yi** (he also made **Legal Innocence** the same year).

Max Mok [Mok Siu Chung] is Jackie Wong, an innocent bystander who witnesses a violent triad street crime. The prosecution is determined to take the case to court, aided by Jackie's testimony. Gangsters try to sway him. When he won't listen to reason, they beat him to a bloody pulp. The whole thing ends in a melodramatic swell as Jackie, wearing a body cast, is propped up in court for the testimony.

Although she has little to do, newcomer Gi Gi became the flavor of the month in the Hong Kong tabloids after this film opened. Maybe she has a good press agent.

WIZARD'S CURSE (1992)
director: **Yuen Cheung Yan.** Lam Ching Ying·Cheung Kwok Keun·Tsui Mon Wah·Cjan Nga Lam·Billy Chow·Chu Mi Mi ★★★½
Talk about a diamond in the rough! Using the unabashed charm of the **Mr. Vampire** series (i.e., the mixture of endearing charm and grisly horror), this film succeeds far beyond its meager budget. Director **Yuen** manages to make *Wizard's Curse* look like a million bucks, creating an immensely satisfying sequel which virtually dwarfs the official **Mr. Vampire '92.**

The setting is contemporary Hong Kong. Master Taoist Lam Chin (one eyedbrowed priest, **Lam Ching Ying**) has just aided the police in destroying La Mit and his girlfriend Kim Sha (Cheung Kwok Keun and Tsui Mon Wah), two criminals who seemed indestructible due their ties with black magic. Lam returns to his home, where he becomes involved in a domestic argument with his daughter, Ting (Cjan Nga Lam) over her choice of boyfriends, perpetuated by her blatant disregard for tradition. [This is a standard theme that runs through the **Mr. Vampire** series.]

Meanwhile, a fiendish wizard, obsessed with dreams of creating an ultimate monster, steals the bodies of the two criminals. He anoints them with the sperm of 99 satyrs and the blood collected from menstrual flow of 99 bitches. The result is the merging of the two bodies into one ultrapowerful, bisexual creature known as the Terrific Vampire. This lustful monster gains knowledge [and strength] by killing and devouring the brains of victims (the first casualties are the wizard and his assistants). Besides using brute force and fangs, the creature also wields its penis as a deadly weapon! More than once, helpless victims are impaled on the humongous organ.

If, within seven days, the vampire can eat the brain of the Taoist's daughter, its power will become insurmountable. So the creature begins the pursuit of Ting.

Master Lam knows the only way to stop the monster is with his daughter's help. She must have sex with a virgin male born at the bewitching hour, and then she will possess the power necessary to defeat the vampire.

Those are the ingredients for this sexually charged, outrageously irreverent horror/comedy. Obviously, it's a delightful surprise. Also starring **Billy Chow** as police officer Keung, the potential male virgin. Chu Mi Mi is Master Lam's estranged wife.

WOLF DEVIL WOMAN (1982)
director: **Chang Ling.** Chang Ling (Pearl Cheong)·Shek Fong·Shek Ying ★★★★
In America she's known as **Pearl Cheong.** Her real name is **Chang Ling** (director and star). But she is *Wolf Devil Woman!*

After being raised by wolves, she attacks the Devil and his evil army of zombies. She can do anything. She can fly. She can swing a mean sword. She can spin around real fast and make her hair turn white.

But, here's the most amazing thing she does: when the Devil sets her boyfriend on fire, she douses the flames by biting (yes, biting) her arm and the spurting blood puts out the fire. (!?!)

WOLF DEVIL WOMAN 2
aka **VENUS: WOLF NINJA**
aka **MATCHING ESCORT** (1983)
director: **Sze Ma Peng.** Chang Ling (Pearl Cheong)·Meng Fei·Chan Kwan Po·Johnny Pang ★★★
This is the second in **Chang Ling's** *Wolf Devil Woman* conceptual series (also see **Miraculous Flower**). It's filled with more fun and action as she unleashes her vengeance on the evil (and rainbow-colored-hair) warlord, plus there's poison spells, walking on water, ghosts, a dethroned good king, and magic mushrooms.

WOLF OF REVENGE (1990)
director: **Lawrence Chu Tsang.** Tang Chen Zong·Wang Yong Fang ★★
Au-Chen's wife, Amy, is killed and his gangster buddies are destroyed by a rival gang. He begins an affair with his dead wife's sister (Wang Yong Fang). She becomes possessed with Amy's spirit and is determined to help him as he takes revenge on the bad guys. Meanwhile, Au-Chen (Tang Chen Zong, trying his damnedest to look like **Chow Yun-Fat**) beats the hell out of the opposing triad. And eventually, in a thunderstorm of bullets, he succeeds. All right, it's different. This is certainly the type of film only Hong Kong could produce—an odd ghost story/gangster hybrid. But is it any good? A guilty pleasure at best; trite junk at worst.

WOMAN•DEMON•HUMAN (1989)
director: **Huang Shuqin.** Gong Li· Pei Yan Ling ★★★★
This is the story of a traveling troupe of actors who play street festivals until the lead actress, Quin Yun, joins a national production. As she becomes famous playing males roles, Quin Yun (beautiful **Gong Li**) begins to doubt her own sexuality, but she finds love (and ultimately disgrace) in the arms of her mentor, Zhang Kui (Pei Yan Ling).

A masterpiece of sensual delights, visuals by cinematographer Xia Lixing with music by Yang Mao. It's not really a genre film. Perhaps it doesn't belong in this book at all. But the images are so majestic, echoed in traditional Chinese opera, its inclusion seems necessary.

A WOMAN, A SHE-WOLF (1991)
director: **Lee Tso Nam.** Lui La · Ng Choi Lai ★½
This whole mess is pointlessly depressing. Here's a film filled with unattractive people having sex and bitching at each other.

It's the story of Yun-Ni and her spiral downward into life's gutter. She gets drunk a lot, but even more, she gets the shit beaten out of her by her various boyfriends and husband.

If, based on the title, you were expecting a horror film, guess again. There's no lycanthropy in this trip through the sewer. Only glimpses at life's horror.

Another mediocre modern film from the legendary chop socky director **Lee Tso Nam**.

WOMEN OF THE JUNGLE (1987)
aka **WOMEN OF THE FOREST**
aka **WOMAN IN THE FOREST STORY**
director: **Wu Chia Chun.** Yue Chan Jun · Long Tian Shiang ★
The only good thing about the movie is the jungle girl (Yue Chan Jun) gets naked a lot. And the hero (Long Tian Shiang) throws up at the film's conclusion.

WOMEN WARRIORS OF KINGMEN (1987)
director: **Xung Fei-Lei.** Wong Kwong Leung · Tsui Sui Keung ★
No one could be desperate enough to watch more than 15 minutes of this awful film about a female band of soldiers protecting Kingmen Island from invading Chinese Communists.

In fact, even the enemy doesn't stick around for the conclusion. Except for a few Commie frogmen, the invaders never show up, and the film ends with the girls going through the paces of a mock scrimmage. Absolutely terrible!

WOMEN'S PRISON (1991).
See *Commando Fury*

WONDER SEVEN (1994)
director: **Ching Siu Tung.** Michelle Yeoh [Khan] · Kent Cheng ★½
Dump the first 80 minutes. Simply fast forward to the end and watch the motorcyle mayhem finale. Everything before the conclusion is instantly forgettable.

The film can be described only as a major disappointment from one of Hong Kong's better directors. It's difficult to believe this is the same filmmaker who made the **Chinese Ghost Story** and **Swordsman** series.

Michelle Yeoh in *Wonder Seven*

WORLD'S FOREMOST BANNED NOVEL (1989)
aka **GOLDEN LOTUS**
director: **Richard Lee [Lee Han Chang].** Charlie Pu·Lee Wan-Su·Fang Yu Ting ★★½

Obviously in the spirit of other recent HK films (e.g., **Sex and Zen** [1991]), this one is based on the famous erotic book *Golden Lotus: The First Book of Wonder in the World* (which was also the inspiration for the classic Chinese opera *Dream of the Red Chamber*), mixing traditional values with heavy doses of sex, bondage, and S&M behavior. The two lead females are Lee Wan Su and Fang Yu Ting, with Charlie Pu as the lucky man in the middle.

WRONGLY KILLED GIRL (1988)
director: **Wong Howg Jang.** Mar San San·Wen Kong Leung·Yam Ho·Cheung Wai ★★

It takes a long while for things to heat up in this medieval horror/fantasy tale. Nothing happens in the first 40 minutes.

After that it's swordplay and sorcery. Plus some very pretty female ghosts.

YELLOW EMANUELLE (1979)
director: **Albert Thomas/Lee Han-Chang.** Chai Lee·Giuseppe Pambieri ★★

A low budget, Italian/Hong Kong co-production capitalizing on the popularity of the *Emanuelle* name. Chai Lee stars as Dr. Emy Wong, and Giuseppe Pambieri is her new patient/boyfriend. The action is a mild soft-core sex romp.

But historically there is something significant about this film. It was the first major movie to play Hong Kong theaters with full frontal nudity, thus starting a tradition that (to this day) separates Hong Kong sex cinema from that of Japan.

YES! MADAM (1987)
aka **POLICE ASSASSIN**
director: **Cory Yuen [Yuen Kwei].** Michelle Khan·Cynthia Rothrock·Tsui Hark·Dick Wei·Samo Hung·Richard Ng ★★★

Often confused with the *In the Line of Duty* series (sometimes considered as either the first or the second entry in that series [see separate reviews]), this film is a girls-with-guns flick produced by **Samo Hung**, who also has a cameo. Starring **Michelle Khan** and Cynthia Rothrock, with guest appearances by **Tsui Hark**, Dick Wei and Richard Ng, it's the story of two female cops on the trail of a microfilm that contains enough top-secret information to topple a gangland empire.

But action is the key word for this film, not plot. And the final showdown at the triad's estate is about as good as it gets.

YES, MADAM '92: A SERIOUS SHOCK (1992)
director: **Stanley Wing Siu.** Moon Lee · Cynthia Khan · Yukari Oshima ★★★

Perhaps the serious shock heralded in the title is **Moon's Lee**'s unconventional portrayal of a villainess in this film. Maybe she's become tired of watching all her peers get meaty bad-girl roles. Regardless, she shines in her portrayal of a cop who kills her boyfriend/boss after he dumps her for another policewoman (**Cynthia Khan**).

Khan goes above the law to get revenge. She and her street-wise friend (**Yukari Oshima**) track down Lee and her corrupt-cop buddies, resulting in an explosive warehouse confrontation.

YOU NEVER DIE TWICE.
See *Aces Go Places 4*

YOUNG HERO (1993)
aka BAREFOOTED KID

director: **Johnny To [To Ke Fung].** Aaron Kwok·Ti Lung·Maggie Cheung ·Kent Tsang Kong ★★★

A tightly constructed, personal film; void of the expansive landscapes and spectacular sets found in filmmaker **To**'s previous **Heroic Trio**. In contrast, this one is directed with a personal charisma usually lacking in chop socky fare. But basically it's a return, in spirit anyway, to the early martial arts films (loosely based on the classic **Invincible One [Chang Cheh]**).

Popular singer-turned-actor **Aaron Kwok**, the villain from **Saviour of Souls**, plays a country rube, Kuan, who journeys to a nearby village after his father's death, seeking help from a family friend, Yuen Nam (**Ti Lung**). He falls in love with Yuen's daughter (**Maggie Cheung**) and enters a local martial arts tournament, which he wins. But as this tragedy unfolds, his victory has only brought attention to himself, and he's framed by the town boss (Kent Tsang Kong, the villain from **Once a Thief**) for murder.

In less capable hands, Young Hero could have been a sentimental disaster. However, **Johnny To** has created a good-looking action film from the simplistic story, filled with strong images and fine performances.

YOUNG MASTER VAMPIRE.

See *Magic Story*

ZEN OF SWORD (1992)

director: **Yuen Chun Man.** Michelle Lee·Cynthia Khan·Waise Lee ★★★
An entertaining B version of **The Swordsman**, with less time dedicated to plot intricacies and story development, and bigger helpings of action and martial arts sequences—marred by a less than robust musical score.

The good cast (**Michelle Li [Lee]**, **Cynthia Khan**, and Waise Lee) is

Michelle Lee (Reis) with Cynthia Khan in *Zen of Sword*

more concerned about individual struggles in the midst of the decaying Ming Dynasty than the political ramifications. As a result, the film is a simplistic tale of betrayal and loyalty punctuated by a slam-bam, battle-terrific ending.

ZODIAC KILLERS (1992)

director: **Ann Hui.** Andy Lau·Cherie Chung ★★
It never gains speed. This film plods along like it has all the time in the world—which wouldn't be bad if it were a love story or a drama—but it's supposed to be an action flick.

Andy Lau and **Cherie Chung** play two Chinese students studying in Tokyo. They are thrown into peril when her former boyfriend is murdered by the Yakuza. Director **Ann Hui** (*Song of the Exile*) seems at home with the segments about the couple's relationship, but sadly ineffective with scenes of corruption and violence inside Japan's dark underbelly.

ZOMBIE VS. NINJA (1987) aka **ZOMBIE REVIVAL: NINJA MASTER**
director: **Charles Lee [Godfrey Ho].** Pierre Kirby·Dewey Bosworth·Renato Sala·Sean Odell·Meike Blischloe·Wei Ping Ao ★

A wacky magician/coffinmaker (with phony Jerry Lewis buckteeth and a terrible haircut) rescues a young man beaten by robbers. Both are constantly threatened by an Anglo fighter (Pierre Kirby) who wears a gold headband with the word Ninja across his forehead.

The film has the look of a composite, the result of three or four different movies strung together. Take producer **Joseph Lai** to court. Sue him. Except for a brief moment during the opening credits, there's not a zombie to be found. Anywhere.

ZU WARRIORS FROM MAGIC MOUNTAIN (1983)
director: **Tsui Hark.** Yuen Biao·Samo Hung·Moon Lee·Meng Hoi·Cheng Siu Tsu ★★★★

This is the epic Oriental fantasy movie filled with extraordinary visual delights. It fluctuates effortlessly from outrageous to ascetic. Almost every scene ambushes the viewer. This is a perfect introduction to the genre.

And a perfect introduction to the directorial talents of filmmaker **Tsui Hark.** For a while now much has been written about his saint or devil status in the Hong Kong production world, but movies like this one solidify his reputation as an adventurous visionary. In many ways, this motion picture set the standard for the countless fantasy films to follow.

The terrific cast adds to the fun. **Samo Hung** gives a wonderful performance as a white-haired priest caught in the middle of this fantasy free-for-all. **Yuen Biao** is a disillusioned soldier who retreats to the Magic Mountains to get a break from a raging civil war. But then, suddenly, he's waist-deep in a frenzied battle for the future of the world against the Blood Monster and his army of demons. He also finds time to fall in love with a beautiful princess (**Moon Lee**) held captive by the savage warriors.

Initially in 1982, the film opened in theaters against **Tsui Hark**'s wishes. He vehemently insisted the movie wasn't finished. But Golden Harvest Films, already behind schedule and over budget, ignored **Tsui**'s plea and released it anyway. This marked the beginning of a continuing dispute between the famous director/producer and Raymond Chow, long-time Golden Harvest boss. Tsui Hark went on to raise additional funds from an independent British company and finished the movie. The international English-language version (called *Zu Time Warriors*) includes a new 25-minute wraparound featuring **Yuen Biao** in modern-day Canada, where he's the top fencing champ at his college. During a freak accident, the student is knocked unconscious and transported, via his dreams, to ancient China for the conflict with the warriors of Magic Mountain. The English version ends with the boy waking from his coma. There's no place like home.

The Roots:
Martial Arts

The following alphabetical list covers martial arts films produced during the genre's most prolific period, from 1966 [with the release of the first modern chop socky movie, **Trail of the Broken Blade**] through the early '80s. Contemporary martial arts films (since the mid-'80s) are listed in the **Review Section** of this book.

Titles identified with this symbol (→) are generally considered the genre's most celebrated and accomplished productions.

ADVENTURE AT SHAOLIN (1980) **director: Wu Ming Hsung.** Shang Kuan Lin Feng·Shi Feng·Tien Feng·Tai Chi Hsien

AGAINST RASCALS WITH KUNG FU. See Wild Bunch of Kung Fu

→ **ALL MEN ARE BROTHERS** (1973) aka **SEVEN SOLDIERS OF KUNG FU** aka **SEVEN BLOWS OF THE DRAGON** aka **WATER MARGIN** **director: Chang Cheh.** David Chiang ·Ti Lung·Chen Kuan Tai·Tetsuro Tanba A troubled project that took three di-

rectors to complete: **Chang Cheh** (listed in the credits) plus **Pai Hsieh Lieh** and **Lui Chia Liang**.

ALL MEN ARE BROTHERS 2 (1974) aka **SEVEN SOLDIERS OF KUNG FU 2** aka **SEVEN BLOWS OF THE DRAGON 2** aka **SEVEN KUNG FU ASSASSINS** **director: Chang Cheh.** David Chiang ·Yang Sze·Ti Lung·Tetsuro Tanba

ALL THE KING'S MEN (1983) **director: King Hu.** Tien Fang·Tan Pao-Yun·Cheng Pei Pei·Chui Tai Ching

AMBITIOUS KUNG FU GIRL (1982)
director: **Lu Chun Ku.** Chen Kuan Tai
·Michelle Mie·Lin Hsai Chun·Hui Tien
Chi

AMSTERDAM CONNECTION (1979)
director: **Lo Ke.** Jason Pai Piao·Wong
Ka Lung·Yang Sze·Fang Mui San

ANGRY RIVER (1970)
director: **Huang Feng.** Angela Mao·
Han Ying Chieh
Golden Harvest's first release and Angela Mao's debut.

ANONYMOUS HEROES (1971)
director: **Chang Cheh.** Ti Lung·David
Chiang·Ching Li·Wang Chung

ART OF WAR BY SUN TZU (1981)
director: **Kam Tao.** Yo Hua·Kao Hsiung

ASSASSIN (1972)
director: **Chang Cheh.** Jimmy Wang
Yu·Chiao Chiao

ASSIGNMENT (1988)
director: **Kuo Nai Hong.** Lung Tien
Sheng·Chen Tien Tai

Alexander Fu Sheng (center) in *Chinatown Kid*

Jackie Chan in *Drunken Master*

Considered one of **Ti Lung**'s best chop socky films

AVENGING NINJA.
See *Zen Kwando Strikes in Paris*

AVENGING WARRIORS OF SHAOLIN.
See *Shaolin Rescuers*

BACK ALLEY PRINCESS (1972)
director: **Lo Wei.** Angela Mao·Cater Wong (Huang)·Shang Kuan Ling Feng ·Sam Hui

BANDITS FROM SHANTUNG (1978)
director: **Chang Yi.** Pai Ying·Huang Feng

BANDITS, PROSTITUTES AND SILVER (1977)
director: **Kao Bo Shu.** Wong Dao·Angela Mao·Lo Lieh·Phillip Kao Fei
Director **Kao Bo Shu** is perhaps the only female chop socky filmmaker

ASSOCIATION (1974)
director: **Cheng Cheh.** Angela Mao· Samo Hung·Byong Yu·Tien Nu

ATTACK OF THE KUNG FU GIRLS (1971)
director: **Lo Wei.** Cheng Pei Pei· James Tien·Lo Wei·Jackie Chan
Best remembered for young **Jackie Chan**'s costarring role as he fights female boxer Cheng Pei Pei and loses.

AVENGER.
See *Queen Boxer*

AVENGING BOXING.
See *Fearless Young Boxer*

➔**AVENGING EAGLE** (1979)
aka **COLD BLOODED EAGLES**
director: **Sun Chung.** Ti Lung·Ku Feng ·Alexander Fu Sheng

BASTARD (1972)
director: **Chu Yuan.** Lily Li·Zhong Hua

➔ **BASTARD SWORDSMAN** (1978)
director: **Lu Chun Ku.** Tsui Siu Keung ·Liu Hsueh Hua·Lo Meng·Sun Chien

BATTLE FOR THE REPUBLIC OF CHINA (1981)
director: **Ting Shansi.** Ti Lung·Wong Dao·Young Wang Yu·Lo Meng

BATTLE WIZARD (1980)
director: **Ching Chun Wu.** Lin Hsiao Lan·Frankie Wei·Linda Tanny Chu·Lo Lieh
Early fantasy kung fu from the Shaw brothers; young **Lin Hsiao Lan** later became the queen of this genre with films like **Magic of Spell** (1986).

→ **BEACH OF THE WAR GOD** (1971)
aka **BLOOD DRAGON**
director: Jimmy Wang Yu. Jimmy
Wang Yu · Lung Fei · Tien Yeh · Shan
Mao
One of the greatest sword-n-fu films
with **Jimmy Wang Yu** as legendary
hero Hsiao Feng, the warrior who protected the China coast from the invading Japanese during the Ming
Dynasty.

→ **BIG BOSS** (1971) known in United
States as **FISTS OF FURY**
director: Lo Wei. Bruce Lee · Nora
Miao
Bruce Lee's first completed film; director **Wu Chia Hsiang** quit after beginning the project, amid complaints
about the minuscule budget; no one
could've predicted its phenomenal success.

BIG BOSS OF SHANGHAI (1979)
director: Chen Kuan Tai. Chen Kuan
Tai · Jimmy Lee · Chen Foo Hung · Chen
Sing

BIG RASCAL.
See Dragon Force

BLACK DRAGON.
See Tough Guy

BLAST OF THE IRON PALM (1979)
aka **BRAVE ARCHER 3**
director: Chang Cheh. Alexander Fu
Sheng · Kuo Chui · Ti Lung · Kuo Chui

BLIND FIST OF BRUCE (1981)
director: Kam Bo. Ho Chung Tao
(Bruce Li) · Tiger Yeung · Yuen Shui Tu
Another in a long list of quickie films
made by Bruce Lee lookalike Ho
Chung Tao (Bruce Li) after the death of
the master. (See special listing in side
bar.)

BLIND FISTS (1972)
director: Chang Sen. Jason Pai Piao ·
Hu Yin Yin

→ **BLOOD BROTHERS** (1973)
aka **DYNASTY OF BLOOD**
aka **KUNG FU INVADERS**
director: Chang Cheh. Ti Lung · David
Chiang · Chen Kuan Tai · Ching Li
Generally considered **Chang Cheh**'s
best film, receiving both fan and critical acclaim. It established Chen Kuan
Tai as a major box office draw and cemented **Ti Lung**'s position.

BLOOD OF THE DRAGON (1978)
director: Kao Bo Shu. Jimmy Wang
Yu · Chi Kuan Chun · Chiao Chiao · Nu
Lung
Pale sequel to **Jimmy Wang Yu**'s orig-
inal **Beach of the War Gods**.

Pretenders to the Throne: Bruce Le, Bruce Li, Dragon Lee, and Bruce Liang

Bruce Lee died, under suspicious circumstances, from a brain aneurysm on July 20, 1973. The entire industry mourned his death. Many filmmakers made movies that today are accepted as homages to the Master. These incorporated elements of the Bruce mystique, but didn't necessarily try to steal his persona. For instance **Samo Hung** made **Enter the Fat Dragon** (1978), the story of an overweight country bumpkin who shaped his life on the principles and fighting techniques of **Bruce Lee**.

But there were a few kung fu boxers who actually tried to become Bruce Lee, decidedly a low road to instant notoriety and fame. The most famous are Ho Chung Tao, a Taiwanese fighter who changed his name to Bruce Li, and Hung Kin Lung from Hong Kong, who became Bruce Le. These two men starred in numerous low-budget chop socky films, often playing characters named Bruce Lee. They weren't bad fighters, but many fans objected to their crass attempt to capitalize on the death of the genre's biggest superstar. A few other martial artists did the same thing, although to a lesser degree. They include Korean Dragon Lee, Bruce Liang, and Bruce Lie (who made only one film, *Bruce Lee Takes Dragon Town* [1980]).

BRUCE LI
(HO CHUNG TAO) films
Blind Fist of Bruce (1981)
Bruce Against Iron Hand (1976)
Bruce Lee, A Dragon Story (1974)
Bruce Lee's Deadly Kung Fu (1977)
  aka **Bruce Li's Jeet Kune Do**
Bruce Lee, Super Dragon (1974)
  aka **The Dragon Dies Hard**
Bruce Lee: The Man, the Myth (1976)
  aka **Bruce Lee. True Story**
  directed by **Ng See Yuen**
Bruce Lee Vs the Supermen (1975)
Bruce Lee, We Miss You (1977)
Bruce Li in New Guinea (1977)
Bruce Li the Invincible (1977)
  aka **Bruce Lee the Invincible China-town Connection** (1984) With Lee Majors, Jr., and Pat McCormick.
Chinese Connection 2 (1984)
Counter Attack (1981)
  aka **Chinese Stuntman**
Deadly Strike (1980)
Dynamo (1979)
Edge of Fury (1981)
  Directed by Lee Tso Nan.
Enter the Panther (1976)
Enter Three Dragons (1979)
  also with Dragon Lee and Bruce Lea
Exit the Dragon, Enter the Tiger (1976)
Fist of Fury 2 (1976)
Fist of Fury 3 (1980)
Fists of Bruce Lee (1978)
Golden Sun (1984)

Bruce Lee's ghost gives clues about his death to a dedicated fan.
Goodbye Bruce Lee (1975)
  aka **Last Game of Death**
Great Hero (1978)
  aka **Bruce Lee's Magnum Fist**
Image of Bruce Lee (1978)
Iron Dragon Strikes Back (1979)
Iron Finger (1977)
  aka **Bruce Lee's Iron Finger**
  Starring Bruce Li and Bruce Liang.
King of Kung Fu (1977)
  aka **The Dragon Lives**
Legend of Bruce Lee (1980)
Master of Jeet Kun Do (1980)
Ming Patriots (1977)
  aka **Bruce Lee's Big Secret**
Return of the Tiger (1977)
  with **Angela Mao.**
Soul Brothers of Kung Fu (1978)
Spirits of Bruce Lee (1979)
Story of the Dragon (1976)
Superdragon vs. Superman (1977)

BRUCE LE
(Hung Kin Lung) films:
Big Boss 2 (1976)
  Listed in credits as Hung Kin Lung.
Bloody Hero (1978)
Bruce and Shaolin Bronzemen (1982)
Bruce and Shaolin Kung Fu (1977)
  aka **Bruce vs Black Dragon**
Bruce and Shaolin Kung Fu 2 (1978)
Bruce and the Dragon Fist (1981)

Bruce Li (aka Ho Chung Tao)

aka **Dragon Fist**
Bruce, King of Kung Fu (1980)
aka **Revenge of the Dragon**
Directed by actor Ho Chung Tao.
Bruce Le Strikes Back (1981)
Filmed in Europe with Harold Sakata.
Bruce Lee Fights Back from the Grave (1976)
Bruce the Super Hero (1979)
Bruce and Bill (1981)
With Bruce Le and Bill Louie.
Bruce's Fingers (1976)
Clones of Bruce Lee (1977)
Also with Dragon Lee and Bruce Lai.
Enter Another Dragon (1981)
With John Saxon and Ron Van Clief.
Enter the Game of Death (1978)
Gymkata Killer (1978)
With Richard Harrison.
Mad Cold Blooded Murder (1981)
With Carter Wong (Huang).
Ninja Strikes Back (1982)
Ninja vs. Bruce Lee (1982)
Re-Enter the Dragon (1979)
Return of Bruce (1977)
Return of Fists of Fury (1977)
Return of Red Tiger (1980)
Salt, Pepper and Soy Sauce (1981)
Super Gang (1982)
Treasure of Bruce Lee (1980)
True Game of Death (1981)
Young Bruce Lee (1982)
Young Dragon (1976)

DRAGON LEE films:
Big Boss 2 (1976)
Also with Bruce Le.
Bruce Lee's Ways of Kung Fu (1978)

Champ Against Champ (1978)
Clones of Bruce Lee (1977)
Also with Bruce Le and Bruce Lai.
Dragon Lee vs. Five Brothers (1982)
Dragon's Showdown (1980)
Enter the Invisible Hero (1981)
Enter Three Dragons (1979)
Also with Bruce Li and Bruce Lea.
Justice of the Dragon (1980)
Kung Fu Fever (1982)
Martial Arts of Shaolin Temple (1983)
Rage of the Dragon (1984)
The Real Bruce Lee (1983)

BRUCE LIANG films:
Broken Oath (1977)
Bruce Lee, D-Day at Macao (1979)
With **Samo Hung** and Carter Wong.
Call Me Dragon (1979)
Fists, the Kicks and the Evil (1979)
Four Shaolin Challengers (1977)
Godfather of Hong Kong (1974)
Incredible Master Beggars (1979)
Invincible Kung Fu (1978)
Ruthless Revenge (1982)
Showdown at the Equator (1984)
Ten Tigers of Shaolin (1979)

Bruce Le (aka Hung Kin Lung)

BLOOD TREASURY FIGHT (1979)
aka **DRAGON DEVIL DIE**
director: **Pao Hsieh Lieh.** David Chiang
·Tan Tao Liang·Wang Chung·Chan Hui
Man
An attempt to broaden the traditional
genre formula by mixing chop socky
action with a treasure hunt caper; it
failed to find an audience.

BLOODY AVENGERS.
See Boxer Rebellion

BLOODY FISTS.
See Heroes Two

BLOODY RING (1973)
aka **MAGIC MAGICIANS**
director: **Yeh Jung Tsu.** Samo Hung·
Bruce Leong·Chang Nam·Helen Ma

BLOODY STRUGGLE (1976)
director: **Jimmy Wang Yu.** Jimmy
Wang Yu·Kang Nam

BOLO (1977)
aka **BOLO THE BRUTE**
director: **Yang Sze.** Jason Pai Piao·
Yang Sze

➔ **BONE CRUSHING KID** (1979)
aka **KUNG FU CRUSHER**
director: **Hsia Cheng Hung.** Chin
Lung · Roy Horan · James Tien (Tsao
Tsan)
Promoted in many markets as a sequel
to **Snake in the Eagle's Shadow** due
to strong similarities.

➔ **BORN INVINCIBLE** (1978)
director: **Joseph Kong.** Carter Wong
·Lo Lieh·Lung Fei·Mark Long (Yo Ming
Tu)
One of Carter Wong's best performances as a ferocious white-haired
kung fu bully; he's challenged by a
righteous trio who discover the secret
to Wong's invincibility lies in his vul-
nerable throat; terrific choreography
by **Yuen Woo Ping**.

BORN INVINCIBLE (1981)
director: **Wong Tai Loy.** Yin Nan Hay
·Kwok Nan Wun

BOXER FROM THE TEMPLE (1980)
director: **Lo Mar.** Wu Yuan Chun·Lam
Fai Wong

BOXER REBELLION (1976)
aka **BLOODY AVENGERS**
director: **Chang Cheh.** Alexander Fu
Sheng · Li Li Hue · Richard Harrison ·
Liang Cha Jen

BRAVE ARCHER.
See Kung Fu Warlords

BRAVE ARCHER 2.
See Kung Fu Warlords 2

BRAVE ARCHER 3.
See Blast of the Iron Palm

BRAVE ARCHER 4.
See Kung Fu Warlords 4

BREAKING DEADLY SWORD.
See Deadly Breaking Sword

➔ **BROKEN OATH** (1977)
director: **Chang Cheung Wo.** Angela
Mao · Bruce Liang · Casanova Wong
(cameo appearance)
Generally considered Angela Mao's
finest performance.

BRUCE AGAINST THE ODDS (1980)
aka **LONE SHAOLIN AVENGER**
director: **Cheng Kay Ying.** Casanova
Wong·Bruce Cheung

BRUCE LEE FIGHTS AGAIN.
See Dragon Lee Fights Again

**BRUCE LEE FIGHTS BACK FROM THE
GRAVE** (1978)
director: **Doo Yong Lee (Umberto
Lenzi).** Bruce K. L. Lea·Anthony Bron-
son·Steve Mak·Deborah Chaplin
Tasteless story of a boxer possessed

by **Bruce Lee**'s soul. Shot in United States by an Italian crew using bogus Chinese names; the director is actually legendary horror filmmaker Umberto Lenzi.

BRUCE VS SNAKE IN EAGLE'S SHADOW.
See *Snake in the Eagle's Shadow*

→ **BUDDHA ASSASSINATOR** (1979)
director: **Tung Kan Wu.** Mang Hoi · Huang Cheng Li · Lung Fei · Chien Yueh Sheng
Promoted in some markets as the sequel to **Dragon and Tiger Kids** due to the reteaming of Mang Hoi and Huang Cheng Li

→ **BUDDHIST FIST** (1980)
director: **Yuen Woo Ping** and **Tsui Siu Ming.** Tsui Siu Ming · Fan Mei Sheng · Simon Yuen (Yuen Hsin Yee)
Tsui Siu Ming is a Taiwanese pop-singer-turned-boxer.

BURNING OF THE IMPERIAL PALACE (1985)
director: **Li Han Hsiang.** Tony Leung (Chiu Wai) · Liu Xiao Ching

BUTCHER WING (1980)
director: **Luk Pak Sang.** Ng Ming Tsui · Hon Kwok Tsui
Another fictionalized account of the Wong Fei Hung story.

BUTTERFLY 18.
See *Invincible Shaolin Kung Fu*

CANNIBALS (1979)
director: **Lo Chun Ku.** Meng Li · Chen Chen · Chen Hung Lieh · Chang Yi
Regardless of the title, this has nothing to do with cannibalism, except in the symbolic sense, as a female casino owner fights the mob.

→ **CANTON IRON KUNG FU** (1981)
director: **Li Chao.** Liang Cha Jen · Wang Chun · Kao Fei · Ting Hua Chung
This film is generally considered the best from Liang Cha Jen.

CAT VS. RAT (1982)
director: **Liu Chia Liang.** Alexander Fu Sheng · Adam Cheng · Hui Ying Hung · Hsaio Ho

CAVALIER.
See *Dancing Kung Fu*

CHALLENGE OF DEATH (1978)
director: **Lee Tso Nam.** Wong Tao · Tan Tao Liang · Chang Yi · Lee Chien Min
sequel to **Hot, Cool and Vicious.**

CHALLENGE OF THE MASTER.
See *Executioners of Death*

→ **CHALLENGE OF THE NINJA** (1978)
aka **HEROES OF THE EAST**
aka **DRUNK SHAOLIN CHALLENGES NINJA**
director: **Liu Chia Liang.** Liu Chia Hui · Liu Chia Liang · Yasuaki Kurata · Yuko Mizuno
One of the few chop socky films that takes *both* Chinese and Japanese martial arts seriously; considered one of the Shaw Brothers' best films. Liu Chia Hui and Yasaki Kurata are both in top fighting form.

CHALLENGER
See *Deadly Challenger*

CHAMP AGAINST CHAMP (1983)
director: **Godfrey Ho.** Dragon Lee · Charles Han · Mark Wong · Doris Tsui
Composite specialist **Godfrey Ho** takes bits and pieces from at least two different films and edits them together into one production. Some of the best scenes are from an unreleased Korean movie about invisible kung fu fighting females.

CHAMPIONS (1979)
director: **Yuen Cheung Yeung.** Jackie Chan·Yuen Biao

→ **CHINATOWN KID** (1977)
director: **Chang Cheh.** Alexander Fu Sheng·Kuo Chui·Wang Lung Wei·Tsai Hung·Sun Chien·Lo Meng
Debut film for Sun Chien and Lo Meng.

→ **CHINESE BOXER** (1970)
aka **HAMMER OF THE GODS**
director: **Jimmy Wang Yu.** Jimmy Wang Yu·Lo Lieh·Lua Szu Yuan·Chan Sing
Early Shaw Brothers' success starring, written by, and directed by **Jimmy Wang Yu** (the first bona fide chop socky superstar). Generally considered the first film to concentrate on fighting techniques as a plot line.

CHINESE HERCULES (1974)
director: **Choy Tak.** Chen Hui Min· Yang Sze·Chiang Fan·Wang Chung
In this case, Hercules is the villain, controlled by a local gangster mob who use the martial arts giant against the rebelling dock workers.

CHINESE PROFESSIONALS.
See One Armed Boxer

CHINESE VENGEANCE (1973)
aka **DYNASTY OF BLOOD**
director: **Chang Cheh.** David Chiang ·Ti Lung·Li Hsiu Hsien·Ching Li

CLAN OF THE WHITE LOTUS.
See Fists of the White Lotus

CLANS OF INTRIGUE (1977)
director: **Chu Yuan.** Ti Lung·Yo Hua· Nora Miao·Li Ching

CLONES OF BRUCE LEE (1977)
director: **Joseph Kong.** Bruce Le · Dragon Lee·Bruce Lai·Bruce Thai
Four Bruce Lee lookalikes created by a mad scientist bent on world domination.

COLD BLOODED EAGLES.
See Avenging Eagle

COME DRINK WITH ME (1965)
director: **King Hu.** Cheng Pei Pei·Yo Hua

COMET STRIKES (1970)
director: **Lo Wei.** Nora Miao·Hsieh Hsien
Kung fu supernatural thriller; couple visits a haunted house.

CONDEMNED (1976)
director: **David Chiang.** David Chiang ·Tsai Hung·Ku Feng·Pai Ying

CONVICT KILLER.
See Iron Chain Assassin.

COUNTDOWN IN KUNG FU.
See Hand of Death

COWARD BASTARD (1979)
director: **Lo Chun Ku.** Meng Yuan Wen·Yuen Wah·Wang Sha·Yu Tsui Ling
Acting debut for HK stuntman Yuen Wah. Shaw Brothers begin inserting slapstick into their chop socky.

CRACK SHADOW BOXERS (1978)
director: **Wan Yao Hua.** Ku Feng · Chou Li Chung

→ **CRANE FIGHTER** (1979)
director: **Raymond Liu.** Judy Lee (Chia Ling)·Raymond Liu·Kam Kong· Ting Hwa Chung·Chia Ling
Generally considered the best film by actor/director **Raymond Liu.** Ironically, the notoriety is due to Judy Lee's crane fist techniques, not Raymond's performance.

CRAZY GUY WITH SUPER KUNG FU (1979)
director: **Wang Lung Wei.** Lee Yi Min ·Pang Gang·Mark Long (in cameo appearance)
Inferior Taiwanese kung fu comedy.

CRAZY KUNG FU MASTER (1984)
director: Kent Cheng. Kent Cheng ·
Wong Ching [Jing]

CRIPPLED AVENGERS.
See Mortal Combat

→ **CRYSTAL FIST** (1979)
director: Hwa Yi Hung. Billy Chong ·
Yuen Siu Tin · Yuen Chun Wai · Chu Tiet
Wo
Billy Chong's first feature film; previously Billy was known as **Willy Dohzan**, an Indonesian pop singer.
Choreographed by future action director **Cory Yuen [Yuen Kewi]**

CUB TIGER FROM KWANGTUNG.
See Snake Fist Fighter

→ **DAGGERS EIGHT** (1980)
director: Cheung Sum. Meng Yuan
Man · Lilly Li · Wilson Tong · Chan Lung

→ **DANCE OF DEATH** (1980)
director: Chan Chi Hwa. Angela
Mao · Chin Pei · Chia Kai · Shi Tien
A costumed kung fu comedy mostly
significant for a fine performance from
Angela Mao. Martial arts choreography by **Jackie Chan**.

→ **DANCE OF THE DRUNK MANTIS**
(1979)
director: Yuen Woo Ping. Yuen Hsin
Yi · Yuen Siu Ting · Huang Cheng Li · Lin
Ying
Promoted by Seasonal Films as the sequel to **Drunken Master**. Starring
Corey Yuen [Yuen Kewi] in a cameo
role.

Liu Chia Hui in *Eight Diagram Pole Fighter*

→ DANCING KUNG FU (1978)
aka **CAVALIER**
director: **Kuo Nai Hong.** Lung Chung Erh·Lo Lieh·Tsai Hung·Lung Fei
An intensive martial arts film from veteran independent producer **Joseph Kuo**, with unique "whoever beats my daughter in a kung fu match has the right to marry her" theme. **Lung Chung Erh** is breathtaking as the fighting maiden.

DANCING WARRIOR.
See *Warrior*

→ DAREDEVILS (1980)
aka **DAREDEVILS OF KUNG FU**
aka **SHAOLIN DAREDEVILS**
aka **VENOM WARRIORS**
director: **Chang Cheh.** Kuo Chui·Chiang Sheng·Sun Chien·Lo Meng·Lu Feng
One of the few times the hero (Kuo Chui) dies.

DEADLY BREAKING SWORD (1979)
aka **BREAKING DEADLY SWORD**
director: **Sun Chung.** Ti Lung·Lilly Li·Alexander Fu Sheng

→ DEADLY CHALLENGER (1980)
aka **CHALLENGER**
director: **Tsang Chi Wai.** David Chiang·Kao Fei·Lilly Li·Tsui Siu Keung

DEADLY DUO.
See *Vengeance*

DEADLY MANTIS (1978)
aka **SHAOLIN MANTIS**
director: **Liu Chia Liang.** David Chiang·Liu Chia Liang

DEADLY SHAOLIN KICKS.
See *Flash Legs*

DEATH CHAMBER.
See *Shaolin Temple*

DEATH DUEL OF KUNG FU (1979)
director: **Cheung Sum.** John Liu·Wong Tao·Philip Ko·Han Ying
Reunites stars of **Secret Rivals**.

DEATH MASK OF THE NINJA.
See *Iron Finger of Death*

DEATH OF BRUCE LEE (1975)
director: **Tommy Loo Chung.** Ron Van Clief·Charles Bonet·Jason Pai Piao·Philip Ko
Black Dragon (Ron Van Clief) conducts his own investigation into the death of Bruce Lee. He comes up with the same confused and conflicting information as everybody else.

DEATH RING (1983)
director: **Chang Cheh.** Chen Kuan Tai·Li Chung·Lu Feng·Ti Lung

DELIGHTFUL FOREST (1971)
director: **Chang Cheh.** Ti Lung·Chu Mu·Yu Feng·Chiang Ling
Based on traditional Chinese novel *Water Margin* by **Shin Nai An**.

→ DEMON FISTS OF KUNG FU (1976)
aka **GRAND MASTER OF DEATH**
aka **GRAND MASTER OF KUNG FU**
director: **Chang Cheh.** Alexander Fu Sheng·Kuo Chui·Wang Lung Wei·Liang Cha Jen
Alexander Fu Sheng shows off his exquisite *Choy Lay Fu* style of martial arts.

DEMON STRIKE (1979)
director: **Sun Chung.** Jason Pai Paio·Liang Cha Jen

→ DESTROYERS OF THE FIVE DEADLY VENOMS (1979)
director: **Chang Cheh.** Alexander Lu Feng·Lo Meng·Wang Li·Chiang Sheng
Director Chang Cheh's sequel to his own **Five Deadly Venoms**, made in 1978.

DEVIL AND ANGEL (1973)
director: Lo Lieh. Lo Lieh·Tien Feng

→ **DIRTY HO** (1979)
director: Liu Chia Liang. Young Wang Yu·Liu Chia Hui·Lo Lieh·Hsiao Ho
One of the best examples of a character driven martial arts film.

DIRTY TIGER AND CRAZY FROG (1978)
director: Karl Maka. Samo Hung·Lui Chia Yung·Karl Maka·Jason Pai Piao

→ **DISCIPLES OF DEATH** (1974)
aka **MEN FROM THE MONASTERY**
director: Chang Cheh. Alexander Fu Sheng·Chen Kuan Tai·Chi Kuan Chun·Tan Yen Tsan
One of **Chang Cheh**'s most celebrated films, the source material for **Johnny To**'s **Barefooted Kid** (see review). Loosely based sequel to **Blood Brothers**.

DISCIPLES OF MASTER KILLER.
See 36th Chamber of Shaolin

DOUBLE CROSSER (1978)
director: Chen Hung Man. Shin I Lung·Chen Hsing

→ **DOWAGER EMPRESS** (1975)
director: Li Han Hsiang. Ti Lung·Lisa Lu·David Chiang·Ku Feng
An impressive costumer martial arts film from the prolific Shaw Brothers, during their kung fu heyday.

→ **DRAGON AND TIGER KIDS** (1979)
aka **HELL'S WIND STAFF**
director: Lo Chun Ku. Mang Yuan Man·Hsu Hsia·Huang Ken Kwang·Jason Pai Piao
This early work from filmmaker Lo (who later made **Haunted Madam** and similar action films) is marred by sloppy direction and hatchet editing;

however, the closing fight sequence is terrific, transcending any technical problems with the movie.

DRAGON BALL
director: Chen Kuan Tai. Ti Kim·Ho Chi Keung

DRAGON DEVIL DIE.
See Blood Treasury Fight

DRAGON DIES HARD (1974)
aka **BRUCE LEE, SUPERDRAGON**
director: Lee Koon Cheung. Bruce Li (Ho Chung Tao)·Lung Fei

DRAGON FIGHT (1988)
aka **DRAGON KICKBOXER**
director: Billy Tang. Jet Li·Dick Wei·Nina Li Chi·Stephen Chow
Chop socky fare from director **Billy Tang**, who later made such controversial films as **Dr. Lamb**, **Run and Kill**, and **Red to Kill** (see Review section). Also an early entry from Chinese boxer **Jet Li**, future star of **Once upon a Time in China**, et al. This film was shot in the Philippines.

DRAGON FIST (1978)
director: Lo Wei. Jackie Chan·Nora Miao
Made on the heels of the successful **Spiritual Kung Fu**, but this one was an unequivocal failure at the box office, disowned by **Jackie Chan** for its lack of humor. Also starring **Bruce Lee**'s cinematic main squeeze, **Nora Miao**.

DRAGON FORCE (1979)
aka **BIG RASCAL**
director: Chi Kuan Chun. Chi Kuan Chun·Wang Ching

→ **DRAGON INN** (1972)
aka **DRAGON GATE INN**
director: King Hu. Shang Kwan Ling Feng·Pai Ying·Ling Fung·Miao Tien
Legendary filmmaker **King Hu** creates a sweeping tale of treachery in the

Ming Dynasty; this story was successfully remade by **Raymond Lee** and producer **Tsui Hark** in 1992 (see separate listing).

DRAGON LEE FIGHTS AGAIN (1978)
   aka **BRUCE LEE FIGHTS AGAIN**
director: To Lo Po. Dragon Lee·Jacky Chang
This one tries to capitalize on both **Bruce Lee** and **Jackie Chan** with bogus lookalikes sporting similar names.

DRAGON MISSILE (1976)
director: Ho Menga (Meng Hua). Lo Lieh·Ti Lung
Standard martial arts mania from Shaw Brothers' notorious horror director (**Black Magic** series).

DRAGON ROOT (1978)
director: Sun Gam Loi. Cheung Kok Keun·Quan Hoi Sa

DRAGON TAMERS (1974)
director: John Woo. Samo Hung·Carter Wong

→ **DRAGON, THE HERO** (1979)
director: Godfrey Ho. John Liu·Tino Wong·Dragon Lee·Phillip Kao·Bolo Yeung
Director **Godfrey Ho** went on to become HK's notorious mix-n-match specialist, the master of creating movies from bits and pieces of unfinished or unreleased projects.

DRAGON, THE LIZARD AND THE BOXER (1977)
director: Lo Ke and **Ngai Lai.** Tan Tao Liang·Meng Fei

→ **DREADNAUGHT** (1981)
director: Yuen Woo Ping. Yuen Biao·Yuen Shen Yi·Phillip Kao·Liang Cha Jen
Generally considered director **Yuen**

Woo Peng's best film; a tour-de force for **Yuan Biao**.

DRUG ADDICT (1974)
director: David Chiang. Ti Lung·David Chiang·Wang Chun·Paul Chin Pei
A precursor to **Chang Cheh**'s **Ten Tigers of Kwantung** (1979), in which **Ti Lung** plays a similar role, a fighter hopelessly addicted to drugs.

DRUNK MONKEY IN TIGER'S EYE.
   See *Drunken Master*

DRUNK SHAOLIN CHALLENGES NINJA.
   See *Challenge of the Ninja*

DRUNKEN ARTS AND CRIPPLED FIST.
   See *Taoism Drunkard*

→ **DRUNKEN CAT'S PAW** (1982)
   aka **FLYING CLAW FIGHTS 14 DEMONS**
director: Ting Shan Si. Chia Ling·Ou Yang Hsieh·Yang Lung·Feng Ling
Blind swordswoman seeks a gang of bandits from Northern China.

→ **DRUNKEN MASTER** (1978)
   aka **DRUNK MONKEY IN TIGER'S EYE**
director: Yuen Woo Ping. Jackie Chan·Yuen Siu Tien
Jackie Chan's humorous rendering of the Wong Fei Hung legend; generally considered the birth of kung fu comedy.

DRUNKEN MONKEY (1979)
   aka **MONKEY KUNG FU**
director: Joe Law. Chen Muk Chuan·Chang Yi
Chop socky comedy obviously inspired by **Drunken Master**; promoted in some markets as a sequel.

→ **DRUNKEN TAI CHI** (1984)
director: Yuen Woo Peng. Donnie Yen·Yuen Cheung Yan
The debut of **Donnie Yen**, an American-born boxer who was studying in Beijing and was discovered by **Yuen Woo Ping**.

DUEL OF FISTS (1971)
director: Chang Cheh. Ti Lung·David Chiang·Ching Li·Ku Feng

DUEL OF IRON FISTS (1969)
director: Chang Cheh. Ti Lung·David Chiang·Ku Feng·Cheng Kang Yeh

DUEL OF THE MASTERS (1981)
director: Wilson Tong. Tsiu Siu Keung·Sonny Yue
Intended as a parody of kung fu films.

DUEL OF THE 7 TIGERS.
See Shadow of the Tigers

DUEL TO THE DEATH (1977)
director: Chu Yuan. Ti Lung·Lilly Li

→ **DUEL TO THE DEATH** (1983)
director: Ching Siu Tung. Tsiu Siu Keung·Liu Sung Jen·Wilson Tong·Casanova Wong
Early film by **Ching Siu Tung**, who later directed the **Chinese Ghost Story** series, the **Swordsman** series, plus **Fists of Fury 1991**.

DUEL WITH DEVILS (1977)
director: Lin Pai. Tan Tao Liang·Angela Mao
The "devils" in the title are those damnable evil Japanese.

DUELS IN THE DESERT (1980)
director: Shiau Mu. Angela Mao·Pai Ying

DYNAMO (1979)
director: Hwa Yi Hung. Bruce Li (Ho Chung Tao)·Ku Feng

The Five Deadly Venoms

DYNASTY OF BLOOD.
See Chinese Vengeance

EAGLE CLAW CHAMPION (1982)
director: Wu Man Hung. Conan Han ·Glenn Choi·Stella Lee·Viola Ku
Poorly made unofficial sequel to the superior **Eagle's Claw**; the credits for the film are suspected to be bogus.

EAGLE CLAW VS BUTTERFLY PALM (1982)
director: Yu Tien Lung. Tien Peng·Yo Hua·Lo Lieh·Yu Tien Lung
Historical chop socky tale of Chinese patriots against the Mongols.

EAGLE WITH A YELLOW FACE (1980)
director: Wu Ma. Yuen Biao·James Tien

→ **EAGLE'S CLAW** (1978)
aka **EAGLE FIST**
director: Lee Tso Nam with **Cheng Kuan Tai.** Chi Kuan Chun·Wang Tao· Phillip Kao·Liang Cha Jen
A highly acclaimed film from Champion Films featuring one of Chi Kuan Chun's best performances. Director Lee Tso Nam never achieved notoriety from the chop socky genre, but he came close with the cult fave **Kung Fu Wonder Child** (1989).

EAGLE'S KILLER (1979)
director: Chang Cheh. John Chang· Huang Cheng Li·Chang Wu Lang· Ching Pei Ling
An example of extensive slapstick kung fu humor.

EAGLE'S SHADOW.
See Snake in the Eagle's Shadow

→ **EIGHT DIAGRAM POLE FIGHTER** (1983)
aka **INVINCIBLE POLE FIGHTER**
director: Liu Chia Liang. Liu Chia Hui ·Alexander Fu Sheng·Liu Chia Liang·

Phillip Kao·Wai Ying Hung·Wong Yue ·Lilly Li
Liu Chia Liang's last film for the Shaw Brothers and probably his best. There were major script revisions during the shoot due to a car accident that took the life of Alexander Fu Sheng.

→ **EIGHT ESCORTS** (1980)
aka **HERO TATTOO WITH NINE DRAGONS**
aka **TATTOO DRAGON CONNECTION**
director: Pao Hsieh Lieh. Chen Kuan Tai·Ching Ling·Hsu Feng·Tan Tao Liang
Generally considered one of the best examples of Shaolin style kung fu fighting in film.

EIGHT MAN ARMY (1976)
director: Cheng Cheh. Ti Lung· Alexander Fu Sheng

8 PEERLESS TREASURES (1979)
director: Pao Hsueh Lieh. Hsu Feng· Chen Hui Min·Wang Chung·Li Hsiu Hsien

EIGHTEEN BRONZEGIRLS OF SHAOLIN (1977)
director: Chian Lai Ya. Sally Chang· Ching Tao·Kam Kong·Yo Hua·Wei Hwa
Chian Lai Ya is a pseudonym used by a director who didn't want to be associated with this film. The filmmaker's true identity remains unknown.

→ **EIGHTEEN BRONZEMEN** (1976)
director: Joseph Kong (Kuo). Carter Wong·Poly Shang Kwan·Chang Yi· Tien Peng·Yi Yuan
Easily **Carter Wong**'s best role. Later this talented boxer was relegated to HK geek shows like Sucabbare (aka Poison Princesses of Cheong Valley).

EIGHTEEN JADE PEARLS (1978)
director: **Cheung Chieh.** Shang Kuan
Ling·Chang Yi·Lo Lieh·Tung Li·Fang
Fang

18 SHAOLIN DISCIPLES (1980)
director: **Hsu Feng.** Carter Wong
(Huang)·Hsu Feng·Meng Fei·Chang
Yi

18 WEAPONS OF KUNG FU (1979)
aka **18 SECRETS OF KUNG FU**
director: **Chen Hung Man.** Li Shao
Hua·Wang Fu Quen·Wang Wing San
·Chen Fei Fei

EMPEROR AND HIS BROTHER (1980)
director: **Chu Yuan.** Ti Lung·Jason Pai
Piao·Lo Lieh·Sun Chien

EMPEROR OF SHAOLIN KUNG FU
(1980)
director: **Liu Chia Liang.** Carter
Wong (Huang)·Lo Lieh

END OF WICKED TIGERS (1984)
director: **Law Ke.** Charles Heung·Lee
Kay Ting·Samo Hung·Wilson Tong

→ **ENTER THE DRAGON** (1973)
director: **Robert Clouse.** Bruce Lee·
John Saxon·Jim Kelly·Angela Mao·
Shek Kin·Bob Wall
The world's most acclaimed martial
arts movie. Besides featuring the king
and queen of kung fu action, **Bruce
Lee** and Angela Mao, many future HK
stars can be seen in cameos (including
**Jackie Chan, Samo Hung, Yuen
Biao,** Lo Lieh, and David Chiang).

EUNUCH OF THE WESTERN PALACE
(1979)
director: **Wu Ma.** Chung Hua·Lo Lieh
·Won Tao·Meng Fei·Lung Fei

→ **EXECUTIONERS OF DEATH** (1976)
aka **EXECUTIONERS OF SHAOLIN**
aka **CHALLENGE OF THE MASTER**
director: **Liu Chia Liang.** Chen Kuan

Tai·Lilly Li·Lo Lieh·Liu Chia Hui·Cheng
Kang Yeh
Generally considered the sequel to **Disciples of Death.** Major early film by legendary director **Liu Chia Liang,** a
former Cantonese master [instructor].

FAST SWORD (1978)
director: **Hwang Feng.** Chang Yi·
Han Hsiang Chin·Samo Hung (also
martial arts director)

FATAL FLYING GUILLOTINES (1983)
director: **Lui Shing Kung.** Chen Sing·
Carter Wong (Huang)·Chen Hsiao
Peng·Kao Chiang

→ **FATAL NEEDLES VS FATAL FISTS**
(1980)
director: **Lee Tso Nan.** Wong Tao·
Chang Yi·Lo Lieh·Li Chiang
Chinese good guys vs drug-trafficking
Mongolians.

→ **FATE OF LEE KHAN** (1973)
director: **King Hu.** Tien Feng·Angela
Mao·Lili Hua·Samo Hung·Mou Ying·
Roy Chiao
King Hu's sprawling story about the
end of the Yuan Dynasty and the rise
of the Ming Dynasty.

→ **FEARLESS HYENA** (1979)
director: **Jackie Chan.** Jackie Chan·
Yen Si Kuan·James Tien·Li Kuan
First film directed by **Jackie Chan.**

FEARLESS HYENA 2 (1980)
director: **Lo Wei.** Jackie Chan·James
Tien·Hon Kwok Choi·Shih Tien
A piecework project, comprised of
outtakes from **Fearless Hyena.**

FEARLESS YOUNG BOXER (1979)
director: **Wong Kwok Chu.** Peter
Chang·Casanova Wong

FEMALE CHIVALRY (1975)
director: **Yang Ou Chen.** Judy Lee
(Chia Ling)·We Tzu Yung

→ FIGHT FOR SURVIVAL (1977)
director: Hu Chin. Shang Kuan Ling Feng·Chia Ling·Wong Tao·Meng Kang
Female boxer **Shang Kuan Ling Feng** is quite impressive as the kung fu student who goes on a mission to recover a sacred book. In an especially odd turn of events, bad guy **Wong Tao** plays his villainous role in drag.

FIST OF DEATH (1977)
director: Lo Wei. Jackie Chan·Tong Lung

FIST OF FEAR, TOUCH OF DEATH (1977)
director: Matthew Mallinson. Aaron Banks · Ron Van Clief · Bill Louie · Teruyuki Higa·Bruce Lee (various film clips)
Aaron Banks gets the opportunity to promote his "search for a new Bruce Lee" at the Martial Arts Expo at Madison Square Garden and talk about "his close and dear friend" Bruce.

FISTS AND GUTS (1980)
director: Liu Chia Yung. Liu Chia Yung·Lo Lieh
Don't be misled by the title; this is a kung fu comedy about the search for the Master of Disguises.

FISTS OF DRAGONS (1980)
aka **KUNG FU KIDS**
aka **RETURN OF 7 NINJA KIDS**
aka **LITTLE RASCALS OF KUNG FU**
aka **LITTLE BIG MASTER**
director: Yen Yung Tsu. Huang I Lung·Ou Ti·Man Li Peng·Chang Hai Fen
Young beggar boys and kung fu shenanigans.

→ FISTS OF FURY (1972) known in United States as **CHINESE CONNECTION**
director: Lo Wei. Bruce Lee · Nora Miao·Lo Wei·James Tien·Tony Liu

Lo Lieh in *Five Fingers of Death*

Generally regarded as one of the most important martial arts films of all time; certainly it's one of the most imitated. **Bruce Lee**'s second film (preceded by **Big Boss** [1971]). This one tells the story of a student who retaliates when his teacher is killed by a gang of arrogant Japanese fighters.

FISTS OF FURY 2 (1976)
director: Jimmy Shaw. Bruce Li (Ho Chung Tao)·Lo Lieh

FISTS OF FURY 3 (1978)
director: To Lo Po. Bruce Li (Ho Chung Tao)·Ku Feng
Obviously, neither of these two sequels was sanctioned.

→ FISTS OF THE WHITE LOTUS (1980)
aka **CLAN OF THE WHITE LOTUS**
director: Lo Lieh. Liu Chia Hui·Lo Lieh·Hui Ying Hung·Lilly Li
Generally considered a sequel to **Executioners of Shaolin**.

FISTS OF VENGEANCE (1980) director: **Chen Hung Man.** Kung Bun ·Shoji Karada

➜ **FIVE DEADLY VENOMS** (1978) director: **Chang Cheh.** Chiang Sheng · Kuo Chui · Lo Meng · Sun Chien · Ku Feng·Wei Pai
Director **Chang Cheh** refused to insert comic relief in his film despite pressure from HK investors. Shaw Brothers Studios backed Chang Cheh in the decision; slapstick kung fu comedy wouldn't come to Shaw Brothers until 1979 with **Coward Bastard.**

➜ **FIVE FINGERS OF DEATH** (1970) aka **IRON PALM** director: **Cheng Chang Ho.** Lo Lieh· Wang Pin·Yang Sze·James Nam·Tien Feng·Chan Shen
Generally considered the film that started the worldwide interest in chop socky. Certainly it was the genre's first major box office hit in the USA before the **Bruce Lee** actioners

5 KUNG FU DAREDEVILS (1980) aka **5 KUNG FU HEROES** director: **Shen Kang.** Meng Fei · Lo Lieh·Liang Cha Jen·Yu Tien Lung
Historical kung fu action as patriots rebel against a Russian liaison during political upheaval in China.

➜ **FIVE MASTERS OF DEATH** (1975) director: **Chang Cheh.** Ti Lung·David Chiang·Meng Fei·Alexander Sheng· Chi Kuan Chun
Another entry in **Chang Cheh**'s Shaolin Temple series, remembered for the vivid reenactment of the destruction of the famous temple in the mid-17th century.

FIVE TOUGH GUYS.
See *Kung Fu Hellcats*

FLAG OF IRON.
See *Spearman of Death*

FLASH LEGS (1977) aka **SHAOLIN DEADLY KICKS** director: **Wu Ma.** Tan Tao Liang · Lo Lieh·Lung Chung Er·Kam Kong

FLYING CLAW FIGHTS 14 DEMONS.
See *Drunken Cat's Paw*

➜ **FLYING GUILLOTINE** (1976) director: **Ho Menga (Meng Hua).** Chen Kuan Tai·Ku Feng·Wei Hung·Liu Wu Chi
Martial arts action is kept to a minimum, instead director **Ho** is more interested in capitalizing on the horrific qualities of a "flying guillotine" as vicious kung fu weapon.

FLYING GUILLOTINE 2 (1977) director: **Cheng Kang.** Ti Lung · Ku Feng·Lo Lieh·Wang Chung

FLYING MASTERS OF KUNG FU (1979) aka **VENGEFUL SWORDSWOMAN** director: **Hwang Feng.** Angelo Mao· Lo Lieh·Chia Ling·Wang Shi

FOUR ASSASSINS (1979) aka **MARCO POLO** director: **Chang Cheh.** Richard Harrison·Carter Wong·Shih Szu·Alexander Fu Sheng
Although promoted as a kung fu film, it is actually a Chinese version of the Marco Polo story.

FOUR INVINCIBLES (1979) director: **Hwa Yi Hung (Hua Jen).** Hon Kwok Choi·Ku Feng·Tai Hsi Yen· Wang Hsing Hsiu

FRIENDS (1974) director: **Chang Cheh.** David Chiang · Lilly Li·Alexander Fu Sheng

FURY OF SHAOLIN FIST (1979) director: **Li Chih So.** Chen Hung Lieh· Shik Chuan·Chiang Pin·Chiao Chiao· Meng Li

Regardless of the title, this one has nothing to do with Shaolin or the fighting methods taught there; instead, it seems to be based on **Shadow Whip** (1977), featuring a whip-cracking villain.

FURY OF SHAOLIN MASTER (1982)
aka **SHAOLIN MASTER AND THE KID**
director: **Lin Fu Di.** Yo Hua·Tsai Tsuan Han·Chen Sing·Pan Yin Tze
Chinese version of the Japanese Lone Wolf and Child series; a swordsman takes his nephew down the path of vengeance.

GAME OF DEATH (1973) (released in 1978)
director: **Robert Clouse.** Bruce Lee· Gig Young · Dean Jagger · Kareem Abdul-Jabbar·Hugh O'Brien · Colleen Camp·Samo Hung
Bruce Lee died during the production of this film; his on screen participation is limited to the final 15 minutes (specifically, a major fight sequence with Kareem Abdul-Jabbar, the basketball player). For the remainder of the film, Bruce Lee's character is played by lookalike **Kim Tai Chung**. The non-Bruce Lee fight scenes were choreographed by Samo Hung. Roy Chiao has a part in the American version; Casanova Wong is in the Asian version only.

GAME OF DEATH 2 (1980)
aka **TOWER OF DEATH**
director: **Ng See Yuen.** Kim Tai Chung·Huang Cheng Li·Roy Chiao· Casanova Wong
Includes **Bruce Lee** outtakes from *Return of the Dragon* (aka *Way of the Dragon*).

GENERATION GAP (1973)
director: **Chang Cheh.** David Chiang ·Ti Lung·Angnes Chan·Helen Ko

→ **GIRL CALLED TIGRESS** (1981)
director: **Wong Hong Chang.** Shang Kuan Ling Feng·Kam Kong
An important transgression film as kung fu movies drifted from mindless fight-oriented segments, reflecting no distinctive boxing style or technique, into a more defined appreciation for the martial arts.

GIRLFIGHTER (1980)
director: **Yang Chin Bong.** Shang Kuan Ling Feng·Tien Peng

→ **GIRL WITH THE THUNDERBOLT KICK** (1970)
aka **MISTRESS OF THE THUNDERBOLT**
director: **Chang Cheh.** Jimmy Wang Yu·Cheng Pei Pei·Lo Lieh·Tang Cheung
Jimmy Wang Yu (called **Wang Yu** for the first 10 years of his career) was the box office name who drew an audience to this feature, but kung fu diva **Cheng Pei Pei** found instant fame because of it.

GOLD CONSTABLES (1980)
director: **Wong Chung.** Carter Wong (Huang)·Lo Lieh·James Tien·Chi Lan
Generally considered Carter Wong's best performance; he plays a sword-fighting policeman named Chu Chi, searching for stolen gold in ancient China.

GOLDEN KEY (1978)
director: **Lo Wei.** Yen Chun · Chin Cheung Lam

THE GOOD, THE BAD AND THE LOSER (1976)
director: **Karl Maka.** Carter Wong (Huang)·Roy Chiao·Lui Chia Yung· Kao Fei.
Karl Maka's directorial debut.

The Five Masters of Death (from left) Meng Fei, Alexander Fu Sheng, Ti Lung, David Chaing, and Chi Kuan Chun

GRAND MASTER OF SHAOLIN KUNG FU (1981)
director: Godfrey Ho. Chang Ling·Philip Cheung
Martial arts frenzy with **Wolf Devil Woman Chang Ling** and Philip Cheung searching for a sacred book in the Temple of the Gold Buddha.

GRAND PASSION (1980)
director: Yang Chi Ching. Shang Kuan Ling Feng·Pai Ying

GREAT GENERAL (1977)
director: Wong Hong Chang. Meng Fei·Chow Gi Ming

HALF A LOAF OF KUNG FU (1978)
director: Chan Chi Hwa. Jackie Chan·Kam Kong·Lung Chung Erh·James Tien
Considered unreleasable upon completion in 1978. It was shelved until 1980, when **Jackie Chan's** name

meant more than the quality of the production.

HAMMER OF THE GODS.
See Chinese Boxer

HAND OF DEATH (1975)
aka **COUNTDOWN IN KUNG FU**
director: John Woo. Jackie Chan·Tan Tao Liang·Samo Hung·James Tien
Jackie Chan's name is listed as **Chan Yuan Lung** in the credits; contrary to popular opinion, this is not his real name. Jackie was born **Chen Gang Sheng** in 1954; Incidentally, this film is the only teaming so far of **Jackie Chan** with popular director **John Woo; Samo Hung** is martial arts director.

HAPKIDO (1972)
aka **LADY KUNG FU**
director: Hwang Feng. Carter Wong

•Angela Mao•Samo Hung•Whang In Sik
Generally thought to be **Samo Hung**'s first starring role; also features a walk-on by **Jackie Chan**. The plot is more Japanese-invading-China phobia.

HARD WAY TO DIE (1979)
   aka **SUN DRAGON**
director: Pal Ming. Billy Chong•Carl Scott
Shot entirely on location in Phoenix Arizona, as **Billy Chong** searches the American desert for his lost grandfather.

HAVE SWORD, WILL TRAVEL (1972)
   aka **THE BODYGUARD**
director: Chang Cheh. Ti Lung•David Chiang

➝ **HEADS FOR SALE** (1969)
director: Chen Chan Ho. Chiao Chiao•Wang Hsia
Terrific early attempt from the Shaw Brothers starring female fighter Chiao Chiao as a street merchant who sells heads in the town square, but it's really part of a plot to gain entrance to an evil warlord's castle and rescue her incarcerated lover. One of the best "sword" movies the genre has to offer.

HEAVEN AND HELL (1977)
director: Chang Cheh. David Chiang•Maggie Li•Alexander Fu Sheng•Lo Meng

HELL'S WIND STAFF.
   See Dragon and Tiger Kids

HERO (1976)
director: Wang Hung Chang. Jimmy Wang Yu•Chiao Chiao

HERO OF BORDER REGION (1982)
director: Pao Hsieh Leih. Chang Ling [Pearl Cheong]•Yuen Cheng Yan•Ti Lung
Sequel to **The Heroic Ones** (aka In-

heritors of **Kung Fu**); film was shelved until 1982).

HERO OF KWANG TONG (1981)
director: Kuo Nai Hong. Man Kong Lung•Yung Sam Sam

HERO TATTOO WITH 9 DRAGONS.
   See Eight Escorts

THE HEROES.
   See Story of Chivalry

HEROES OF THE EAST.
   See Challenge of the Ninja

HEROES OF THE LATE MING DYNASTY (1978)
director: Hwa Yi Hung. Carter Wong•Han Ying Chieh

➝ **HEROES OF SHAOLIN** (1979)
director: William Chang. Chen Sing•Ting Hua Chung•Lo Lieh•Yuen Biao•Corey Yuen
Yuen Biao has a mere cameo role, but he wa also martial arts director.

➝ **HEROES TWO** (1973)
   aka **KUNG FU INVADERS**
   aka **BLOODY FISTS**
director: Chang Cheh. Chen Kuan Tai•Alexander Fu Sheng•Wang Chung•Liu Chia Yung
Legendary filmmaker **Liu Chi Liang** is the action director/choreographer for this impressive Cheng Cheh vehicle.

HEROIC FAMILY (1978)
director: Liu Chia Liang. Liu Chia Liang•Yung Wang Yu•Alexander Fu Sheng•Lily Li

➝ **HEROIC ONES** (1971)
director: Chang Cheh. David Chiang•Ti Lung
Not to be confused with **Heroic Ones** (**Inheritors of Kung Fu**), directed by **Pao Hsieh Leih**, which also stared **Ti Lung**.

HIMALAYAN (1975)
director: **Hwang Feng.** Angela Mao·
Tan Tao Liang·Chen Sing·Samo Hung

HIS NAME IS NOBODY (1980)
director: **Karl Maka.** Liu Chia Yong·
Dean Shek
Director **Karl Maka**, easily recogniz-
able due to his completely bald head,
found notoriety as an actor in the **Aces
Go Places** series (1982 thru 1990)
and later became a HK producer.

→ **HITMAN IN THE HAND OF BUD-
DHA** (1980)
director: **Huang Cheng Li.** Huang
Cheng Li·Kao Hung
Director Huang Cheng Li, tired of
being typecast as a villain, puts himself in the hero's role.

HONG KONG PLAYBOYS (1983)
director: **Wong Ching [Jing].** Alexander Fu Sheng·Cherie Cheung·Chen
Pai Hsiang·Shi Kien
Alexander Fu Sheng's last movie; he
died in the summer of 1983, during the
filming of **Eight Diagram Pole Fighter**.

→ **HOT, COOL AND VICIOUS** (1976)
director: **Lee Tso Nam.** Wong Tao·
Tan Tao Liang·Sun Chia Lin·Corey
Yuen
Loads of kung fu action, fight scene after
another; one of the first films to capitalize on and distinguish fighting skills,
specifically the famed Southern Fist and
North Legs.

HOUSE OF TRAPS (1981)
director: **Chang Cheh.** Lu Feng·Wang
Li·Kuo Chui·Chiang Sheng

HURRICANE (1970)
director: **Lo Wei.** Nora Miao·Hsieh
Hsien

→ **IMPERIAL SWORD** (1977)
aka **KUNG FU SHADOW**
aka **BRAVE IN KUNG FU SHADOW**

director: **Chan Chi Hwa.** Tien Peng·
Chia Ling·Chang Yi·Lung Fei
Two swordsmen attempt to clear their
father's name by exposing the real
thief who snatched the sacred imperial
sword.

INCREDIBLE KUNG FU MASTER (1979)
director: **Joseph Cheung.** Samo
Hung·Tung Wei·Phillip Kao·Tung Wei
·Lee Hoi San

INCREDIBLE KUNG FU MISSION
(1979)
aka **KUNG FU COMMANDOS**
director: **Chang Hsin Yi.** John Liu·
Robert Tai·Chen Lung

→ **INCREDIBLE MASTER BEGGARS**
aka **TWELVE KUNG FU KICKS**
(1979)
director: **To Lo Po.** Bruce Liang·Larry
Lo·Hon Kwok Choi·Li Hai Sheng
Generally considered **Bruce Liang**'s
best film, demonstrating his unique
high-powered, but graceful, kung fu
boxing ability.

INHERITOR OF KUNG FU (1978)
aka **HEROIC ONES**
director: **Pao Hsieh Lieh.** Ti Lung·
Chang Ling
See review in text portion.

INSIDE THE FORBIDDEN CITY
director: **Kao Li.** Ivy Ling Po·Li Ching

INSTANT KUNG FU MAN (1980)
director: **Tung Kan Wu.** John Liu·
Huang Cheng Li

→ **INSTRUCTORS OF DEATH** (1980)
aka **MARTIAL CLUB**
director: **Liu Chia Liang.** Liu Chia Hui
·Hui Ying Hung·Ku Feng·Wang Lung
Wei
Liu Chia Liang is folk hero Wong Fei
Hung in the **Shaw brother**'s humanis-
tic variation of the myth.

INVINCIBLE (1976)
aka **SWIFT SHAOLIN BOXER**
director: **Chen Hung Man.** Lo Lieh·
Angela Mao·Wei Tze Yung·Chia Ling
Most likely, this film wasn't called *Invincible* or *Swift Shaolin Boxer* when it
was released to HK theaters. Both titles
are misleading; it's really a slasher
film with some fleeting martial arts sequences.

INVINCIBLE (1980)
director: **Lo Jun.** Jimmy Wang Yu·
Helen Ma

→ **INVINCIBLE ARMOR** (1977)
director: **Ng See Yuen.** John Liu·
Hwang Jan Lee · Phillip Kao · Tino
Wong
Choreographed by **Corey Yuen** and
Yuen Biao.

INVINCIBLE EIGHT (1971)
director: **Lo Wei.** Angela Mao·Nora
Miao·Shien Tien Sha·Chang Chung
This costume revenge tale was the second movie released in Golden Harvest's long and impressive repertoire.

INVINCIBLE IRON FIST (1970)
aka **RUTHLESS IRON HAND**
director: **Chang Cheh.** Chen Kuan Tai
·Ti Lung·David Chiang·Ching Li

INVINCIBLE KUNG FU BROTHERS.
See *Shaolin Advengers*

INVINCIBLE KUNG FU LEGS (1980)
aka **LEG FIGHTERS**
director: **Lee Tso Nan.** Tan Tao Liang
·Hsai Kuang Li

→ **INVINCIBLE KUNG FU TRIO** (1974)
aka **DRAGON'S FATAL FIST**
director: **Joe Law.** Meng Fei·John Lui
·Angela Mao·Kam Kong
This time Meng Fei plays legendary
hero Fong Sai Yuk.

→ **INVINCIBLE ONE** (1975)
aka **DISCIPLES OF SHAOLIN**
director: **Chang Cheh.** Alexander Fu
Sheng·Feng Ko An·Chi Kuan Chun·
Chen Ming Li
Remade as **Young Hero (Barefooted
Kid)** [1993].

INVINCIBLE POLE FIGHTER.
See *8 Diagram Pole Fighter*

INVINCIBLE SHAOLIN.
See *Unbeatable Dragon*

INVINCIBLE SHAOLIN KUNG FU
(1979)
aka **SECRET OF SHAOLIN KUNG
FU**
aka **BUTTERFLY 18**
director: **Ko Shih Hao.** Li Yi Min·Sher
Pu Liao·Ko Chun

INVINCIBLE SWORD (1971)
director: **Tsu Tsan Hong.** Jimmy
Wang Yu·Yo Hua

INVISIBLE FIST (1969)
director: **Chang Cheh.** Lo Lieh·Kuo
Chui
This was Lo Lieh's first starring role.

INVISIBLE TERRORISTS (1976)
director: **Kao Bo Shu.** Carter Wong·
Ku Lung·Lo Lieh·Wang Chung
Despite the title, this film has no supernatural qualities; rather, it's the story of
Buddhist priests fighting the aggressively evil Ching rulers.

IRON BODYGUARD (1973)
director: **Chang Cheh.** Chen Kuan Tai
·Lilly Li

IRON CHAIN ASSASSIN (1979)
aka **CONVICT KILLER**
director: **Chu Yuan.** Ti Lung·Jason Pai
Piao·Ching Li·Ku Kuan Chung

→ **IRON FINGER OF DEATH** (1975)
aka **DEATH MASK OF THE NINJA**

Chen Kuan Tai in *The Flying Guillotine*

director: Tang Chi Li. Ti Lung·Er Tung Sheng·Jason Pai Piao·Ai Fei·Ku Feng
Early directorial effort from future filmmaker Tang (**Legend of Wisely, Bury Me High**, et al.).

→ **IRON FIST MONK** (1978)
director: Samo Hung. Samo Hung· Chen Sing·Dean Shek
Directorial debut for **Samo Hung**. **Jackie Chan** is martial arts director and has a walk-on part.

IRON MAN (1972)
director: Chang Cheh. Chen Kuan Tai ·Ching Li·Wang Chung·Chu Mu

→ **IRON MONKEY** (1977)
director: Chen Kuan Tai. Chen Kuan Tai·Kam Kong·Wilson Tong·Chi Kuan Chun
Actor Wilson Tong later became a HK genre director. This film was remade in 1993 by **Yuen Woo Ping** and **Tsui Hark**.

IRON PALM.
See Five Fingers of Death

JADE DAGGER NINJA (1979)
aka **NINJA JADE DRAGON**
director: Li Siu Wah. Tien Peng·Lung Chung Er

JADE TIGER (1977)
director: Chu Yuan. Ti Lung·Lo Lieh· Lilly Li·Ku Feng

JUST JACKIE (1978)
director: Lo Wei. Jackie Chan·Yen Shi Kwan
Depending on who's telling the story, this is or is not an unfinished project; it has never been officially released.

KARATE EXTERMINATOR.
See Killer Constable

KICK WITHOUT A SHADOW.
See Magnificent Kick

KID ACE IN THE HOLE.
See Kung Fu Ace

KIDNAP IN ROME (1976)
director: Ng See Yuen. Bruce Liang· Mang Hoi
Shot entirely on location in Italy by a Hong Kong crew.

KIDS FROM SHAOLIN.
See Shaolin Temple 2

→ **KID WITH GOLDEN ARM** (1978)
director: Chang Cheh. Kuo Chui·Lo Meng·Wei Pai·Lu Feng·Sun Chien
Strong Shaw Brothers cast with **Lo Meng** demonstrating a wide variety of kung fu techniques as he plays both a sighted and a blind fighter within the intricacies of the plot.

→ **KILLER ARMY** (1979)
director: Chang Cheh. Kuo Chui·Lo Meng·Lu Feng
Yet another terrific Chang Cheh film, this time highlighting the distinctive martial arts talents of boxer Kuo Chui; a combination of unarmed and sword fighting in this costume actioner about civil war in China.

KILLER CONSTABLE (1980)
aka **KARATE EXTERMINATOR**
aka **LIGHTNING KUNG FU**

director: Kuei Chih Hung. Chen Kuan Tai·Ku Feng·Jason Pai Piao·Chaing Tao
The film has received a cult status over the years, but the story of Constable Liang (Chen) and his search for thieves and stolen gold is less than memorable today.

KILLER ELEPHANTS (1980)
director: Hwa Yi Hung. Sung Pa·Alan Yen·Nai Yen
This time the title isn't a metaphor; it's really a movie about a farmer who uses elephants to protect his land from an evil baron.

→ KILLER FROM SHANGTUNG (1971)
director: Chang Cheh. Ching Li·David Chiang·Wang Chung·Ku Feng
A very different kind of **Cheng Cheh** film, relying on strong characterizations as people go through their everyday life on the eve of the Sino/Nippon War, with little preparation for the unexpected attack on Shanghai.

KILLER METEOR (1977)
director: Lo Wei. Jimmy Wang Yu·Jackie Chan
Jackie Chan (called **Chen Lung** in the credits) plays the villain.

KING BOXER (1972)
director: Kung Min. Meng Fei·Shoji Karata
Not to be confused with **Five Fingers of Death** (which is called *King Boxer* in some markets), this humdrum modern-day actioner is Meng Fei's debut film. Shot in Thailand.

KING EAGLE (1971)
director: Chang Cheh. Ti Lung·Li Ching·Wang Chung

KING OF BOXERS.
See *Ten Fingers of Steel*

KNIGHT ERRANT (1974)
director: Jimmy Wang Yu. Jimmy Wang Yu·Yasuaki Kurata·Chen Pei Ling·Shan Mao

→ KNOCKABOUT (1977)
director: Samo Hung. Samo Hung·Yuen Biao·Liang Cha Jen·Karl Maka
Debut film for **Yuen Biao**.

KUNG FU ACE (1979)
aka **KID ACE IN THE HOLE**
director: Chung Leung. John Liu·Kwon Young Moon

KUNG FU COMMANDOS.
See *Incredible Kung Fu Mission*

KUNG FU EMPEROR (1980)
director: Pao Hsieh Lieh. Ti Lung·Tan Tao Liang·Shih Szu·Chen Sing
Big-budget chop socky produced by actor Phillip Kao. Many genre fans insist this is **Ti Lung**'s finest film.

KUNG FU EXECUTIONER (1980)
director: Lin Chin Wei. Billy Chong·Carl Scott

KUNG FU HELLCATS (1974)
aka **FIVE TOUGH GUYS**
director: Pao Hsieh Lieh. Chen Kuan Tai·Ku Feng·Wang Chung·Lily Ho

→ KUNG FU INFERNO (1974)
director: Chen Hung Man. Yasuaki Kurata·Chen Chang
Recommended only for the amazing fight sequences with Yasuaki Kurata (star of **Challenge of the Ninja**).

KUNG FU INSTRUCTOR (1978)
director: Sun Chung. Ti Lung·Yung Wang Yu·Wand Lung Wei·Ku Feng

KUNG FU INVADERS.
See *Heroes Two*

KUNG FU KIDS BREAK AWAY (1980)
aka **LEE'S KILLER KIDS**

242

director: **Chang Cheung Wo.**
Casanova Wong·Huang I Lung

→ **KUNG FU KILLERS** (1971)
aka **ANGRY GUEST**
director: **Chang Cheh.** Ti Lung·David
Chiang·Yasuaki Kurata·Ku Feng
The action switches from China to
Thailand to Japan in this fast-paced
martial arts extravaganza.

KUNG FU: MONKEY, HORSE, TIGER
(1980)
director: **Lee Geo Shou.** Lo Lieh·
Carter Wong (Huang)

KUNG FU OF 8 DRUNKARDS (1980)
director: **Mu Wa.** Meng Fei·Chen
Sing·Lung Fei
Yet another imitation of **Snake in the
Eagle's Shadow**.

KUNG FU OF SEVEN STEPS (1979)
director: **Ting Shan Si.** Chen Tien Tse
·Chang Chen Lan

KUNG FU VENGEANCE (1973)
director: **Chang Cheh.** David Chiang
·Ti Lung·Wang Ping·Lo Lieh·Ku Feng·
Wang Chung

KUNG FU VS. YOGA (1979)
director: **Chan Chi Hwa.** Chien Yueh
Sheng·Alan Hsu

→ **KUNG FU WARLORDS** (1978)
aka **BRAVE ARCHER**
director: **Chang Cheh.** Alexander Fu
Sheng·Lo Meng·Helen Yu·Ku Feng
Terrific cast, including Helen Yu as a
blind female freedom fighter; but,
even though Ti Lung is listed in the
credits, he's nowhere to be found; the
film inspired three sequels, sometimes
released internationally under the
Brave Archer moniker.

KUNG FU WARLORDS 2 (1979)
aka **BRAVE ARCHER 2**
director: **Chang Cheh.** Alexander Fu

Sheng·Chang Cheh·Wang Lung Wei·
Ku Feng

KUNG FU WARLORDS 4 (1981)
aka **BRAVE ARCHER 4**
director: **Chang Cheh.** Alexander Fu
Sheng·Kuo Chui·Chiang Sheng·Lu
Feng

LACKEY & LADY TIGER (1980)
director: **Norman Law.** Tien Niu·Huo
Hsing
Yet another **Snake in the Eagle's
Shadow** clone.

→ **LADY CONSTABLE** (1978)
director: **Chang Yi.** Angela Mao·
Chia Ling·Wang Kuan Hsing
Policewoman and her swordswoman
assistant find a gang of jewel thieves.

LADY GENERAL HUA MU LAN
(1969)
director: **Yuan Feng.** Ivy Ling Po·Chin
Han

LADY HERMIT (1970)
director: **Ho Menga (Meng Hua).**
Cheng Pei Pei·Shih Szu

LADY IS THE BOSS (1980)
director: **Liu Chia Liang.** Hui Ying
Hung·Liu Chia Liang·Liu Chia Hui·Ku
Feng
This project marked the beginning of a
two-year lean period for director **Liu
Chia Liang**. Against his wishes, he
made a series of light kung fu actioners; but he returned with a vengeance
in 1982, riding the explosive **Legendary Weapons of China**.

→ **LADY WHIRLWIND** (1971)
director: **Hwang Feng.** Angela Mao·
Chang Yi·Samo Hung·Chien Yueh
Sheng
The original fighting diva flick, inspiration for the countless imitators to follow through the years. Angela Mao's

ASIAN CULT CINEMA

Bruce Lee fights Kareem Abdul Jabbar in *Game of Death*

first starring role; **Samo Hung** is martial arts director.

LAND OF THE BRAVE (1974)
director: Hsiao Yung. Cheung Lik ·
Wilson Tong · Meng Chiu · Liang Shao
Hua
Very unusual martial arts film about
patriots fighting the invading Japanese
army, with emphasis on nudity and
sexual sadism, including whip and torture sequences.

LAST DUEL (1975)
director: Hsu Tsang Hung. Jimmy
Wang Yu · Tang Lan Hua

LAST HURRAH FOR CHIVALRY
(1982)
director: John Woo. Wei Pai · Liu
Sung Ren · Lee Hoi San · Choy Chung
Sun
See review in text section.

LAST TEMPEST (1975)
director: Li Han Hsiang. Ti Lung · Lisa
Lu · Hsiao Yao

LEE'S KILLER KIDS.
See *Kung Fu Kids Break Away*

LEG FIGHTERS.
See *Invincible Kung Fu Legs*

→ LEGEND OF A FIGHTER (1980)
director: Yuen Woo Ping. Leung Kar
Yan · Phillip Kao · Yasuaki Kurata · Kao
Fei
Some publications translate Leung Kar
Yan as Leung Cha Jen.

LEGEND OF THE FOX (1979)
director: Chang Cheh. Kuo Chui · Lu
Feng · Chiang Sheng

→ LEGENDARY STRIKE (1978)
director: Hwang Feng. Angela Mao ·

Carter Wong (Huang) · Chu Kong · Casanova Wong
A mixture of murder mystery and kung fu action.

→ **LEGENDARY WEAPONS OF CHINA** (1982)
aka **LEGENDARY WEAPONS OF KUNG FU**
director: **Liu Chia Liang.** Lau Kar Leung · Jui Ying Hung
A comeback movie for director **Liu Chia Liang**, who, against his wishes, made a series of unsuccessful kung fu comedies, including **Lady Is the Boss, My Young Auntie**, and **Cat Vs. Rat.** This film is often cited as the best kung fu movie of them all.

→ **LIFE GAMBLE** (1978)
aka **LIFE COMBAT**
director: **Chang Cheh.** Kuo Chui · Alexander Fu Sheng · Lo Meng · Wang Lung Wei
Here's a kung fu film constructed more like a traditional western, as a weaponsmith tries to retire and mask his identity in a sleepy village only to spring into action when the town is threatened by a gang of thieves.

LIGHTNING KUNG FU.
See Killer Constable

LONE SHAOLIN AVENGER.
See Bruce Against the Odds

LOST KUNG FU SECRET (1982)
director: **Regis Liew.** David Chiang (credited as **Garth Lo**)
Regis Liew is a pseudonym; the filmmaker's true identity is unknown, although it was most likely **Joe Law**.

LOST SAMURAI SWORD (1970)
director: **Lei Chu.** Tien Peng · Pai Ying · Wang Ping

MA SU CHEN.
See Rebel Boxer

MAD MAD KUNG FU (1980)
director: **Chia Chun.** Chin Long · Simon Yuen Hsiao Tien

→ **MAD MONKEY KUNG FU** (1979)
director: **Liu Chia Liang.** Liu Chia Liang · Lo Lieh
Director **Liu**'s debut as a star.

MAFIA VS. NINJA (1983)
director: **Robert Tai.** Alexander Lo Rei · Charlema Hsu
A surprise hit for filmmaker **Robert Tai**, giving him the green light for his eight-hour extravaganza **Ninja's Final Duel** (see review section).

MAGIC BLADE (1976)
director: **Chu Yuan.** Ti Lung · Lily Li · Lo Lieh · Linda Tanny Chu · Ching Li

MAGNIFICENT (1980)
director: **Lo Lieh.** Lo Lieh · Carter Wong (Huang) · Casanova Wong · Bruce Lai
A kung fu-style movie dealing with acupuncture and pressure points.

MAGNIFICENT BODYGUARDS (1978)
director: **Lo Wei.** Jackie Chan · Bruce Liang
Original version was in 3-D Stereovision.

→ **MAGNIFICENT BUTCHER** (1980)
director: **Yuen Woo Ping.** Samo Hung · Yuen Biao · Kwan Tak Hing · Lam Ching Ying · Fan Mei Sheng · Lee Hoi San
After the success of **Dance of the Drunk Master** (1979), boxer Yuen Siu Ting was slated to star in this film, but a fatal heart-attack cut his career short. He was replaced by **Fan Mei Sheng**.

MAGNIFICENT FIST (1978)
director: **Kam Aug.** Carter Wong (Huang) · Cheung Wai

The entire invading Japanese army is thwarted by karate fighting **Wong**.

MAGNIFICENT KICK (1980)
aka **KICK WITHOUT A SHADOW**
director: **Daniel Lau**. Kwan Tak Hing·Jason Pai Piao
Yet another variation of "fight for the honor of our school"

MAGNIFICENT KUNG FU WARRIORS (1979)
director: **Chang Cheh**. David Chiang·Alexander Fu Sheng·Chi Kuan Chun·Lu Feng
Comedy comes to **Chang Cheh** films.

→ **MAGNIFICENT TRIO** (1970)
director: **Chang Cheh**. Jimmy Wang Yu·Lo Lieh·Ching Ping·Cheng Lei
Chinese version of Hideo Gosha's *3 Outlaw Samurai* [1966]. Three swordsmen aid a village of peasants against an evil ruler.

MAGNIFICENT WONDERMAN (1979)
director: **Godfrey Ho**. Casanova Wong·Charlie Hyun
Unlike many **Godfrey Ho** films, this one is not a composite; it's a cohesive story of a mute who learns Shaolin kung fu and avenges his father's death at the hands of Mongolian terrorists.

MAN CALLED TIGER (1973)
director: **Lo Wei**. Jimmy Wang Yu·Maria Yi

MANCHU BOXER (1975)
director: **Lin Shew Hua**. Tony Liu Yung·Tao Ming Ming
Samo Hung is martial arts director.

→ **MAR'S VILLA** (1978)
director: **Ting Shan Si**. John Liu·Phillip Kao·Tung Wei
Considered one of the best Taiwanese chop socky films.

MARTIAL ARTS OF SHAOLIN.
See *Shaolin Temple 3*

MARTIAL CLUB.
See *Instructors of Death*

MARVELOUS KUNG FU (1981)
director: **Raymond Lui**. Raymond Lui·Wei Ping Ao
Some of this kung fu comedy (especially the slapstick scenes with the bucktoothed thief [Wei Ping Ao] wound up in **Zombie Vs Ninja**.

→ **MASKED AVENGERS** (1980)
director: **Chang Cheh**. Kuo Chui·Lu Feng·Chiang Sheng
Very similar to Chang Cheh's earlier **Five Deadly Venoms**, especially in plot and the incredible fight sequences; the biggest difference, however, is some of the masked heroes aren't alive when the final credits roll.

MASTER KILLER.
See *36th Chamber of Shaolin*

MASTER KILLER (1980)
director: **Wong King Fang**. Phillip Kao·Yuan Lung·Ka Sa Fa [Casanova Wong]

MASTER OF DEATH (1975)
director: **Yu Han Sang**. Chi Kuan Chun·Lo Lieh·Wai Hseng·Chia Ling

MASTER OF DISASTER (1982)
aka **TREASURE HUNTERS**
director: **Liu Chia Yong**. Alexander Fu Sheng·Gordon Liu·Chang Chan Peng·Wang Lung Wei
One of the prime examples of Shaw Brother's kung fu comedy.

→ **MASTER OF FLYING GUILLOTINE** (1976)
aka **ONE ARMED BOXER 2**
director: **Jimmy Wang Yu**. Jimmy Wang Yu·Liu Chia Yong

An FX-laden extravaganza; the purists complained vigorously about gimmicks over substance, but the film has stood the test of time.

MASTER OF KUNG FU (1973)
director: Ho Menga (Meng Hua). Ku Feng·Chen Ping·Wang Hsieh
This time Ku Feng plays legendary hero Wong Fey Hung.

→ **MASTER STRIKES** (1979)
director: Kao Bo Shu. Casanova Wong·Ching Siu Tung
Generally considered kickboxer Casanova Wong's best performance.

MASTER STRIKES BACK (1982)
director: Sun Chung. Ti Lung·Lu Chun Ku·Ku Feng

MASTER WITH CRACKED FINGERS.
See Snake Fist Fighter

MEN FROM THE GUTTER (1983)
director: Kao Fei. Kao Fei·Yuen Shen Yi

MEN FROM THE MONASTERY.
See Disciples of Death

Cheng Pei Pei and Jimmy Wang Yu in *Girl With the Thunderbolt Kick*

MEN OF THE HOUR (1981)
director: Chen Ming Hua. Chang Ling·Chin Hsiang Lin·Lo Lieh·Nora Miao

MERCENARIES FROM HONG KONG (1981)
director: Sun Chung. Ti Lung·Jimmy Wang Yu
One of the first modern-day gun movies.

MING PATRIOTS (1977)
aka **BRUCE LEE'S SECRET**
director: An Yeung Chia. Bruce Li (Ho Chung Tao)·Chang Yi·Judy Lee (Chia Ling)
This Ming Dynasty tale was called *Bruce Lee's Secret* in some markets, probably because of Bruce lookalike **Ho Chung Tao [Bruce Li]** in the starring role. But genre fans say the real secret is the true identity of the director. **An Yeung Chia** (a one-shot listing) is a suspected alias for **Liu Chia Liang**, who supposedly didn't want to be associated with the film; some prints list him as the action supervisor.

→ **MIRACLE FIGHTER** (1982)
director: Yuen Woo Ping. Yuen Yat Chor·Leung Kai Yen
This mixture of wizards-n-fu found big numbers at the box office, and paved the way for the countless imitators that followed. Official sequel was **Taoism Drunkard**.

MISTRESS OF THE THUNDERBOLT.
See Girl With the Thunderbolt Kick

MONKEY IN THE MASTER'S EYES (1979)
director: Chen I Shin. Pan Yin Tze·Chin Lung
Obviously intended as a satire of the Jackie Chan hit **Drunken Master** [aka **Drunk Monkey in Tiger's Eye**]

MONKEY KUNG FU.
See *Drunken Monkey*

MOONLIGHT SWORD AND JADE LION (1981)
director: **Kwong Lam.** Angela Mao·Wong Tao

→ **MORTAL COMBAT** (1978)
aka **CRIPPLED AVENGERS**
director: **Chang Cheh.** Wang Lung Wei·Chen Kuan Tai·Kuo Chui·Lu Feng
Armless cripple unites other handicapped specialists into his army against an evil ruler.

→ **MY REBELLIOUS SON** (1982)
director: **Sun Chung.** Alexander Fu Sheng·Ku Feng·Chan Wei Man·Wang Lung Wei
One of Alexander Fu Sheng's last performances before his death in 1983; this time, he manages to successfully mix his martial arts skill with his natural talent for comedy.

MY SON (1967)
director: **Joe Law.** Jimmy Wang Yu·Margaret Hsing

MY YOUNG AUNTIE (1981)
director: **Liu Chia Liang.** Liu Chia Liang·Wang Lung Wei
More lightweight fluff from legendary director **Liu Chia Liang** during his two-year (studio imposed) bleak comedy period.

MYSTERIOUS ISLAND (1982)
director: **Chang Cheh.** Kuo Chui·Ku Feng

NA CHA, THE GREAT.
See *Shaolin Hellgate*

NAKED FISTS OF TERROR.
See *Spiritual Boxer*

NEW FISTS OF FURY (1976)
director: **Lo Wei.** Jackie Chan·Nora Miao
Jackie's screen name previously was **Chan Yuan Lung**, now he's credited as **Chen Lung**.

→ **(NEW) ONE ARMED SWORDSMAN** (1973)
director: **Chang Cheh.** David Chiang·Ti Lung·Ku Feng·Li Ching
Insiders believe this was **Chang Cheh** and Shaw Brothers' personal vengeance motion picture. Angry over **Jimmy Wang Yu**'s departure from the studio, Chang Cheh agreed to remake the actor's best-known film, replacing him with his new martial arts triumvirate David Chiang, **Ti Lung**, and Ku Feng.

NEW SHAOLIN BOXERS (1976)
director: **Chang Cheh.** Alexander Fu Sheng·Hsieh Hsing

NEW SOUTH HAND AND NORTH KICK BLOWS (1981)
director: **Chang Yi.** John Lui·Chin Lung·Alexander Lou

NINJA HUNTER (1984)
director: **Wu Kuo Jen.** Alexander Lou·Mark Long·Chung Ling·Lau Hoi Yin
Another variation on the destruction of Shaolin Temple

→ **NINJA IN A DEADLY TRAP** (1983)
aka **HERO DEFEATING JAPS**
director: **Chang Cheh.** Ti Lung·Shoji Karata

NINJA IN THE CLAWS OF THE CIA (1982)
aka **KUNG FU EMANUELLE**
director: **John Liu.** John Liu·Casanova Wong·Mirata Miller·Raquel Evans
Boxer John Liu directs and writes this absurd tale of a kung fu teacher who is hypnotized by the CIA; he manages

to escape to France but now women find him irresistible.

→ **NINJA IN THE DRAGON'S DEN** (1982)
    aka **NINJA WARRIORS**
director: Yuen Kwei [Corey Yuen]. Conan Lee·Kiroyuki Sanada
One of few Chinese genre films that paints Japanese as good guys; Hiroyuki Sanada finally gets to be the hero, aided by Conan Lee, against a fascist religious sect.

NINJA WOLVES (1979)
director: Joe Law. Chang Yi·Yo Hua·Chin Po·Chen Mu Chuan

→ **ODD COUPLE** (1979)
director: Liu Chia Yong. Samo Hung·Liu Chia Yung·Leung Kai Yen·Li Hai Sheng
Aside from the **Jackie Chan** vehicles, this is generally considered the best chop socky comedies, with humor derived from character sketches and well-written sequences rather than lowbrow slapstick. Produced by **Karl Maka; Jackie Chan** is martial arts director.

→ **ODE TO GALLANTRY** (1981)
director: Chang Cheh. Kuo Chui·Sun Chien·Lu Feng
Tale of mistaken identities (Lu Feng plays two roles) during the Ming dynasty. Plot is too complicated for its own good, but martial arts sequences are amazingly good (as expected in a **Chang Cheh** film).

OF COOKS AND KUNG FU (1979)
director: Ting Shan Si. Jacky S. Chan·Li Kuen·Wu Ma·Chia Kai

OLD MAN AND THE KID (1982)
director: Sun Chung. Alexander Fu Sheng·Meng Fei

OLD MASTER (1980)
director: Joseph Kuo. Yu Chan Yuan·Bill Louie
The Old Master is played by Yu Chan Yuan, who was **Jackie Chan**'s martial arts teacher.

Lo Meng (Center) in *Kid with the Golden Arm*

ONE ARMED AGAINST NINE KILLERS
(1981)
director: **Hsu Tsan Hung.** Jimmy Wang Yu·Lo Lieh

→ **ONE ARMED BOXER** (1971)
aka **CHINESE PROFESSIONALS**
director: **Jimmy Wang Yu.** Jimmy Wang Yu·Lung Fei·Tien Yeh·Tang Shin
Although heavy on martial arts action, this film was criticized for its similarity to **Chinese Boxer.** However, this is generally considered the last truly great **Jimmy Wang Yu** film.

ONE ARMED BOXER 2.
See Master of Flying Guillotine

ONE ARMED CHIVALRY (1976)
director: **Jimmy Wang Yu.** Jimmy Wang Yu·Liu Chia Yung

→ **ONE ARMED SWORDSMAN** (1967)
director: **Chang Cheh.** Jimmy Wang Yu·Chiao Chiao·Liu Chia Liang·Pan Ying Tze
Not the first martial arts film but recognized as the first successful one, making **Jimmy Wang Yu** an overnight sensation and creating the concept of action for action's sake as an acceptable criterion for genre films. The first official sequel was **Return of One Armed Swordsman,** followed by a Japanese/Hong Kong coproduction, **Zatoichi And The One Armed Swordsman** (aka **Zatoichi Meets His Martial Match**).

ONE ARMED SWORDSMEN (1976)
director: **Jimmy Wang Yu.** Jimmy Wang Yu · David Chiang · Lo Lieh · Chang Yi·Li Mang
Three one-armed swordsmen fight each other in this far-fetched sequel

PERILS OF SENTIMENTAL SWORDS-MAN (1981)
director: **Chu Yuan.** Ti Lung·Teng Wei Hao·Lo Lieh·Ku Feng·Linda Chu

Third entry in series; preceded by **249** **Sentimental Swordsman** and **Return of Sentimental Swordsman.**

PIRATE (1973)
director: **Chang Cheh.** Ti Lung·David Chiang·Yu Feng
A Chinese variation on the Robin Hood legend, told by prolific **Chang Cheh.**

POINT THE FINGER OF DEATH (1978)
director: **Jimmy Wang Yu.** Jimmy Wang Yu·Liu Chia Yung

→ **POLICE FORCE** (1973)
director: **Chang Cheh.** Alexander Fu Sheng·Wang Chung
Alexander Fu Sheng's first starring role; the beginning of a 10-year relationship with director Chang, ending with Fu Sheng's accidental death in 1983.

PRODIGAL BOXER (1972)
director: **Cai Yang Ming.** Meng Fei· Lee Lam Lam
First starring role for Meng Fei.

PRODIGAL BOXER 2 (1977)
director: **Yueng Kuen.** Meng Fei·Yasuaki Kurata

→ **PRODIGAL SON** (1981)
aka **PULL NO PUNCHES**
director: **Samo Hung.** Samo Hung· Frankie Chan·Lam Ching Ying·Yuen Baio
Generally considered the birth of modern chop socky. Long recognized as **Samo Hung's** masterpiece; he directed and choreographed.

PROUD TWINS (1979)
director: **Chu Yuen.** Alexander Fu Sheng·Meng Chiu
Perhaps the inspiration for **Jackie Chan's** Twin Dragons (1992).

PULL NO PUNCHES.
See Prodigal Son

PURSUIT OF VENGEANCE (1977)
director: **Chu Yuan.** Ti Lung·Er Tung
Sheng·Lo Lieh

→ **QUEEN BOXER** (1974)
aka **AVENGER**
director: **Yuen Feng Chi.** Judy Lee
(Chia Ling)·Yeung Kwan
Debut film for opera-performer-turned-
actress Judy Lee (Chia Ling). See
Crane Fighter for her best, most acclaimed performance.

RAIDERS OF BUDDHIST KUNG FU
(1982)
director: **Godfrey Ho.** Lui Chia Hui·
Mike Wong
More mix-n-match nonsense from
Godfrey Ho, with a bogus title to infer
Indiana Jones stylized action.

RAINING IN THE MOUNTAIN (1979)
director: **King Hu.** Hsu Feng · Tien
Feng

→ **RAPE OF THE SWORD** (1969)
director: **Yueh Feng Chi.** Lili Hua·Li
Ching
A true novelty for the Shaw Brothers: a
martial arts musical, big-budget production in the tradition of the Peking
Opera.

REBEL BOXER (1979)
aka **MA SU CHEN**
director: **Ting Shan Si.** Jimmy Wang
Yu·Kang Nan

→ **REBELLIOUS REIGN** (1980)
director: **Fong Ching.** Lung Fong·Tsiu
Siu Keung
Dazzling martial arts choreography in
a tired Ching Dynasty plot, originally
written by Lo Wei for Bruce Lee.

RED PHOENIX (1989)
director: **Tyrone Hsu.** David Chiang·
Lo Lieh

RENDEZVOUS WITH DEATH (1980)
director: **Sun Chung.** Chen Kuan Tai·
Yung Wang Yu·Lo Lieh·Lin Hsiu Chun

→ **RENEGADE MONK** (1981)
aka **SHAOLIN EX-MONK**
director: **Chang Yi.** John Liu·Huang
Hsing Hsiu
John Liu's tour de force, his best performance marred only by director
Chang's annoying use of gimmicks.

RETURN OF CHINESE BOXER (1975)
director: **Jimmy Wang Yu.** Jimmy
Wang Yu·Lung Fei

→ **RETURN OF DEADLY BLADE** (1981)
director: **Hwang Feng.** David Chiang
·Yasuaki Kurata·Lo Lieh·Tsui Siu Keung
Deadly Blade is a spin-off character
from **Sentimental Swordsman,**
played both there and here by David
Ciang.

→ **RETURN OF ONE ARMED SWORDS-
MAN** (1968)
director: **Chang Cheh.** Jimmy Wang
Yu·Chiao Chiao·Tien Fong·Ku Feng·Ti
Lung

RETURN OF SECRET RIVALS (1980)
aka **FILTHY GUY**
director: **Kam Yuen Wah (Yong).**
Samo Hung·Carter Wong (Huang)

**RETURN OF SENTIMENTAL SWORDS-
MAN** (1980)
director: **Chu Yuan.** Ti Lung·Alexan-
der Fu Sheng·Er Tung Sheng·Lo Lieh
Sequel to **Sentimental Swordsman.**
Another sequel followed, called **Perils
of Sentimental Swordsman.**

RETURN OF THE DEADLY BLADE
(1980)
aka **SHAOLIN FIGHTERS VS NINJA**

director: **Wong Tai Loy.** David Cheung
·Kurata Yasuaki·Lo Lieh·Wan Jan Lee

RETURN OF THE DRAGON.
See Way of the Dragon

RETURN OF THE EIGHTEEN BRONZE-MEN (1975)
director: **Joseph Kuo.** Carter Wong (Huang)·Chia Ling

RETURN OF THE MASTER KILLER
See Return to the 36th Chamber

RETURN TO THE 36TH CHAMBER (1980)
    aka **RETURN OF THE MASTER KILLER**
director: **Liu Chia Liang.** Liu Chia Liang·Wang Lung Wei
Unlike the original **36th Chamber of Shaolin** (1978), this one is speckled with many (misplaced) scenes of humor. Shaw Brothers finally acquiesced to pressure from the marketplace, forcing Director Liu to include comedy in his films. Thus began a streak of mediocre movies for the filmmaker until his **Legendary Weapons of China** in 1982.

REVENGE OF A SHAOLIN MASTER (1979)
director: **Joe Law.** Tan Tao Liang·Chan Sing

REVENGE OF DRAGON (1983)
director: **Robert Tai.** Alexander Lou·Liu Hao Yi
Kids-n-kung fu **Robert Tai**-style.

→ **REVENGER** (1979)
director: **Pao Hsieh Lieh.** Ti Lung·Tan Tao Liang
Ti Lung in a dual role.

RIDER OF REVENGE (1979)
director: **Hwang Feng.** Shang Kuan Ling Feng·Tien Peng

RING OF DEATH (1980)
director: **Ng See Yuen.** Cliff Lok·Wong Jan Lee

RIVALS OF SILVER FOX (1982)
director: **Godfrey Ho.** Casanova Wong·Barry Lam

→ **ROAR OF THE LION** (1981)
director: **Chia Chun.** Lo Meng·Yung Wang Yu
Features one of the most impressive Lion Dances ever caught on film.

ROVING SWORDSMAN (1980)
director: **Chu Yuan.** Ti Lung·Ching Li·Ku Feng

ROYAL FIST (1974)
director: **Ting San Shi.** Jimmy Wang Yu·Chang Ching

SAMURAI BLOOD, SAMURAI GUTS (1979)
Kong Pun·Lee Shue·Ng Pun
Undoubtedly, this Taiwanese film had a name change before its release in the United States, since samurai are distinctly Japanese warriors and there's not a Nippon in the film. Instead, this is a bloodless, gutless story of swordsmen who attempt to kill Devil's Knight in exchange for a sacred book.

→ **SAVAGE FIVE** (1974)
director: **Chang Cheh.** Ti Lung·David Chiang·Chen Kuan Tai·Li Hsiu Hsien

SCORCHING SUN, FIERCE WIND, WILD FIRE (1978)
director: **Hwang Feng.** Angela Mao·Lo Lieh·Tien Peng

SCREAMING TIGER.
See Ten Fingers of Steel

SECRET EXECUTIONERS (1983)
director: **Godfrey Ho.** Huang Cheng Li·Jim Norris

More composite mix-n-mix junk from **Godfrey Ho.** This time, even the credits are a bogus collection of unlikely Anglo/Chinese composites (Alan Kong, Peggy Min, Sam Kong, Mandy Yong, and Tung Wagner)

SECRET OF CHINESE KUNG FU (1980)
director: **Sun Gam Loi.** Lo Lieh·Hsia Ling Ling

SECRET OF SHAOLIN KUNG FU.
See Invincible Shaolin Kung Fu

→ **SECRET OF TAI CHI** (1982)
director: **Chick Hung.** Lee Hoi Yin· Kwok Leung
Generally considered the ultimate tai chi movie.

SECRET RIVALS (1976)
director: **Ng See Yuen.** John Liu·Wong Tao·Huang Cheng Li·James Nam

SECRET RIVALS 2 (1977)
director: **Ng See Yuen.** John Liu · Hwang Jing Lee

→ **SENTIMENTAL SWORDSMAN** (1977)
director: **Chu Yuan.** Ti Lung·David Chiang·Ku Feng·Yo Hua·Ching Li·Er Tung Sheng

Yuen Biao (R) in *Magnificent Butcher*

Director **Chu Yuan's** masterpiece trilogy (followed by **Return of Sentimental Swordsman** and **Perils of Sentimental Swordsman**). It also inspired a spin-off **Return of Deadly Blade,** featuring the character played by David Chiang.

SEVEN BLOWS OF THE DRAGON.
See All Men Are Brothers

SEVEN BLOWS OF THE DRAGON 2.
See All Men Are Brothers 2

SEVEN COMMANDMENTS OF KUNG FU (1979)
director: **Ng See Yuen.** Lee Yi Min· Chang Yi
A chop socky remake of the Lee Van Cleef spaghetti Western *Day of Anger.*

→ **SEVEN GRAND MASTERS** (1978)
director: **Kuo Nai Hong.** Mark Long· Lee Yi Min
Generally considered one of the best independently produced chop socky films of the '70s (by Hong Hwa Films, Taiwanese production).

SEVEN MAN ARMY (1975)
director: **Chang Cheh.** Ti Lung · Alexander Fu Sheng·David Chiang· Chen Kuan Tai

72 DESPERATE REBELS (1972)
director: **Lin Pai.** Pai Ying·Chen Sing ·Lung Fei
A story liberally borrowed from the legendary Japanese folk tale *Chushingura (Loyal 47 Ronin).*

→ **SHADOW OF THE TIGERS** (1979)
aka **DUEL OF THE 7 TIGERS**
director: **Yeung Kuen.** Kim Tung · Phillip Kao·Yang Pan Pan·Casanova Wong
Financed by the Hong Kong Kung Fu Federation and featuring many instructors in cameo roles.

SHADOW WHIP (1977)
director: Lo Wei. Cheng Pei Pei·Ku Feng·Yue Hua
Interesting variation on tradition as whips take the place of swords. It inspired a sequel, **Whiplash.**

SHANGHAI MASSACRE (1979)
director: Lee Tso Nam. Wang Kuan Hsing·Yasuaki Kurata

→ **SHANGHAI 13** (1981)
director: Chang Cheh. Ti Lung·David Chiang·Chen Sing·Jimmy Wang Yu·Chen Kuan Tai·Lu Feng·Li Hsiu Hsien
A star-studded martial arts cast presenting the superstars of the '60s and '70s in a political actioner, as patriots steal a secret treaty proving a conspiracy between Japan and China.

→ **SHAOLIN AVENGERS** (1975)
aka **INVINCIBLE KUNG FU BROTHERS**
director: Chang Cheh. Alexander Fu Sheng·Lung Fei·Chi Kuan Chun·Tang Yen Tsan
This film is generally considered the advent of "incorporating true kung fu styles" rather than relying on swinging-arms techniques of previous chop socky productions.

SHAOLIN BOXER (1976)
director: Chang Cheh. Alexander Fu Sheng·Wang Lung Wei

SHAOLIN CHASTITY KUNG FU (1981)
director: Robert Tai. Alexander Lo Rei·Liu Hao

SHAOLIN DAREDEVEILS.
See Daredevils.

SHAOLIN DEADLY HANDS (1978)
aka **SHAOLIN INVINCIBLE GUYS**
director: Raymond Lui. Raymond Lui·Chi Kuan Chun

SHAOLIN DEADLY KICKS.
See Flash Legs.

SHAOLIN DISCIPLE (1980)
director: Min Ming. Liu Chia Yung·Kuan Chung·Li Wen Tai·Lu Ying

SHAOLIN DRUNK MONKEY (1979)
director: Godfrey Ho. Elton Chong·Eagle Han

SHAOLIN EX-MONK.
See Renegade Monk.

SHAOLIN FIGHTERS VS. NINJA.
See Return of Deadly Blade.

SHAOLIN FIST FIGHTER (1980)
director: Godfrey Ho. Elton Chong·Mike Wong

SHAOLIN HANDLOCK (1978)
director: Ho Menga (Meng Hua). David Chiang·Chen Hui Min·Chen Ping·Lo Lieh
A vengeful son uses his perfected shaolin handlock against the villain who kicked his father. Notable only because it's directed by **Ho Menga.**

→ **SHAOLIN HELLGATE** (1974)
aka **NA CHA, THE GREAT**
director: Chang Cheh. Alexander Fu Sheng·Chaing Tao
Supernatural thrills and magic fu in story of Na Cha, the 3000-year-old savior who founded Peking; he battles the Ming emperor who's in cahoots with the Ocean Demon and other nasty Taoist gods.

→ **SHAOLIN INVINCIBLE STICKS** (1979)
director: Lee Tso Nan. Wong Tao·Chang Yi·Kam Kong
Probably director **Lee**'s best film.

SHAOLIN INVINCIBLES (1977)
director: Yuen Cheung Yeung. Carter Wong·Judy Lee (Chia Ling)

Memorable for the kung fu fighting gorillas.

SHAOLIN IRON CLAWS (1978)
aka **SHAOLIN IRON EAGLE**
director: **Ko Shih Hao.** Wong Tao·Li Yi Min·Chang Yi

→ **SHAOLIN KING BOXER** (1976)
aka **IRON FISTS**
director: **Karl Maka.** Chen Kuan Tai·Meng Fei·Liu Chia Yung·Liang Cha Jen
Effective example of Taiwanese chop socky film with breathtaking fight scenes between Liu Chia Yung (using 2 swords) and Chen Kuan Tai.

SHAOLIN KUNG FU MASTER (1978)
director: **Jimmy Shaw [Lin Shew Hua].** Wang Kuan Hsing·Chang Yi·Wong Tao·Lung Fei·Tsai Hung
Some publications have translated Wang Kuan Hsing as Wang Chiang Lung.

→ **SHAOLIN MARTIAL ARTS** (1973)
director: **Chang Cheh.** Chi Kuan Chun·Liu Chia Hui·Alexander Fu Sheng·Chiang Tao
Acting debut of Liu Chia Hui.

SHAOLIN MASTER AND THE KID.
See Fury of Shaolin Master.

SHAOLIN PLOT (1977)
director: **Huang Feng.** Carter Wong·Chan Sing·Samo Hung·James Tien

SHAOLIN RESCUERS (1979)
aka **AVENGING WARRIORS OF SHAOLIN**
director: **Chang Cheh.** Jason Pai Piao·Lu Feng·Lo Meng·Kuo Chui

→ **SHAOLIN TEMPLE** (1976)
aka **DEATH CHAMBER**
director: **Chang Cheh.** Alexander Fu Sheng·Kuo Chu·Ti Lung·Chi Kuan Chun

Alexander Fu Sheng plays legendary hero Fong Sai Yuk in this 122-minute kung fu epic.

SHAOLIN TEMPLE (1980)
director: **Chan Hsin Yeh.** Jet Li·Yu Hai·Yu Cheng Hu
Jet Li's **[Li Lian Ji]** debut film.

SHAOLIN TEMPLE 2 (1983)
aka **KIDS FROM SHAOLIN**
director: **Chan Hsin Yeh.** Jet Li·Wong Chiu Yin·Din Nan

SHAOLIN TEMPLE 3 (1985)
aka **MARTIAL ARTS OF SHAOLIN**
director: **Liu Chia Liang.** Jet Li·Yu Hai·Yu Cheng Hu

SHAOLIN TEMPLE STRIKES BACK (1983)
director: **Joseph Kuo.** Chen Chiang Chang·Chang Shan

SHAOLIN VS. LAMA (1983)
director: **Lee Tso Nam.** Alexander Lou·Chang Shan

SHAOLIN VS. WU TANG (1981)
director: **Liu Chia Hui.** Liu Chia Hui·Wang Lung Wei·Adam Cheng·Ching Li
Liu Chia Hui's spite project. After Shaw Brothers forced him to turn his official sequel to **36th Chamber of Shaolin** (**Return to 36th Chamber** [1980]) into a light comedy, director Lui made this true sequel for Golden Sun.

SHAOLIN WOODEN MEN (1976)
director: **Lo Wei.** Jackie Chan·Kam Kong·Lung Chung Er·Yuen Biao
Decidedly bad movie with some exceptional fight scenes; **Jackie** always shines.

SHARP FISTS OF KUNG FU (1977)
director: **Chang Cheung Wo.** Chung Pei·Chung Cheng

SHOWDOWN AT COTTON MILL
(1978)
director: Wu Ma. Chi Kuan Chun·Tan
Tao Liang·Chang Kun Lung·Chang
Pong

SILENT SWORDSMAN (1977)
director: Kao Li. Chang Yi·Cheung
Pei Pei

**SILVER HERMIT FROM SHAOLIN
TEMPLE** (1979)
    aka **SILVER HERMIT MEETS THE
    BLOODY FANGS OF DEATH**
director: Tien Peng. Tien Peng·Chen
Sing·Meng Fei
Martial artist meets vampires.

SINGING KILLER (1970)
director: Chang Cheh. Ti Lung·David
Chiang·Ku Feng
Contemporary tale of a nightclub
singer (Chiang) who is muscled by the
mob. A sequel to **Singing Thief.**

SINGING THIEF (1968)
director: Chang Cheh. David Chiang
·Ti Lung·Wang Ping

SIX DIRECTION BOXING (1977)
director: Tyrone Hsu. David Chiang·
Simon Yuen

SKYHAWK (1976)
director: Samo Hung. Samo Hung·
Yuen Biao·Nora Miao

→ **SLEEPING FIST** (1978)
director: Yip Wing Tsui. Leung Kai
Yen·Wong Yat Lung
An unofficial sequel was produced,
Thundering Mantis.

SLICE OF DEATH (1978)
director: Ho Menga (Meng Hua).
David Chiang·Lo Lieh·Lilly Li

→ **SNAKE AND CRANE ARTS OF
SHAOLIN** (1978)
director: Chan Chi Hwa. Jackie Chan·

Wang Lung Wei in *My Young Auntie*

Nora Miao·Kam Kong·Kim Ching
Lam
Probably Jackie Chan's best chop
socky film, but ironically it was a box
office disaster, grossing only a small
percentage of what his goofy martial
arts comedy **Half a Loaf of Kung Fu**
did later the same year (by the same
director).

SNAKE DEADLY ACT (1979)
director: Wilson Tong. Ng Kun Lung·
Angela Mao·Phillip Kao·Chan Wei
Man

SNAKE FIST FIGHTER (1971/81)
    aka **LITTLE TIGER FROM CANTON**
    aka **MASTER WITH CRACKED FIN-
    GERS**
    aka **STRANGER IN HONG KONG**
director: Wei Hoy Fung. Jackie Chan·
Hon Kwok Choi
Original title: *Little Tiger of Canton.*
Featuring a very young **Jackie Chan**
[he was 16 years old and called **Chan**

Yuan Lung in the credits]. The film was shelved, then released when Chan became a star (1981).

→ SNAKE IN THE EAGLE'S SHADOW (1978)
aka **BRUCE VS SNAKE IN EAGLE'S SHADOW**
aka **EAGLE'S SHADOW**
director: **Yuen Woo Ping.** Jackie Chan·Yuen Siu Tien·Hwang Jing Lee·Tino Wong
Based on a script by **Jackie Chan;** it started a new phase of martial arts films: the kung fu comedy.

→ SNAKE IN THE MONKEY'S SHADOW (1979)
director: **Cheung Sum.** John Cheng·Wilson Tong
Superb martial arts action as Johnny Chang learns a perfected kung fu style by watching a monkey fight a cobra.

→ SNUFF BOTTLE CONNECTION (1977)
director: **Shen Liu Li.** John Liu·Huang Cheng Li·Yip Fai Yang·Ko Fei
Lots of impression kung fu action and fighting styles; Huan Cheng Li uses a combination of Snake and Eagle, with each hand engaging in different techniques, similar to Jackie Chan's work in **Snake and Crane Arts of Shaolin.**

SOUL OF THE SWORD (1977)
director: **Hua Shan.** Ti Luing·Lin Chen Chi

SPEARMAN OF DEATH (1980)
director: **Chang Cheh.** Kuo Chui·Lu Feng

→ SPIRITUAL BOXER (1974)
aka **NAKED FISTS OF TERROR**
director: **Liu Chia Liang.** Lui Chia Liang·Lu Ah Tsai
Debut film by acclaimed director **Lui Chia Liang.**

SPIRITUAL BOXER 2 (1979)
director: **Lui Chia Liang.** Lui Chia Liang·Yung Wang Yu

→ SPIRITUAL KUNG FU (1978)
director: **Lo Wei.** Jackie Chan·James Tien·Roy Chiao·Kao Chiang
Highly regarded **Jackie Chan** film and general considered **Lo Wei's** best movie.

SPY RING KOKUNYAKAI (1978)
director: **Ting Shan Si.** Judy Lee (Chia Ling)·Chang Yi

→ STORY OF CHIVALRY (1980)
aka **THE HEROES**
director: **Wu Ma.** Ti Lung·Shi Szu·Tan Tao Liang
The directer is popular character actor **Wu Ma.**

STRANGER IN HONG KONG.
See Snake Fist Fighter

STREET GANGS OF HONG KONG (1979)
director: **Chang Cheh.** Wang Chung·Alexander Wu Feng

STRIKE 4 REVENGE (1972)
director: **Chang Cheh.** David Chiang Wang Chung·Ti Lung·Lilly Li·Yasuaki Kurata

STRIKE OF THE THUNDERKICK TIGER (1978)
director: **Henry Wong.** Casanova Wong·Charles Han

→ SUPER NINJAS (1981)
director: **Chang Cheh.** Chien Tien Chi·Lo Meng

SUPER POWER (1979)
director: **Lin Chin Wei.** Billy Chong·Liu An Li·Lau Tan
Billy Chong is credited under the Chinese moniker Chung Chuan Li. His

real name is Willy Dohzan, from his Indonesian heritage.

SWORD (1972)
director: **Pan Lu.** Jimmy Wang Yu·Lee Kuen·Mian Tien·Chi Lung Wu

SWORD OF SWORDS (1968)
director: **Chang Cheh.** Jimmy Wang Yu·Li Ching·Tien Fong

SWORD STAINED WITH ROYAL BLOOD (1980)
director: **Chang Cheh.** Kuo Chui·Lu Feng·Ching Li
Yet another clan vs. clan tale with some very impressive martial arts. Remade in 1993 by **Brandy Yuen.**

SWORDSMAN WITH AN UMBRELLA (1979)
director: **Chang Cheung Wo.** Chiang Sheng·Yui Wang

→ **TAI CHI MASTER** (1983)
director: **Yuen Ho Ping.** Donnie Yen· Yuen Chung Yan
The debut role for Donnie Yen; a silly tale of a boy who learns tai chi kung fu from a puppeteer, but the martial arts is terrific.

→ **TAOISM DRUNKARD** (1983)
aka **DRUNKEN ARTS AND CRIP-PLED FIST**
director: **Yuen Cheung Yeung.** Yuen Yat Chor (Simon Yuen)·Li Yi Min·Yuen Cheung Yan
Sequel to **Miracle Fighter.**

TATTOOED DRAGON (1974)
director: **Jimmy Wang Yu.** Jimmy Wang Yu·Tien Fong

TEN FINGERS OF STEEL (1973)
aka **SCREAMING TIGER**
aka **KING OF BOXERS**
director: **Cheng Cheh.** Jimmy Wang Yu·Lung Fei·Wong Lung

Again, those nasty Japanese pirates are invading the Chinese coast.

→ **TEN TIGERS OF KWANTUNG** (1979)
director: **Chang Cheh.** Alexander Fu Sheng·Ti Lung
Ti Lung would star in an unusual sequel in 1984, **Opium and the Kung Fu Master** (see review section).

36 CRAZY FIST (1979)
director: **Chan Chi Hwa.** actor director: **Jackie Chan.** Leung Siu Hung·Ku Feng
Jackie Chan can be seen during the opening credits as he choreographs fight sequences.

→ **36TH CHAMBER OF SHAOLIN** (1978)
aka **MASTER KILLER**
aka **DISCIPLES OF MASTER KILLER**
director: **Liu Chia Liang.** Gordon Liu· Lo Lieh
Another Shaw Brothers' actioner directed with intense heroics by chop socky great **Liu Chia Liang.** A sequel was called **Return to the 36th Chamber.** Liu's unofficial sequel was called **Shaolin Vs. Wu Tang.**

THREE EVIL MASTERS (1980)
director: **Lo Chun Ku.** Yuan Tak·Chen Kuan Tai

3 SHAOLIN MUSKETTERS (1978)
aka **THREE SWORDSMEN**
director: **Ou Yang Chun.** Lo Lieh·Meng Fei·Liang Chia Jen

→ **THUNDERING MANTIS** (1979)
director: **Tsia Wing Choy [Yip Wing Bui].** Leung Kai Yen·Won Yat Lung· Kao Hung·Chien Yueh Sheng
An unofficial sequel to **Sleeping Fist.**

TIGER AND CRANE FIST (1977)
director: **Jimmy Wang Yu.** Jimmy Wang Yu·Lung Fei·Liu Chia Yong

TIGER KILLER (1981)
director: **Li Han Hsiang.** Ti Lung·
Wang Ping

TO KILL WITH INTRIGUE (1978)
director: **Lo Wei.** Jackie Chan (Cheng
Lung in credits)
Weak **Jackie Chan** pic shot in Korea.

→ **TOUCH OF ZEN** (1971)
director: **King Hu.** Shi Jun·Hsu Feng·
Pai Ying
One of the longest martial arts films, at
2 hours, 55 minutes.

TOUGH GUY (1974)
aka **BLACK DRAGON**
director: **Tommy Loo Chun.** Jason Pai
Piao·Gorge Estrada·Nancy Veronica·
Ron Van Clief
Standard drug-trafficking kung fu action with Ron Van Clief in a cameo
role. Shot in the Philippines.

TOURNAMENT (1974)
director: **Huang Feng.** Samo Hung·
Angela Miao

TOWER OF DEATH.
See Game of Death 2

TRAIL OF BROKEN BLADE (1966)
director: **Chang Cheh.** Jimmy Wang
Yu·Chiao Chiao·Tien Fong
One of the first contemporary martial
arts films.

TRAITOROUS (1976)
director: **Ting Shan Si.** Carter Wong·
Samo Hung·Polly Shang Kwan·Chang
Yi

TREASURE HUNTERS.
See Master of Disaster

TRILOGY OF SWORDSMANSHIP
(1972)
director: **Chang Cheh.** Ti Lung·David
Chiang · Li Ching · Ku Feng · Wang
Chung

A departure in cinematic style for director **Chang Cheh.** This is an omnibus movie, with three different short
stories based on swordfighting.

TWELVE DEADLY COINS (1969)
director: **Hsia Cheng Hung.** Lo Lieh·
Tien Fong

TWELVE KUNG FU KICKS.
See Incredible Master Beggars

2 ASSASSINS OF DARKNESS (1977)
director: **Ting Shan Si.** Wang Tao·
Chang Yi·Tung Wei

2 CHAMPIONS OF SHAOLIN (1979)
aka **2 CHAMPIONS OF DEATH**
director: **Chang Cheh.** Chiang Sheng
·Lu Feng·Lo Mang

2 FISTS AGAINST THE LAW (1980)
director: **Chang Cheung Wo.** Choy
Chung Sin·Wong Jan Lee

2 ON THE ROAD (1980)
director: **Chia Chun.** Leung Kai Yen·
Wang Lung Wei

2 WONDROUS TIGERS (1980)
director: **Cheung Sum.** Phillip Kao·
John Chang

→ **UNBEATABLE DRAGON** (1978)
aka **INVINCIBLE SHAOLIN**
director: **Chang Cheh.** Kuo Chui·Lu
Feng·Chiang Shang·Wei Pei
Because of the similarities in the cast,
this film was promoted as a sequel to
Five Deadly Venoms in some markets.

→ **UNICORN PALM** (1972)
director: **Hwang Feng. codirector:**
Bruce Lee. Wong Sung Leung·Chan
Wei Man
Mostly significant because of **Bruce
Lee's** involvement. Lee's credit is listed
as **Little Dragon Lee:** stunt co-ordina-
tor and action director. The film stars

Bruce's friend and personal wing chun instructor Wong Sung Leung (Unicorn).

VALIANT ONE (1974)
director: King Hu. Samo Hung·Roy Chiao·Yuan Biao
Samo plays a bad-guy Japanese in this simplistic tale of Nippon pirates versus the Chinese zealots by famed director **King Hu.**

→ **VENGEANCE** (1971)
aka **DEADLY DUO**
director: Chang Cheh. David Chiang ·Ti Lung·Chen Sing
Generally considered David Chiang's best role, earning him a HK Best Actor Award in 1972. The first teaming of **Ti Lung** and David Chiang.

VENOM WARRIORS.
See Daredevils

VICTIM (1980)
aka **LIGHTNING KUNG FU**
director: Samo Hung. Samo Hung·

Ti Lung in *Ten Tigers of Kwangtung*

Leung Kai Yen · Karl Maka · Wilson Tong

VICTIMS OF THE KILLER (1980)
director: Chu Yin Ping. Adam Cheng ·Lin Ching Hsia

WANDERING SWORDSMAN (1970)
director: Chang Cheh. David Chiang ·Ti Lung·Lilly Li

WARRIOR (1983)
aka **DANCING WARRIOR**
director: Chang Cheh. Cheng Tien Chi·Jimmy Wong

→ **WARRIORS TWO** (1978)
director: Samo Hung. Samo Hung· Casanova Wong·Leung Kai Yen·Liu Chia Yong
The original inspiration for **Samo Hung'**s more successful **Prodigal Son.**

WATER MARGIN.
See All Men are Brothers

→ **WAY OF THE DRAGON** (1972)
aka **RETURN OF THE DRAGON**
director: Bruce Lee. Bruce Lee·Nora Miao·Chuck Norris·Bob Wall
Although made before **Enter the Dragon,** it was not released in America until after *Enter's* success; thus the title was changed to **Return of the Dragon** (U.S.). This film marks **Bruce Lee'**s directorial debut. It was followed by **Unicorn Palm,** which he codirected but did not act in.

WHEN TAE KWON DO STRIKES (1973)
aka **STING OF THE DRAGON**
director: Huang Feng. Angela Mao· Carter Wong (Huang)·Samo Hung· Jhoon Rhee
Featuring tae kwon do master Jhoon Rhee in a costarring role as a boxing church gardener.

WHIPLASH (1978)
director: **Chung Leung.** Cheng Pei Pei·Yi Yuen
Sequel to **Shadow Whip.**

WILD BUNCH OF KUNG FU (1982)
aka **AGAINST RASCALS WITH KUNG FU**
director: **Chen Pan Wen.** Simon Yuen Hsiao Tien·Fang Chung·Lung Hsiun

→ **WOMAN AVENGER** (1979)
director: **Lee Tso Nam.** Hsia Kwan Lee·Pang Gang

WONG FEI HUNG BRAVELY CRUSH-ING THE FIRE FORMATION (1972)
director: **Chang Cheh.** Chen Kuan Tai Fu Sheng
Chen Kuan Tai plays legendary hero Wong Fei Hung.

→ **WORLD OF THE DRUNKEN MAS-TER** (1979)
director: **Joseph Kuo.** Lee Yi Min· Chan Hui Lau·Lung Fei·Yuen Siu Tin

YELLOW FACED TIGER (1977)
aka **SLAUGHTER IN SAN FRAN-CISCO**
director: **Lo Wei.** Chuck Norris·Sylvia Chang

YOGA AND KUNG FU GIRL (1979)
aka **OCTAGON FORCE**
director: **Sun Gam Loi.** Chi Kuan Chun·Phoenix Chen

YOUNG AVENGER (1980)
director: **Wilson Tong.** Wong Yue· Wilson Tong

→ **YOUNG MASTER** (1980)
director: **Jackie Chan.** Jackie Chan· Wei Pai·Yuen Biao·Lilly Li
Jackie Chan's first film for Raymond Chow's Golden Harvest Films, an ex-clusive agreement that spanned over a decade.

YOUNG TIGER (1980)
director: **Wu Ma.** Ko Tai Lung·Meng Fei

→ **ZATOICHI AND THE ONE ARMED SWORDSMAN** (1970)
aka **ZATOICHI MEETS HIS MATCH**
director: **Kimiyoshi Yasuda.** Jimmy Wang Yu·Shintaro Katsu
This Japan/Hong Kong coproduction is generally considered **Jimmy Wang Yu's** finest performance.

ZEN KWANDO STRIKES IN PARIS (1979)
aka **AVENGING NINJA**
director: **John Liu.** John Liu·Alan Hsu
Far-fetched autobiography by and about HK boxer John Liu.

Director Filmography

Hong Kong's film production technique is considerably different from that of the Western world. Commonly, producers take an active role in the hands-on directorial chores, and often cinematographers or second unit directors are largely responsible for exterior shooting. Sometimes multiple directors (usually uncredited) work on the same project, signing it with an unrelated pseudonym. Their true identities remain a mystery.

For the purpose of this book, however, we are tabulating according to the formal standards of the industry. If someone is identified as a director in the opening credits of the film, we have listed that person accordingly (except in certain instances where known multiple participation occurred). At the same time, it should also be noted that many HK directors work in conventional fashion, helming their own projects.

For technical information regarding interpretation and transcription of names, see **Deciphering the Chinese Language.** The following list is in alphabetical order according to the director's family (last) name. Thus, as examples, **Lan Nai Kai** can be found under **L,** for **Lan; Tsui Hark** under **T** for **Tsui;** anglicized **John Woo** is under **W** for **Woo;** and, a bit more confusing, combination anglicized/ traditional **Clifton Ko Sum** is under **K** for **Ko.** Variations in spelling or interchangeable names are indicated with parentheses (   ); an Anglo alias is listed in brackets [   ].

Note: This is an expanded list reflecting most titles encompassing a director's career. If the film is *italicized,* it has not been covered in this volume.

Aag Mang
Daughter of the Devilfish
An Yeung Chia
see **Liu Chia Liang**
Bierium, Jon
War Victims
Bunnag, Rom
Pregnant by a Ghost
Buo Fong
Love with the Ghost in Lushan
Cann, Richard
War of the Wizards
Cha Chuen Yee [Cha Fu Yi]
Awakening
Chinese Copout
In the Line of Duty 2
Legal Innocence
Mr. Fortune
Witness
Chan, Benny
Code of Honor
Magic Crane
Moment of Romance
Moment of Romance 2
Chan, Charles W. M.
Gangland Odyssey
Chan Chi Hwa
Dance of Death
Half a Loaf of Kung Fu
Imperial Sword
Kung Fu Vs. Yoga
Retreat of the Godfather
Skin-Stripper
Snake and Crane Arts of Shaolin
36 Crazy Fist
Vampires Settle on the Police Camp
Chan Chi Suen
Fatal Love
Tangled Love
Chan, Frankie
Armour of God 2 ·
Burning Ambition
Criminal Hunter
Fun and Fury
Good, Bad and the Beautiful
Oh! Yes Sir
Outlaw Brothers
Warrior's Tragedy
Warrior's Tragedy 2

Wrath of Silence
(·) codirected by Chan
Chan, Gordon
see **Wong Ching [Jing]**
Chan, Henry
Obsessed
Chan, Henry S. K.
Mixed Up
Chan Ho Sun [He Fan]
(aka **Peter Chan Ho Sun**)
Erotic Nights
He Ain't Heavy, He's My Father
He's a Woman, She's a Man
Pickles Make Me Cry
Temptation Summary
Tom, Dick and Harry
Trouble, I've Had It All My Days
Chan Hsin Yeh
Shaolin Temple
Shaolin Temple 2
Chan, Jackie
Armour of God
Armour of God 2 ·
Dragon Lord
Drunken Master 2 ·
Fearless Hyena
Hidden Hero
Inspector Wears a Skirt
Inspector Wears a Skirt 2
Mr. Canton and Lady Rose
Police Story
Police Story 2
Police Story 3: Supercop
Project A
Project A (Part 2)
Protector ·
Young Master
(·) codirected by Chan
Chan Kar Sheung [Gordon Chan]
Final Option
Game Kids
Inspector Pink Dragon
King of Beggars
Long and Winding Road
Unfaithfully Yours
Yuppie Fantasia
Chan Kwok [Ricky Chan]
Finale in Blood
Friend from Inner Space
Return to Action

Chan, Norman
Inside Track
Nobles
Pretty Woman
Chan, Otto
Final Judgement
Key to Fortune
Pink Lady
Screwball '94
Stooges in Hong Kong
Under the Roses
Chan, Phillip
Carry on Yakuza
Mr. Sunshine
Night Caller
Tongs
Chan, Veronica
Taste of Killing and Romance
Chang Cheh
All Men Are Brothers
All Men Are Brothers 2
Assassin
Blood Brothers
Boxer Rebellion
Chinatown Kid
Chinese Vengeance
Daredevils
Death Ring
Delightful Forest
Demon Fists of Kung Fu
Destroyers of Five Deadly Venoms
Disciples of Death
Duel of Iron Fists
Eagle's Killer
Eight Man Army
Five Deadly Venoms
Five Element Ninja
Five Masters of Death
Four Assassins
Friends
Generation Gap
Girl with Thunderbolt Kick
Have Sword, Will Travel
Hero Defeating Japs
Heroes Two
Heroic Ones
House of Traps
Invincible Iron Fist
Invincible One

Iron Body Guard
Iron Man
Kid with Golden Arm
Killer Army
Killer from Shangtung
King Eagle
Kung Fu Killers
Kung Fu Vengeance
Kung Fu Warlords
Kung Fu Warlords 2
Legend of the Fox
Life Gamble
Magnificent Kung Fu Warriors
Magnificent Trio
Masked Avengers
Mistress of the Thunderbolt
Mortal Combat
Mysterious Island
(New) One Armed Swordsman
New Shaolin Boxers
Nine Demons
Ninja in Ancient China
Ode to Gallantry
One Armed Swordsman
Pirate
Return of One Armed Swordsman
Savage Five
Seven Man Army
Shanghai 13
Shaolin Avengers
Shaolin Boxer
Shaolin Daredevils
Shaolin Hellgate
Shaolin Martial Arts
Shaolin Rescuers
Shaolin Temple
Singing Killer
Singing Thief
Slaughter in Xian
Spearman of Death
Street Gangs of Hong Kong
Super Ninjas
Sword of Swords
Ten Fingers of Steel
Ten Tigers of Kwantung
Trail of Broken Blade
Trilogy of Swordsmanship
Two Champions of Shaolin
Unbeatable Dragon

Vengeance
Wandering Swordsman
Warrior
Wong Fei Hung Bravely
  Crushing the Fire Formation
Chang Cheung Wo
[Derek W. Cheung Chang]
Broken Oath
Kung Fu Kids Break Away
My Dream Is Yours
Sharp Fists of Kung Fu
Swordsman with an Umbrella
Two Fists Against the Law
Chang Chun (also **Chung Leung)**
Dragon Pearl
Kung Fu Ace
Man of Nasty Spirit
New Mr. Vampire 1
Thrilling Bloody Sword
Whiplash
Chang Ling
[Sze Ma Peng]
Dark Lady of the Butterfly
Invincible (General Invincible)
Matching Escort
Miraculous Flower
Monkey War
Wolf Devil Woman
Chang Peng Ye
  see *Chu Yin Ping*
Chang, Silvia
Mary From Beijing
Once upon a Time
Chang, Tommy [T. Chang]
Devil's Box
Escape From Coral Cove
Satanic Crystals
Chang, William
  see *Ding Shan Yu*
Chang Yi (Chang Hsin Yi)
Bandits from Shantung
Eagle's Killer
Incredible Kung Fu Mission
New South Hand, North Kick Blows
Renegade Monk
Shaolin Ex-Monk
Chen Chan Ho
Devil's Treasure

Five Fingers of Death
Heads for Sale
Chen Chi Hui
  see *Chan Chi Hwa*
Chen Chi Liang [Lawrence Chen]
Dream Lover
Lover's Tear
Murder
Never Ending Summer
Pearl of the Orient
She Starts Fire
Chen Hung Man
Double Crosser
Fists of Vengeance
Invincible
Kung Fu Inferno
Chen I Shin
Iron Fan and Magic Sword
Chen Kuan Tai
Big Boss of Shanghai
Dragon Ball
Eagle's Claw
Iron Monkey
Chen, Ranwood
Trouble Couple
  also see *Yau, Pierre*
Chen Wen Sun
Death Cage
Cheng Jui Si [Kent Cheng]
Code of Fortune
Crazy Kung Fu Master
Dragon in Jail
Easy Money
Fortune Code
Heartbeat 100
Lethal Contact
Magic Amethyst
Mermaid Got Married
Why Me
Cheng Siu Keung [John Cheong]
[*sometimes* **Kevin Cheung**]
[*sometimes* **Jacob Cheung**]
Assassin
Bet on Fire
Bullet for Hire
Dragon Chronicles
Drugs Area
Eternal Combat
Forbidden Arsenal

Killer Lady
Killers Must Die
Return Engagement
Returning
Sea Wolves
Will of Iron
Cheng Ren Sheng
see **Li Siu Wah**
Cheung, Alex
Cops and Robbers
Cheung, Alfred
see **Hung, Samo**
Cheung, James
Amazons of Hong Kong
Cheung, Joseph
see **Cheung Tung**
Cheung, Lionel
Rape and Die
Cheung, Nilson
see **Wong Ching [Jing]**
Cheung Sum
Daggers Eight
Death Duel of Kung Fu
Snake in the Monkey's Shadow
Two Wondrous Tigers
Cheung Tung [Joseph Cheung]
Flaming Brothers
Hot Hot and Pom Pom
Incredible Kung Fu Master
Chia Chun [Lei Chu]
Bruce Lee in New Guinea
Bruce Lee Vs. Supermen
Mad Monk Kung Fu
Roar of the Lion
Two on the Road
Chian Lai Ya
Eighteen Bronzegirls of Shaolin
Chiang Sheng
Attack of Joyful Goddess
Chin Chung Wu
Heroic Fight
Magic Of Spell
Twelve Animals
Chin Sing Wai [Stanley Wing Siu]
Avenging Quartet
Cruel Kind
Guys in Ghost's Hand
Thou Shalt Not Swear
Vampire Buster

Winner Takes All   **265**
Yes! Madam: Serious Shock
Chin Wing Keung
Apartment for Women
Right Here Waiting
Sisters-in-Law
Victory
Ching, Mason
(suspected pseudonym for **Chang Chun Liang)**
New Mr. Vampire 2
Ching Siu Tung
Chinese Ghost Story ·
Chinese Ghost Story 2 ·
Chinese Ghost Story 3 ·
Duel to the Death
Fists of Fury 1991
Heroic Trio ·
Moon Warriors
The Raid
Swordsman ·
Swordsman 2
Swordsman 3: East Is Red
Terre Cotta Warrior
Witch from Nepal
Wonder Seven
(·) codirected by Ching Siu Tung
Chiu Son Kee [Samson Chiu]
News Attack
Oh! My Three Guys
Rose
Yester-You Yester-Me
Choi Kai Kwong [Maisy Choi]
Grow up in Anger
Naughty Couple
Sisters of the World Unite
Chong Sha Shiong
see **Lai Guo Jian**
Chou Ming Hung
South Seas Blood Letter
Chow Lo Wen
Unpublicized Case
Choy Fat
Cheetah on Fire
Chu Chi Hung
Spiritual Martial
Chu Ken In
My Wife's Lover

266 **Chu Mu**
All in the Family
Chu Yin Ping
Book of Heroes
China Dragon
Demon Fighter
End of the Road
Fantasy Mission Force
Flying Dagger
Ghost's Sword
Golden Queen Commando
Home Too Far
Hunting List
I Have a Date with Spring
Island of Fire
Island Warriors
My Flying Wife
Phoenix the Raider
Pink Force Commando
Requital
Shaolin Popey 2
Slave of the Sword
To Miss with Love
Victims of the Killer
Chu Yuan
Bastard
Bloodstained Tradewind
Buddhist Spell
Challenge of the Lady Ninja
Clans of Intrigue
Descent of The Sun
Duel to the Death
Emperor and his Brother
Jade Tiger
Magic Blade
Perils of Sentimental Sowrdsman
Proud Twins
Pursuit of Vengeance
Return of Sentimental Swordsman
Roving Sowrdsman
Sentimental Swordsman
White Haired Devil Lady
Chuen Hui San
Diary of a Serial Rapist
In Between Loves
Chung, Billy, and China
Teenage Trap
Chung, David
In the Line of Duty

Magnificent Warriors
Royal Warriors
Clouse, Robert
Battle Creek Brawl
Enter the Dragon
Game of Death
Ding Shan Yu (William Chang [Kee])
Calamity of Snakes
Ghostly Vixen
Heroes of Shaolin
Host for a Ghost
Our Neighbors are Phantoms
Vampire Kids
Djalili, H. Tjuit
Mystics in Bali
Warrior 2
Fan Tsui Fen [Tommy Fan]
Battle in Hell
Godfather's Daughter Mafia Blues
Last Duel
Phantom Killer
Firmanstan, Maman
Hell Hole
I Want to Get Even
Fok Yiu Leung [Clarence Fok Yiu Leung]
Before Dawn
Black Panthen Warriors
Dragon from Russia
Greatest Lover
Iceman Cometh
Naked Killer
Passion 1995
Remains of a Woman
They Came to Rob Hong Kong
Young Wai See Lee
Fong Ching
Rebellious Reign
Full, Lawrence
see **Chu Yin Ping**
Fung Pak Yuen
Sam the Iron Bridge 1
White Lotus Cult
Gautama, Sisworo
Primitives
Gui Zhi Hong
see **Lai Guo Jian**

Hao Lee
Curse of the Zombi
He Chi Chiang [T. F. Mous]
Last Breath
Man Behind the Sun
Man Behind the Sun 2
Man Behind the Sun 3
He Fan
see **Chan Ho Sun**
He Lian Chow
Devil and the Ghostbuster
He Ping
Swordsman in Double Flag
Ho, Benny
see **Ho, Chung Sing**
Ho Chung Sing [Godfrey Ho]
(sometimes **Charles Lee, Benny Ho, Gordon Chan**)
Angel the Kickboxer
Angel's Blood Mission
Bloody Mary Killer
Champ Against Champ
Dragon the Hero
Golden Destroyer
Grand Master of Shaolin Kung Fu
Hitman the Cobra
Lethal Panther
Magnificent Wonderman
Ninja the Protector
Ninja Thunderbolt
Princess Madam
Raiders of Buddhist Kung Fu
Rivals of Silver Fox
Scorpion Thunderbolt
Secret Executioners
Shaolin Drunk Monkey
Shaolin Fist Fighter
Zombie Vs. Ninja
Ho, David
Fatal Passion
Ho Fong
Ghost Ballroom
Shocking!
Ho, Godfrey
see **Ho Chun Sing**
Ho Meng Hua [Ho Menga]
Black Magic
Black Magic 2
Broken House

Dragon Missile
Flying Guillotine
Goliathon
Jade Ramshak
King with My Face
Lady Hermit
Lady of Steel
Maid from Heaven
Master of Kung Fu
Monkey Goes West
The Rape After
Shaolin Handlock
Slice of Death
Susanna
Ho Wang Muri
Cripple Masters
Hong Lu Wong
Cannibal Mercenary
Hsia Cheng Hung
Bone Crushing Kid
Twelve Deadly Coins
Hsu Hsia [Tyrone Hsu]
Beauty Investigator
Demons from Flame Mountain
Ghosts Galore
Golden Nun
Lung Wei Village
Red Phoenix
Six Direction Boxing
Who's the Ghost in Sleepy Hollow
Hsu Tsang Hung
Last Duel
One Armed Against Nine Killers
Huang Feng
see **Hwang, Feng**
Huang Shuquin
Woman•Demon•Human
Hui, Ann
Song of Exile
Spooky Bunch
Swordsman
Zodiac Killers
Hung, Samo
(sometimes pseudonyms: **Raymond Sen, Terry Tong,** or **Lee Yao Ting**)
Best Is the Highest
Blade of Fury
Cash on Delivery
Don't Give a Damn

268 Dragons Forever
Eastern Condors
Encounters of Spooky Kind
Encounters of Spooky Kind 2
Enter the Fat Dragon
First Mission
Gambling Ghost
Ghost Nursing (Ghost Renting)
Gigolo and Whore
Her Fatal Ways
Her Fatal Ways 2
Into the Fire
Iron Fist Monk
Knockabout
License to Steal
Moon Warriors
My Lucky Stars
Owl and Bumbo
Pantyhose Heroes
Paper Marriage
Pedicab Driver
Prodigal Son
Queen's Bench
Talk to Me, Dicky
Twinkle Twinkle Lucky Stars
Seven Warriors
Shanghai Express
Skyhawk
Sleazy Dizzy
Slickers Vs. Killers
Spooky! Spooky!
Victim
Warriors Two
Wheels on Meals
Winners and Sinners
Huoy King
Snake Girl Drops In
Hwa Hu
(suspected pseudonym for **Hwa I Hung**)
Impetus Fire
Impetus Fire 2
Hwa Yi [I] Hung (Li Zhao)
Crystal Fist
Dynamo
Four Invincibles
Ghost Killer
Gory Murder
Killer Elephants

Kung Fu from Beyond the Grave:
Kung Fu Zombies
Jade Claw
Prince of the Sun
Sun Dragon
Hwang Feng [Huang Feng]
(also **Hwang Ting Wu**)
Angry River
Fast Sword
Flying Masters of Kung Fu
Hapkido
Himalayan
Lady Whirlwind
Legendary Strike
Naked Came the Huntress
Return of Deadly Blade
Scorching Sun, Fierce Wind
Shaolin Plot
Stoner
Unicorn Palm
Hwang Hang Lee
Hitman in the Hand of Buddha
Martial Arts master: Wong Fei Hung
Jin Weng
Leech Girl
Kam, Andrew
see **Kam Yuen Wah**
Kam Bum Koo
Strange Dead Bodies
Kam Ling Ho
Ghost School
Kam Yoo Tu
Graveside Story
Vampires Strike Back
Kam Yuen Wah [Andrew Kam]
Big Heat
Fatal Terminator
Red and Black
Return of Secret Rivals
Swordsman
Kao Bo Shu
Bandits, Prostitutes and Silver
Blood of the Dragon
Invisible Terrorists
Master Strikes
Kao Fei
Bitter Taste of Blood
Cyprus Tiger
Men From The Gutter

Kao Li [Phillip Kao]
Final Run
Hard To Kill
Inside The Forbidden City
Killer's Romance
Mermaid
Mirror And The Lichee
Phantom War
Silent Swordsman
Ke Sing Pui
Dream Of Desire
Easy Money
Eye For An Eye
Kim Young [Si] Hyo
Capriciousness
Valley Of Ghosts
Vengeful Vampire Girl
King Hu
All The King's Men
Fate Of Lee Khan
Legend Of The Mountain
Painted Skin
Raining In The Mountains
Swordsman ·
Touch Of Zen
Valiant One
Ko, Phillip
    see *Kao Li*
Ko Shih Hao
Days Of Being Dumb
Invincible Shaolin Kung Fu
Shaolin Iron Claws
Ko Shou Liang [Blackie Ko]
Curry And Pepper
Nobody's Hero
Ko Sum [Clifton Ko Sum]
All's Well That Ends Well
City Squeeze
Daddy, Father, Papa
Happy Ghost
Happy Ghost 2
Happy Ghost 4
How to Be a Billionaire
I Will Wait for You
It's a Mad, Mad, Mad World
It's a Wonderful Life
Laughter of Water Margins
One of the Lucky Ones

Satin Steel   **269**
Summer Lover
Kong, Joseph
    see *Kuo Nai Hong*
Kong Yeung
Angel Delight
Curse
Haunted Romance
King of Gamblers
Kuei Chih Hung
Bamboo House of Dolls
Killer Constable
Killer Snakes
Kung Ming
King Boxer
Kuo Nai Hong [Joseph Kong]
Born Invincible
Bruce's Fingers
Clones of Bruce Lee
Dancing Kung Fu
Eighteen Bronzemen
Hero of Kwang Tong
Old Master
Seven Grand Masters
Shaolin Temple Strikes Back
World of the Drunken Master
Kwan Kum Ping [Stanley Kwan]
Center Stage
Love unto Waste
Rouge
Kwan, Teddy Robin
All the Wrong Spies
Cops and Robbers
Flesh and the Bloody Terror
Shanghai Shanghai
To Spy with Love
Lai, Albert
Bitter Taste of Blood
Death Triangle
Young Dreams
Lai Dai Wai [David Lai]
Lost Souls
Possessed
Possessed 2
Runaway Blues
Savior of Souls
Spiritual Love
Sworn Brothers
Tian Di

Lai Guo Jian [Guy Lai]
Bewitched
Boxer's Omen
Detective In The Shadows
Ghost For Sale
Hex
Point Of No Return
She Shashou
Sister Cupid
Super Cop: Female
Lai, Ivan
  see **Lan Nai Kai**
Lai Yat Ching
Call Girls '94
Lam Ching Ying
Vampire Vs. Vampire
Lam, David
  see **Lam Tak Luk**
Lam, Eddie
Mountain Warriors
Lam Hing Lung [Bosco Lam]
Underground Banker
Lam Ling Tung [Ringo Lam]
Aces Go Places 4
Burning Paradise
City on Fire
Cupid One
Espirit d'Amour
Full Contact
Happy Ghost 3
People's Hero
Prison on Fire
Prison on Fire 2
School on Fire
Touch and Go
Twin Dragons
Undeclared War
Wild Search
Lam, Ringo
  see **Lam Ling Tung**
Lam Tak Luk [David Lam]
Bomb Disposal Officer: Baby Bomb
Doctor's Heart
First Shot
Four Loves
Hong Kong Gigolo
Modern Love
Powerful Four
Tears and Triumph

Lam Wuah Chuen
Beauty Evil Rose
Devil Girl 18
Lam Yee Hon
Home for an Intimate Ghost (Liu Jai)
Lan Dei Tsa
(*suspected pseudonym* for **Lan Nai Kai**)
Seventh Curse
Lan Nai Kai [Nam Nai Choi]
(*sometimes* **Peter Ngor** *and* **Ivan Lai**)
Cat
Daughter of Darkness
Daughter of Darkness 2
Erotic Ghost Story
Erotic Ghost Story 2
Erotic Ghost Story 3
Ghost Snatcher
Her Vengeance
No Regrets, No Returns
Peacock King
Rikki O (Story of Ricky)
Saga of the Phoenix
Thank You, Sir
Lau, Andy
Crocodile Hunters
In the Blood
Lau Chang Wei [Ricky Lau]
Encounters of Spooky Kind 2
Lethal Contact
Magic Story
Mr. Vampire
Mr. Vampire 2
Mr. Vampire 3
Mr. Vampire 4
Mr. Vampire '92
Naked Killer 2: Raped by an Angel
Nocturnal Demon
Romance of the Vampires
Skinned Girl
Spooky Family
Spooky Family 2
To Live and Die in Tsimshatsui
Treasure Hunt
Twilight Siren
Ultimate Vampire
Vampire Strikes Back

Lau, Jeff
Chinese Odyssey
Days of Tomorrow
Eagle Shooting Heroes
Hong Kong Butcher
Love and the City
Mortuary Blues
Operation Pink Squad
Operation Pink Squad 2
Top Bet
Lau Kar [Karl] Leung
Aces Go Places 5
Drunken Master 3
Fury in Red
Lantern
New Kids in Town
Raining Night's Killer
Skinny Tiger and Fatty Dragon
Tiger on the Beat
Tiger on the Beat 2
Lau Kar Wing
City Cops
Dragon Family
Til Death Us Do Scare
Lau Ku Chang [Lawrence Lau]
Arrest the Restless
Cageman
Gangs
Gangs '92
He Who Chases After the Wind
Lee Rock
Lee Rock 2
Lee Rock 3
Three Summers
Lau Kwok Hung
Devil of Rape
Erotic Journey
Lau Shing Hon
Headhunter
House of the Lute
Lau Sze Yu
Forced Nightmare
Ghost Busting
Magic Story
Law, Alex
Love, Now You See It . . .
Painted Faced
Law, Clara
Farewell China

Fruit Bowl **271**
Reincarnation of Golden Lotus
Temptation of a Monk
Law, Joe (Lo Chen)
Incredible Kung Fu Trio
Last Kung Fu Secret
My Son
Revenge of a Shaolin Master
Law Man
Hearty Response
Law, Norman
Family Honor
Kung Fu Scholar
Scheming Wonders
Vampire Busters
Law, Rocky
Dragons of the Orient
Lee, Bruce
Way of the Dragon
Lee, Charles
    see **Ho, Godfrey**
Lee Chin Gai
Doctor Mack
Marked for Murder
Lee, Danny
Dr Lamb
Twist
Untold Story
    (·) codirected by Danny Lee
Lee Han Chang [Richard Lee]
Dances with Snakes
Dress off for Life
Erotic Dream of Red Chamber
Flower Drums of Fung Yang
Love on Delivery
My Better Half
World's Foremost Banned Novel
Yellow Emanuelle
Lee, Jimmy
    see **Lee Tso Nan**
Lee King Chu
Mission Kill
No Way Back
Lee, Raymond
    see **Li, Hui Min**
Lee, Richard
    see **Lee Han Chang**
Lee Tso Nan (Jimmy Lee)
Challenge of Death
Challenge of Lady Ninja

Diamond Fight
Eagle's Claw
Edge of Fury
Exit the Dragon, Enter the Tiger
Hot, Cool and Vicious
Invincible Kung Fu Legs
Kung Fu Wonder Child
Love in the Big Country
Magic Warriors
Shaolin Invincible Sticks
Shaolin Massacre
Shaolin Vs. Lama
Takes Two to Mingle
Woman, a She-Wolf
Woman Avenger
Lee Yao Ting
    see **Hung, Samo**
Lei Chu
    see **Chia Chun**
Len Tsu Chow
Blood Demon
My Pretty Companion
Leo Po Chih
    see **Leung Po Chih**
Leung, George
Night Evil Soul
Return of the Evil Fox
Leung, Kay
Bloody Hand Goddess
Leung Lee
Cat Living Ten Times
Magic Needles
Scare the Living
Leung, Lionel
(*suspected pseudonym for* **Hwa I Hu**)
Dragon Vs. Vampire
Leung Pasan
Anger (Angels with Golden Guns)
Fatal Love
Leung Po Chih [Raymond Leung]
Angel
Angel 2
Angel or Whore
Banana Cop
Black Butterfly
Blue Lightning
First Time Is the Last Time
He Lives by Night
Incorruptible

Shanghai 1920
Weakness of Man
Leung Siu Hung
Heart Stealer
Insanity
Vendetta
Leung Tung Ni [Henry Leung]
Demons
Hello Dracula
Hidden Passion
High Voltage
Li Hui Min [Raymond Lee]
Dragon Inn
Killer's Blues
Li Kin Sang [Chris Li]
Angel Mission
Crystal Fortune Run
From Beijing with Love
In the Line of Duty 5
Legend of Emperor Yan
Li Siu Wah [Keith Li]
[sometimes Cheng Ren Sheng]
Blood Ritual
Centipede Horror
Crazy Blood
Crazy Spirit
Fire Fight
Freedom from the Greedy Grave
Hocus Pocus
Isle of Fantasy
Jade Dagger Ninja
Li Yuen Ching [Jimmy Li]
Blue Jean Monster
China Dolls
Strange Rape Case
Liew, Regis
Lost Kung Fu Secret
Lin Hui Huang
Ms Butterfly
Lin Pai
Duel with Devils
72 Desperate Rebels
Lin Yixiu
Leech Girl
Ling Akuri Lu
Crippled Heroes
Liu Chia Liang
Cat Vs. Rat
Challenge Of The Ninja

City Cops
Cypress Tiger
Deadly Mantis
Dirty Ho
Eight Diagram Pole Fighter
Emperor Of Shaolin Kung Fu
Executioners Of Death
Fists And Guts
Instructors Of Death
Killer Angels
Lady Is The Boss
Legendary Weapons Of China
Mad Monkey Kung Fu
Master Of Disaster
Ming Patriots
My Young Auntie
Odd Couple
Operation Scorpio
Return To the 36th Chamber
Shaolin Temple 3
Shaolin Vs Wu Tang
Spiritual Boxer
Spiritual Boxer 2
36th Chamber Of Shaolin
Liu, Chin Wei
Kung Fu Executioner
Malevolent Mate
Super Power
Liu Hung Chuen
Devil Fetus
Liu, John
Ninja In Claws Of The CIA
Zen Kwando Strikes in Paris
Liu Kuo Shin
Ali Baba
Devil's Owl
Devil's Vendetta
Liu, Raymond
Crane Fighter
Liu Shew Hua [Jimmy Shaw]
Fist of Fury 2
Manchu Boxer
Portrait in Crystal
Shaolin Kung Fu Master
Lo Chun Ku [Tony C. K. Lo]
Cannibals
Crack Shadow Boxers
Devil Hunters
Dragon and Tiger Kids

Haunted Madam
Three Evil Masters
Lo Ke
Amsterdam Connection
Final Run
In the Lap of God
Lo Lieh
Black Magic with Buddha
Devil and Angel
Edge of Darkness
Fists of the White Lotus
Hong Kong Godfather
Magnificent
Summons to Death
Lo Mar
Boxer from the Temple
Lo Wan Shing
Hypocrite
Lo Wei
Angry Ranger
Attack of Kung Fu Girls
Back Alley Princess
Big Boss
Chinatown Capers
Comet Strikes
Fist of Fury
Golden Key
Heart of a Teenage Girl
Invincible Eight
Just Jackie
Killer Meteor
Little Shantung Arrives in Hong Kong
Magnificent Bodyguards
Man Called Tiger
Naughty Naughty
New Fists of Fury
Rainbow
Seaman Number 7
Shadow Whip
Shaolin Wooden Men
Spiritual Kung Fu
To Kill with Intrigue
Yellow Faced Tiger
Lo Weng Tung
Crazy Safari
Spooky! Spooky!
Long Shao Ji
Devil Twin
Uncle Ken's Angels

Lu Bin
Elusive Song of the Vampire
Lu Jian Ming
Doctor Vampire
Into the Night
Lu, Kenneth
Ghost's Love
Lu Tung Lo
Animation Sexitation
Asylum of Love
Lu Wong Tu
Toothless Vampires
Luk, Jamie
Bomb Disposal Officer: Baby Bomb
Killer's Love
My Will . . . I Will
We Visited Southeast Asia
What a Small World
Luk Pak Sang
Brave Young Girls
Butcher Wing
Luo Lin
Figures from Earth
Fury of the Heaven
Ma Sui Wai
Circus Kids
Don't Call Me Gigolo
Mak Don Hung [Johnny Mak]
Long Arm of the Law
Mak Dong Kit [Michael Mak]
[sometimes **Poon Man Kit**]
Everlasting Love
Hero of Hong Kong 1949
Hero of Tomorrow
Long Arm of the Law 2
Long Arm of the Law 3
Lung Fung Restaurant
Sex and Zen
Shootout
Sword of Many Loves
To Be #1
Truth (television series)
Truth: Final Chapter
Mak, Peter
see **Mak Yai Kit**
Mak Yai Kit [Peter Mak]
All Night Long
Chinese Legend

Loves Of The Living Dead
Wicked City
Maka, Karl
The Good, the Bad, and the Loser
His Name Is Nobody
Man Gon [Derek Chang]
Heavenly Spell
Run
Mang Hoi
Blonde Fury
Mous, T. F.
see **He Chi Chiang**
Nam Nai Choi
see **Lan Nai Kai**
Ng See Yuen
Aloha, the Little Vampire
Bruce Lee True Story
Game of Death 2
Haunted House
Kidnap in Rome
Ring of Death
Secret Rivals
Secret Rivals 2
Seven Commandments of Kung Fu
Vengeance of the Snow Maiden
Ni, John
see **Wang Lung Wei**
Oli, Nicole
Blood Bath 23
Pal, Ming
Hard Way to Die
Pan Ling Tong [Pan Fung]
Blood Sorcery
Brutal Sorcery
Lover's Rock
Poison Rose
Pao Hsieh Lieh
Blood Treasury Fight
Deadly Angels
Eight Escorts
Eight Peerless Treasures
Hero of Border Region
Heroic ones (Inheritors)
Kung Fu Emperor
Kung Fu Hellcats
Revenger
Park Yoon Kyo
Bloody Smile
Two Women from Netherworld
Wedding Dress of the Ghost

Poon Man Kit
  see **Mak Dong Kit [Michael Mak]**
Putra, Sisworo
Hell Raiders
Warrior
Ratno, Timoer
Blind Swordswoman
Blind Warrior
Devil's Sword
Revenge of the Ninja
Rotar Ru Tar
Ginseng King
Ry Man
Lady Tiger
Sen, Raymond
  see **Hung, Samo**
Shao Jun Huang
Armageddon
Shaw, Jimmy
  see **Liu Shew Hua**
Shen Liu Li
Devil Yielded to God
Ninja Holocaust
Snuff Bottle Connection
Shek Ping
Satyr Monks
Shin, Stephen
BB 30
Bite of Love
Black Cat
Black Cat 2
Brotherhood
Great Conqueror's Concubine
Happy Together
Heart Against Hearts
Love Me and My Dad
Perfect Match
Tiger Cage 2
Shin Ren
Tale of a Female Ghost
Soo Kim In
Grudge of Moon Lady
Su, William
Kickboxer Tears
Sudjio, L.
Black Magic 3
Sui Ming
Demi Gods and Demi Devils

Suma, Worod
Warrior 3
Sumat, Saichur
Raiders of Doomed Kingdom
Sun Chung [William Sun]
Angel Hunter
Avenging Eagle
City War
Deadly Breaking Sword
Demon Strikes
Human Skin Lanterns
Kung Fu Instructor
Lady in Black
Master Strikes Back
Master's Necklace
Mercenaries from Hong Kong
Murder of Murders
My Rebellious Son
Old Man and the Kid
Rendezvous with the Devil
Wind, Forest, Fire, Mountain
Sun Gam Loi
Dragon Root
Secret of Chinese Kung Fu
Yoga and Kung Fu Girl
Sze Ma Peng
  see **Chang Ling**
Tai Ng Ok [Robert Tai]
Death Cage
Girls in the Tiger Cage
Girls in the Tiger Cage 2
Legend of a Drunken Tiger
Mafia Vs. Ninja
Ninja's Final Duel
Revenge of Dragon
Shaolin Chastity Kung Fu
Tan Hua Xiong [Fred Tan]
No Fear for Loving
Split of the Spirit
Tang, Billy
  see **Tang Hin Sing**
Tang Chi Li
Bury Me High
Butterfly and Sword
Iron Finger of Death
Legend of Wisely
Once upon a Time: A Hero in China
Opium and the Kung Fu Master

276   **Tang Hin Sing [Billy Tang]**
Dr. Lamb
Dragon Fight
Red to Kill
Run and Kill
Those Were the Days
Vengeance Is Mine
Tao Ten Hong
Girl Gang
Money Game
My Crazy Love for You
Ting Shan Si
Beheaded 1000
Drunken Cat's Paw
800 Heroes
Kung Fu of Seven Steps
Magic Sword
Mar's Villa
Of Cooks and Kung Fu
Queen Bee
Queen's Ransom
Rebel Boxer
Royal Fist
Seven Coffins
Spy Ring Kokunyakai
Two Assassins of Darkness
To Ke Fung [Johnny To]
All About Ah-Long
Barefooted Kid
Big Heat
Fun, Luck and the Tycoon
Heroic Trio
Heroic Trio 2
Justice, My Foot
Lucky Encounter
Seven Years Itch
To Lo Po
Fist Of Fury 3
Incredible Master Beggars
Tong Kwai Lai [Stanley Tong]
Blood of the Black Dog
Police Story 3: Supercop
Project S
Rumble in the Bronx
Stone Age Warriors
Tong Ky Ming [Wilson Tong]
Bloody Fight
Duel of the Masters

Fatal Love
Fatal Rose
Ghost Ballroom
Ghost Nursing
Nomad
Snake Deadly Act
Spirit of Love
Young Avenger
Tong, Stanley
   see ***Tong Kwai Lai***
Tong, Terry
Seven Warriors
Tong Wai Sing
Blood Maniac
Tong, Wilson
   see ***Tong Ky Ming***
Tsang, Eric
Aces Go Places 1
Aces Go Places 2
Fatal Vacation
Handsome Siblings
Little Cop
Strange Bedfellows
Tigers
Vampire Family
Tsang, Kenneth
Au Revoir, Mon Amour
Tsui Hark
A Better Tomorrow 3
Aces Go Places 3
All the Right Clues
Banquet
Butterfly Murders
Chinese Feast
Chinese Ghost Story ·
Chinese Ghost Story 2 ·
Chinese Ghost Story 3 ·
Deception
Don't Play with Fire
Green Snake
I Love Maria (Roboforce)
Iron Monkey ·
Happy Ghost 3 ·
King of Chess
Laser Man ·
Love in the Time of Twilight
Lovers
Magic Crane ·

Master
Once upon a Time in China
Once upon a Time in China 2
Once upon a Time in China 3
Once upon a Time in China 5
Peking Opera Blues
The Raid ·
Shanghai Blues
Spy Games ·
Swordsman ·
Swordsman 2 ·
Twin Dragons ·
We Are Going to Eat You
Wicked City ·
Zu Warriors from Magic Mountain
· codirected by Tsui Hark
Tsui Wing Choy
see **Yip Wing Tsui**
Tu Wah Wu
Mind Fuck
Tung Kan We [Richard Tung]
Buddha Assassinator
Instant Kung Fu Man
Lady Wolf
Magic Cop
Umbara, Danu
Five Deadly Angels
Wai Hon To
Sam the Iron Bridge 2
Wai Ka Fai
Peace Hotel
Wai Li
Angel Terminator
Club Girls
Wan Quan Bao
Blood of Indian Fetish Cult
Wang Chung Kuan
July Spirit
Vampire Child
Wang, Irene
Love Me Vampire
Wang Lung Wei [John Ni]
Crazy Guy with Super Kung Fu
Escape from the Brothel
Fury in Red
Widow Warriors
Wang, Peter
Laser Man

Wang Yu [Jimmy Wang Yu]   **277**
Beach of the War God
Chinese Boxer
Golden Swallow
Man Called Tiger
Man from Hong Kong
Master of Flying Guillotine
One Armed Boxer
Sword
Tattooed Dragon
Tiger and Crane Fist
Wang Yung Ling [Hsiung]
Fire Fist of the Incredible Dragon
Lewd Lizard
Many Faced Woman
Night of Obsession
Wei, Dick
Visa to Hell
Wei Hoy Fung
Snake Fist Fighter
Wen Lap Kuen
Black Sheep
Wong Che Keung [Benny Wong]
Angel Force
Dreaming the Reality
Robotrix
Story of a Gun
That's Money
Wong Chi Chang [Kirk Wong]
Club
Crime Story
Flash Future Kung Fu
Gunmen
Love to Kill
Organized Crime and Triad Bureau
Rock 'n' Roll Cop
True Colors
Wong, Ching [Jing]
(sometimes **Gordon Chan**)
(sometimes **Nilson Cheung**)
Big Score
Born to Gamble
Boys Are Easy
Chinese Torture Chamber Story
City Hunter
Crocodile Hunters
Dances with Dragons
Deadly Dream Woman
Fight Back to School

278   Fight Back to School 2
Fight Back to School 3
Fortune Hunters
Future Cops
Ghost Busting
Ghost Fever
God of Gamblers
God of Gamblers 2
God of Gamblers 3
God of Gamblers Returns
Hail the Judge
Holy Weapon
Hong Kong Playboys
Jailhouse Eros
Kung Fu Cult Master
Last Blood
Last Hero in China
Liquid Sword
Magic Crystals
Modern Romance
Money Maker
Mr. Possessed
New Legend of Shaolin ·
Return of the Demon
Return to a Better Tomorrow
Royal Tramp
Royal Tramp 2
Saint of Gamblers
The Sting
Tricky Brains
Truant Heroes
    (·) codirected by Wong Ching
[Jing]
Wong Chung
Angel Enforcers
Fire Phoenix
Fractured Follies
Gold Constables
Mission of Justice
Run, Don't Walk
Vampire's Breakfast
Wong Hong Chang
Girl Called Tigress
Great General
The Hero
Wong Kam Tin
Guilty or Innocent
Most Wanted
Shoot to Kill

Wrongly Killed Girl
Wong Kar Wei [Wai]
As Tears Go By
Ashes of Time
Chungking Express
Days of Being Wild
Fallen Angels
Wong King Fang
Curse of Wicked Wife
Guardian
Master Killer
Wong, Kirk
   see **Wong Chi Chang**
Wong Kong
Comfort Women
Excessive Torture in a Female Prison
   Camp
Ghost of the Fox
Wong Kwok Chu
Fearless Young Boxer
Whore and the Policewoman
Wong, Parkman
Exposed to Danger
Passionate Killing in a Dream
Red Shield
Unmatchable Match
Wong Tai Loy [Taylor Wong]
Born Invincible
Fai & Chi: Kings of Kung Fu
Fantasy Romance
Girls from China
Girls Unbuttoned
Man of the Times
Return of the Deadly Blade
Rich and Famous
Sentenced to Hang
Three Swordsmen
Tragic Hero
Triads: Inside Story
Wild Party
Wong Tsing
Return of the Demon
Transmigration Romance
Woo, John
A Better Tomorrow
A Better Tomorrow 2
Broken Arrow (American Production)
Bullet in the Head
Dragon Tamers

From Riches to Rags
Hand of Death
Hard Target (American Production)
Hard-boiled
Heroes Shed No Tears
Just Heroes
The Killer
Last Hurrah for Chivalry
Once a Thief
Peace Hotel ·
Plain Jane to the Rescue
Run Tiger Run
Time You Need a Friend
To Hell with the Devil
   (·) listed as producer
Woo Ka Chi
Sex of the Imperial
Women of the Jungle
Woo Lian Sing
Witch with the Flying Head
Wu, David
Bride with the White Hair 2
From Zero to Hero
Once a Blacksheep
Spy Games
Sunshine Friends
Wu Kuo Ren
Ghostly Love
Hong Kong Eva
Twinkle Twinkle Little Star
Who's (the) Killer
Wu Ma
Burning Sensation
Chinese Ghostbuster
Dead and the Deadly
Eagle with a Yellow Face
Exorcist Master
Flash Legs
Kickboxer
Kung Fu of Eight Drunkards
My Cousin the Ghost
Portrait of a Nymph
Showdown at Cotton Mill
Stage Door Johnny
Story of Chivalry
Story of Kennedy Town
Young Tiger
Wu Su Man [Stephen Wu]
Ghost Festival
One Step Beyond

Xen Chu Lung
Magic Needles
Xin Ren
Beautiful Dead Body
Xung Fei Lei
Excuse Me, Please
Ghost Snatchers
Women Warriors of Kingmen
Yang Chin Bong [Chester Yang]
Commando Fury
Girl Fighter
Lunatic Frog Women
Pretty Women at War
Revenge for Rape
Searching for Love
Yang Ou Chen [Richard Yang]
Female Chivalry
Ghost Story of Kam Pin Mui
Seeding of a Ghost
3 Shaolin Musketeers
Yao Feng Pan
All in Dim Cold Night
Blue Lamp in a Winter Night
Evil Black Magic
Horror Inn
Spirit Vs. Zombi
Yau, Herman
Chez 'n' Ham
Cop Image
Don't Shoot Me, I'm Just a Violinist
Fearless Match
Taxi Hunter
Untold Story
Yau, Pierre
Killer and the Cop
Trouble Couple
Yee Chik Ki
Fatal Chase
Midnight Angel
Yee Tung Sing [Derek Yee Tung Sing]
Bachelor Swan Song
C'Est la Vie, Mon Cheri
Full Throttle
Lunatic
People's Hero
Yip Wing Tsui [Tsui Wing Choy]
Sleeping Fist
Thundering Mantis

Yu, Antonio
Snake Devil
Yu, Jimmy Wang
see **Wang Yu**
Yu Kong Yun [Dennis Yu]
Evil Cat
Flesh and the Bloody Horror
Ghost Hospital
Imp
Sketch of a Psycho
Yu Ren Tai [Donnie Yu]
Bless This House
Scared Stiff
Yu Ronnie (Yu Tan Tai)
Bride with the White Hair
Bride with the White Hair 2 ·
China White
Dead End of Besiegers
Great Pretenders
Jumping Ash
Legacy of Rage
Occupant
Phantom Lover
Postman Strikes Back
Savior
Shogun and Little Kitchen
Trail
    (·) codirected by Ronnie Yu
Yuen, Alan
Touches of Love
Yuen, Brandy
In the Line of Duty 3
Sword Stained with Royal Blood
Three Against the World
Yuen Bun
Once upon a Time in China 4
Yuen Cheung Yan
Bloody Ghost
Caged Beauties
Devil Design
Ghost Mansion
Haunted Cop Shop 2
Wizard's Curse
Yuen Cheung Yeung
Champions
Dark Side of Chinatown
Live Hard
Master of Zen: Tamo Monk
Shaolin Invincibles
Taoism Drunkard

Yuen, Corey
  see **Yuen Kwei**
Yuen Feng Chi
Lady General Hua Mu Lan
Pink Rose
Queen Boxer
Rape of the Sword
Story of Rose
Yuen Kwei [Corey Yuen]
Fist of Legend
Fong Sai Yuk
Fong Sai Yuk 2
Fortune Hunters
Ghost Renting ·
My Father Is a Hero
New Legend of Shaolin ·
Ninja in the Dragon's Den
On the Run
Raging Thunder
Revenge of Angel
Righting Wrongs
Savior of Souls ·
Savior of Souls 2 ·
She Shoots Straight
Women on the Run
Yes! Madam
    (· co-directed by Yuen Kwei)
Yuen Woo Ping
Buddhist Fist
Dance of the Drunk Mantis
Drunken Master
Fire Dragon
In the Line of Duty 4
Iron Monkey
Legend of a Fighter
Magnificent Butcher
Miracle Fighters
Mismatched Couples
New Age of Living Together
Snake in the Eagle's Shadow
Steel Horse
Tai Chi Master
Tiger Cage 3
Wing Chun
Yueng Kuen
Bloody Beast
Forbidden Arsenal
Ghost's Lover
Prodigal Boxer 2

Shadow of the Tigers
Super Lady Cop
Zen of Sword
Yueng, Simon
Easy Money
Phantom War

Yun Ching [Simon Yun Ching]   **281**
Angel Terminators 2
Zhang Yimou
Raise the Red Lantern

The Major Players

This alphabetical listing tabulates the films in the career of a specific actor or actress. Not all of these titles were reviewed in this volume.

If a movie is listed in nonbold, nonitalic type, it was reviewed in the "Film Section" of this book; if the title is in **boldface** type, it can be found under "Roots: Martial Arts" and if it's in *italic* type, the film was not reviewed in this volume.

Frankie Chan [Chan Fan Kay]

Burning Ambition
Carrying on Pickpocket
Dream of Desire
Fun and Fury
Good, the Bad, and the Beauty
Oh! Yes Sir!
Outlaw Brothers
Teenage Trap
Warrior's Tragedy 1
Warrior's Tragedy 2

Jackie Chan pseudonyms: Chan Yuan Lung, Jackie Lung, Chen Lung, real name: Chen Gang Sheng

All in the Family
Armour of God
Armour of God 2
Attack of the Kung Fu Girls
Battle Creek Brawl
Champions
City Hunter
Crime Story
Dragon Fist
Dragon Lord
Dragons Forever
Drunken Master
Drunken Master 2
Fantasy Mission Force
Fearless Hyena
Fearless Hyena 2
First Mission
First Strike: Police Story 4
Fist of Death
Half a Loaf of Kung Fu
Hand of Death
Hapkido
Inspector Wears a Skirt (*director only*)
Inspector Wears a Skirt 2 (*director only*)
Iron Fist Monk
Island of Fire
Just Jackie
Killer Meteor
Magnificent Bodyguards
Millionaire Express
Mr. Canton and Lady Rose

My Lucky Stars
New Fists of Fury
Police Story
Police Story 2
Police Story 3: Supercop
Pom Pom
Project A
Project A 2
Project S
Protector
Rumble in the Bronx
Shaolin Wooden Men
Snake and Crane Arts of Shaolin
Snake Fist Fighter
Snake in the Eagle's Shadow
Spiritual Kung Fu
36 Crazy Fist
Thunderbolt
To Kill with Intrigue
Twin Dragons
Twinkle Twinkle Lucky Stars
Wheels on Meals
Winners and Sinners
Young Master

Chang Ling (Pearl Cheong)

Dark Lady of the Butterfly
Fantasy Mission Force
Grand Master of Shaolin Kung Fu
Hero of Border Region
Heroic Ones

Invincible
Matching Escort
Men on the Hour
Miracle of the Crystal Rose
Miraculous Flower
Wolf Devil Woman

Sisters of the World Unite
Story in Sorghum Field
That Day on the Beach
White Jasmine
Yellow Faced Tiger

Silvia Chang [Chang Ai Chia]

Kent Cheng [Cheng Chuen Yan]

Aces Go Places
Aces Go Place 2
Aces Go Place 3
Aces Go Place 4
All About Ah-Long
Cabaret Tears
Double Trouble
Eight Tales of Gold
Fun, Luck and the Tycoon
Funniest Movie
Funny Face
Golden Age
He Lives by Night
Kidnapped
Killer Lady
King of Stanley Market
Legend of the Mountain
My Grandfather
New Age of Living Together
Once upon a Time
Passion
Rascal's Tale
Seven Year Itch

Beloved Daddy
Beloved Son of God
Blood of the Black Dog
Body Guard from Beijing
Code of Fortune
Copbusters
Crime Story
Dr. Lamb
Easy Money
Family Day
Family Strikes Back
Fun and Fury
Ghost Legend
Give Me Back
Heartbeat 100
Hero of Hong Kong 1949
Imp
Lethal Contact
Lifeline Express
Lord of East China Sea
Lord of East China Sea 2
Lucky Encounter
Man of the Times
Mermaid Got Married

Most Wanted
Mr. Smart
Mr. Sunshine
Oh My Cops
Once upon a Time in China
Once upon a Time in China 5
Powerful Four
Run and Kill
Run, Don't Walk
Sentenced to Hang
Sex and Zen
Spooky Family
Spooky Family 2
Those Merry Souls
Turning Point
Vampire Buster
Vampire's Breakfast
Vendetta
Why me?

Jacky Cheung [Cheung Hok Yau]

As Tears Go By
Ashes of Time
Banquet
Best Friend of the Cops
Boys Are Easy
Bullet for Hire
Bullet in the Head
Bury Me High
Chinese Ghost Story 2
Chinese Ghost Story 3
Chinese Legend
Couples, Couples, Couples
Curry and Pepper
Days of Being Dumb
Deadly Dream Woman
Demoness from 1000 Years
Eagle Shooting Heroes
Flying Dagger
Future Cops
Haunted Cop Shop
High Risk
Hot Hot and Pom Pom
Mr. Canton and Lady Rose
My Dream Is Yours
Nobles
Once upon a Time in China
Point of No Return
Private Eye Blues
Raid
Seven Warriors
Sister Cupid
Slickers Vs. Killers
Swordsman
Tiger Cage

Olivia Cheng

Crazy Blood
Family Affair
I Will . . . My Will
Killer's Blues
Til Death Do We Scare

To Live and Die in Tsimshatsui
True Love
Vampire Buster
Where's Officer Tuba?
Wicked City
Will of Iron

Nomad
Once a Thief
Phantom Lover
Rouge
Tristar

Leslie Cheung [Cheung Kwok Wing]

Maggie Cheung [Cheung Man Yuk]

A Better Tomorrow
A Better Tomorrow 2
A Better Tomorrow 3
Aces Go Places 5
All's Well That Ends Well
All's Well That Ends Well, Too
Arrest the Restless
Ashes of Time
Banquet
Bride with the White Hair
Bride with the White Hair 2
Chatter Street Killer
Chinese Feast
Chinese Ghost Story
Chinese Ghost Story 2
Chinese Ghost Story 3
Days of Being Wild
Eagle Shooting Heroes
Fatal Love
Final Encounter of the Legend
For Your Heart Only
He's a Woman, She's a Man
Intellectual Trio
It's a Wonderful Life
Long and Winding Road

Alan and Eric: Between Hello
As Tears Go By
Ashes of Time
Bachelor Swan Song
Banquet
Barefooted Kid (Young Hero)
Beloved Son Of God
Boys Are Easy
Call Girls 1988
Center Stage
Days Of Being Wild
Double Fattiness
Dragon From Russia
Dragon Inn
Eagle Shooting Heroes
Farewell China
First Shot
Fishy Story
Flying Dagger
Green Snake
Happy Ghost 3
Heartbeat 100
Hearts, No Flowers
Heroic Trio
Heroic Trio 2: Executioners
Holy Weapon

How to Pick Girls Up
Iceman Cometh
Inbetween Love
It's a Drink! It's a Bomb!
Last Romance
Love Soldier of Fortune
Lovelorn Expert
Mad Monk
Moon, Stars, Sun
Moon Warriors
New Age of Living Together
Paper Marriage
Perfect Match
Police Story
Police Story 2
Police Story 3: Supercop
Project A (Part 2)
Rose (Blue Valentine)
Seventh Curse
Sister Cupid
Song of the Exile
Story of Rose
Today's Hero
True Love
Twin Dragons
What a Hero
Will of Iron

Crystal Fortune Run
Dances with the Dragon
Deadly Dream Woman
Devil's Vendetta
Dragon Chronicles
Fatal Passion
Fight Back to School
Fight Back to School 2
Fight Back to School 3
Fists of Fury 1991
Gangland Odyssey
God of Gamblers 2
God of Gamblers' Return
Holy Weapon
Invincible
Last Hero in China
Lee Rock
Lee Rock 2
Lee Rock 3
Operation Pink Squad 2
Our Neighbors Are Phantoms
Romantic Dream
Royal Tramp
Sword of Many Loves
Sword Stained with Royal Blood
Swordsman
Tiger Cage 3
Vampire Family

Cheung Man

All for the Winner
Bet on Fire
Cheetah on Fire
Chinese Legend

Billy Chong [Willy Dohzan]

Crystal Fist
Hard Way to Die
In the Line of Duty 2

Jade Claw
Kung Fu Executioner
Kung Fu Zombie
Paper Marriage
Pedicab Driver
Sun Dragon
Super Power
Wind, Forest, Fire, Mountain

Banquet
Chinese Odyssey: Pandora's Box
Chinese Odyssey 2: Cinderella
Curry and Pepper
Dragon Fight
Fight Back to School
Fight Back to School 2
Fight Back to School 3
Fists of Fury 1991
From Beijing with Love
God of Gamblers 2
God of Gamblers 3
Hail the Judge
He Who Chases After the Wind
Justice My Foot
King of Beggars
Last Conflict
Legend of the Dragon
Love Is Love
Love on Delivery
Lung Fung Restaurant
Mad Monk
Magnificent Scoundrels
Out of the Dark
Royal Tramp
Royal Tramp 2
Thief of Time
Tricky Brains
Unmatchable Match
When Fortune Smiles

Cathy Chow [Chow Hoi Mei]

Cathy Chow [Chow Hoi Mei]
Don't Give a Damn
Fruit Punch
Holy Virgin Versus the Evil Dead
Insanity
Private Eye Blues

Vivian Chow

**Stephen Chow (Stephen Chiao)
[Chiauo Sing Chi]**

Angel Hunter
Arrest the Restless
Family Affairs
Fruit Bowl
Fun and Fury
No Regret, No Return
Top Banana Club
Tulips in August
Unmatchable Match

Chow Yun-Fat

A Better Tomorrow
A Better Tomorrow 2
A Better Tomorrow 3
All About Ah-Long
An Autumn's Tale
Cherry Blossoms
City on Fire
City War
Club Girl Story
Code of Honor
Diary of a Big Man
Dream Lovers
Eight Happiness
Executor
Flaming Brothers
Fractured Follies
Full Contact
Fun, Luck and the Tycoon
God of Gamblers
God of Gamblers' Return
Greatest Lover
Hard-boiled

Headhunter
Hearty Response
Hong Kong 1941
Killer
Love: Now You See It . . .
Love unto Waste
Lunatics
Miss O
My Will . . . I Will
Occupant
Once a Thief
Peace Hotel
Postman Strikes Back
Prison on Fire
Prison on Fire 2
Rich and Famous
Scared Stiff
Seventh Curse
Spiritual Love
Story of Rose
Story of Wu Yiet
Tiger on the Beat
Tragic Hero
Treasure Hunt
Triads: Inside Story
Why Me?
Wild Search
Witch from Nepal

Cherie Chung [Chong Chu Hung]   **Gong Li**

Cherie Chung	Gong Li

Banana Cop
Banquet
Bet on Fire
Carry on Hotel
Chaos by Design
Couples, Couples, Couples
Dead and the Deadly
Eighteen Times
Fatal Love
Golden Swallow
Good, the Bad and the Beauty
Goodbye Darling
Happy Din Don
Happy Together
Heaven Can Help
Last Romance
Moon, Stars, Sun
Once a Thief
Peking Opera Blues
Postman Strikes Back
Spiritual Love
Wild Search
Witch from Nepal
Zodiac Killers

Dragon Chronicles
Empress Dowager
God of Gamblers 3
Great Conqueror's Concubine
Mary from Beijing
Raise the Red Lantern
Terra Cotta Warrior
Woman•Demon•Human

Sibelle Hu [Hu Hui Chung]

Angel Terminators 2
Bury Me High
Devil Hunters
Dreaming the Reality
Drugs Area
Fong Sai Yuk
Fong Sai Yuk 2

Holy Virgin Versus the Evil Dead
Inspector Wears a Skirt
Inspector Wears a Skirt 2
Lethal Contact
Lethal Panther
Magic Amethyst
My Lucky Stars
My Lucky Stars 2

Samo Hung (Sammo Hung) [Hung Kam Bo]

Association
Banquet
Best Is the Highest
Blades of Fury
Bloody Ring
By Hook or by Crook
Carry on Pickpocket
China's Last Eunuch
Code of Fortune
Daddy, Father, Papa
Dead and the Deadly
Dirty Tiger and Crazy Frog
Dirty Tiger Kung Fu
Don't Give a Damn
Dragon Tamers
Dragons Forever
Eastern Condors
Eight Taels of Gold
Encounters of the Spooky Kind
Encounters of the Spooky Kind 2
End of Wicked Tigers
Enter the Fat Dragon
Fast Sword

Fate of Lee Khan
First Mission
Fortune Code
Gambling Ghost
Game of Death
Hand of Death
Hapkido
Heart of the Dragon
High Calibre
Himalayan
Incredible Kung Fu Master
In the Blood
Iron Fist Monk
Island of Fire
Knockabout
Kung Fu Cult Master
Lady Whirlwind
License to Steal
Lover's Tear
Magnificent Butcher
Manchu Boxer
Man from Hong Kong
Millionaire Express
Moon Warriors
Mr. Vampire 3
My Flying Wife
My Lucky Stars
My Lucky Stars 2
Odd Couple
Owl and Bumbo
Painted Faces
Painted Skin
Pantyhose Heroes
Paper Marriage
Pedicab Driver
Pom Pom
Prodigal Son
Project A
Return of Secret Rivals
Seven Warriors
Shanghai Express
Shanghai Shanghai
Shaolin Plot
She Shoots Straight
Skinny Tiger and Fatty Dragon
Skyhawk
Slickers Vs. Killers
Stoner
Tai Chi Master
To Err Is Human

Touch and Go
Tournament
Traitorous
Valiant One
Victim
Warriors Two
Wheels on Meals
Where's Officer Tuba?
Winners and Sinners
Yes Madam
Zu Warriors from Magic Mountain

Rosamund Kwan [Kwan Ji Lam]

Adventurers
Armour of God
Assassin
Banquet
Bite of Love
Blade of Fury
Dr. Wei and the Scripture with No
    Words
End of the Road
Ghost Fever
Gigolo and the Whore
Great Adventurer
Great Conqueror's Concubine
Headhunter
Inspector Pink Dragon
Last Duel
Love Among the Triads
Magic Crane
Mr. Smart
Once upon a Time in China
Once upon a Time in China 2
Once upon a Time in China 3
Once upon a Time in China 5
Pretty Ghost
Project A 2
Proud and Confident
Saviour of Souls 2
Swordsman
Swordsman 2
Three Against the World
Tiger Cage 2
Touch of Love
Undeclared War
Vengeance Is Mine

Cynthia Khan (Cynthia Yang) [Yang Li Chiang]

Angel on Fire
Avenging Quartet
Blade of Fury
Dead End of Besiegers
Death Triangle
Forbidden Arsenal
In the Line of Duty 2
In the Line of Duty 3
In the Line of Duty 4
In the Line of Duty 5
Sea Wolves
Super Lady Cop
Thirteen Cold Blooded Eagles
Tiger Cage 2
Tough Beauty and Sloppy Slop
Transmigration Romance
Yes, Madam '92
Yes, Madam 5
Zen of Sword

Aaron Kwok [Kwok Fu Shing]

Barefooted Kid
Future Cops
Game Boy Kids
Gangs '92
Kung Fu Scholar
Liquid Sword
Moment of Romance 2
Rhythm of Destiny
Savior of Souls
Shootout
Whatever Will Be, Will Be

Leon Lai [Lai Ming]

City Hunter
Fallen Angels
Fruit Bowl
Fun and Fury
Love and the City
Magic Touch
Run
Sword of Many Loves
Wicked City

Amy Kwok [Kwok Ai Ming]

Gleam of Hope
No Fear for Loving
Obsession
Will of Iron

Lam Chang Ying [Lam Ching Ying]

Best Is the Highest
China Dolls
China Dragon
Chinese Connection
Crazy Safari
Dead and the Deadly

Eastern Condors
Encounter of the Spooky Kind 2
Enter the Dragon
Exorcist Master
Eye for an Eye
First Mission
First Vampire in China
Fists of Fury
Forced Nightmare
Her Vengeance
Heroes Shed No Tears
Hocus Pocus
Hot Hot and Pom Pom
Last Vampire in China
Lover's Tear
Magic Cop
Magnificent Butcher
Martial Arts Master: Wong Fei Hung
Mr. Vampire
Mr. Vampire 2
Mr. Vampire 3
Mr. Vampire 1992
Mr. Vampire: New Mr. Vampire 2
Painted Faces
Prince of the Sun
Prodigal Son
Project A 2
Red and Black
Return of the Dragon
Roboforce (I Love Maria)
Sad Story of Saigon
School on Fire
Skin Stripper
Slickers Vs Killers
Spooky Family 2
Swordsman
Ultimate Vampire
Vampire Strikes Back
Vampire Vs. Vampire
Wizard's Curse

Andy Lau [Lau Tak Hwa]

As Tears Go By
Bloody Brotherhood
Casino Raiders
Casino Raiders 2
Casino Tycoon
Casino Tycoon 2
China White
City Kids
Code of Fortune
Crazy Companions
Crazy Companions 2
Crocodile Hunter
Dances with the Dragon
Days of Tomorrow
Dragon Family
Dragon in Jail
Drunken Master 3
Everlasting Love
Fortune Code
Full Throttle
Future Cops
Game Kids
Gangland Odyssey
God of Gamblers
God of Gamblers 2
Great Adventurers
Handsome Siblings
Home Too Far
Hong Kong Godfather
I Am Sorry
In the Blood
Island of Fire
Kawashima Yoshiko
Last Blood

Lee Rock
Lee Rock 2
Lee Rock 3
Little Cop
Long Arm of the Law 3
Magic Crystal
Moment of Romance
Moon Warriors
My Lucky Stars
My Lucky Stars 2
News Attack
No Risk, No Gain
Proud and Confident
Return Engagement
Rich and Famous
Romancing Star
Runaway Blues
Saviour of Souls
Saviour of Souls 2
Seventh Curse
Sworn Brothers
Taste of Killing and Romance
Thief of Time
Three Against the World
Three Swordsmen
Tian Di
Tigers
Tragic Hero
Tricky Brains
What a Hero
What a Wonderful World
Zodiac Killers

Carina Lau

City Warriors
Days of Being Wild
Detective in the Shadows
Eagle Shooting Heroes
Gigolo and Whore
Girls Without Tomorrow
He's a Woman, She's a Man
Holy Weapon
Lover of the Swindler
My American Grandson
Naughty Boys
Profiles of Pleasure
Queen's Bench III
Shadow Cop
She Shoots Straight
Supercop: Female

Lau Ching Wan

Angel Hunter
Bloody Hand Goddess
Bomb Disposal Officer: Baby Bomb
C'est la Vie, Mon Cheri
Doctor Mack
Don't Shoot Me, I'm Just a Violinist
Golden Girls
Happy Massage Girls
I Wanna Be Your Man
I've Got You Babe
Legal Innocence
Live Hard
Most Wanted
Oh! My Three Guys
Only Fools Fall in Love
Return to a Better Tomorrow
Tears and Triumph
Third Full Moon
Thou Shalt Not Swear
Tragic Fantasy: Tiger of Wanchai

Bruce Lee [Lee Jun Fan]

Big Boss (Fists of Fury)
Enter the Dragon
Fist of Fury (Chinese Connection)
Game of Death
Way of Dragon (Return of Dragon)

Danny Lee [Lee Shiu Shian] or [Lee Sau Yin]

Aces Go Places 5
Against All
Asian Connection
Big Score
Blue Lightning
Brotherhood
City Cops
City Cops 2
City on Fire
Code of Honor

298   *Cop of the Town*
Criminal Hunter
Diary of a Serial Rapist
Dr. Lamb
Executor
Fearless Match
Final Justice
Goliathon
Great Cheat
Just Heroes
Killer
Law Enforcer
Law with Two Faces
Love to Kill
Nobody Ever Cheats
No Compromise
No Way Back
Organized Crime and Triad Bureau
Parking Service
Powerful Four
Red Shield
Rhythm of Destiny
Rich and Famous
Road Warriors
Shaolin Heroes
Shoot to Kill
Stunning Gambling
Sword Stained with Royal Blood
Takes Two to Mingle
Thank You Sir
Tiger on the Beat 2
Twist
Undeclared War
Untold Story
Water Tank Murder Mystery

Loletta Lee [Lizhen Lee]

Angel of the Road
Before Dawn
Bless This House
Chicken à la Queen
Crazy Love
Devoted to You
Final Victory
Forbidden Arsenal
For Your Heart Only
Girls Unbuttoned
Happy Together
Isle of Fantasy
Jailhouse Eros
Kiss Me Goodbye
Mr. Vampire 4
Remains of a Woman
Sexy and Dangerous
Spirit of Love
Student Union
Summer Lover
Why Wild Girls
Young Wisely: Legend of Cosmos
Young Wisely: Son of the Devil

Michelle Lee (Michelle Reis)

Black Morning's Glory
Drunken Master 3
Fallen Angels
July 13th (100 Ways to Kill Yourself)
Other Side of the Sea
Sword of Many Loves
Wicked City
Zen of Sword

Big Deal
Bury Me High
Death Hunters
Death Triangle
Dreaming the Reality
Fatal Termination
Kickboxer Tears
Killer Angels
Lady Reporter
Little Heroes Lost in China
Mission Kill
Mission of Justice
Mr. Vampire
Mr. Vampire 2
New Kids in Town
Nocturnal Demons
Princess Madam
Protector
Revenge of Angel
Yes, Madam '92
Zu Warriors From Magic Mountain

Moon Lee [Lee Choi Fung]

Angel
Angel 2
Angel 3
Angel Force
Angel Terminators 2
Angel the Kickboxer
Avenging Quartet
Beauty Investigator

Jade Leung

Black Cat
Black Cat 2
Enemy Shadow
Satin Steel
Spider Woman

Tony Leung [Leung Chiu Wai]

All Men Are Brothers: Blood of the Leopard
All the Winners
Ashes of Time
Blind Romance
Blue Lightning
Bullet in the Head
Burning of Emperor's Palace
Chungking Express
Doctor Mack
Eagle Shooting Heroes
Farewell China
Flying Dagger
Gunmen
Hard-boiled
Island of Fire
Lady in Black
Laser Man
Magic Crane
Master's Necklace
People's Hero
Pretty Ghost
Prison on Fire
The Raid
Returning
Roboforce (I Love Maria)
Rose Rose I Love You
Seven Warriors
She Shoots Straight
Three Summers
Tom, Dick and Harry
Tomorrow
Touch of Love

Tony Leung [Leung Kar Fai]

Ashes of Time
Au Revoir, Mon Amour
Boys Are Easy
Dragon Inn
Eagle Shooting Heroes
God of Gamblers 2
God of Gamblers' Return
He Ain't Heavy He's My Father
He and She
Her Fatal Ways
It's a Wonderful Life
I Will Wait for You
Long and Winding Road
Lover of the Last Empress
Lover of the Swindler
Lover's Lover
Once upon a Time: Hero in China
Queen's Bench III
Roof with a View
Sentenced to Hang
Skinned Girl
Sting
Tigers
To Live and Die in Tsimshatsui
Touch of Evil

Jet Li [Li Lian Ji]

Abbot Hai Teng of Shaolin
Body Guard from Beijing
Dragon Fight
Dragons of the Orient
Dr. Wei and the Scripture with No Words
Fist of Legend
Fong Sai Yuk
Fong Sai Yuk 2
High Risk
Kung Fu Cult Master
Last Hero In China
Master
My Father Is a Hero
Once upon a Time in China
Once upon a Time in China 2
Once upon a Time in China 3
Shaolin Kung Fu
Shaolin Temple
Shaolin Temple 2
Shaolin Temple 3
Swordsman 2
Tai Chi Master

Brigitte Lin (Venus Lin) [Lin Ching Hsia]

All the Wrong Spies
Ashes of Time
Boys Are Easy
Bride with the White Hair
Bride with the White Hair 2
By Love Possessed
Chungking Express
Deception
Demon Fighter
Different Love
Dragon Chronicles
Dragon Inn
Dream Lovers
Eagle Shooting Heroes
Eight Hundred Heroes
Encouraging Melody
Fantasy Mission Force
Fire Dragon
Flaming Brothers
Golden Queen Commando
Handsome Siblings
Lady in Black
Lily Under the Muzzle
Love Affair
Lover Beware
Magnificent 72
Misty Dizzle
Orchid in the Rain
Other Side of Gentlemen
Peking Opera Blues
Phoenix the Raider
Pink Force Commando
Police Story
Red Dust

Royal Tramp 2
Starry Is the Night
Swordsman 2
Swordsman 3: East Is Red
Thirty Million Rush
Three Swordsmen
True Colors
Victims of the Killer
Wild Goose on the Wing
Women Warriors of Kingmen
Zu Warriors From Magic Mountain

Max Mok [Mok Siu Chung]

Angel of the Road
Apartment for Women
Assassin
Bloodbath 23
Blood Call
China's Last Eunuch
City Kids
Close Escape
Dangerous Duty
Dragon Family
Eye for an Eye
Fire Dragon
Heart of a Killer
Hero of Tomorrow
Lantern
Long Arm of the Law 3
Lucky Stars
Lung Fung Restaurant
Magic Crystal
Mission Kill
Never Say Regret
No Regret, No Return
No Way Back
Once upon a Time in China 1
Once upon a Time in China 4
Once upon a Time in China 5
Outlaw Brothers
Path of Glory
Pedicab Driver
Seven Warriors
Slave of the Sword
Son on the Run
That's Money
Twilight of the Forbidden City

Lu Hsiu Ling

Hidden Passion
Kickboxer
Morning Date
Runaway Blues
Who's the Killer

Whampoa Blues
Witness

Three Wishes
Top Bet
Trouble Couples
Why Why Tell Me Why

Anita Mui (Anita Mei) [Mui Yim Fong]

Carrie Ng [Ng Kar Lee]

A Better Tomorrow 3
Au Revoir, Mon Amour
Banquet
Beheaded 1000
Center Stage
Chocolate Inspector
Code of Fortune
Drunken Master 2
Fight Back to School 3
Fortune Code
Golden Destroyers
Greatest Lover
Happy Bigamist
Heroic Trio
Heroic Trio 2
Justice My Foot
Kawashima Yoshiko
Magic Crane
Moon Warriors
Mr. Canton and Lady Rose
My Father Is a Hero
One Husband Too Many
Prince of Portland Street
Rouge
Rumble in the Bronx
Saviour of Souls
Scared Stiff

Angel Hunter
Angel Terminators
Black Panther Warriors
Bloodstained Tradewind
Call Girl '92
Candlelight's Woman
Changing Patner
Cheetah on Fire
City on Fire
Crystal Hunt
Days of Tomorrow
Dragon from Russia
Family Day
Fight to Survive
First Time Is the Last Time
Fishy Story
Forsaken Cop
Girls Without Tomorrow
Gunmen
Hero Dream
He Who Chases after the Wind
Incorruptibles
Inside Track
Justice My Foot
Lady Killer
Mission of Justice

Mistaken Identity
Modern Romance
Mountain Warriors
Naked Killer
Never Ending Love
Rascal's Tale
Remains of a Woman
Return Engagement
Right Here Waiting
Rock 'n' Roll Cop
Sentenced to Hang
Sex and Curse
Sex and Zen
Skinny Tiger and Fatty Dragon
Story of Pei Li
Twilight of the Forbidden City
Ultimate Vampire
Weakness of Man
Woman Killer's Rampage

Devil Girl 18
Dreaming the Reality
Fatal Chase
Final Run
Godfather's Daughter Mafia Blues
Hard to Kill
Kickboxer Tears
Kung Fu Wonder Child
Lethal Panther 2
Lover's Tear
Midnight Angel
Mission of Justice
Outlaw Brothers
Project S
Punch to Revenge
Rikki O
Shanghai Express
Yes, Madam '92

Oshima, Yukari (Cynthia Luster)

Angel
Angel Mission
Angel Terminators 2
Angel the Kickboxer
Avenging Quartet
Beauty Investigator
Book of Heroes
Brave Young Girls
Burning Ambition
Close Escape
Deadly Target
Death Triangle

Ti Lung

A Better Tomorrow
A Better Tomorrow 2
All Men Are Brothers
All Men Are Brothers 2
Anonymous Heroes
Avenging Eagle
Banquet
Barefoot Kid (Young Hero)
Battle for the Republic of China
Black Magic
Black Magic 2
Blade of Fury
Blast of the Iron Palm

Blood Brothers
Chinese Vengeance
City War
Clans of Intrigue
Deadly Breaking Sword
Death Ring
Delightful Forest
Dowager Empress
Dragon Missiles
Drug Addict
Drunken Master 2
Duel of Iron Fists
Duel of the Fists
Duel to the Death
Eight Man Army
Emperor and His Brother
First Shot
Five Masters of Death
Flying Guillotine 2
Friend from Inner Space
Generation Gap
Have Sword, Will Travel
Hero Defeating Japs
Hero of Border Region
Heroic Ones
Inheritors of Kung Fu
Invincible Iron Fist
Iron Chain Assault
Iron Finger of Death
Jade Tiger
Killer's Blues
King Eagle
Kung Fu Emperor
Kung Fu Instructor
Kung Fu Killers
Kung Fu Vengeance
Kung Fu Warlords
Last Temptest
Legend of Wisely
Love Me and My Dad
Magic Blade
Master Strikes Back
Mercenaries from Hong Kong
My Pretty Companion
(New) One Armed Swordsman
Ninja in a Deadly Trap
Opium and Kung Fu Master
People's Hero
Perils of Sentimental Swordsman
Pirate

Pursuit of Vengeance   305
Return of One Armed Swordsman
Return of Sentimental Swordsman
Revenger
Run, Don't Walk
Savage Five
Sentimental Swordsman
Seven Blows of the Dragon
Seven Man Army
Shanghai 13
Shaolin Heroes
Shaolin Temple
Singing Killer
Singing Thief
Soul of the Sword
Story of Chivalry
Strike 4 Revenge
Ten Tigers of Kwantung
Tiger Killer
Trilogy of Swordsmanship
True Colors
Vengeance
Wandering Swordsman
Warrior's Tragedy

Joey Wang (Joey Wong) [Wong Ki Chang]

Banquet
Beheaded 1000
Bet on Fire
Big Heat
Big Score
Butterfly and Sword
Carry on Hotel

Casino Tycoon
Chinese Ghost Story
Chinese Ghost Story 2
Chinese Ghost Story 3
Chinese Legend
City Hunter
Cypress Tiger
Deception
Demoness from 1000 Years
Eagle Shooting Heroes
Eternal Combat
Eye for an Eye
Fai and Chi: Kings of Kung Fu
Family Honor
Fantasy Romance
Flowery Love
Foxy Spirits
Fractured Follies
Ghost Snatchers
God of Gamblers
Green Snake
Hearty Response
Killer's Response
Lady Wolf
Ming Ghost
My Dream Is Yours
My Heart Is That Eternal Rose
100 Ways to Murder Your Wife
Painted Skin
Point of No Return
Portrait of a Nymph
Red and Black
Reincarnation of Golden Lotus
Spirit Love
Spy Games
Swordsman 3: East Is Red
Working Class

Wang Yu (Jimmy Wang Yu)

Assassin
Battle for the Republic of China
Beach of the War God
Beheaded 1000
Blood of the Dragon
Bloody Struggle
Chinese Boxer
Dirty Ho
Dress off for Life
Fantasy Mission Force
Girl with Thunderbolt Kick
Golden Swallow
Hero
Heroic Family
Invincible
Invincible Sword
Island of Fire
Killer Meteor
Knight Errant
Kung Fu Instructor
Last Duel
Magnificent Trio
Man Called Tiger
Man from Hong Kong
Master of the Flying Guillotine
Mercenary from Hong Kong
My Son
One Armed Against Nine Killers
One Armed Boxer
One Armed Chivalry
One Armed Swordsman
Point the Finger of Death
Requital
Return of One Armed Swordsman

Return of the Chinese Boxer
Roar of the Lion
Royal Fist
Shanghai 13
Spiritual Boxer 2
Sword
Sword of Swords
Tattooed Dragon
Ten Fingers of Steel
Tiger and Crane Fist
Trail of Broken Blade
Zatoichi and the One Armed Swordsman

Our Neighbor Detective
Retribution Sight Unseen
Rock 'n' Roll Cop
Setup
Taxi Hunter
Top Banana Club
Underground Banker
Untold Story
Wuniu

Anthony Wong [Wong Chou San]

Angel Hunter
Awakening
Bomb Disposal Officer: Baby Bomb
Cop Image
Daughter of Darkness
Erotic Ghost Story 2
Final Judgement
Full Contact
Gleam of Hope
Hard-boiled
Heroic Trio
Heroic Trio 2: Executioners
Lamb Killer
Legal Innocence
Love to Kill
Moment of Romance 2
Now You See Me, Now You Don't
Organized Crime and Triad Bureau

Simon Yam [Yam Tat Hwa]

Awakening
Banquet
Black Cat
Bullet for Hire
Bullet in the Head
Burning Ambition
Cash on Delivery
Chinese Copout
Crossings
Crystal Fortune Run
Cypress Tigers
Day Without Policeman
Devil's Box
Dr. Lamb
Doctor's Heart
Dragon Killer
Drunken Master 3
Final Judgement
Final Run
First Shot
Framed
Full Contact

Future Cops
Gigolo and Whore
Gigolo and Whore 2
Goodbye Mammie
Great Pretenders
Green Killer
Guns and Roses
Hard to Kill
Holy Weapon
Hong Kong Gigolo
Incorruptible
Insanity
Killer's Love
Killer's Romance
Legendary Couple
Live Hard
Love Among the Triad
Lucky Stars
Man Wanted
Mission Kill
Mistaken Identity
My Crazy Love for You
Naked Killer
Osmanthus Alley
Passion 1995
Powerful Four
Prince of Portland Street
Raped by an Angel
Return Engagement
Run and Kill
Sacred Memory
Sea Wolves
Tiger Cage
Tongs
Tragic Fantasy: Tiger of Wanchai
True Hero
Twist
Wild Ones

Chingmy Yau [Yau Su Jun]

Blind Romance
Boys Are Easy
City Hunter
God of Gamblers' Return
High Risk
Legendary Couple
Liquid Sword
Love of the Last Empress
Naked Killer
Raped by an Angel
Return Engagement
Return to a Better Tomorrow
Saint of Gamblers
She Starts Fire
Skinned Girl
They Came to Rob Hong Kong
Truant Heroes

Charlie Yeoh (Charlie Young)

Apartment for Women
Dr. Wei and the Scripture with No
    Words
Fallen Angels
High Risk
Love in the Time of Twilight
Lovers

Amy Yip (Amy Ip) [Yip Chi May]

Blue Jean Monster
China Dolls
Easy Money
Erotic Ghost Story
Ghostly Vixen
Inspector Wears a Skirt 2
Jailhouse Eros
Lethal Contact
Magnificent Scoundrels
Our Neighbors Are Phantoms
Queen of the Underworld
Requital
Robotrix
Saviour of Souls
Sex and Zen
To Be #1
Vampire Kids
Vampire Strikes Back

Michelle Yeoh (Michelle Khan) [Yeoh Chu Kheng]

Butterfly and Sword
Easy Money
Heroic Trio
Heroic Trio 2
Holy Weapon
In the Line of Duty 1
Magnificent Warriors
Police Story 3: Supercop
Project S

Cecilia Yip [Yip Tong]

Amnesty Decree
Espirit d'Amour
Final Judgement
Fumbling Cops
King of the Sea
Legal Innocence
Peace Hotel
Right Here Waiting
To Be #1
Weakness of Man

Sally Yip (Sally Heh) [Yip Tze Man]

Banquet
Cupid One
Diary of a Big Man
Golden Queen Commando
Just For Fun

The Killer
Laser Man
Marianna
Occupant
Peking Opera Blues
Pink Force Commando
Roboforce
Sisters of the World Unite
Welcome

Veronica Yip

01:00 AM
Bogus Cop
Call Girls '92
Cash on Delivery
Eagle Shooting Heroes
Hero Beyond Boundary of Time
Hong Kong Show Girls
Law on the Brink
Pretty Woman
Retribution Sight Unseen
Rose (Blue Valentine)
Run
Sacred Memory
Summer Lover
Vendetta
Watch Out!

Yu Rong Guang

Combo Cops
Dead End of Besiegers
Heart of a Killer
High Voltage
Iron Monkey
My Father Is a Hero
Project S
Rock 'n' Roll Cop
Swordsman 3
Wind Beneath My Wings

From Beijing with Love
Golden Girls
He and She
He's a Woman, She's a Man
I Want to Go on Living
I Will Wait for You
I've Got You Babe
Incorruptible
Just Married
Taste of Killing and Romance
Tears and Triumph
Thunderbolt
Tragic Commitment
Tricky Business
Tristar
True Hero
Whatever You Want
Wrath of Silence

Anita Yuen

01:00 AM
C'est la Vie, Mon Cheri
Chinese Feast
Crossings
Crystal Fortune Run

Yuen Biao

Champions
Circus Kids
Descendant of the Sun
Don't Give a Damn
Dragon from Shaolin
Dragons Forever
Dreadnaught
Eagle with a Yellow Face
Eastern Condors
Encounters of the Spooky Kind
Enter the Fat Dragon
Ghost Renting

Heroes of Shaolin
Iceman Cometh
Invincible Armor
Kickboxer
Knockabout
License to Steal
Magic Crystal
Magnificent Butcher
Mr. Canton and Lady Rose
Mr. Vampire
Mr. Vampire 2
Mr. Vampire 3
My Lucky Stars
My Lucky Stars 2
On the Run
Once upon a Time in China
Peacock King

Portrait of a Nymph
Project A
Righting Wrongs
Rosa
Saga of the Phoenix
Shanghai Express
Shanghai Shanghai
Shaolin Wooden Men
Shogun and Little Kitchen
Skyhawk
Sword Stained with Royal Blood
Those Merry Souls
Tough Beauty and Sloppy Slop
Winners and Sinners
Young Master
Zu Warriors from Magic Mountain

Sources

Most of the films reviewed in this book are available by mail order from **Video Search of Miami,** P.O. Box 16-1919, Miami FL 33116 (305) 279-9773. Call or write for a free catalog.

Wholesalers should contact **Tai Seng Video,** 170 South Spruce Ave #200, South San Francisco, CA 94080 (415) 871-8118. Call or write for a free catalog.

For further information on Oriental films, subscribe to **Asian Cult Cinema®** (formerly **Asian Trash Cinema®**) [published bimonthly]. Send a check or money order for $30, payable to Vital Books, Inc., P.O. Box 16-1917, Miami FL 33116.

Bibliography

Other recommended books and publications on Hong Kong cinema:

Cineraider Magazine, edited by Richard Akiyama. P.O. Box 240226, Honolulu HI 96824-0226.

Encyclopedia of Martial Arts Movies, by Bill Palmer, Karen Palmer and Ric Meyers. Published by Scarecrow Press, Metuchen NJ.

Essential Guide to Hong Kong Movies, by Rick Baker and Toby Russell. Published by Eastern Heroes Press, P.O. Box 409, London SE 18 3DW, UK.

Jackie Chan Fan Club magazine. P.O. Box 2281, Portland OR 97208.

Oriental Cinema Magazine, edited by Damon Foster. Draculina Publishing, P.O. Box 587, Glen Carbon, IL 62034.

About the Author

Thomas Weisser has an M.A. in English and Communications from the University of Dayton. For twenty years after his graduation in 1970, he became involved in the entertainment business and has been recognized as one of the industry's top promotion consultants and record producers. In the early 1990s, he taught at Miami Dade University in Miami, Florida. Today he edits his own magazine, *Asian Cult Cinema*, and is the co-author, with his wife, Yuko Mihara, of various Asian film books.